Books by Elmer Rice

Nonfiction

THE LIVING THEATRE *1959*

Novels

ON TRIAL *(novelization of play)* *1915*
A VOYAGE TO PURILIA *1930*
IMPERIAL CITY *1937*
THE SHOW MUST GO ON *1949*

Plays

ON TRIAL *1919*
THE ADDING MACHINE *1923*
THE PASSING OF CHOW-CHOW *(one act)* *1925*
WAKE UP, JONATHAN *(with Hatcher Hughes)* *1928*
CLOSE HARMONY *(with Dorothy Parker)* *1929*
COCK ROBIN *(with Philip Barry)* *1929*
STREET SCENE *1929*
THE SUBWAY *1929*
SEE NAPLES AND DIE *1930*
THE LEFT BANK *1931*
COUNSELLOR-AT-LAW *1931*
THE HOUSE IN BLIND ALLEY *1932*
WE THE PEOPLE *1933*
THREE PLAYS WITHOUT WORDS *(one act)* *1934*
THE HOME OF THE FREE *(one act)* *1934*
JUDGMENT DAY *1934*
TWO PLAYS (BETWEEN TWO WORLDS and NOT FOR CHILDREN) *1935*
BLACK SHEEP *1938*
AMERICAN LANDSCAPE *1939*
TWO ON AN ISLAND *1940*
FLIGHT TO THE WEST *1941*
A NEW LIFE *1944*
DREAM GIRL *1946*
SEVEN PLAYS BY ELMER RICE *1950*
THE GRAND TOUR *1952*
THE WINNER *1954*
CUE FOR PASSION *1959*

Pamphlets

THE SUPREME FREEDOM *1949*
CONFORMITY IN THE ARTS *1953*

Minority Report:

An Autobiography

by ELMER RICE

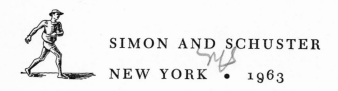

SIMON AND SCHUSTER
NEW YORK • 1963

To my children: Robert, Peggy, John, Judy, Paul
and
my grandchildren: Andy, Ann, Josh, Dickie, Rachel

Contents

I   A New York Childhood   /   9

II   Family Life   /   20

III   Toward an Education   /   33

IV   To Make My Bread   /   53

V   Office Boy to an Attorney's Firm   /   66

VI   When I Went to the Bar as a Very Young Man   /   78

VII   The Jackpot   /   98

VIII   A New Life: I   /   120

IX   Peace and War   /   133

X   To Hollywood and Back   /   163

XI   The Nineteen-Twenties   /   187

XII   The Discovery of Europe   209

XIII   The Play That Had No Chance   /   235

XIV   Work and Play   /   256

XV   The Future at Work   /   286

XVI   A Time of Turmoil   /   326

XVII   Life as an Ex-Playwright   /   343

XVIII Fellowship   /   374

XIX   A New Life: II   /   400

XX   Catastrophe   /   434

XXI   A New Life: III   /   450

XXII   Credo and Coda   /   461

Minority Report:

An Autobiography

CHAPTER

I

A New York Childhood

1

One afternoon a few years ago, as I left the Dalton School in East
Eighty-ninth Street, which my three youngest children were attending, I suddenly decided to pay a visit to the place of my birth. No
long journey was required, for my objective was only a block away,
at 127 East Ninetieth Street, between Park and Lexington avenues.
I knew the address because it appeared on the birth certificate
which I had needed for admission to the bar. Though I must have
passed the corner of that block hundreds of times, I had never
stopped, always telling myself that someday I must. Now the day
had come.

I thought that probably the flathouse was no longer there—sixty-
odd years is a long life for a Manhattan building. I knew that it
was a flathouse; if maternity hospitals existed when I was born,
their use was restricted to the homeless and to the sophisticated
rich, and my family was in neither category.

After a brisk minute's walk, I reached my destination. The house
had indeed survived: one of a pair of five-story walk-ups, with a
railed stoop and a vestibule, an unmistakable relic of the late nineteenth century. It bore its age well, no doubt because the tone of
the neighborhood had come up rather than down. The beige-colored
brick was fresh, the windows were clean, there was no litter.

I resisted an impulse to cross the street and go inside, for obviously there was nothing to see or do there. Had some helpful or suspicious person asked me if I were looking for someone, I would not have known whether to answer yes or no. So I went about my business. The whole operation had consumed less than five minutes.

I had no association with the place, since we had moved away in my infancy; nevertheless, it seemed to me that I should have felt *something*. But I didn't, unless it was the satisfaction of crossing "Visit birthplace" off my mental list of Things I Must Do. My indifference typified my almost complete lack of interest in my antecedents. I know next to nothing about my ancestry, and very little about my own family, except for those of its members among whom I grew up; for I paid little attention to their reminiscences and asked few questions about the past.

All that I know about my great-grandparents is that they were natives of Germany. I do not know their given names, what they looked like, what their occupations were. For me, family life begins with my grandparents, all of whom emigrated to the United States in the mid-nineteenth century.

My maternal grandfather, whose name was Lion, and who came from Berlin, died long before I was born. I must have been told something about his background and means of livelihood, but all that I can remember is that in the 1850s he settled in Warrenton, Virginia, where my mother was born in 1858. I recall seeing a photograph of him: a kindly, gentle face.

Both my grandmothers died when I was four or five. Though my mother's mother lived in Baltimore, where I saw her only occasionally, while my father's was a member of my childhood household, I remember the former far more vividly—perhaps because she was warm, cheery and loving, while my paternal grandmother was stiff, morose and forbidding, like a seventeenth-century Dutch portrait.

My father's father was the only grandparent I knew well. He had been apprenticed to a tailor, but in 1848, when Europe was swept by an epidemic of revolutions, he put down his needle and joined the rebels. I have sometimes wondered whether my own lifelong rebelliousness is due to hereditary influences.

When the revolution collapsed, Grandpa was taken prisoner. Given the choice of going to jail or emigrating to America, he emigrated. Whether he regarded it as the lesser evil or as a golden opportunity, I do not know. Almost penniless, he arrived in New York in 1850, after a month in the hold of a sailing vessel. He was an energetic and strong-willed man, and by the outbreak of the Civil War he had established himself as a storekeeper in Clearfield, Pennsylvania. By that time he was the father of four living children —one or two others had died in infancy—of whom my father, Jacob, born in 1861, was the youngest. Grandpa was drafted, but was able to buy a substitute—a permissible procedure. Some seventy-five years later, I was lunching with Robert Sherwood and Sidney Howard. We were getting ready to produce Sherwood's play *Abe Lincoln in Illinois*. He remarked that his grandfather had served in the Civil War. I said that mine had avoided service by buying his way out. "So did mine," said Howard. "And, what's more, he stole the money to do it with."

Grandpa must have continued to prosper in a modest way, for at fifty—a dozen or so years before my birth—he "retired," and he remained in that state for the rest of his life. He died at ninety-three.

My parents were cousins, though I am not clear about the exact degree of relationship. I grew up in the belief that their mothers were half sisters; but both were named Hannah, and it seems unlikely that a common parent would give two children the same name. However, there is no doubt about the cousinship, for I often heard it referred to and sometimes was a little uneasy about the possible effects of a consanguineous marriage upon myself. At the time of the marriage in 1891, my mother was thirty-three, my father not quite thirty-one.

2

I was born, in the Ninetieth Street walk-up, on September 28, 1892, and given the awkward and inharmonious name Elmer Leopold Reizenstein. I do not hold it against my mother, for it was almost obligatory to honor both grandfathers in the naming of a firstborn son. My grandfathers were respectively Isaac and Elkan, so I might have become Elkan Isaac or Isaac Elkan, but she spared me that. Instead she took Grandpa's middle name for mine and substituted Elmer for Elkan, in the belief that it was "a fine old Southern name," rather elegant and distinguished. Little did she suspect, dear soul, that it subjects its unfortunate possessor to facetious comment and condescending smiles.

Early in 1893, perhaps because another child was expected, or because my father's parents came to live with us, we moved from the German enclave of Yorkville to the neutral and relatively undeveloped territory of upper Madison Avenue. Our new home, where we lived for ten years, was in one of a row of five-story brownstone-front walk-ups, which had been built in the expectation that the 1892 Columbian Exposition would be held in Central Park. Chicago got the exposition, but there was no lack of tenants for the new buildings. They were a cut above the general run of brownstone fronts, for they contained no shops and there was only one flat to a floor.

Our third-floor flat consisted of seven rooms and bath, strung along a narrow hallway: the type known as a railroad flat. The living room and the small hall bedroom overlooked the street; the kitchen, at the other end, the back yard; the other rooms, a darkish inside court. These quarters somehow accommodated my parents, my grandparents, my father's brother William, myself, my younger brother (during his brief lifetime) and the "servant girl." My brother died when I was about three, my grandmother a year or two later, so I have no memory of the earlier arrangements. But until I was twenty-two, whatever seven-room flat we occupied housed my parents, Grandpa, Uncle Will, the servant girl and, of course, myself.

The house was well kept. The stairways and halls were neatly carpeted, there was abundant hot water and steam heat. Every year the entire apartment was redecorated at the landlord's expense: wallpaper, paint, plaster. I enjoyed watching the painters at work, particularly in the kitchen, where they artistically superimposed brown paint upon the yellow to give the effect of graining. Once a painter to whom my mother offered a cup of tea asked if she had any rum to put in it, a request that so outraged and amused her that she never tired of recalling it. It may interest present-day Manhattanites to know that our monthly rental was twenty-eight dollars.

The household appurtenances were of the period. All the bathroom appliances were of tin or zinc and heavily encased in wood painted to simulate mahogany. A little cabinet under the washbasin provided storage for pails and scrub brushes, as well as harborage for cockroaches, against which my mother waged relentless warfare. Electricity had not yet been installed. Mellow, soothing gaslight was filtered through Welsbach mantles, which blazed up occasionally, causing momentary excitement but no real fire hazard.

Like the boy in *A Child's Garden of Verses,* I used to stand at the window to watch the lamplighter make his swift rounds, turning up the jets of the street lamps with a deft twist of his long rod.

It is hard to re-create an image of New York at the turn of the century. There was something small-townish, even placid, about it. The era of skyscrapers was just beginning. The twenty-one story Flatiron Building, a civic wonder, dates only from 1902. Elevators in residential buildings were still something of a novelty. Most people lived in walk-up flathouses, or, if they could afford it, in private houses, mainly of the brownstone-front, English-basement variety. Many survive as shabby rooming houses or rookeries swarming with the most depressed elements of the population.

The telephone was still regarded as a luxury in private life. There was one at the corner drugstore, available for use by regular customers—no charge, of course. But it was a privilege one reserved for special occasions: a hurry call for the doctor, perhaps. If he had no telephone, you sent someone around to his office, which was always in his home. If it wasn't urgent, you wrote a postcard, and he usually showed up next day, or at any rate the day after. Office visits were a dollar, house visits were two dollars. Specialists were only for the rich or to be "called in for consultation" in moments of crisis. The family doctor was obstetrician, pediatrician, internist, externist and often surgeon. Drugstores were drugstores. I suppose their prices were high, for whenever my mother wanted to convey that any sort of establishment was expensive she called it "a regular drugstore." I miss the great globular glass jars filled with bright-colored translucent liquids.

The motion picture was in its mechanical and ideological infancy, a flickering novelty exhibited in nickelodeons for the diversion of children and a sprinkling of adult curiosity seekers. These auditoriums were usually vacated stores equipped with a screen, a projector, folding chairs and an upright piano. As their name indicates, the admission price was five cents.

It was transport, though, that made the real difference. Except for the network of ugly, noisy, light-obscuring elevated railways, there was little mechanized transportation. The automobile was still an object of mild amazement and amusement. However, by the time I was in the fifth grade there were signs on upper Fifth Avenue limiting speed to eight miles per hour. An agile boy could keep pace with the high, chugging vehicles—their occupants clad in veils, gloves, goggles and long coats called dusters—shouting as he ran, "Get a horse! Get a horse!" Very often they had to.

The horse was king of the road. Streetcars, buses, fire engines, moving vans, delivery wagons were all horse-drawn. As late as 1915, I took a hansom cab from Grand Central Station to Morningside Heights. On a return from a childhood holiday, I found trolley cars being installed on Madison Avenue. I used to walk over to Lexington Avenue for the thrill of watching the "cable" cars scale the steep hill at 102nd Street. Even more exciting was a ride on the cars, clutching one's seat and shutting one's eyes during the ascent or descent. On Park Avenue, one could mark the progress of the underground trains by the puffs of smoke that came up through the circular vents in the central grassy strip.

Horsecars continued in use well on into the present century: on 110th Street, Chambers Street, East Broadway and the waterfront "Belt Line." They were not without charm, particularly when there were wood fires in the potbellied iron stoves. And what could be more fun than to scramble to the upper deck of a Fifth Avenue bus and sit on the long bench beside the driver?

The traffic was noisy even then; but the noises were different: the whinnying and snorting of horses, the clatter of wheels and clangor of iron-shod hoofs upon the cobbled streets. Runaways were not infrequent; I saw many a cart go careening wildly up the avenue, sometimes pursued by a mounted policeman, sometimes stopped by a bold citizen who leaped out and seized the horse's bridle. Fires were frequent, too; every day the engines charged by at the gallop, with their swinging brass bells clamoring, the spotted Dalmatian running alongside. The ambulance bells were staccato, the harness bells of the heavy brewery horses merely tinkled.

In winter it was jingle bells; for sleighs, private and commercial, thronged the streets. On a hill in Central Park a sort of roadhouse, known as MacGowan's Pass Tavern—a relic of Revolutionary times, I believe—presented to the driver of the season's first sleigh a bottle of champagne. Horses often lost their footing on the ice-coated cobblestones. As they kicked and plunged, the driver, usually with volunteer assistance, would try to free them from the shafts—a dangerous business. Sometimes a horse broke a leg, and the gathering crowd awaited the arrival of a policeman who applied his service revolver to the animal's head. Often the corpse would lie at the curb for several days, the frozen legs stiffly distended, until the removal cart happened along.

Even with the installation of electric cars, getting out of Manhattan was a cumbersome business. There was one bridge across the East River, none across the Hudson, and of course no under-river tunnels. The Pennsylvania Railroad terminated in Jersey City, the Long Island Railroad in Long Island City. To reach my Aunt Fannie's summer cottage in Far Rockaway, my mother and I took the Madison Avenue streetcar to Twenty-third Street, the crosstown car to the East River ferry, and a train on the other side to the Far Rockaway station, whence we walked to the cottage. When we went to Baltimore, we followed the same procedure to get to Jersey City. There we really had a long wait, for my mother, who believed in punctuality, was usually an hour early.

Sanitary conditions were even worse sixty years ago than they are today. The sidewalks were befouled with dog droppings and the streets with heaps of horse manure, which attracted hordes of English sparrows. The white-uniformed street cleaners, trundling their canvas receptacles, could never get things really tidy. They were known as "white wings" (in 1926 Philip Barry wrote a play about a street cleaner, with that title), and their occupation was facetiously referred to as "following the ponies." Equine corpses were a rarity, but dead dogs and cats were abundant, lying for days in the gutters or on the blackened snow heaps. In summer swarms of flies buzzed about the loathsome remains. Lidless barrels of ashes and reeking garbage awaited collection by uncovered garbage carts. On windy days ashes filled the air; exuberant small boys upset the garbage containers. Coal for the furnaces was delivered through sidewalk apertures, impeding both pedestrians and vehicular traffic. As the coal slid down the chutes, clouds of coal dust arose. Expectoration, as Charles Dickens had observed fifty years earlier, was a universal practice; the streets were coated with spittle. Vacant lots, numerous in my neighborhood, were depositories for discarded household gear of every sort. Often, too, they served as places of public convenience. In fact, wherever you went you had to watch your step.

The streets were alive with providers of refreshment, services and entertainment. Madison Avenue was far above the level of the pushcarts, those colorful, aromatic street markets of the immigrant quarters, but there was a steady procession of itinerant vendors and performers: the roasted-chestnut man, the peanut man, the pretzel man, the hokey-pokey man—who sold paper cones filled with shaved ice that was doused with brightly colored liquids—and the man who cried, "Corn! *Sweet* corn!" or "*Straw*berries! Straw*berries!*" The dealer in pots and pans made his periodic rounds. So did the scissors-grinder; when you heard his bell, you gathered up your edged implements and hurried downstairs, standing by while he sharpened them in the efficient little workshop that his cart housed. The old-clothes man, coatless, vest unbuttoned, a folded newspaper under his arm, timed his daily visit for mid-morning, when the housewives, their beds made, their children off to school, were taking a breather, leaning out the parlor window on folded arms to view the street pageant or to gossip with a next-door neighbor. "I kesh klo'" was his plaintive cry, supplemented by a direct appeal to the protruding heads. At the least sign of encouragement he came dashing up the stairs to begin the bargaining process.

Hurdy-gurdies were numerous, the humble hand-borne variety, with or without the monkey and his tin cup, and the wheeled ones that ground out Italian opera. The children gathered about, pennies in hand; sometimes they danced. German musicians, small brass ensembles, performed in the back yards, blaring forth "Du, Du liegst mir im Herzen" and "Ach, Du liebe Augustine." You flung your penny, wrapped in newspaper, out the kitchen window, waiting anxiously for the retrieval and the wave of acknowledgment. Sometimes a Salvation Army band took up its post at the street corner, the women in poke bonnets rattling tambourines, the men beating drums or blowing trumpets. They provided little enjoyment; the trickle of pennies was thin.

The streets were alive, too, with people going about their various errands; walking had not yet become obsolete. Shopping, especially for food, took a lot of time. There were no chain stores or supermarkets. Iceboxes were small, and the ice melted fast; large quantities of fresh food could not be kept on hand. Good housewives scorned canned food, unless they put it up themselves. So there were frequent visits to the provision shops, and often long waits until the man you were used to was free. For each merchant was an individual, whose personality and practices were subjects of dinner-table conversation. When I accompanied my mother, I could be sure of an apple or a banana from the grocer, a cupcake or a cruller from the baker. I particularly remember Mr. Fehskens, the grocer, a white-aproned, sober man with thinning hair, a neat mustache, steel-rimmed spectacles and, most memorable of all, a pencil worn slantingly behind the ear—a dashing, exotic touch, I thought. At Christmas he would send us a great basket of dates or a large box of almond-shaped chocolate-filled cookies. The butcher sent a goose or a turkey, the baker a rich layer cake.

Most fascinating was the Chinese laundryman, across the avenue. Family wash was, of course, done at home, by the housewife, the servant girl or, in wealthy families, a day worker known as a "washwoman"—laundresses did not come in until later—so I suppose the laundryman's clientele consisted entirely of improvident bachelors. I sometimes went into his shop for a bag of litchi nuts. (They looked and tasted like raisins; I could not understand why they were called nuts.) I gazed in wonder at the laundry tickets inscribed with Chinese characters—"No tickee, no washee" was a popular catch phrase, though I doubt that its users knew exactly what it meant— and at the pigtailed proprietor, in his blue blouse and loose, ankle-length cotton trousers. I liked to watch him spray a mouthful of water over the shirt he was ironing. The neighborhood boys devised many ways of teasing him. Most annoying was a device called a "ticker": a porcelain beer-bottle cap with a rubber disk, attached to a long string. The cap adhered to the shop window, and when the string was tautened the glass vibrated clatteringly. At last the laundryman's patience gave out; he came charging out of the shop, pigtail flying, flatiron in hand, with no chance, of course, of catching his tormentors. Though I laughed, I always felt a little sorry for him, and still do.

Household activities kept my mother and the servant girl on the go the week round. The cooking, mending and other skills came within my mother's province, the heavy work was done by the servant girl, invariably a "greenhorn," a newly arrived young peasant—a German or a German-speaking Hungarian or "Böhmische," as my family called the natives of Bohemia. She was buxom, thick-fingered, strong, and wholly innocent of English and of city ways. My mother undertook the instruction of this clumsy field hand in the mores and speech of America. (The girl usually began by picking up the taboo words, which she proudly imparted to me.) She had a seven-day, eighty-four-hour work week, with one night "out" and every other Sunday off—after the midday dinner dishes were washed. Her monthly wage was twelve dollars. After a while she became sufficiently Americanized to ask for fourteen, an inflationary trend that my mother firmly resisted, preferring to begin all over with the training of a new immigrant. So all through my childhood there was a steady stream of Lenas and Annas and Kunegundes.

Each day had its general and its specialized duties. While my mother went marketing, the servant girl made the beds, emptied the numerous spittoons and chamber pots and answered the repeated summons of the dumbwaiter whistle. Provisions, merchandise, ice and garbage were all hauled up or down in that binlike lift operated by pulley ropes. The collectors and deliverers were known only by the voices that ascended from the basement's depths. In the holiday season there was likely to be found among the groceries a slip of paper that read: "Christmas is coming with all its joys, and don't forget the order boys," a lyrical effort certain to elicit a dollar.

Monday was washday. Linen for six beds, towels, table linens (my mother would have scorned paper napkins or towels), all washable wearing apparel—everything went into the kitchen washtubs and was then carried in baskets to clotheslines on the roof; I don't know how they managed in a prolonged rainy spell. Tuesday was the day for ironing, an arduous task with all those sheets, tablecloths and shirts. Wednesday and Thursday were dedicated to cleaning: a thoroughgoing application of mop, broom, carpet sweeper and scrub brush. Cockroaches and mice had to be dealt with, and in summer the houseflies that swarmed in through the unscreened windows, too numerous for the sheets of sticky flypaper called Tanglefoot. Friday was reserved for silver polishing and other odd jobs. For my mother it was baking day; everything but bread was home-baked. She was an excellent German cook: hearty soups, dumplings, stews, roasts and schnitzels. On Saturday, in deference to the Sabbath, she let the servant girl carry on alone, while she went shopping, visited friends or made sick calls. Most of Sunday was taken up with the preparation of the huge midday meal and the cleaning up afterward. If relatives called in the afternoon, they were urged to stay for supper, which meant getting up a collation of cold meats and salads.

Spring cleaning was a major operation. The mess left by painters and paperhangers had to be cleaned up; there were draperies to be taken down, rugs to be carried to the back yard and thoroughly beaten, winter woolens to be packed in camphor, closets to be scrubbed and lined with fresh shelf paper. My mother was likely to judge her acquaintances by the degree of their adherence to these household rituals. One of her favorite anecdotes was about the family from whose table a dumpling rolled unobserved behind the sideboard one autumn day, not to be discovered until the spring cleaning, a story that never failed to evoke laughter from the members of my household, even on its hundredth repetition.

In late-summer canning time, bushel-basketfuls of fruits and vegetables were cleaned, cut up and processed, then sealed in Mason jars, dozens and dozens of them, enough to last all winter: peas, corn and beans, peaches, plums and cherries, strawberry jam and a delicious jelly made of raspberries and currants; and great quantities of dill pickles, greatly relished by my family, but loathed by me, then and now.

3

This was the small world of my early childhood. It was unlike the world of today. The tempo, the rhythm were different; so were many of the standards and attitudes. Does this explain my ability to relax almost completely between spells of tension and hard work? Or that beneath a good many layers of acquired sophistication there lurks a ludicrous naïveté? I would like to know.

One gets to be the way one is, I suppose, by the operation of everything that happens from the moment of conception: the combination of the parental genes; nurture and parental behavior; education and environment; the influence of elders and contemporaries; fortunate or unfortunate accidents. No one can evaluate these complex and divergent agencies, particularly with respect to himself. Yet everyone can, to some extent, recognize factors that have contributed to his development.

In my own case, I am aware of certain circumstances that went into shaping my character and the course of my life: my relationship to my mother; the illness of my father; the death, in infancy, of my brother, which made me in effect an only child; and the financial situation of my family.

CHAPTER

II

Family Life

1

I do not remember my younger brother, Lester, who died of diphtheria and scarlet fever when I was about three. But I do remember coming back to Madison Avenue from Brooklyn, where I had been sent to stay with some relatives known to me only as Uncle and Aunt. The return home is clearly fixed in my mind: I almost see myself mounting the stairs and entering the flat. I seem to recall, too, the lingering odor of the disinfectant sulphur candles, though perhaps this memory relates to one of my own childhood illnesses. What, if anything, was said to me about my brother's death, I do not remember. But for many years his photograph, mounted on stiff cardboard and unframed, stood on my mother's dresser: a round-faced, round-eyed baby. The anniversaries of his birth and death were days of mourning for her. She never got over the loss.

Strangely enough, neither did I, though I had no conscious memory of him. I always felt a sense of deprivation, of something missing in my life. Had I been the only child, I would have accepted aloneness as a matter of course; but that brief infantile association must have had some deep meaning for me. Anyhow, I never became reconciled to the loss of a companion and playmate. A continuing fantasy had to do with his resurrection; not in a religious sense, of course, but merely in a physical one. I pretended that he was not really dead, or that somehow he would come back to life, and then suddenly one day there he would be. Even had there been no brother, I would have been inward-turning; as it was, my solitariness was accentuated. To compensate for it, I had to build up resources within myself. What effect my brother's survival would have had upon my emotional attitudes and my relationships there is no knowing; but that my life would have been very different I have not the slightest doubt.

I believe firmly in the law of compensation. Everything must be paid for in one way or another. There is no absolute, no unmixed good or evil. We all have the weaknesses of our strengths, the strengths of our weaknesses. Platitudinous though it may be, it is a philosophy that has helped me through life, by enabling me to accept boons with caution, disasters with fortitude. A solitary child, a bereft child, I had many hours of loneliness, of self-pity, no doubt. I was shy, aloof and secretive. (I am still secretive and am sometimes accused of aloofness—but never shyness!) Yet my loneliness made it imperative for me to develop self-reliance and self-sufficiency.

Also—fortunately for myself and for those with whom I have had love relationships—jealousy, though perhaps latent in me, has never asserted itself. For I had no rival to compete with. I was the sole recipient of the love and attentions of everyone around me: my parents, Grandpa, Uncle Will. I never felt unwanted or in the way, never was "put in my place" or treated as though I were mean or ridiculous. I cannot recall ever being struck. Punishments, as I was able to recognize, were not vindictive, but the inevitable consequence of misbehavior; so I had no sense of injustice or mistreatment. I was not on the best terms with my father. He was ill-tempered and constantly nagged me about table manners and other details of conduct. But he was never cruel, and perhaps I knew, even then, that he had a deep love for me. Whatever was lacking in the paternal relationship was supplied by Grandpa and Uncle Will, who were unfailingly kind and for whom I had the liveliest affection.

Nothing was lacking in the maternal relationship. My mother and I had almost nothing in common except our mutual love, but that was a potent force indeed. It was a love that never waned; fifteen years after her death, there is hardly a day in which I do not think of her with tenderness and longing. Yet there was no "momism" about the relationship, nothing "Freudian," nothing morbid or incestuous. Her love was unselfish and undemanding. She imposed no restrictions, made no claims. When I was ready to go my own way, she did not try to hold me; there were no apron strings to be unloosed, no silver cord to be severed. I rarely asked her advice, and she never proffered it. My way of life and my career were wholly outside the range of her experience. Over the years, my ideas and attitudes became increasingly incomprehensible to her. Though I must have said and done many things that shocked her, she never complained or reproached me. Her effulgent and nourishing love gave me a sense of security and trustfulness that has served me well all my life.

I have known many people who preached goodness, but relatively few who practiced it. My mother's precepts were matched by her deeds. There was no mawkishness or self-righteousness about her; it was simply her nature to be good. She was devoid of malice, harshness or ill-will. She enjoyed people, believed in them, cheered and helped them. She thought that everyone had good intentions, and she put the best possible construction upon everyone's behavior. (In later years, when on rare occasions she took a taxi, she would say, "He was a very nice driver. He only charged me forty cents." It would have been useless to explain that the fare was regulated by the meter.) I have always wished that I had profited more by her example. But at least she instilled in me the belief that goodness is the goal humanity must strive to attain. Without her early guidance, my own shortcomings would have been even greater.

2

The composition of the household and its economic level were determined by the fact that my father was an epileptic. His illness impaired his earning capacity so greatly that my parents could make ends meet only by taking in Grandpa and Uncle Will as boarders. They lived with us as far back as I can remember; so I assume that my father's ailment began soon after my birth, or perhaps after my brother's conception. Had it been earlier, I am certain there would have been no marriage, or at any rate no children.

From overheard snatches of conversation, I surmised that my father had been engaged in some business of his own. However, my birth certificate lists his occupation as bookkeeper. Earlier in life he had certainly been a traveling salesman, for I often heard him speak with distaste of his experiences. He dismissed as childish nonsense my desire to travel. To him, travel meant lugging sample cases about the country, and living, for weeks at a time, in one wretched small-town hotel after another.

I am even more vague about the origin of his ailment. Epilepsy, I have been told, can result from a variety of aberrations: brain injury, alcoholism, venereal disease; but I have no reason to believe that any of these caused my father's illness. Heredity seemingly is another possible factor. I have sometimes suspected that my maternal grandmother was mentally disturbed; however, none of her other children showed any sign of mental or nervous disorder.

At the time of my father's death, an attending physician suggested a psychiatric explanation. The sufferer, seeking escape from reality, engages in daydreams that bring about complete withdrawal, amounting even to momentary loss of consciousness. Gradually these pleasurable interludes increase in intensity until they become involuntary, leading to major seizures and resulting eventually in physiological changes. At least, that is how I understood it. Anyhow, my father being dead, it was a matter of only academic interest to me.

To live with an epileptic is, for a child, a trying, not to say terrifying, experience. There are two forms of epileptic seizure: the petit mal, or brief lapse from consciousness, to which I have referred, and the grand mal. In the former, the sufferer, suddenly and without warning, in the middle of a sentence or while walking along the street, goes completely blank: his eyes become expressionless, he smiles vacuously and nods mechanically. In less than a minute it is over. He becomes normal again, apparently unaware of the momentary abstraction. To those about him these occurrences are disconcerting, but not particularly alarming. The grand mal, or epileptic fit, is quite another matter. If you are on the lookout for it—and if you live with an epileptic you must be—it is heralded by a glazing of the eyes and a stiffening of the body, followed by a piercing, inhuman cry. The victim, completely unconscious now, falls to the ground, frothing at the mouth, his rigid body writhing convulsively. Gradually the seizure subsides, the body relaxes, the eyes open; but he is spent and somnolent and must be assisted to bed.

During my childhood and adolescence I must have seen hundreds of these fits. Often they occurred at the dinner table. The meal would be violently disrupted, then resumed perfunctorily, without savor. Sometimes a glass had been overturned or a plate sent crashing to the floor. There were nights when I was torn from sleep by that stricken animal cry, and lay listening in the dark until all was quiet in the adjoining room. I have often wondered why I suffered none of the ill effects one reads about in psychiatric case histories. At least, none that I am aware of: I have never been "nervous" or subject to fears and anxieties. Perhaps it was because there was no hysteria or excitement. My mother remained calm, and the presence of Grandpa and Uncle Will gave me security. I was always sure they would protect me from harm.

The incidence of the seizures was irregular and unpredictable. Sometimes there would be none for months, sometimes several in one week, even two in one day. The reason for this variability was a mystery. No doubt there were aggravating causes, for often the attacks came after a period of mounting tenseness and irritability. I knew I must avoid exciting or angering my father; but there was no telling what might inflame his overwrought mind.

Frequently he had seizures away from home. If he was in an office or a shop, he could usually remain there until he was able to board a streetcar. He arrived home pale and shaken, saying nothing about the attack. Sometimes he fell down in the street and was carried off in an ambulance. While we anxiously awaited his homecoming, a policeman rang the doorbell to give us the news. Uncle Will would hurry to the hospital to bring my father home. So whenever he was late for dinner there was mounting uneasiness. Aware of this, and resentful of what he regarded as surveillance, he would sometimes deliberately stay out late, just to make us worry.

A Dr. Williams, who looked like the Phiz drawings of Mr. Dombey, paid periodic visits. All he seemed to dispense were words of cheer and what I suppose was a sedative: a foul-smelling concoction that poisoned the breath. But so far as I know, no cure was attempted. After twenty-five years of affliction, my father died.

I did not hate my father, but I disliked him. He was physically repulsive to me; for children are repelled by ugliness, and I found him ugly. In photographs taken at the time of his marriage he was presentable enough, but when I became aware of him he was already showing the ravages of illness: sunken, almost cadaverous cheeks; prominent forehead veins; blackened and decaying teeth. (He could not visit a dentist, lest he have a seizure while the instruments were in his mouth.) I did not like him to kiss or embrace me. He knew it and resented it, which did not help matters.

Furthermore, he was forever nagging away at me, partly in exercise of his parental authority, but mainly, I think, because he had a quarrelsome nature. My mother's assurances that in former days he had been quite amiable did not impress me. I judged him by his present behavior and reacted accordingly. I am sure that he worried continually about his inability to make contact with me. On my side, I believed that I should love my father, and probably even wanted to, but I could not overcome the antagonism he aroused. We were seldom in open conflict, but there was always an undercurrent of hostility.

In those days thirty or thirty-five dollars per week was a respectable family income; fifty was quite handsome. I am sure that at the time of his marriage my father was well able to support a household. But nobody wants to employ a hypersensitive and quarrelsome epileptic. Increasingly he had to rely upon relatives and acquaintances for part-time jobs or other money-making expedients, and upon the contributions of Grandpa and Uncle Will to the household finances. This dependence stung his pride; he fancied he was being patronized, an object of charity.

3

Whatever Grandpa and Uncle Will paid, however, could hardly have been regarded as charity. They got more than their money's worth. Uncle Will would have had to live in a boardinghouse, and so would Grandpa after my grandmother's death, for it is unlikely that his married children would have taken him in. While my father fumed inwardly at his humiliation, my mother devoted herself to providing a comfortable home life for our boarders. She catered to their tastes and whims, and warmed them with womanly affection and companionship.

I found the "intruders" very agreeable housemates. Uncle Will was good-humored and phlegmatic. Though he came to what was almost a pauper's end, he must have been fairly well-to-do in his earlier years. He was something of a sport—in the popular, not the biological, sense. A believer in taking life easy, he frequented the theatre and race track, went on fishing trips to Maine and Canada, traveled as far as Florida, Cuba and California. He wore a gold ring with a diamond in it, smoked Rameses II cigarettes—I remember the Egyptian figures on the box—and liked a drink. I assume there were women in his life, but I never heard a reference to them. He always treated me with generosity, seldom reprimanded me and never tried to direct my course in life. We were very good friends.

Even closer was my relationship to Grandpa. All through my preschool years we were constant companions. He had "retired" some fifteen years before I was born. With his savings he had bought some flathouses in Brooklyn, which brought him enough income to live on. (I suspect that they were rather horrible slum dwellings.) Once a month he took a trip to Brooklyn to collect the rents. The rest of the time he had on his hands, where it hung heavily, I am sure.

Every fair morning, Grandpa and I went to Central Park, just a block away. While he settled down on a bench with some other old gentlemen, smoking, spitting, exchanging reminiscences about the old country and the Civil War, I roamed about within eyeshot, amusing myself in one way or another. I suppose I had playmates, but I do not remember them. However, there was always something for a boy to do: chasing squirrels or feeding them peanuts; rolling in the grass or the fallen leaves; trying to balance on a railing; building a snow man or coasting down a gentle slope. The high point of the morning was the purchase of a large, delicious pretzel, fat and doughy at the bottom, thin and crisp at the top, heavily salted. Sometimes I was treated to a ride on the little steam railroad that ran just inside the park wall, from 106th to 110th Street. The round trip cost five cents, but it was worth it.

We returned home for lunch, and as we neared the end of the meal the doorbell announced the arrival of Mr. Oppenheimer. My mother, resigned to his premature appearance, offered him fruit or a slice of coffee cake, while we hurriedly finished eating so that the table could be cleared for the afternoon-long pinochle session. I remember Mr. Oppenheimer very well, though for me he had no life away from the pinochle table. He seemed much older than Grandpa, perhaps because of his enormous white beard. He looked something like Brahms, though of course the resemblance was not apparent to me at the time. Grandpa's clipped iron-gray hair was worn en pompadour, and he was clean-shaven except for sideburns that came halfway down his cheeks. I thought him rather distinguished-looking.

I often watched the game until the smoke became too thick for comfort. Two-handed pinochle is not an intricate game, and I soon mastered it. The antagonists concentrated on the play, watching each other suspiciously and speaking little except for a sort of ritualistic patter. If you melded four queens you said, "*Etwas die ladies*"; a full suit was "*Rock, Hosen und Weste.*" Sometimes, when the game went on almost until suppertime—one had dinner only on Sunday—my mother waited a little impatiently for Mr. Oppenheimer's departure so that the ashes and the spittoons could be removed. No one would have dared interrupt the game. On Sundays Mr. Oppenheimer did not appear, but sometimes Grandpa, Uncle Will, my father and some casual outsider would play skat, a game I never understood, perhaps because four smokers and spitters in the unventilated room soon drove me out.

Once Grandpa took me to Philadelphia, where he had relatives. We spent several days doing the sights: the Liberty Bell, the Mint and so on. Most exciting was Electric Park, whose fountains were played upon by varicolored lights. It excited me far more than did later visits to Versailles and Tivoli. I remember nothing about my relatives, except that their house contained a book about the Mohawk chief Joseph Brant, by far the most fascinating story I had ever read. I still mourn my inability to finish it before we left. Like most young readers, I paid little attention to the book's title and the author's name, so I could never take it up again.

4

My mother's infancy had been spent in the shifting Civil War battleground of northern Virginia, where her home had been raided by foragers from both armies. Later her family moved to Baltimore, where she grew up. She took me there almost every year, trips that

I greatly enjoyed. We shared a chair in the parlor car; as I grew up, it became a rather tight squeeze. We carried our lunch with us: chicken sandwiches and homemade layer cake. (There was a prescribed diet for every occasion. Illness is associated in my mind with chicken broth and calf's-foot jelly; the first full meal after convalescence, with a squab and chocolate ice cream.)

Being in Baltimore was even better than getting there. I was the only grandchild and only nephew, so of course I was the center of attention. I adored my grandmother; she was so affectionate, so quietly charming. She knew exactly what I liked to eat and saw that I got it. Outside the dining room was a cupboard, well stocked with cookies and brownies, to which I had free access. I can still smell the warm spiciness that assailed me when the door was opened.

It was delightful to have the run of a large house, so different from the cramped New York flat. It was one of a long row of identical houses, brick-fronted, with three gleaming white marble steps which were scrubbed every morning by the Negro servant girls. The sidewalks were of brick, too, laid in V-shaped patterns. If you stepped on a loose brick after a rainfall a small geyser drenched you. After supper we all sat on grass mats on the steps, taking the air, eating watermelon and gossiping with the neighbors on either side. There was little traffic, for all deliveries were made through the alleys to which the long back yards led. The Negro delivery-men were, of course, not permitted to come to the front door. There were few Negroes in our New York neighborhood, and it seemed strange to see so many of them. I was not frightened or repelled, but I did believe that if you touched a Negro the black came off on you, a notion I must have acquired from my paternal Uncle Charlie's wife, Aunt Sarah, who was a native of New Bern, North Carolina. I wonder how much adult prejudice against Negroes, Jews, Catholics and foreigners is the outgrowth of just such idiotic childhood misconceptions!

I liked my three Baltimore uncles. The middle one, Uncle Albert, a good-looking, energetic man generally regarded as head of the family, gave me presents and took me to amusement parks and restaurants. The oldest, Uncle Ben, was a taciturn, self-effacing, beaten man who had some minor job in Uncle Albert's successful business. Uncle Edwin, the youngest, was something of a character:

the only person on either side of the family who could even remotely be called eccentric. He was a complete extravert, voluble,
demonstrative and erratic. His "den" was something to amaze and
delight a small boy, an incredible hodgepodge of bizarre furnishings and bric-a-brac: rugs, bed coverings and draperies from the
Middle East; a doorway curtain of strings of cylindrical beads
that rattled in the breeze; "swords" fashioned from perforated
Chinese coins; little teakwood tables and hanging shelves crammed
with knickknacks; and, most prominent of all, a painting of a
crouching lion—the family name was Lion—with metal bars inserted in the frame to represent a cage. The whole was dimly
lighted by a wrought-iron lamp with red glass panels. I think the
family worried a little about him; but he married quite young
and settled down to respectable middle-class life. (My mother told
me that on his wedding day she inspected him carefully to make
sure that he had washed behind the ears.) His wife was the eldest
of five daughters of a bearded, one-eyed Alsatian bravo known as
Colonel Jerome Lang, whose title presumably had been acquired
in the Civil War. Uncle Eddie's wife was Mathilde, called Tillie.
The names of all the girls fascinated me: Hortense, Léocadie,
Clementine, Camille.

The only person in Baltimore I disliked was my mother's sister,
Aunt Emma. She always tried to be friendly and affectionate, but,
like my father, she was physically unattractive to me. She was one
of those unfortunate women without any grace or charm: a con-
genital old maid with protruding teeth, a shrill voice and small
eyes that peered through lenses half an inch thick. One of my chief
grievances was that she persisted in calling me "Ellie." I was not
pleased, either, when on her annual visits to New York I had to
vacate my bed in the living room and move in with Grandpa. My
mother was saddened by my hostility, but she could not make me
relent.

I shudder now when I think of the poor creature's lonely, futile
life. When my grandmother died, she went on living with Uncle
Albert, whose wife, a cold, petulant, selfish woman, made no attempt to conceal her resentment at having the inept spinster foisted
upon her. So Aunt Emma lived on for endless years, acceptable to
no one but my mother, whom she idolized. One tragicomic little
episode is revealing. Always before embarking on one of her rare

visiting or shopping expeditions she made sure that her under-
clothing was fresh, against the possibility of an accident that required hospitalization. She frequently alluded to this precaution,
unaware that it made her an object of ridicule. Then one day she
did have an accident and was taken to a hospital. It was probably
the only triumphant moment of her miserable life.

5

My entourage of loving adults was not limited to my relatives.
It included a family of three who lived on the top floor of the
Madison Avenue flathouse—Henry Weiss, his wife Frances and her
sister, Julia Apolant. They were intimate friends as far back as I
can remember and remained so as long as they lived. As each died,
it became my task to make the funeral arrangements and manage
the small estates. Henry Weiss, Hungarian-born, a slow-moving,
slow-thinking man with a heavy bronze mustache and features
that seemed too large for his face, was a distributor of shoemakers'
supplies. His business was located in East Forty-second Street, and
he commuted to work on the New York Central, walking over to
the station at Park Avenue and 110th Street to take the steam train to
the terminus. His wife was an exceptionally good-looking woman—
even as an old lady—with a lively, warm disposition. Her sister
was an agile, bright-eyed little hunchback.

The Weisses were childless, a condition to which Frances reconciled herself as best she could by her attentions to the children of
her numerous friends, all of whom adored her. She was a second
mother to me and second in my affections only to my own mother.
In later years she looked more and more to me for advice and consolation, as a mother might.

The Weiss family was economically and culturally a cut above
mine. Mr. Weiss was an amiable dullard, but the sisters had some
acquaintance with the amenities of living and a certain sense of
aesthetics that was completely lacking in my family. They had
bright carpets, frilly curtains, china closets filled with ornaments and
porcelain of European origin, quantities of iridescent cut glass—very
much in vogue then. It all seemed beautiful to me; spacious too,
with only three people occupying the flat.

The two women were forever knitting, tatting and embroider-

ing: decorating handkerchiefs and napkins with bright-red straw-
berries that sprang from bright-green stems and were picked out
with bright-yellow seeds; making things of leather too; and burning
designs on boxes with a special kind of needle heated in an alcohol
flame—an art, I have learned, known as xylopyrography. The
kitchen was busy, too; for a small visitor from the third floor there
was always an assortment of cookies, layer cakes, strudel, fudge,
taffy, peanut brittle. In the holiday season there was store-bought
marzipan, cunningly shaped and tinted to resemble various fruits,
and excruciatingly delicious.

Sunday mornings I would pad upstairs in my pajamas and climb
into the Weisses' bed. We conversed almost entirely in German,
which I spoke fluently, having learned it simultaneously with
English. (It was a peculiarity of mine to refer to myself in the
third person. I never said "ich," always "der Elmer.")

As my parents' birthdays or wedding anniversaries approached,
Frances would secretly coach me in some doggerel verse appropriate
to the occasion. On the day itself I would arise early, enter my
parents' bedroom, plant myself at the foot of the bed with arms
folded behind me, and speak my piece. I still remember snatches
of some of these filial tributes. One began: "Liebe Eltern, höre
mich," after which exhortation it went on, like a New Year's resolution, to enumerate the virtues I intended to practice during the
coming year. I was going to be "artig und gehorsam" and much else.
Sometimes, in the course of the year, when my performance did not
quite measure up to the prospectus, my mother would give me a
gentle reminder.

All that coddling and cuddling undoubtedly nourished my ego
and built up my sense of self-importance. I never suffered from
those childhood feelings of being unwanted or forced to play
second fiddle that seem to be at the bottom of so many adult maladjustments and neuroses. Nevertheless, I lived almost entirely in a
world of adults and always longed for that absent brother-playmate.
I worried about Grandpa too, my only daily comrade. He seemed
very old, and the death of my grandmothers may have suggested
that his end was near—a groundless fear. My father's illness disturbed me greatly, too. I never confided these troubles and misgivings to anyone, but I did make them the subjects of prayer. I do
not know who taught me to pray; my mother, I suppose, for it could

hardly have been anyone else. Nor do I remember the substance of the prayer; it was probably the sort of routine that children repeat automatically. Whatever it was, I added three specific petitions of my own invention: that my father get well, that Grandpa go on living forever, and that my brother be restored to life. I went on with this for a long time, until I came to doubt the efficacy of prayer and gave it up. I have never gone back to it.

III

Toward an Education

1

Presumably because I was "delicate," I did not begin school until I was seven. I have no recollection of being sickly, though I do remember consuming great quantities of malted-milk tablets and a vile concoction called Scott's Emulsion. Several doctors have told me that my chest formations suggest a history of juvenile rickets, which, according to Webster, is a disease of malnutrition, characterized by restlessness, fever and profuse sweating. I certainly never had any of those symptoms, and it is inconceivable that anyone who ate at my mother's table could have been undernourished.

Getting into school was a bit of a problem, for my mother was unwilling to have me go to the school nearby, because most of the pupils were children of Irish or Italian immigrants, whom she considered "tough." (My own later observation confirmed her judgment.) With the assistance of a family acquaintance, Eva Kosminsky, I was admitted to Public School 57, in 115th Street near Third Avenue, presumably a more genteel neighborhood. (The school is still there, now attended by a newer breed of "undesirables," the Puerto Ricans.) Since I could read and write, I was put in the second grade, of which Miss Kosminsky was the teacher.

The school was nearly three quarters of a mile from my home, and there were two streetcar lines to cross, so Grandpa was elected my escort. Every morning I trudged off with him, clutching my lunchbox, a handsome tin affair brightly lacquered with a Scotch plaid; when empty, it could be folded flat. At the end of the school day Grandpa was waiting for me. It meant a lot of walking for him, but he liked to walk. I think he also liked being entrusted with with so important a responsibility. I forget how the afternoon trip affected the pinochle game; I suppose Mr. Oppenheimer just sat and waited. When the streets were icy and the crossings ankle-deep in snow it took quite a while.

Those two years at P.S. 57 seem to have left no memories. Even my impression of Miss Kosminsky, though pleasant, is shadowy. Undoubtedly she helped me through the difficult period of adjustment, but whether I was happy or unhappy, interested or bored, I am unable to remember.

Since all the other children lived near the school, I had no contact with them outside the classroom. My mother, in protecting me from the toughs, had intensified my introversion and aloneness. From the welter of my schoolmates not a name, not a face emerges. Yet schoolgoing released me from the confines of the family circle and put me, to some extent, on my own. I now had the privilege of seeking diversion and adventure in the streets. By "streets" I mean not only the thoroughfares themselves, but the cellars, the roofs, the back yards and the vacant lots. Over this extensive territory I ranged freely, joining the neighborhood boys and girls in a great variety of activities.

The sidewalks and the stoops were forums for powwows and arenas for those indeterminate free-for-alls in which small boys love to engage. For all sorts of games too: hopscotch; leapfrog; stoop ball; prisoner's base; I spy the woolly, woolly wolf; kick the stick; red rover; a tisket, a tasket; around the mulberry bush; water, water, wildflower; London Bridge; ring-around-a-rosy; cops and robbers. Jacks, rope skipping and ball bouncing—the latter two accompanied by ritualistic chants—were favored by girls, whereas marbles was exclusively a game for boys. On the first warm spring day the cry of "Immy up!" would draw an eager crowd. The owner of the "immy" or "realer"—a relatively valuable pellet of imitation or real marble —sat on the sidewalk, the marble between his spread legs a target for kneeling sharpshooters. I always began with a fine supply of marbles and ended with none, for I was deficient in all manual skills. In slippery weather we made long "sliding ponds" on the side-walks—hazards to inattentive or shortsighted pedestrians.

Cellars, dimly lighted and stinking of the urine of cats, served as hiding places or shelters in rainy weather. Sometimes an ambitious group staged a theatrical performance in an empty storage bin—a sort of loosely constructed revue or variety show, to which admission could be gained for the modest sum of five pins. I do not remember how the proceeds were divided, or what the recipients did with their shares.

Back yards were good for games that involved hiding or chasing. You could dodge in and out of the cellars, scramble over dividing fences or squeeze through holes in them. Roofs were mostly forbidden ground, partly because of a supposed element of danger, partly because they were usually filled with laden clotheslines. But the attraction of the housetops was irresistible. You could crouch behind the chimneys or the low parapets that separated the roofs, or hide among drying sheets and tablecloths. Sometimes you tried on the billowing union suits, male or female, over your outer clothing.

Best of all playgrounds were the vacant lots. Fifth Avenue was undeveloped from Ninety-sixth Street all the way to 110th. (On 105th Street, near Fifth, there was still a small wooden farmhouse with palings and a little kitchen garden.) The sand lots made good baseball fields, the irregularities of the terrain adding to the hazards of the game. I was never a good baseball player, partly because of my myopia, which went undetected all through my school life. When sides were chosen up, I was always picked last and accepted with resignation by my teammates. After a while I gave up playing, and without regret.

There were other lots, rocky wastes or miniature jungles, ideal for all sorts of adventurous and imaginative play—piracy, banditry, battles and sieges; especially in winter, a season of great snow forts and snowball fights. There were also treasure houses of junk and, like the excavators at Delphi, one never knew what one might find. From the clumps of burdock we gathered the little adhesive "stickers," fashioning them into big balls, stockpiles of ammunition with which to pepper the backs of passers-by. Sometimes the victim detected us and laughed good-humoredly or made a feint at pursuit. We often debated the ethics of throwing the burrs into the long hair of little girls. The belief that they could be removed only by cutting off the hair was not, I am afraid, a very effective deterrent.

Life in the streets had its heartaches and perils too. I was constantly twitted about my lack of athletic prowess and about my bright-red hair, admired by adult females but derided by juvenile males. I was Red, Bricktop, Carrots. Then once I went out wearing a beautiful new derby, which was promptly snatched from my head and used as a football—one of the unhappiest moments of my whole life. (I have seen a photograph of myself, at the age of three, dressed in a Little Lord Fauntleroy suit, with lace collar and plumed hat. Fortunately, I do not remember myself in it.) Again, I was held up in Central Park, in broad daylight, by two bandits a year or so older than myself. I offered no resistance and suffered no harm beyond the loss of my pocketknife and some coins.

Neither juvenile crime nor gang warfare was unknown sixty years ago. Every street had its gang. The members were younger than those of today's gangs, perhaps because the compulsory school age was lower; at fourteen many boys were already at work. But the youngsters were not lacking in toughness or belligerence. When the grapevine warned that the "Hun'red and Fift's" were about to engage the "Hun'red an' Nint's" in a fight—they were not yet called rumbles—timid little boys stayed indoors. These encounters were often savage. I never heard of knives or firearms being used, but a brick, a baseball bat, a bottle or a frozen snowball can be a dangerous weapon. There were many fractured limbs, jaws and skulls.

Perhaps my early acquaintance with street gangs accounts for my antipathy to mobs or crowds. I believe that when an individual becomes a unit in a parade, a mass demonstration, a military organization, a convention, a religious assemblage, a sports event gathering, he functions on a lower intellectual and moral level than when he acts independently of group pressure and the fear of being a nonconformist. He is far more likely to respond to clichés and banal slogans, to howl down dissent, to engage in antisocial or even violent behavior. The egg-throwing heckler, the lyncher, the trooper who shoots down strikers, the American Legionnaire who drops water-filled paper bags on the heads of passers-by may in private be a tolerably decent citizen. Anyhow, from the time I first ventured into the streets, I have distrusted and shunned crowds. The minority man I have always been is just a grown-up minority boy.

2

The ordinary run of schooldays was set off by special occasions that called for special activities. On Halloween, you wore your jacket inside out and, chalk in hand, sallied forth to mark up your contemporaries and be marked up by them. At dusk you went willingly indoors, for then the marauding gangs appeared, armed with flour-filled knit stockings that sometimes contained a small rock too.

Election night was the time of the big bonfires. For weeks, boxes, crates and barrels had been begged or filched from storekeepers and householders and stored in cellars, whence they were hauled to the vacant lots and heaped high, ready to be ignited when night fell. The blazes roared and soared, giving off welcome warmth too, for the night was likely to be chilly. Around the big fires the attendants whooped and danced, in nonpartisan celebration. Nobody cared who had won the election; indeed, nobody knew, for it sometimes took days for decisive returns from the outlying areas to come in. As the fires died down, the bolder spirits leaped through the flames. I enjoyed watching them.

Even longer preparation preceded the Glorious Fourth. For a month all savings and pocket money went into the piling up of a supply of fireworks. Eager patriots began celebrating on the eve of the holiday, or even a few days before. On the day itself, the uproar began at dawn. Everybody, young and old, was in the streets, armed with red firecrackers of all sizes, which were ignited, singly or in packs, by smoldering sticks of punk. There were cap pistols; there were torpedoes, twists of paper filled with pebbles and a percussion cap that exploded upon contact with the pavement. No matter how lavish the hoard of explosives had seemed, it always became necessary to plead for replenishments. The racket went on until far into the night. The air was acrid, the streets littered. After dark, the magical fireworks appeared: Roman candles, pinwheels, rockets. You watched the rocket balls sail into the sky, and as they descended in a burst of stars you responded with a deeply exhaled "Aaaah!"

It was a day marked by accidents and casualties. Bad burns were common; people were blinded. It was said that the careless use of cap pistols could cause lockjaw, but I did not understand why. Horses, stampeded by the noise of explosions, dashed off frantically, injuring people and property. Awnings and lace curtains at open windows became ignited; if there was a breeze, the flames spread quickly. The fire engines were constantly on the go, their plangent bells contributing to the general din. Rain on the fifth was attributed to the smoke and fumes, as current climatic conditions are attributed to nuclear blasts.

My favorite holiday was Thanksgiving, a day for masquerading. Every child and many adults donned a costume, put on make-up or a papier-mâché false face, tooted a brightly colored tin horn. The streets swarmed with strutting couples and lockstepping columns: hoboes, harlequins, fairy princesses, cowboys, Chinese coolies, burnt-cork Negroes. One year I was a clown, in a cone-shaped hat, a mountebank's mask, and a pair of polka-dotted white flannel pajamas stuffed out with a pillow. But I was not allowed to solicit pennies from passing adults.

Christmas had no special public features, nor was it observed in my family, though I received many gifts. Also, Grandpa used to take me to the German Theatre in Irving Place, managed by that fine actor Rudolf Christians. In the holiday season there were dramatizations of Andersen's fairy tales. I wish I had kept the programs, but that is a practice I began only at twelve.

The Eden Musée, in West Twenty-third Street, was a waxworks museum, like Madame Tussaud's in London and the Musée Grevin in Paris. You got off to a fine start by laughing at the unsuspecting patrons whose inquiries the uniformed attendant ignored, or who waited for the young lady in the summer frock to rise from the bench with the "Wet Paint" sign. It was disappointing, though, to be barred from the famous Chamber of Horrors—an arbitrary prohibition, for I do not believe that children are greatly disturbed by gruesome and sanguinary scenes. But by way of compensation there was the mechanical chess player, an imposing Oriental automaton who signalized his victories over one and all by sweeping the pieces from the board. On a gallery around the exhibition hall were stereoscopes whose twin lenses afforded three-dimensional views of the Pyramids, the Parthenon, the Grand Canyon and Mont Blanc. I could not be torn away until I had feasted my eyes on every one of them. Perhaps this was the genesis of my determination to see the world.

The Buffalo Bill Show was an annual event at Madison Square

Garden, then located on Madison Square. Part of the fun was the ride downtown on top of the horse-drawn Fifth Avenue bus. Buffalo Bill himself, the famous Indian fighter Colonel William F. Cody, always made a personal appearance: a fine figure of a man, goateed, mustachioed, in a close-fitting embroidered white uniform and wide-brimmed Stetson, circling the arena on a snowy-white high-stepping horse. Annie Oakley, the crack sharpshooter, later immortalized by Ethel Merman, was on hand, too. (Free admission tickets, pasteboards punctured by round holes, used to be called Annie Oakleys.) Besides sharpshooting, roping, fancy riding and "bulldogging" of bison, there were dramatic episodes: an attempted stagecoach robbery, or an attack upon a covered wagon by yelling half-naked Indians in war paint. The finale was a spectacular re-creation of a recent historic event. One year the Rough Riders, led by a thespian Teddy Roosevelt, charged victoriously up a ramp representing San Juan Hill. Another year it was the attack upon the legation-quarter wall in Peking: the Allied troops, bearing their national colors, thrust their bayonets into the wall's crevices and by these improvised ladders scaled the barrier to rescue their compatriots who were menaced by the infamous Boxers.

These dramas had meaning to one who was able to spell out the headlines in the New York *Herald*. Whenever there was a big story, newsvendors roamed the streets carrying armfuls of a special edition and hoarsely shouting, "Extra! Extra! Big battle in Cuba! Read all a-bout it!" There has always been a war somewhere; in my early schooldays there were three: the Spanish-American War, the Boxer Rebellion and the Boer War. All I remember about the Boer War is a splendid joke about General De Wet. You asked why the Boer soldiers wore rubber boots, and when everyone gave up you said, "To keep De Wet from defeat." From the Boxer episode, I learned that the Chinese, commonly known as the Chinks, are a mysterious, treacherous and nefarious people, a concept long perpetuated by Hollywood and the pulp magazines. In my novel *A Voyage to Purilia* there is a chapter on the cinematic development of this thesis.

The Spanish-American War I remember clearly: the sinking of the *Maine;* the battle of Manila; the redoubtable Teddy, "alone in Cuba," as Mr. Dooley put it. We used to sing, "Spain, Spain, Spain, you oughtta be ashamed, for doing such a thing as blowing up the

Maine." I knew all the war songs, of course: "Dolly Gray," "Good-bye, Little Girl, Goodbye" and "There'll be a Hot Time in the Old Town Tonight." They supplanted the Civil War songs my mother had taught me: "Tenting on the Old Camp Ground," "Rally Round the Flag, Boys" and "Just Break the News to Mother" ("Tell her not to wait for me, for I'm not coming home").

My own children have always had difficulty in restraining me from singing the songs I learned at my mother's knee: "Annie Rooney," "The Bowery," "Daisy Bell" ("a bicycle built for two"), "The Sidewalks of New York," "Come, Birdie, Come" ("and live with me"), "Down Went McGinty" ("to the bottom of the sea"), "My Sweetheart's the Man in the Moon," "Grandfather's Clock" ("It stopped short, never to go again, when the old man died"), and her favorite, "After the Ball" ("Many a heart is aching, if you could read them all; many the hopes that have vanished, after the ball"). I preferred the schoolyard version that began: "After the ball is over, Jennie takes out her glass eye."

One day I heard the vendors shouting the news of Queen Victoria's death, but the name meant little to me. More vivid is the memory of President McKinley's assassination, which occurred in the same year. I associate it with an accident that happened to my mother. While waiting for a streetcar she was kicked in the leg by a horse, a painful though not serious injury. As she limped from room to room to do her household chores, I accompanied her, reading aloud the reports of McKinley's lingering death. It had been my impression that an inflammatory editorial in one of the William Randolph Hearst newspapers had been found in the pocket of the assassin, Leon Czolgosz. But Walter Lord, whose lively book *The Good Years* describes the assassination, thinks I am mistaken. Anyhow, the editorial, which said that "if bad men can be got rid of only by killing, then the killing must be done," led Theodore Roosevelt to charge Hearst with responsibility for McKinley's death.

3

At nine I was transferred to a big new school, P.S. 171, only two blocks from my home. I no longer needed an escort: a big advance along the road to self-dependence. It was at 171 that I first fell in love. The object of my devotion was my fourth-grade teacher, Ella

McNair, who had rosy cheeks, dimples, prominent teeth, unruly hair and bright eyes that flashed when she lost her temper, which was not seldom. I knew her as "Teacher" until the end of her life, by which time I was an author, husband and father. Reciprocally, I was her favorite pupil, perhaps because I took great pains not to incur her displeasure. When I was promoted to the fifth grade, presided over by Mr. Keresey, a cadaverous man with a booming voice and a mobile Adam's apple, I still saw Teacher at recess and often slipped into her room at the end of the school day.

The principal of the school, William J. O'Shea, a portly man, filled me with awe. I took a somewhat less exalted view of him when I encountered him as superintendent of schools thirty-five years later. As regional director of the Federal Theatre Project, I tried to enlist his aid in a plan for making theatrical performances available to schoolchildren; but I failed even to capture his attention. I was so disgusted by his denseness and bureaucratic apathy that I did not bother to bring up the good old days at P.S. 171.

My schoolmates were now neighborhood boys whom I could see outside school hours, though not many house visits were exchanged. I was reluctant to invite my friends, partly because there was no telling when my father might have a fit, partly because he criticized the table manners and speech of my guests or commented on their failure to show him sufficient respect. Disturbing, too, were his objections to my association with the three sons of his brother, Uncle Charlie. The boys, Chester, Allen and Wilbur—we were a great family for names!—lived only a few blocks away. Normally we would have been close companions. But the relationship was far from normal; our fathers were bitter enemies. Apparently my father believed that Uncle Charlie had cheated him in some business transaction. The only time Uncle Charlie entered our house was when my grandmother was dying. Upon his arrival my father withdrew with me to the other end of the flat, where we sat until Uncle Charlie left. Too young to understand what was happening, I sensed that something was not as it should be.

As I grew older, I was shocked by the virulence of my father's hatred. He never referred to his brother by name, always as "It," his lips trembling, his throat constricted: an ugly spectacle. Sometimes my cousins came in to play table games, but if my father arrived home early he either greeted them curtly or ignored them completely, to my great embarrassment. By contrast, on the rare occasions when, more or less in defiance of my father, I visited them, I was always cordially received by Uncle Charlie.

As successive waves of immigrants swarmed into the slums of the lower East Side and pushed their predecessors uptown, our neighborhood became noisier and more congested. It continued to deteriorate, until it became one of the city's most depressed sections. Recently whole blocks of the crumbling, insanitary flat-houses have been razed to make room for towering housing projects, cheerless segregated warrens occupied by Negroes and Puerto Ricans. When our landlord began converting the ground floor to stores, my family decided to move. It was an important event in my life: a new neighborhood, new living quarters, a new school.

I found it a change for the worse. Our new flat was in a narrow side street, West 114th Street, instead of on a wide avenue. Central Park was no longer around the corner, but four blocks away. There were almost no vacant lots; no big rectangle of back yards, only dingy inside courtyards, dismally called airshafts. To make matters worse, our flat was on the ground floor, so that the size of the front rooms was reduced by the vestibule. There was no bright, sunny kitchen; the sun rarely entered any of the rooms. We were exposed to all the dirt and noise of the street. There was, of course, no bedroom for me; I slept in the living room on a folding iron bedstead, for which there was hardly space among all the cumbersome furniture. In the three years we lived there, I never got used to the glaring electric street lights and the confused din of traffic, footfalls and voices.

At the time I transferred to my new school, P.S. 10, at 117th Street and St. Nicholas Avenue, the elementary-school span was increased from seven years to eight. All reasonably good pupils were advanced a year, so, having completed the fifth grade, I entered the seventh. I now had specialized teachers for mathematics, history and grammar, which made school life a little more interesting; but I had no sense of attachment to the school.

One redeeming feature of the new neighborhood was the branch of the New York Public Library, just a block away. Nothing in my life has been more helpful to me than the simple act of joining the library. It would be impossible for me to overstate my indebtedness to that noble institution. It was my university and my shrine. It brightened and enriched my life by introducing me to a world in which I have spent some of my happiest hours: the world of books. It provided me with knowledge, entertainment, exaltation, solace, ideas and ideals; stimulated my curiosity and imagination; shaped my philosophy and paved the way for my career.

School must have taught me something, too, but I cannot say what. What I remember chiefly about P.S. 10 are my two appearances as an actor. Each year, at graduation, a scene from Shakespeare was performed. When I was in the seventh grade I was the First Citizen, arrayed in a toga fashioned by my mother from a sheet, in the forum scene from *Julius Caesar*. It is not a fat part; in fact, the citizen is little more than one of the mob, with the usual ad libs. However, at the very end of the scene I had one fine ringing speech: "Come, away, away! We'll burn his body in the holy place, and with the brands fire the traitors' houses. Take up the body!"

At my graduation I fared better. I was Antonio in *The Merchant of Venice* courtroom scene. He is a dull, unattractive character, but he talks a lot, so from an actor's point of view it is a good part. This time we were provided with period costumes; I wore a fine velveteen doublet and long tight-fitting hose. I still can recite some of the speeches and sometimes do, amid cries of protest from my children.

Nobody saw anything amiss about performing *The Merchant of Venice;* indeed, many of the children who acted in it were Jewish. The best portrayal of Shylock I have ever seen was by the famous Jewish actor Jacob P. Adler (father of Luther and Stella). He spoke Yiddish, while the rest of the company spoke English: incongruous but effective. Yet today overzealous Jewish organizations have made it almost impossible for the play to be performed or even studied in schools and colleges. A few years ago Margaret Webster had to drop it from her repertory, because certain campus groups theatened to boycott her entire program. As an opponent of censorship, I have fought many battles on this issue. Most recent was my involvement in a public controversy over the attempt of the New York Board of Rabbis to prevent Joseph Papp's tasteful Shakespeare-in-the-Park production from being televised.

Except for fleeting appearances in plays of my own, I did not go on with acting. Once during the London run of *Judgment Day* I sat on the stage as a courtroom spectator. On another occasion I startled the cast of *Two on an Island* by announcing that I intended to play seven parts—really not a great feat, for they were all cross-overs with almost no lines. Some of the actors tried unsuccessfully to break me up; and I did get one laugh that nobody had got before. But acting as a career never appealed to me.

4

At the end of my two uneventful years at P.S. 10, I entered the High School of Commerce. I would have preferred Townsend Harris Hall of the College of the City of New York, which was reputed to have high scholastic standards; besides, my closest friend, Abraham Allenberg, the class valedictorian, was going there. My second choice was De Witt Clinton High School, mainly because I wanted to study Latin, which was not taught at Commerce.

But Commerce, as its name suggests, specialized in the teaching of business subjects, which made it best qualified to prepare me for my destined career. I say "destined," for it had always been taken for granted that I was to become a businessman. I do not recall that any other possibility was considered, or that the matter was discussed at all. All the men in my family were engaged in business; it seemed obvious that I would follow their example. I assumed I would, too; at twelve one is not likely to have very affirmative ideas about a career. In my childhood I had a passion for building blocks. I owned a fine set of German-made Richter blocks of varicolored stone in all shapes and sizes. Everyone admired my elaborate fabrications, and my mother predicted that I would grow up to be an architect (pronounced "arch-itect") By the time I was graduated from P.S. 10, the blocks had long been abandoned. The possibility of becoming a writer never entered my mind; if it had, my elders would have dismissed it as a childish whim.

The High School of Commerce, abutting today's Lincoln Center for the Performing Arts, was a long way from my home. To get there I used New York's new transportation marvel, the subway, which had begun operation on October 27, 1904. I remember the date well, because it was my mother's birthday. The inauguration of the subway, described by its financial genius, August Belmont, as "this splendid arcarde," was a gala occasion that vied for front-page honors with the Roosevelt-Parker Presidential campaign and the Japanese assault upon the Russian fortress of Port Arthur. The sedate *Herald*, under the heading "Carnival Spirit to Open Subway," said "The celebration promises to equal in picturesqueness, the outbursts of enthusiasm and good-natured jostling, for which New York is famous on election nights and New Year's eves. The reaches of the tunnel will resound with the tooting of horns and the din of all sorts of noise-making devices." In the Aldermanic Chamber, after benedictions by Coadjutor Bishop Greer and Archbishop Farley, Mayor George B. McClellan, son of the famous Union general, optimistically declared, "The spirit of New York built the subway, as it will meet and solve every problem in our municipal development." Next day the *Tribune* reported: "Fully seventy-five per cent of those who rode on the subway last night were out for the experience. Many of them went into the train with a guilty self-conscious look on their faces, for the New Yorker does not like to admit that he is curious about anything. Once seated, however, they gazed out of the windows brazenly and did not attempt to stifle the exclamations of wonder."

My family, though sharing the general curiosity, deferred its investigation until the opening of the Lenox Avenue branch, some weeks later. On the appointed Sunday my parents, Grandpa, Uncle Will and I entered the kiosk at 116th Street and inhaled for the first time that acrid mephitic air that is the daily inspiration of millions of New Yorkers. The dimly lighted interior, with its tile mosaics and steel pillars, was magical and awesome, the train a splendid chariot. In order to get a good view of every station, we took a local. The train switched over to Broadway, down to Times Square, over to Grand Central and down to City Hall. Since we were not going anywhere, but were just out to see the sights, we kept our seats and made the return trip, station by station. Eventually we reached home, tired but happy.

By the time I entered high school, nearly a year later, the subway had become just another means of transportation. I soon learned how to cheat on fares. You purchased tickets in strips of five, which you tore into six parts, dropping the segments quickly into the "ticket chopper's" glass receptacle. Sometimes a group of football-playing students would simply "rush" the ticket chopper and board the train.

The High School of Commerce, now coeducational, with "honor" classes specializing in the fine arts (one of my granddaughters is a student), in my day concentrated on such subjects as business arithmetic, double-entry bookkeeping, and stenography. I never got as far as speed writing, but I did master the Pitman system of notation and am probably the only member of the Authors' League of America who has read all of *Robinson Crusoe* in shorthand. Of the other subjects, I particularly disliked biology, which consisted largely of messing about with earthworms and other fauna preserved in evil-smelling formaldehyde. My favorite subject was English, not because of the books we studied, most of which I had already read, but because I had a good teacher, John B. Opdycke, whom I met again later in life and who became the author of well-known textbooks on the writing and teaching of English. Once I wrote a story which I called "Honesty Is the Best Policy," a rather clever title, I thought. But Opdycke pointed out that since "best" is superlative, it implied that with respect to probity there is a "good" policy and a "better" policy, obviously not what I had intended. It was the first time anyone had suggested to me that I should think about the words I used. I profited by the lesson, but with many lapses, I am afraid.

Emotionally and socially, high school meant little to me. Though I got on well enough with my fellow students, I made almost no friends. I was not on any school team, nor do I remember participating in any extracurricular activity. Gymnasium attendance was a sore trial to me; to avoid chinning myself and vaulting over horses, I spent most of the hour in the lavatory. I was bored by the long assembly periods in which we rehearsed songs and cheers in preparation for interschool games, none of which I ever attended.

Outside school hours, I had plenty of activities: playing on the streets with the neighborhood boys and girls, reading, busying myself with various collections. My favorite collection was of picture postcards, mostly views of the principal streets of American cities and of summer resort hotels. But there were some fine foreign ones from a friend of my mother's, a buyer for an importing house. On her frequent trips to Europe she wrote me letters on sets of postcards, mostly from Switzerland, depicting Alpine scenes in which each mountain was represented as a grotesque animal or giant. I longed to see the original scenes; when I did at last, they

failed to measure up to the postcard images. Now and then the
sender, very elegant and worldly, came to visit us. Through that
curious process of osmosis by which children absorb information
not intended for them, I gathered that she not only smoked cigarettes and drank wine but was the mistress of her employer. I admired her, but not unreservedly, for she always spelled my name
"Elma."

I was the organizer of a rather exclusive club, consisting of only
five members. It was called the Henry Clay Literary Society. Why
Henry Clay I do not know. It was the brand name of the cigars
my father smoked, but that could hardly have been the reason. The
club provided badges for its members: swatches of blue satin, with
gilt paper letters—HCLS—of the sort that haberdashers used to
paste inside their customers' hats. Unfortunately, the letters did
not stick very well to the smooth satin. There were officers, of
course: president, vice-president, secretary and treasurer; I believe a fifth office was created to provide for the odd member—
perhaps a second vice-president or a sergeant at arms. Thanks to a
copy of *Roberts' Rules of Order,* our meetings were parliamentary
models. Motions were made, seconded, amended, debated, tabled
or voted up or down. There were many points of order and more
often than not an appeal from the chairman's ruling. These formal
proceedings left little time for the club's literary activities, whatever they were meant to be; but that early training has served me
well in the course of a lifetime filled with committee and board
meetings.

I was a baseball fan too. There were Giants in the earth in those
days; and I was fortunate enough to see the mighty team assembled by the great John J. (Muggsy) McGraw. Dan McGann,
Larry Doyle, Arthur Devlin, Roger Bresnahan, Mike Donlin—I
saw them all. And those pitchers: Iron Man McGinnity, who could
win both games of a double-header; deaf-mute Dummy Taylor;
eccentric Rube Marquard; godlike Christy Mathewson. My heart has
always belonged to the Giants, even in the days of their migration.
The Yankees, originally known as the Highlanders—because their
first park was on Washington Heights, where the Columbia Presby-
terian Medical Center now stands—I still regard as aliens and up-
starts. The Dodgers, once the Superbas, in honor of their owner, Ned
Hanlon, producer of a musical extravaganza called *Superba,* have

always seemed to me unworthy of notice. I knew the names and records of all the players. Whenever my sons try to put me in my place, I remind them that I saw Ty Cobb, Babe Ruth, George Sisler, Rogers Hornsby, Honus Wagner, Walter Johnson, Cy Young, Ed Walsh, Napoleon Lajoie, Grover Cleveland Alexander and many other immortals.

Another sport in which I became interested was horse racing, mainly because my friend Abe Allenberg's father, generally known as Klondike—he had gone to Alaska in the gold-rush days—was a bookmaker. He had a thick neck, a thick skull, thick hands and a thick accent, but he was a friendly, likable man. He had an implacable hatred of Governor Charles Evans Hughes—always referred to by him as "Pink Whiskers"—who was trying to make race track betting illegal. I never saw a race—perhaps children were barred from the track—but sometimes when the meeting was at Brighton Beach the Allenbergs invited me to the Brighton Beach Hotel for a luxurious meal. I was as well acquainted with the records of all the thoroughbreds as I was with those of the ballplayers. Whenever I visit the Museum of Natural History the rearing skeleton of the great Sysonsby evokes a flood of memories.

But it was theatregoing that gradually became my dominant interest. My program collection dates from 1905, but I had seen plays before that. Once, as a birthday treat, I was given the choice of seeing Richard Mansfield in one of his famous roles or Victor Herbert's operetta *Babes in Toyland*. I chose the latter, so I never saw the great Mansfield, who died shortly afterward. I did not regret my choice, for *Babes in Toyland* was an exciting show and I learned early in life that you can't have everything.

My first program was that of *A Society Circus,* the opening production, I believe, of that magnificent showplace the Hippodrome. Like so many other notable structures, it has succumbed to New York's compulsion to demolish. No child could ever forget the Hippodrome's dazzling stage spectacles, now dwarfed but not excelled at the Radio City Music Hall. What comic has ever matched that hilarious clown Marceline? What has been more thrilling or mysterious than the descent of that line of beautiful chorus girls into a water-filled tank from which they were never seen to emerge?

Not long afterward I saw *The Count of Monte Cristo,* in which

Eugene O'Neill's father, James O'Neill, appeared perennially, preferring financial success to the development of his talents. I had read the novel several times and was disappointed in the necessarily attenuated stage version. When Edmond Dantès clambered upon a rock to proclaim that the world was his, I was annoyed because the sea's agitation was obviously produced by stagehands crawling about under the painted groundcloth. Even at that age my acceptance of the theatre's illusions was tempered by my rejection of its absurdities. Once I made an excursion through the choppy waters of Marseilles harbor to the Château d'If, where a guide obligingly pointed out the cell that had been occupied by the fictional Dantès, a bit of pseudo history in which the tourists displayed great interest.

These early visits to the theatre were not frequent. Most of my evenings were spent at home. I had homework and I read a lot, but even so the evenings were long. Uncle Will was always out—gambling or enjoying female society, I suppose. My parents never went out and nobody ever came to see us. My mother had innumerable friends, but she saw them only by day; they preferred not to be subjected to my father's testiness and sarcasm. So evening after evening we just sat home by ourselves. There was no phonograph, all conversational possibilities had been exhausted at the supper table. To relieve the tedium, we played games: parcheesi, lotto, a variety of dominoes called muggins, and a simplified form of anagrams. I usually won, so it was not an altogether disagreeable activity, but, after months and years of it, it became really irksome. Sometimes my father had a minor seizure that interrupted the game, or a major one that terminated it.

5

During this period I made an important decision; it had to do with religion. I had had no religious instruction, had never been to a synagogue—or temple, as my family called it. There was no family observance of religious holidays, except that I was kept from school and that on the Day of Atonement my mother fasted. While the rest of the family sat at table, she remained in her room, silently mourning her baby and her parents. When I was eight or nine I joined in the fast, not because the ritual or the day had any meaning for me, but because I wanted to show the men that though they were deserting my mother I was not. I sat with her, and we talked, or I read.

If my father or Uncle Will had opinions on the subject of religion, I never heard them voiced. Grandpa, however, had very definite opinions, which he expressed freely. He was a sort of village athe-ist, though perhaps that is not the correct term, for he questioned the factual accuracy of the Scriptures rather than the principles of theology. He often spoke scornfully of his disbelief in the Creation, Noah's Ark, the parting of the waters of the Red Sea, the Virgin Birth, the miracles of Jesus, and the Resurrection. I had not yet read the Bible, so much of his argument was unintelligible to me, but I was impressed by the forcefulness of his delivery. Far along in life, while working on a play about Thomas Paine, I read *The Age of Reason;* in spite of my great admiration for Paine, I simply could not take the book seriously, for in his strictures on the miracu-lous and the supernatural I heard again the authoritative voice of Grandpa.

My only contact with organized religion had been trivial but antagonizing. On one of the holidays, Abe Allenberg and I set off on a walk around Central Park, a favorite exercise, which I kept up for many years. On our way uptown along Fifth Avenue, it started to rain. We had no money to waste on carfare, so we sought shelter in the synagogue at Seventy-sixth Street. We hurried up the steps, only to be met by a demand for our tickets, followed by rapid expulsion. Drenched and shivering, we trudged on home, in-furiated by our treatment. Of course, no religious sentiment had prompted our entry, nor did we take into account that on holidays payment was required. On the other hand, no one would have been incommoded if we had stood in a corner of the vestibule until the rain stopped. The whole episode was inconsequential, but not un-influential.

Shortly after this incident, my mother suggested that I attend Sunday school, in preparation for confirmation. At first I refused, but she seemed so distressed that I yielded and was inducted into a temple near my home. Presumably admission was restricted to children of congregation members, so I suspected that my mother knew somebody who made it possible for me to attend without payment. Again I saw an unsavory association between religion and commerce.

I heartily disliked Sunday school. The other boys belonged to a social group of higher economic status. I had no contact with them and wanted none. I did not feel inferior, merely aloof and indifferent. I was even more indifferent to the course of instruction—if it could be called that—conducted by a Mr. Asher, a man with a toothbrush mustache who wore a morning coat and an Ascot tie. While he discoursed on various Biblical subjects, we busied ourselves making spitballs, little paper pellets moistened with saliva. Much of Mr. Asher's time was consumed in trying to detect the projectors of these missiles.

Even more distasteful than the class was the succeeding religious service in the temple: the unctuous dissertation of the rabbi; the singing of Hebrew hymns, no word of which I understood; and again the systematic collection of money. When my year of durance finally ended, I was astonished to receive an award for my Sunday-school achievement! Perhaps I had thrown fewer spitballs than the others or had been luckier in escaping detection. I never read the book which was awarded me.

Now came a crucial moment for me—the first of many. When it was time to make arrangements for my confirmation, I flatly refused to go through with it. My mother pleaded with me, but, though it pained me to oppose her, I could not bring myself to pledge allegiance to a creed that meant nothing to me. I rather think my father was relieved by my decision, for I am sure he had spent sleepless nights worrying about where the money would come from to pay for new clothes, a celebration of some sort and probably a contribution to the temple.

For me the importance of my refusal was symbolic rather than actual. It would have been easy enough to do what so many boys did: take the confirmation in stride and then forget about it. My declination was a different sort of stride, a step along the road of independent thought and behavior, the first decisive expression of a determination to live as I chose.

6

At the end of my second year of high school, another decision was made—not by me this time—that had a far greater immediate effect upon my life. I was told that my parents could no longer afford to keep me in school; the time had come for me to begin to earn my living. It was a hard blow. I was not yet fifteen, and I wanted an education. But, knowing my family's economic situation, I could not protest. So my eight years of school life—six in grade school, two in high school—came to an end, neither with a bang nor with a whimper, but just in the manner appropriate to my station in life.

IV

To Make My Bread

1

Our financial situation presented some curious contradictions. Thanks to the contributions of Grandpa and Uncle Will, we were not poverty-stricken. We always had a servant girl; the linens were fresh and the furniture was in good repair; our table provided the best cuts of meat, the choicest fruits and vegetables. Yet other expenditures were minimal, and every penny was discussed and argued about. My mother bought a new dress every three or four years; my father was always shabby. When I outgrew a suit or an overcoat, Uncle Will bought me a new one; twice a year I received a box of shirts and pajamas from Uncle Albert, who was a partner in the Faultless Nightshirt Company of Baltimore. I had almost no pocket money. Once when a teacher suggested the purchase of a history book for supplementary reading, it took me weeks to bring myself to ask my father for the required seventy-five cents. He gave it to me, but with such an air of harassment that I regretted the request. So it went: maintenance of a false standard of living, and worry, worry, worry. All this had its effect upon me, of course—how could it not have had?—and it led me to formulate two rules for the conduct of my own life: never to be dependent upon anyone, and never to live beyond my means. Fortunately, I have been able to adhere to both.

Uncle Will, our financial mainstay, was not a very good business-man. He lacked the drive and single-mindedness that make for business success; he was always ready to take time out for a tour or a fishing trip. He was never in any one business for long. At one time he was proprietor of a retail liquor store on Amsterdam Avenue. I enjoyed spending Saturdays there. We lunched in a restaurant; in the store, I was allowed to draw upon a little keg of reddish syrup—grenadine, perhaps.

Later he became one of the first to profit from the craze for Teddy bears. He established a small factory on West Broadway and for several years made a fine thing of it. But, as so often happens under our free-enterprise system, large manufacturers entered the field, forcing out Uncle Will, who had neither the capital nor the aggressiveness to meet the competition. His next undertaking was the marketing of relief models of the Panama Canal—then nearing its completion—for use as advertising devices. This did not go well at all and after a year or so was abandoned.

It was followed by a more successful venture. A fad developed for making ashtrays by pasting cigar bands on glass saucers and backing them with felt. As the mania for this extraordinary handicraft spread, Uncle Will undertook to supply the frantic demand for materials. He organized our household as a sort of cottage industry. For months my parents, Grandpa and I, forsaking the parcheesi board, spent the evening hours stuffing transparent envelopes with assorted cigar bands, squares of felt and of tinfoil, and instructional leaflets. We were paid for our work, and since my fingers were more deft than those of my elders, my output far exceeded theirs, so that I made several dollars per week—a small fortune! But soon every home in the land boasted a cigar-band ashtray; again Uncle Will had to turn to something else.

He conducted these various operations from one of the decaying buildings on lower Broadway. Further, he employed my father in various minor capacities, thereby providing him with something to do and somewhere to spend his time, as well as with a small salary. As a sideline, my father sold cigars by the box to acquaintances and acquaintances of acquaintances, who were quite willing to help a needy man whose prices were no higher than a tobacconist's. He spent part of each day trudging about, taking orders and making deliveries. During the Christmas season, when the demand was heavy, I was pressed into service to help with the deliveries.

2

When the time came for me to go to work, I was offered a job
in the law office of my cousin Lillian's husband. He was Moses
H. Grossman (known to me as Cousin Moe), senior partner of the
well-known firm of House, Grossman and Vorhaus. But I had no
interest in a legal career. What little I knew about the law derived
mainly from *The Pickwick Papers, Little Dorrit* and *Bleak House;*
it did not attract me to the bar. I felt a little ungrateful about turning down what was presumably a golden opportunity. I did not
know that it was common practice among law firms to take in boys
who gave promise of becoming useful.

So I sought a business job and soon found one—whether through
some connection or simply through answering an advertisement, I
do not remember. My employers were Samstag and Hilder Brothers, occupants of an entire six-story building in the same run-down
area in which Uncle Will's office was located. The firm was in the
jobbing business, middlemen who acted as distributors for small
manufacturers with no sales force of their own. A corps of salesmen traveled to every corner of the United States, taking orders
from retailers for all sorts of merchandise, which was shipped from
the New York headquarters. My pay was four dollars and fifty cents
for a six-day, fifty-four-hour week. That worked out to seventy-five
cents per day, or a little better than eight cents an hour.

I was in the claim department, whose head was a bald, prematurely fat young man named Yondorf. To his desk came complaints
from customers in Oregon, Kentucky or Maine about shortages,
breakages, defects, substitutions. It was my duty to investigate the
merits of these claims. I moved about the building, interviewing
stock clerks, packers and shipping clerks. Sometimes there were ad-
missions of error or substitutions were justified by stock shortages.
Usually culpability was denied—the goods had been closely examined for defects, had been carefully counted, had been securely
packed. I reported my findings to Mr. Yondorf, who then wrote offering the complainant an adjustment or, more often, trying to persuade him that the firm was not at fault.

At first I found my job rather exciting. Being out of knee pants
and a wage earner gave me a sense of importance. I applied myself
to mastering the mysteries and techniques of the business world. I

was fascinated by the great stocks of merchandise that filled the building: clothing, crockery, tools, linens, toys. Sometimes I saw salesmen's reports from Yakima, Sioux Falls, Biloxi, Dubuque, Tallahassee. I awaited the return of these men, eager to see in the flesh mortals who were privileged to visit such exotic, romantic places. I saw myself as proprietor one day of an establishment even more elaborate than that of Samstag and Hilder Brothers. The lower floor was somehow to contain a canal or winding rivulet, along which prospective customers would proceed by barge or canoe to inspect the merchandise tastefully displayed upon the banks.

But, as the novelty wore off, it became apparent to me that I was engaged in a dull routine, in unpleasant surroundings, among people with whom I felt no contact. I wondered dismally if this was to be the pattern of my life.

The building had windows only on the Broadway front. The vast recesses were artificially lighted and quite airless. The claim department was on a balcony, almost within touching distance of the ceiling; neither light nor air could possibly enter. Much of my workday was spent among the packers and shippers in the basement, a gloomy, dusty, littered cavern. In winter I hardly saw the sun; I left home shortly after dawn and quit work after dark. No wonder everybody in the place looked pasty. (Women workers had not yet taken to using make-up.)

What troubled me most was loneliness; I seemed unable to establish contact with my co-workers. Occasionally I went to lunch with a young man about ten years my senior. Except that his name was Singer and that he wore glasses, I remember nothing about him: what his job was, what drew us together, what we talked about. Of course I never saw him outside working hours. I exchanged smiles and pleasantries with two or three female clerks who seemed sympathetic, but they could hardly have been expected to take much interest in an introverted fourteen-year-old. Mostly I ate alone, at places within my fifteen-cent limit. For a while I patronized Bernarr MacFadden's Vegetarian Restaurant, operated by the magazine publisher and health faddist. But when a cockroach walked out of my date sandwich I concluded that the place was misnamed and went there no more.

Though I did not know it, I badly wanted a hero, an older man whom I could admire and emulate. He was not to be found at

Samstag and Hilder Brothers. My employers were formidable but not impressive. Samstag, a stout bearded man, was seldom visible. But the brothers, little men with fiery mustaches and tempers, were always flitting about, finding fault with everyone. When they were heard approaching—they could always be heard!—the workers wriggled about like maggots under an upturned stone.

Mr. Yondorf was affable enough, but I disliked his perpetual smirk and unfunny wisecracks, mostly of a sexual nature. When the salesmen came home, they turned out to be not knights errant with tales of high adventure, but rather shoddy fellows who boasted in crude and explicit terms of their erotic exploits. Throughout the establishment, sex—or, at any rate, reference to it—was rife. The men continually directed sexual innuendoes at the women, who either tittered self-consciously or pretended not to understand. Among themselves the males seemed never to tire of the subject. Typical was the conversation—if that is the word for it—of three invoice clerks stationed in the cellar, where they sat on high stools, wearing green eyeshades to lessen the glare of the naked electric lamps. One was paunchy, bald, bespectacled; another, tall and cadaverous; the third, a twitchy, pimpled youth. They talked as they worked, and apparently they were under compulsion to give every remark a sexual connotation. Each sally, though devoid of wit or joy, evoked laughter. Frequently the older men twitted the boy about his supposed aberrations. He protested feebly, but obviously enjoyed the attention he was receiving.

3

Like any product of the New York public schools, or like any school-boy anywhere, I suppose, I was well informed about sex. By the time I was twelve, the conversation of older boys, supplemented by graphic and literary material, had made me acquainted with the nature of the sexual act in all its variations. Within my family circle I had never heard the subject referred to, even indirectly. Once when I was perhaps eleven, a neighborhood girl of twelve or thirteen, whose parents were out for the evening, invited me to have supper with her. I was quite taken aback by mother's curt refusal of permission, for she seldom spoke sharply to me. Later, when the incident assumed significance, I speculated on what might have happened if I had been allowed to accept.

I do not believe that my school indoctrination had any of the ill effects envisaged by advocates of censorship. Of course, I was greatly interested in what I learned, but it all seemed very remote and even a little unappetizing. I do not mean that I was revolted or that I had any lofty sexual ideal. It was the sly, leering tone of the schoolboy discussions that offended me, rather than the subject matter. Therefore it was disturbing to hear adults, presumably my superiors in wisdom and experience, talking about it in grade-school terms and with grade-school lubricity. I had been thrust unprepared from a sheltered home. My household members were uncultivated and perhaps not too well-mannnered, but there was nothing coarse-grained or cheap about them.

Yet, at the time, I was more conscious of their shortcomings than of their virtues. The discomforts and inadequacies of my home life were growing more irksome. We had moved away at last from the dark, noisy ground-floor flat, to one just a few blocks away, on the third floor of a group of houses that surrounded a large, airy court. Though the new flat was superior to the old, there was, as usual, no bedroom for me. I had to share Grandpa's room, smallish and dark, with one window that opened on a narrow airshaft. At night the window was always shut. It was worse in winter than in summer, for, with the radiator full on, the heat was almost unbearable. I hated going to bed and stayed up as late as I could. The night noises and habits of an old man are neither pleasant nor conducive to repose, so I never had enough sleep. At six, Grandpa awoke, sang lustily, coughed, spat, got up for a shot of whiskey. At last I asked to be transferred back to the folding cot in the living room. There I slept for the next eight years.

The waking hours were not enjoyable, either. When I dragged myself, half asleep, to the breakfast table, the room was already hazy with cigar smoke; I ate to the accompaniment of hawking and spitting. I had always minded it, but now I was more fastidious, or more rebellious. So I hastily swallowed a few mouthfuls and hurried off to the Ninth Avenue El. Sometimes I could not eat at all, and, since my budgeted lunch was meager, I was underfed. The hearty evening meal was not enough to satisfy the needs of a growing boy. At twenty-one I weighed 130 pounds, though I was nearly six feet tall.

My most acute hunger, though, was emotional and intellectual. Unknowingly, I craved aesthetic sustenance; knowingly, I craved learning and new horizons. My family circle provided none. In my childhood my mother had vaguely suggested piano lessons, but, knowing nothing about music, I had had no incentive. Even at fifteen, I had heard only hurdy-gurdies, street and school bands and theatre orchestras. My father detested music; Grandpa and Uncle Will seemed unaware of its existence. Though my mother loved it, particularly if it was romantic or sentimental, she had no opportunity to hear it. We had no piano or phonograph; to spend money for a concert or an opera was unthinkable.

The only art object in our home was a Rogers group, in gold-flecked white bisque, representing a shepherdess and her flock—a wedding gift, I suppose. On my walks around Central Park, I sometimes strayed into the Metropolitan Museum of Art. But, without guidance, the profusion of Egyptian sarcophagi, medieval armor, Grecian vases, Renaissance paintings and Roman portrait busts bewildered me. I was impressed by Rosa Bonheur's *Horse Fair* and the oversized *Washington Crossing the Delaware* (painted, it seems, by a German). Perhaps other things impressed me, for I kept going back.

In the theatre my family, except my father, took a greater interest. Before her marriage my mother had enjoyed theatregoing. She often spoke of Edwin Booth, Lawrence Barrett and other great actors she had seen. Uncle Will occasionally took me to see a play; so did my visiting Baltimore relatives, and now and then Grandpa. I suppose I went five or six times a year—exciting events! On my own, I went sometimes to vaudeville shows, though I could hardly afford it. Out of my four-fifty per week, ten cents daily went for El fare, fifteen for lunch. That left three dollars for clothing, birthday gifts for members of my family, newspapers, an occasional ice-cream soda, haircuts, and contingencies. There was not much over for recreation. My widely spaced visits to the theatre whetted my appetite for cultural fare.

Home life, once so snug, so warm, so reassuring, now had little to offer. At the end of a long day spent mostly in trying to account for a mysterious shortage in soup plates to the Simpson Emporium in Kansas City, all there was to look forward to was the vapidity of domestic table talk. The hours, the weeks, the years of those dinner-table conversations! The same platitudes, endlessly repeated;

the same illogical discussions based upon profound misinformation; the same heated arguments about the degrees of kinship between remote relatives, often long deceased; the same recollection of pointless happenings of twenty, thirty, forty years ago; the same retelling of comic anecdotes, apropos of nothing.

My mother, by far the most loquacious, usually led the conversation. A typical opening gambit was her announcement of an afternoon visit to a friend; but before she could develop the subject Uncle Will would ask what means of transportation she had used. If she replied that she had taken the Eighth Avenue streetcar and transferred at Eighty-sixth, he would suggest that she should have taken the 116th Street line and transferred at Madison. While my mother defended her choice of route, my father intervened, either in her support or to propose a third possibility. Voices rose; tempers shortened. At length, my mother pointed out that since she was now back home the question was moot (though she did not put it in those terms). She now proceeded with a description of her visit, a more or less verbatim account of what had been said: a long, rambling stream of inconsequentialities and irrelevancies that covered births, deaths, marriages, domestic squabbles, bright sayings or awful behavior of children, health notes, cooking hints. At the conclusion of this recital my father would either condemn the persons discussed or else dismiss them as unworthy of notice. Grandpa, more judicious and temperate, would remark, "Well, I don't know the people, so I can't say."

When an election was in progress, there were sharp political exchanges, usually unrelated to the issues of the campaign. Grandpa and Uncle Will were Democrats, which accounts for my father's being a Republican. That was how it ordinarily worked out; if one brother took a certain view, the other automatically took an opposing one. There were no hard feelings, no aftermath; it was argument for argument's sake. Apparently for them, as for Nietzsche, a good war hallowed any cause.

Sometimes the sheer absurdity of these discussions struck me as funny; mostly, though, I was bored and even angered. Of course, I should have been more tolerant, should have taken the meaningless chatter in my stride. But a teen-ager floundering in a bog of frustration is not likely to be so objective. To mitigate the excruciating tedium, I developed the art of not listening, a technique that enables you to busy yourself with your own thoughts while paying just enough attention to avoid being caught unawares. It is a skill that has served me well through many a dinner party, lecture, political speech, committee meeting, religious service, telephone conversation and broadcasting commercial.

4

What saved me during those sterile years was the word. I do not mean Holy Writ, but just the printed word: books, books, books. I learned to read long before I went to school. My earliest books were German picture stories. I particularly remember a horrible one called *Struwwelpeter,* whose text and illustrations made only too clear the fate that awaited the juvenile delinquent. The thumb sucker was confronted by a shears wielder, who snipped off the offender's digit. An unfortunate who refused his soup faded quickly from chubbiness to an emaciation that led but to the grave. All this should have scared me out of my wits and landed me eventually on an analyst's couch. But, being neither a thumb sucker nor a soup shunner, I felt only smug superiority to the victims.

I suppose my reading in English began with the funnies. The New York *Herald* had a fine colored Sunday supplement that presented Foxy Grandpa, Buster Brown and his dog Tige, Little Nemo and *The Dreams of a Welsh Rarebit Fiend.* Occasionally access to the *World* or the *American* made me acquainted with Happy Hooligan, the Katzenjammer Kids and Maud (a fractious mule). I soon graduated to the works of Horatio Alger, Oliver Optic, Edward Stratemeyer and G. A. Henty, and then went on to Dumas, Hugo, Cooper, Irving and Scott; eventually I progressed to Dickens, Thackeray, Poe, Conan Doyle, Mark Twain, the narrative poems of Longfellow, Whittier, Matthew Arnold and Tennyson. Favorite books I reread three or four times: the d'Artagnan series, *Les Misérables, The Wandering Jew, Ben-Hur, Quo Vadis, David Copperfield,* the Leatherstocking Tales.

From the time I began reading no one had to ask me what I wanted for my birthday or Christmas. Soon I began to assemble a little library. Whenever I had a few spare dollars, I added another section to my Globe-Wernicke bookcases. My library has grown, but few of the original volumes, I regret to say, have survived.

Literature was as alien to my family's world as were the other arts. There was never a book in my home until I introduced one. I never knew my father or Uncle Will to read a book or make reference to one. Grandpa never read, either, though he must have been a reader in his youth, for sometimes he quoted in German from the works of Lessing or Schiller. My mother enjoyed popular fiction of the wholesome variety. In later years I kept her supplied. But in my childhood she would have thought it wasteful to buy books, and entering a library would have seemed rather unfeminine.

My own preoccupation with books struck my family as abnormal and somewhat unhealthy. I was always being asked why I did not go out and play, or warned that stooping over books would make me round-shouldered—and round-shouldered I certainly was—or that I would ruin my eyes. (But no one thought of sending me to an oculist.) My mother sometimes expressed the fear that I was straining my mind. I don't know what she meant by that; I'm not sure that she did, either.

The possibility of becoming a writer never suggested itself to me. Reading was for me both an anodyne and a stimulant, an escape from and compensation for the dullness of daily life, a vicarious gratification of my stifled emotions. Books were not literature, but mental and spiritual fare. I knew they did not write themselves, but authorship was still nebulous and impersonal. I sometimes scribbled doggerel or wrote inept schoolboy parodies of "Barbara Frietchie" or "The Midnight Ride of Paul Revere," but I did not connect that with authorship. Once, by accident, I saw a great author in the flesh. I went up to City College the day the Great Hall was dedicated. Unable to get into the building—I had no ticket!—I watched the academic procession cross the campus. It was headed by Mark Twain, who was receiving an honorary degree. I still see vividly the snow-white hair and mustache, and the scarlet gown and mortarboard. My program book reminds me that on November 30, 1910, I attended a Mark Twain memorial service in Carnegie Hall, at which William Dean Howells presided and the speakers were Joseph H. Choate, Champ Clark, Joseph G. Cannon, Henry Watterson, Joseph H. Twichell and Henry van Dyke. "A most impressive ceremony" is my notation. It must have been, yet I am unable to remember anything that was said or what any of the celebrities looked like.

I was no longer interested in the old family games; as soon as supper was over, I buried my nose in a book. Now and then, touched by Grandpa's loneliness—his old card partners had died off—I played pinochle with him. It was a labor of love, for it would be hard to think of a duller game than two-handed pinochle, especially when your opponent is almost stone deaf. Grandpa always thought I might be cheating him. If I turned a trick quickly, he would make me turn it back so that he could verify it. I am afraid I did not play with him as often as I should have.

However, next to reading, card playing was my chief recreational activity. Every Sunday I went around to the Allenbergs', where I spent the entire afternoon and evening—with a brief supper interlude—playing cards with Abe and his brother. Sometimes their mother or a girl cousin joined in. We played bridge, auction pinochle, hearts, twenty-one, bezique, euchre, écarté, five hundred, and several varieties of poker. At eleven I staggered home and tumbled into bed, bleary-eyed and depressed by the prospect of another week at Samstag and Hilder Brothers.

My relations with my father continued to worsen. I wanted to admire and respect him and was resentful because I could not. He was by no means a stupid man; indeed, he was far more intelligent than his sister or either of his brothers. But he was ignorant—ignorant and obscurantist: he knew nothing, was interested in nothing. He even took pleasure in recalling that he had formerly been known as "the woman hater." When anyone referred to it, he grinned delightedly. It did not seem funny to me; I was rather shocked.

I was shocked, too, and repelled, by his racial prejudices. He was always fulminating against the niggers and the dirty dagoes. But his most vitriolic comments were directed against the kikes, the recent Jewish immigrants from Eastern Europe. That was not exceptional. There is a sort of pecking order among Jews, as among other peoples. In general German Jews look down upon their Russian and Polish coreligionists. The process operates in reverse, as is indicated in Abraham Cahan's novel *The Rise of David Levinsky:* "I often convict myself of currying favor with the German Jews. But then German Jews curry favor with Portuguese-American Jews, just as we all curry favor with Gentiles and as American Gentiles curry favor with the aristocracy of Europe."

I rejected my father's arrogant assumption that he was superior to anyone whose background differed from his. Among my school-mates and street companions were many immigrants or children of immigrants. I liked some, disliked others, was indifferent to most. But my feelings had nothing to do with their race, religion or nationality. When I visited their homes, I often discovered that their fathers were more amiable and better informed than my own. If I suggested to my father that his sweeping generalizations were un-justified, I was told to keep quiet about things I did not understand.

Increasingly I resented his querulousness toward my mother. Once I lashed out at him, telling him that his behavior was inexcusable, that he showed no awareness of her devotion to his care and comfort. To my surprise, he listened meekly and in silence, even tried for a while to moderate his conduct. I think that my mother, though quite shocked by my onslaught, was also proud of my championship.

Sensing my dissatisfaction with my job and with my life in general, my mother tried to comfort and hearten me. But since she did not know what I was striving for—how could she, when I did not know myself?—her attempts merely added to my rebelliousness. Though my love for her was undiminished, I was developing a kind of intellectual snobbery, growing more and more weary of her shopworn adages, delivered each time with an air of discovery: "It's a long lane that has no turning," "If at first you don't succeed, try, try again," and her favorite, "Everything comes to he who waits." I am afraid I was often guilty of the very petulance and un-graciousness to which I objected in my father.

5

After eight or nine months of work, my pay was raised to six dol-lars, an increase that provided an occasional theatre ticket, a maga-zine or even a book. But it did not lessen my distaste for the job. I wondered how long I would be entrapped in it. I soon found out. The recession of 1907—it was called a panic then—had resulted in a general slackening of trade. As usual, employers "retrenched" at the expense of their workers. As one of the latest to be employed, I was one of the first to go.

My joy at being dismissed was mitigated by the knowledge that I had to find another job. I began the search immediately, going about town to answer help-wanted ads. Soon I was engaged as office boy by a small firm, the nature of whose business I have forgotten. The job seemed as unattractive as the one I had lost; I groaned at the prospect of beginning work next day. On the way home I made another of those decisions that have, from time to time, altered the course of my life. I told my parents that I did not intend to become a businessman. Then, having been taught by my mother to be considerate of others, I wrote a note to the man who had engaged me, telling him that I had changed my mind.

V

Office Boy to an Attorney's Firm

1

The only alternative that suggested itself to the business career on which I had arbitrarily turned my back was the law, though I still had no interest in becoming a lawyer. Cousin Moe's offer held good, so I entered the service of House, Grossman and Vorhaus as file clerk at five dollars per week. Only fifty cents better off than I had been a year before, I had to console myself with the prospect of a brilliant career at the bar.

The firm's offices were on lower Broadway near Trinity Church, a few blocks from the complex of courthouses at City Hall Park. The titular head of the firm, Frederick House, had retired to preside over the newly created Traffic Court. He came to the office now and then: an austere man, to whom everyone showed great deference.

The actual head was Cousin Moe—Mr. Grossman, now that he was my employer, but generally referred to by the staff as M.H.G. He was about thirty-five, with the physique of a jockey; but he made up for his diminutiveness in nervous energy. He looked a little like a comic-section character named Mr. Peewee: small black mustache and bulging forehead with prominent blue veins. His nasal voice was too big for his body; he had a stammer that he could not keep under control in moments of intensity. I shall have much more to say about him, most of it derogatory.

One of his partners was his brother William, a taciturn man who seldom came to the office and had little contact with the staff. The third senior partner was Louis J. Vorhaus, the firm's chief trial lawyer, a gruff-voiced man with a piratical black beard. He suffered from asthma, which may have accounted for his chronic irascibility. His brother was married to M.H.G.'s sister, so the firm was more or less a family affair.

Besides two junior partners, who had little authority, there were six or eight salaried lawyers in charge of various branches of the firm's business. Also in the office, though not connected with it, was Samuel S. Koenig, Republican boss of New York County, who usually had a political sinecure of some sort, serving once as New York's secretary of state. The nonlegal staff consisted of secretaries, stenographers and miscellaneous clerks, thirty-five or forty people in all. In contrast to my previous job, where at the end of a year I had known almost no one, I was soon on fairly familiar terms with everyone. But these people were more intelligent and on the whole better educated and better mannered. Five or six were preparing for a legal career; with two of them I quickly formed lasting friendships.

One of my new friends, Frank W. Harris—not to be confused with Oscar Wilde's biographer—was four years my senior. Nevertheless, we took to each other instantly and remained close friends until his death fifty years later. The other, James S. Watson, was a Jamaican Negro in his early twenties, a handsome man with very black glossy skin, a neat mustache and strong white teeth. He had a rich voice and a broad British accent. I saw little of him in later years, but I did have the pleasure of speaking at a dinner at the Hotel Astor that honored the tenth anniversary of his election to the bench of the Municipal Court.

My new job was interesting. I was in complete charge of the cabinets that filled most of the file room from floor to ceiling. At the end of the room, by the window, was the bookkeeper's cage, which Miss Lueders always kept locked. No daylight ever reached my end, for though we were on the ninth floor there was another tall building on the opposite side of canyonlike Cedar Street. But it was better than the low-ceilinged balcony and the dismal cellar of Samstag and Hilder Brothers.

As each new case came in I opened a file for it, a red manila envelope bearing a serial number which was entered upon a card and placed in a catalogue file. All papers relating to the case were filed in its envelope, which I supplied to anyone who wanted to consult it. I was kept busy all day, for the quantity of legal paperwork is staggering. My wire reception baskets were never empty. Working almost without supervision gave me a gratifying sense of responsibility. The misfiling of a document could have serious consequences. In a short time I memorized all the case numbers, and I never had to refer to the index. (I still take pride in my personal files, which are voluminous and well organized.) When a case was closed, the papers were sent to a storage warehouse in Brooklyn. If it became necessary to refer to them, I went to the warehouse to search among the fading, crumbling records.

I read a good deal of the material I handled: pleadings, affidavits, contracts, letters, judgments, briefs, transcripts of testimony. Though much was dull and much at first unintelligible, I rapidly became acquainted with the varieties of legal activity, the underlying principles and the relevant procedures. The firm's staff included specialists in real estate, divorce, damage suits, bankruptcy, administration of estates, contracts, and criminal law; each branch had its own techniques. Without being aware of it, I acquired haphazardly the rudiments of a legal education, in the course of which I stumbled upon many new situations and relationships and many unfamiliar aspects of human nature, often disconcerting. I learned, too, the importance of the precise word, of exact definitions that provided safeguards against ambiguity and evasion. At the same time I became aware of cumbersomeness and tautology, and sometimes I amused myself by rephrasing a complex statement in simple language.

My interest in the documents was not entirely intellectual. Among them were depositions, usually in divorce proceedings, whose nature called for transcription by a male stenographer. Naturally, I read them with avidity. These were not schoolyard jokes, but graphic accounts of specific behavior involving identifiable individuals. In fact, I sometimes saw in the outer office persons referred to in the depositions. It was hard for me to believe that the lady quietly waiting, a model of elegance and decorum, could indeed be the one whose conduct the hotel bellboy had described in crude, minute detail. I blushed for her as I wondered how she would have felt had she known that a little office boy was cognizant of her indiscretions.

Of great interest to me was the firm's extensive theatrical clientele, which included the Broadway managers Oliver Morosco and A. H. Woods, and the famous opera impresario Oscar Hammerstein (grandfather of Oscar Hammerstein II, who was three years my junior and also studied law for a time). The old man was a striking figure, with his tight-waisted coat, glossy top hat and cane. Other clients were the vaudeville headliner Taylor Granville; one of my baseball heroes, Mike Donlin, who left the Giants to go on the stage with his wife, Mabel Hite; and that great team of comics, Joe Weber and Lew Fields. Long afterward, I used to see them almost every day lunching at the Hotel Astor, old men surrounded by their surviving cronies.

Though my work was not dull, and my relations with my office mates were pleasant and even stimulating, I was not content. The wretched pay allowed little for my needs and desires and nothing for the family budget. The hours were long, too: eight-forty-five to six. Occasionally we had Saturday afternoon off; usually we had to stay until four or five. Most law offices closed daily at five, and on Saturdays at noon.

M.H.G. was responsible for our time schedule. The son of penniless immigrants, he had overcome poverty, diminutive stature and a speech impediment to attain a certain position in his profession and a substantial degree of financial success. Having "come up the hard way," he could not see why anyone else should come up any other way, particularly anyone who was dependent upon him for a livelihood. He expected all his employees to be zealous about the firm's welfare and personally devoted to him. Anything short of that he regarded as base ingratitude amounting almost to treason.

He was all for efficiency and getting things done. A framed legend in the outer office read: "The fellow who says it can't be done is always interrupted by the fellow who's doing it." An admirer of Elbert Hubbard, the popular "philosopher," he presented to every member of the staff Hubbard's best-known literary creation, *A Message to Garcia*. It dealt with an American soldier who was ordered to deliver a message to a Cuban general. No one knew where Garcia was, but the soldier found him and fulfilled his mission. The point of the story, a favorite with employers, was that the resourceful underling can accomplish the seemingly impossible. Interestingly enough, everyone who reads the story remembers the name of Garcia, but not that of the intrepid hero.

As a Christmas present, M.H.G. gave me a year's subscription to *The Philistine*, a magazine published by Hubbard, with a format derived from William Morris' typographical innovations: an odd little publication containing miscellaneous information and bits of advice on efficiency and other subjects. The only one I remember is "Never run after a trolley car or a woman; there'll be another one along in a minute."

Those Saturday afternoons were really irksome. The courts and all other law offices were closed; the Wall Street area was deserted. Everybody wanted to go to a ball game or a matinee. Instead we had to pretend to be busy, cleaning up or writing reports. Sometimes there was a staff conference, with M.H.G. presiding at the head of the long library table. He pointed out the need for efficiency and teamwork, for putting more effort into the job, getting more results. After all, we were one big family, all interested in the common good. The force of all this was somehow lost upon the married men who were trying to support their own families on twenty-five dollars a week. Nothing was said about pay increases or participation in the firm's profits.

2

During my sixteenth year I corrected two long-neglected physiological defects. Just before I changed jobs, a raging toothache sent me to a dentist for the first time in my life. He discovered numerous cavities, some almost beyond remedy. No parent, teacher or doctor had ever suggested that I have my teeth looked after!

Also, it had begun to dawn upon me that I was not seeing as well as I should. I had always been bad at games that called for acute vision; at bat or in the field, I never saw the ball coming. In the classroom, unless I sat up front, I could not read the blackboard. On a walk, my father or Uncle Will would point out a funny dog across the street, but I saw no dog. I was then told sharply that of course I saw him; not liking to be rebuked, I looked again and reported that I saw him now and that he was indeed a funny dog.

So I consulted an oculist, who told me that I was congenitally nearsighted and should have been wearing glasses for the past ten years. When I put on the glasses, I literally could not believe my eyes. The world took on a wholly new aspect. I could see dogs not only across the street but a block away. I could read signs, bill-boards and subway ads. For the first time, from my customary seat in the second balcony I could actually see the faces of the actors. I can think of few experiences more exciting than putting on those glasses.

Seeing the actors was especially important to me, for, thanks to Uncle Will, visiting relatives and an occasional cash gift, I was going to more and more plays. Many of them, like *The Count of Monte Cristo*, were hardy perennials to which stars devoted a large part of their careers: Joseph Jefferson in *Rip Van Winkle*, E. H. Sothern in *If I Were King*, James K. Hackett in *The Prisoner of Zenda*, David Warfield in *The Music Master*, William Gillette in *Sherlock Holmes*. As I have often pointed out to drama students and lecture audiences, the scene in the Stepney gas chamber, where Holmes is pursued by the fiendish Professor Moriarty, is a fine example of the difference between reading a play and seeing it. Holmes puts out the lights, leaving visible only the glowing end of his cigar. "Follow the cigar!" cries the professor. But when the lights go on it appears that the invincible detective has put the cigar on the window sill and escaped by the door. No description of that scene could possibly equal the effect of its enactment.

I saw many other great successes: Rose Stahl in *The Chorus Lady*, Otis Skinner in *Kismet*, John Mason in *The Witching Hour*, William Hodge in *The Man from Home*, Douglas Fairbanks in *The Man of the Hour*, John Barrymore in *The Fortune Hunter* and Ethel in *Trelawney of the Wells*, Johnston Forbes-Robertson in *The Passing of the Third Floor Back*, Walter Hampden in *The Servant in the House*. The two last-named plays, parables dealing reverently and rather mawkishly with the appearance of Christ in a modern setting, were responsible for the enactment of a New York State law prohibiting the representation of any member of the Trinity upon the stage. During the successful run of *The Green Pastures* in the 1930s, I asked Marc Connelly what he would think of my instituting a criminal proceeding against the play to test the constitutionality of the law. He had no great enthusiasm for my idea.

Eventually I met many of the actors whom I had seen from afar in my youth: Hampden, Fairbanks and the Barrymores; the great musical-comedy stars Fritzi Scheff and Lina Abarbanell; Frances Starr, still on the stage, who won fame in *The Easiest Way;* and a demure middle-aged lady who was introduced to me at a party at Antoinette Perry's as Doris Keane, glamorous heroine of Edward Sheldon's *Romance*.

I saw musical comedies that starred Blanche Ring, Nora Bayes, Emma Trentini, Valli Valli, Julia Sanderson and Bessie McCoy, the Yama-Yama girl; and the comedians: DeWolf Hopper, famous for his recitation of "Casey at the Bat"; Montgomery and Stone, as the tin woodman and the scarecrow of *The Wizard of Oz*; James T. Powers; Sam Bernard; Jefferson De Angelis. Some of the shows were importations from Vienna or Budapest adapted to American tastes; the native products made up in vitality and innocent gaiety what they lacked in wit and originality. Some were tuneful, especially if the composer was Victor Herbert. I became a Savoyard too, and can still intone many of Gilbert's lyrics: singing has always been beyond me.

And vaudeville! Perhaps its delights have been overpraised, but it provided me with many, many hours of enjoyment. The Alhambra Theatre was only a few blocks from my home, and I went often, usually with the Allenberg boys. They bought fifty-cent orchestra seats; all I could afford was standing room at a quarter. When the lights were lowered I would slip down the aisle and squeeze in between the brothers, a buttock on each seat and the chair arm in the small of my back. All my memories of vaudeville are associated with that pressure on my spine. Sometimes an usher routed me out, but usually I was undisturbed.

Vaudeville fare was rich and varied: bands, song-and-dance teams, animal acts, instrumentalists of every sort, jugglers, monologists, ballad singers, opera singers, prestidigitators, playlets, capsule musical comedies, impersonators, swimmers, bicyclists, minstrel troupes, cartoonists, quick-change artists, infant prodigies. At the end of the performance a screen was lowered for the exhibition of a motion picture—a signal for most of the adults to leave. A theatrical journal defined an artist as "any act on a vaudville bill that is not a trained seal."

The names of the performers, remembered now only by the aging, were as widely known as are the movie and TV stars of today, for every sizable town had its vaudeville house. Many of the acts were European importations. There was an English troupe of knockabout acrobats, Fred Karno's comedians, who presented slapstick pantomimes, such as *A Night in a Music Hall* and *A Night in a Lodging House*. The company's funniest and most agile member was a youth named Charlie Chaplin. Once at a Hollywood party I was convulsed by Chaplin's imitations of the English music-hall stars I had often seen: Vesta Victoria singing "Waitin' at the Church," Alice Lloyd singing "I'm Looking for the Lovelight in Your Eyes," Harry Lauder singing "I Love a Lassie."

Vaudeville performances, unlike today's popular entertainments, were carefully prepared and technically perfected. The performers did not have to make themselves heard over the loud talk of drinkers in a smoky room, or cater, in the intervals of hard-sell, to an insatiable craving for novelty. Highly sensitive to the response of their attentive, critical audience, they put everything they had into their work. The material was not hastily assembled, inadequately rehearsed, tossed off at one fleeting performance. Whatever its quality, it was organized and projected with close regard for detail. Every line, gesture, inflection, pause was carefully planned and tested. Routines were created not to be discarded but to be nurtured and perfected. An act could tour for two years without a repeat engagement. When it did come back, the patrons were glad to see an old friend, delighted to hear the old jokes and songs, pleased by the new material that had been cautiously and skillfully introduced. It was like seeing an old girl in a new hat.

One feature of vaudeville was the dialect comedians: German, Irish, Swedish, Jewish, Negro (the last often a white in blackface). They imitated accents and speech patterns and poked fun at characteristic traits and usages. There was nothing malicious or inimical about these caricatures; they were often enjoyed most by those who recognized their own idiosyncrasies. Today such good-humored raillery is taboo. Every racial, national and religious group has its zealous spokesmen who object to any allusion that might conceivably offend the most hypersensitive of their constituents. Where animosity does exist, censorship only intensifies it. Ridicule, or even invective, is often a good safety valve.

It was at the Alhambra that I first went backstage. One of the firm's clients, Taylor Granville, had a prize-fight playlet, *The Star Bout*. At its climax a small crowd gathered around the ring, extras picked up by the stage manager at fifty cents a head. One night Frank Harris and I arranged to be included. Though all I had to do was make crowd noises, it was exciting to be on the stage, getting the feel of the unseen audience. This is what most actors live for, the reason many prefer the discomforts and insecurity of the theatre to well-paid miming before a motion picture or television camera.

Viewing the show backstage was exciting, too: the stagehands, the changing lights and scenery, the actors waiting to make their entrance. I had seen some of the acts from the front, and here I was almost rubbing elbows with the performers. From the wings I watched Eddie Leonard, a popular blackface comedian, go through his act. In response to the laughter and applause he bowed, then turned smilingly to his female partner. The moment the curtain was down he heaped abuse and profanity upon her, charging her with some error. She hurried off weeping; he followed, keeping up his tirade. I was deeply shocked, as I still am by disparities between profession and behavior. I know very well that an exquisite poet may be a drunkard or a drug addict, that a brilliant scientist may be a swindler or a boor, that a great spiritual leader may be cruel and selfish in his personal relationships. I know, too, that these anomalies and irrelevancies should not disturb me; yet disturb me they always do.

A nontheatrical but highly dramatic event was Teddy Roosevelt's triumphal parade up Broadway upon his return from an African safari. These processions, now commonplace, were then still novel. I remember the bristling mustache, the toothy grin, the gleaming spectacles, the waving hat. The Bull Moose campaign, when he stood at Armageddon and battled for the Lord, lay ahead.

Another spectacular event was the fire that destroyed the Equitable Building on lower Broadway. One bitter-cold morning, the streets were blocked with fire-fighting apparatus, the air was filled with clouds of smoke. The burning building, six stories high and constructed in the form of a hollow square, was just across Broadway from the Trinity Building, where I worked; from our office windows I could look down into the heart of the fire. The streams of water that a hundred hoses played upon it froze instantly, turning the exterior of the building into a glistening crater from whose depths the flames soared: a scene from some Inferno or Walpurgis Night. By the end of the day the fire was under control, but the hard weather persisted and the gutted shell was ice-coated for weeks.

3

After a year at the files, my application for a promotion was granted; I was advanced to a clerkship. I still did not want to be a lawyer, but, as it seemed the only career open to me, I felt I had better prepare for it. I could not, of course, attend a university law school, since I had no college degree; anyhow, I had to go on working. The only school open to me was New York Law School, which was located near my office and had late-afternoon classes. Even there a high-school diploma was required. But it was possible to obtain its equivalent by passing a sufficient number of the examinations given periodically by the State Board of Regents. I could have taken credit for my two years of high school, but the point allowance was so small that it was better to claim no credit and to take the examinations subject by subject.

With my promotion went a desk in the outer office, new duties and a salary increase of two dollars—a forty per cent raise! I kept one dollar for myself and contributed the other to the household, as a token acknowledgment of my responsibility. The extra dollar provided more theatre tickets and left a little over for the opening of a savings bank account, which later became vitally important.

Part of my new job was the preparation of procedural documents, mostly a matter of filling up printed forms or dictating prescribed formulas—routine work, but it increased my knowledge of legal terminology and practice. Most of my working day was spent outside the office, a welcome change from artificial light and airless quarters. Not yet eighteen, I could not serve process—summonses and subpoenas—but I made the rounds of attorneys' offices, delivering the legal papers that lawyers are always exchanging. Sometimes I went to the Hall of Records to trace a chain of real-estate titles or to search for an old will.

After a while I was entrusted with the answering of court calendars, a phase of my work I enjoyed, for it took me all over the greater city. The principal courts were at City Hall Park, but the municipal and magistrates' courts were scattered throughout the city's boroughs. Sometimes I went to the county court in Jamaica or White Plains, and the Appellate Division, which had its own building at Madison Square. I was impressed by the five black-robed figures on the dais, and by the air of austere dignity that pervaded the chamber where I might one day be sworn in as a member of the bar.

My excursions provided a slight increase in spending money. If I went to an office or court more than ten blocks away, I was allowed ten cents carfare. By walking one way I could pocket half of it. I liked being assigned to Queens County Courthouse, across the Queensborough Bridge, a trip that called for a twenty-cent round-trip fare. By leaving home at eight and walking the six miles or so, I netted a ten-cent profit. With a nickel here and a dime there, I sometimes added fifty or seventy-five cents to my weekly income. Since the carfares were charged to the clients, questions were seldom asked about the petty-cash vouchers, known to the office staff as "swindle sheets"; today, in the higher circles of the tax-conscious, they are described by the elegant euphemism "expense accounts."

To accumulate the sixty points required for the Board of Regents' certificate, I had to pass a dozen or more examinations, a severe task, for I had only the evening hours for study. I could not afford a tutor; attending evening high-school courses would have been too time-consuming; so I went ahead on my own. Every night when the family retired—fortunately at an early hour—I sat at the dining-room table and toiled away, until I could get through the sample examinations supplied by the Regents. Frequently I was distracted, for the servant girls across the court often disrobed without pulling down the shades. But I made good progress with my studies.

My preparatory work was based on the hope that the firm would give me time off to attend law-school classes and would pay my tuition; obviously I could not pay it myself. This arrangement was quite customary. Large law firms found it advantageous to train promising young clerks, who knew the office routines and were likely to accept smaller salaries than newcomers would demand. Several other clerks in my office also wanted law-school privileges. We applied to M.H.G., who told us he would consider our applications and let us know when he had made up his mind. As the months dragged on, our anxiety increased. If we were turned down, we would have to give up the study of law or try to find jobs with some firm that would see us through.

The Regents' Examinations gave me no trouble. By applying

myself, I was able to amass the needed points in less than a year— half the time I had allowed myself. This was accomplished by taking, at each session, more examinations than I had prepared for. If I failed, I lost nothing. Finding the first-year English paper so elementary that I could complete it in half an hour, I went on to pass the second-, third- and fourth-year papers, for none of which I had prepared. By spending a few hours after work each night studying without guidance I had in a year satisfactorily done the equivalent of four years' full-time work at high school. Even assuming that I am above average in intelligence and diligence, it seems a sad commentary upon our educational system.

The completion of my examinations in the spring qualified me to enter law school in the fall. Everything now hinged on M.H.G.'s decision. It was not until midsummer that I learned that my application was one of four that had been approved. I was relieved but not grateful, for of course he had decided months before and simply put off telling us so that we would have a becoming sense of the great favor that was being bestowed. The effect was just the opposite: our respect for him was lowered, if that was possible.

VI

When I Went to the Bar as a Very Young Man

1

In the fall of 1910, aged eighteen, I entered New York Law School. Its two-year course of study made no attempt to supply a rounded legal education, with excursions into philosophy, history and sociology. It was a trade, rather than a professional, school, which efficiently performed the practical job of drilling students in the rudimentary knowledge of law required for passing the state bar examinations.

I had received another two-dollar raise, bringing my pay up to nine dollars. My expendable income remained the same, for I turned over the additional two dollars to my mother. The firm also paid my law-school tuition of a hundred dollars per year, which came to another two dollars a week. I attended late-afternoon classes, thereby reducing my work week to about forty-four hours. So after three years of work I had raised my earning capacity to twenty-five cents an hour.

My employers were somewhat less munificent than these figures make them appear. I was now legally entitled to serve process, for which the client was customarily charged a fee of a dollar fifty for each service, one of the disbursements incidental to litigation.

Most firms turned over the fee to the process server; not so mine. The client was billed, but the clerk got nothing. If I served process eight times a week, which was not unusual, the firm collected twelve dollars, a dollar more than I cost them for a full week's work. Much of the service was made at night, after class, canceling out my excused time. For this night work I was allowed fifty cents for dinner. Once, returning cold, tired and hungry from a remote part of Brooklyn, I ate a substantial meal that cost seventy-five cents. I was sharply reprimanded and warned not to repeat the extravagance. Consequently, I was not too responsive to the frequent reminders that I was the recipient of law-school "privileges."

Process serving often taxes one's ingenuity and broadens one's knowledge of human nature. When the whereabouts of the person sought is unknown (*cf. A Message to Garcia!*) or he is evasive, a good deal of detective work may be necessary. Once after spending many hours tracing, from one address to another, a woman with a common name like Mary Jones, I was informed that she was at the city maternity hospital on Blackwell's Island (now Welfare Island). At the hospital I was told that there was a Mary Jones there, and that she would be sent for. The fifty women in the last stage of pregnancy who crowded the reception room all focused their attention upon me during what was, I suppose, the most embarrassing fifteen minutes I have ever spent. When Mary Jones appeared, even more pregnant than the rest and obviously terrified, it took only a moment to discover that she was not the person I was after. So I apologized and fled.

When it is a case of evasion, the server sometimes resorts to fantastic devices. I knew one youth who slipped by a stage doorman while a performance was in progress, walked on stage in the middle of a scene, handed an actor a summons, and walked off. The audience probably thought it was part of the play.

I had a somewhat less colorful backstage experience with Arnold Daly, a brilliant actor with a flamboyant personality, whose conversation was likened by Bernard Shaw to American railroads, because "it passed through a varied and fertile country, but had poor terminal facilities." After he had eluded me for months, I went to the stage door of the Hudson Theatre at the end of a performance and was directed to his dressing room. The door was opened by a baldish man, whom I took for Daly, for I had seen him play, but always wearing a toupee. Wanting to make sure, I said, "Mr. Daly?" Instantly he turned, shouted, "Arnold!" and bolted into the inner room, locking the door behind him. Frustrated, I called his press agent and said I wanted to interview Mr. Daly for the New York *Times*. An appointment was arranged, but my office would not let me go through with it, so I had only the satisfaction of imagining Daly exercising his vivid vocabulary at the expense of the press agent and the *Times*. I then went to his apartment house and sent up word that I had a package for him. Evidently he had tired of evading me, for he stood in the doorway with outstretched hand. I caught a glimpse of a luncheon table, at which an attractive young woman was seated. All my efforts were wasted, for shortly afterward Daly was declared bankrupt.

In another pursuit, I never did catch my quarry, a well-known gambler, whom I was not alone in trying to run down. Suddenly his name and likeness were on every front page: "Billiard Ball" Jack Rose, whose testimony was mainly responsible for the conviction of Police Lieutenant Charles Becker for the murder of the gambler Herman Rosenthal.

By now I knew my way around all the courts. I could identify all the judges and was familiar with their respective reputations for punctuality, asperity or tolerance, legal knowledge, and integrity. I sometimes lingered to listen to a trial, especially if it involved divorce, murder or rape. Once I heard an attractive woman testify in defense of her husband, who was charged with the murder of their lodger. Calmly she faced the crowded courtroom and, in a cultivated voice, told how she had arisen from beside her presumably sleeping husband and had gone to the lodger's bed. I could not stay to the end of the trial and never found out what the verdict was.

Often I was interested more in the behavior of some well-known trial lawyer than in the subject matter of the case, as one might go to see a star, no matter what the play. The analogy is close, for the conduct of a jury trial depends more upon the art of acting than upon the science of law. Frequently all the legal knowledge a trial lawyer needs is an acquaintance with the rules of evidence, which are fairly simple. The day is often won by obfuscation, trickery and histrionics. I saw some of the notable courtroom performers of the time, among them Francis L. Wellman, who wrote several books on the technique of cross-examination, and Dudley Field Malone, a smooth rhetorician, who later appeared in the Scopes evolution trial in Tennessee. When I lived in Paris, I saw him sometimes, elegantly clad, en route to his Place Vendôme office, divorce headquarters for the American upper class. Perhaps the most famous of all trial lawyers was Max D. Steuer. Though his methods of practice were considered dubious, he always managed to avoid overstepping the permissible. I have had personal dealings with some of his disciples and I can testify that they learned their lessons well. Typical of Steuer's tactics was a cross-examination I once heard him conduct. A key witness whose testimony was damaging to Steuer's client had mentioned that while waiting for someone he had sat on the edge of a table. Steuer, ignoring the substance of the testimony, seized upon this irrelevant detail. Why had the witness sat on the table? Was it a habit of his? Were there no chairs? The witness grew confused, lost his temper, spluttered, contradicted himself, while Steuer, calm and soft-spoken, pressed the attack, discrediting the entire testimony without going beyond this one inconsequential remark. The incident did not diminish my misgivings about the practice of law.

Now and then I was assigned to one of our trial lawyers as a sort of courtroom assistant, a real sinecure, especially if the trial lasted several days, for there was little to do except carry the brief bag and make an occasional telephone call. The rest of the time I sat at the counsel table, acquiring a knowledge of courtroom procedure that has been very useful to me as a dramatist.

Many of the firm's important cases were tried by the office counsel, ex-Judge Herman Joseph, a lecherous old reprobate, but good-humored and jolly. I considered it a privilege to be assigned to him, for he treated me almost as an equal, even including me in the luncheon parties of clients and witnesses at Haan's, a famous restaurant near the courthouse. Once I was quite overwhelmed to find myself sitting beside John Barrymore, then still in his twenties. I had seen him only recently in *The Fortune Hunter,* a great farce-comedy success. He paid no attention to me, nor did he say anything memorable, but it was an exciting hour. Some twenty years later he appeared in the film version of my play *Counsellor-at-Law.* By that time, his brilliant career was nearing its tragic end.

2

It did not take me long to discover that law school was a bore and a waste of time. I was already familiar with much of the subject matter, and the two-hour lecture sessions merely rehashed a textbook chapter that could be read and absorbed in half an hour. The basic text was, of course, *Blackstone's Commentaries*, in an edition copiously annotated and related to modern instances by George Chase, dean of the school. I was interested far more in the quaintness of Blackstone's eighteenth-century prose than in the legal principles he expounded. I did rather enjoy real-property law, much of which stems from the complex land tenures of the feudal system. It pleased me to learn that real property consists of land, tenements and hereditaments, and that hereditaments may be corporeal or incorporeal. I had read some novels with medieval settings, so this branch of the law seemed quite romantic. Not so with long discussions of what was and what was not adequate consideration for a contract. Negotiable instruments, to which we were introduced by a booming-voiced, very thin young man named Stout, I found excruciating.

To relieve the tedium and to employ the school hours usefully, I developed a technique for reading in class. The recitations were in strictly alphabetical order, so by concentrating for ten minutes or so before your turn came you could easily pick up the thread of the discussion and be well prepared to carry on. Once you had done your bit, you were safe for the rest of that day. In fact, the classes were so large that sometimes your name was not reached at all.

I shall always be grateful to New York Law School for the knowledge of literature I acquired there. In two years I must have read hundreds of books. Most of them were plays, because I could finish a play in a two-hour session, and because I was becoming interested in the drama as an art form and a medium for the expression of ideas. I read every play I could lay my hands on. When I had gobbled up everything on the drama shelves of my branch library, I went to other branches or to Central Circulation.

A classmate, Bertram Bloch, lived only a few blocks from me. On our trips uptown together on the Ninth Avenue El we discovered that we had many interests and problems in common. Bert too was employed in a law office and was preparing reluctantly for a legal career. Like me, he had a passion for the theatre and spent his school time reading plays. We were soon exchanging books after class or, if the plays were short, during the recess. There was also a great similarity in our social outlook and political beliefs, and we both liked to play bridge. We began spending evenings together, mostly at Bert's house, ostensibly to assist each other in preparation for next day's class. But soon the dreary textbooks would be pushed aside, we would discuss books or plays for a while, then a deck of cards appeared, and we recruited Bert's mother or uncle to join us; if no one was available, we played double dummy. Sometimes we made no pretense at study at all, but arranged an evening at cards with Frank Harris, Abe Allenberg or some other friend. All my youthful playing finally made any game of cards unendurable.

3

Law school and my job kept me busy but did not provide satisfactions for my emotional, intellectual and spiritual needs. Nor did religion or sex. I found them in a passionate interest in the arts and in the development of a social philosophy.

There is little to be told of my youthful sexual experience. When I was about sixteen Uncle Will told me, without preliminaries, that I was old enough to "have a woman," and that if I needed money he would supply it. I assume my mother had prompted him to speak to me, though not in those terms! I was too embarrassed to reply, and the subject never came up again. However, I decided to gratify my normal curiosity about the sexual relationship. Indirectly, and without divulging my intention, I obtained from a fellow clerk the address of a young woman whom he visited. One Sunday afternoon I went there, not without trepidation, for I did not know what sort of person I would be dealing with. My fears were groundless. My hostess, if I may call her that, received me amiably and with an air of social decorum; indeed, she was genteel almost to a fault. I had been told that she was a graduate nurse who had given up hospital work for this more lucrative and presumably more agreeable career. I could readily believe it, for the whole proceeding was conducted in an efficient, clinical, impersonal manner. It was all rather like a visit to a physiotherapist or an X-ray technician. I paid the stipulated fee and was politely invited to call again.

I was neither elated nor repelled, merely puzzled. I don't know just what I had expected, but the experience seemed without significance. Reluctant to form a hasty judgment, I made several return visits, but always came away with the feeling that something was lacking. What was lacking, of course, was emotion. In its absence I felt no inclination to pursue my investigations, preferring to find vicarious satisfaction in drama, fiction, poetry and music. Consequently I developed a kind of romantic idealism and a behavioral puritanism, though in the realm of ideas I was unconventional, unorthodox and revolutionary.

Thanks to the indifference of my family, I was almost entirely free of religious pressures and escaped indoctrination of any sort, so religion never played a part in my life. I have never regretted my refusal to adopt the Jewish faith; nor have I ever embraced any other faith. In adolescence, when I sought an anchorage for my turbulent mind and spirit, I was drawn momentarily toward various religious disciplines: Quaker, Christian Science, Catholic. But I could never overcome my skepticism or accept any creed or body of doctrine. I have never believed in the efficacy of prayer, the survival of personality after death, or the existence of a supreme being that is concerned with the minutiae of our daily lives.

I am not an atheist, for I regard atheism as a form of religion: an affirmation of the *non*existence of God, in which I cannot join, since it is not susceptible of proof. Indeed, it seems to me impossible that the organization and the relationships that are discernible throughout the universe can be the result of mere chance. But since the nature and purpose of the directive force are unknown, and probably unknowable, I see no reason for concerning myself with it, particularly since I do not believe that anything I think, say or do can affect it or alter its effect upon me.

I feel that religion, like all beliefs, is good for those for whom it has meaning. Though I have known many who have been distorted and scarred by bigotry, sectarianism and superstition, and by childhood indoctrination of destructive concepts of guilt, sin and eternal punishment, there are certainly many who find solace in worship, or inspiration and guidance in a religious creed. It seems to me these are matters each individual must decide for himself. I quarrel with no man for holding to his own beliefs, no matter how baseless or outrageous they may seem to me. It is only when he attempts to force those beliefs upon others, or to suppress opinions and behavior that run counter to his, that I take exception.

Not occupied with my relationship to God or with preparations for the hereafter, I centered my aspirations and dreams upon man's relationship to himself and to his fellow men. My emotional goals were self-improvement and social betterment, two aspects of one objective. I was profoundly influenced by the living example of my mother's goodness: forbearance, honesty, decency, loving-kindness. While I was under her wing, I thought her behavior quite normal —or, more accurately, I just accepted it unquestioningly. Thrust into the world, I was shocked to find in the conduct of most adults a lack of dignity and of integrity, and a disregard for the sensibilities and well-being of others.

It became apparent to me that most people found no satisfaction in their daily occupation, not only because they were economically exploited, but because they took no pride or joy in their work. My own working conditions, though far from unendurable, were sufficiently irksome to produce a critical, even revolutionary, attitude toward the economics, politics, morals and ethics of the existing social order. The concept of freedom began to take shape; eventually it dominated my thought and action.

My rebelliousness made me particularly responsive to books that exposed the social structure's weaknesses and evils, or the hypocrisy, slavishness and sterility of human behavior. My haphazard reading was omnivorous. Sometimes one author led to another; sometimes I chose at random. Many writers, past and present, influenced my thinking, but it was Bernard Shaw who far exceeded all the others. I had occasion to describe that influence at a luncheon given by the British Authors' Society on the centenary of Shaw's birth. The other speakers—Sybil Thorndike, St. John Ervine and Clement Attlee—were able to give revealing personal glimpses of Shaw. But I had never met him, for I was sure that he would have no interest in me and I had refrained from seeking an introduction. So I could speak only about what his writings had meant to me. In the course of my remarks I said:

One day, in rummaging in the drama shelf . . . , I came across two volumes called *Plays, Pleasant and Unpleasant* . . . The effect was cataclysmic. Doors and windows opened, bells rang, lights went on and horizons widened. It was the most revolutionary event to happen in my life, in an intellectual sense. I immediately went after everything I could lay my hands upon which Shaw had written. I read his *Novels of My Nonage*, the Fabian Tracts, *The Quintessence of Ibsenism*, . . . and those two wonderful volumes of *Dramatic Opinions and Essays*, from which I learned more about the theatre than from all the treatises I have read, before and since.

Also, Shaw then began to have a hold in America and his plays began to be produced. I was fortunate enough to see Robert Lorraine in *Man and Superman;* the original English company in the first production in New York of *Fanny's First Play;* Arnold Daly in *Arms and the Man,* Forbes-Robertson and Gertrude Elliott in *Caesar and Cleopatra,* and Mrs. Patrick Campbell and Philip Merivale in *Pygmalion.*

All this was before World War I, and I can say without exaggeration that the total effect completely altered my life, my way of thinking, my mode of life—everything. For one thing, I became a socialist. I still am, I think, though perhaps with a few reservations! There was opened to me a whole new world and a whole new orientation in politics, in religion, in education, science, art and sex—in all these things completely new ideas, new ways of thinking and new attitudes toward life, which have colored everything that has happened to me, everything I have done and everything I have thought since.

I went on to say that if this sounded excessive to younger listeners it was because Shaw's ideas had influenced the thinking of so many people that his revolutionary opinions of fifty years ago had become widely accepted, even commonplace. Thus I was able, after many decades, to pay public tribute to my most provocative teacher.

Though Shaw was dominant, many other writers impressed me profoundly. I read and studied all the plays of Ibsen and of other dramatists who were writing "problem plays"—that is, criticisms of society as a whole or studies of individuals who found themselves in conflict with social institutions. The authors included Galsworthy, Stanley Houghton, St. John Hankin, Granville Barker, Strindberg, Björnsen, Hauptmann, Sudermann, Brieux, Henri Becque, Pinero and Henry Arthur Jones; Chekhov I did not discover until later. Of course, in all this reading I unconsciously learned a great deal about the technique of play construction.

I saw many of these plays performed. Almost every Saturday night three or four of us would occupy second-balcony seats in a Broadway theatre, or in one of the Harlem theatres where plays could be seen immediately after their Broadway run. By this time I was seeing twenty-five or more plays in a season, so I became well acquainted with the work of the leading contemporary playwrights and actors. When a new play by Shaw, Pinero, Barrie, Rostand or Maugham was announced we went to the box office the day the ticket sale opened, getting first-night seats whenever possible.

Often I am asked whether the actors were better than those of today. It is hard to answer, because standards change. On the whole, I think not. Undoubtedly they had opportunities in good repertory and stock companies for a kind of training that is not available today. Yet I do not believe that the general level of performance was higher. Some stars appeared in the same play year after year, neglecting the development of their talents; others confined themselves to parts that were strictly tailored to their personalities.

Nearly all the theatres I frequented in my teens have disappeared: Charles Frohman's two famous houses, the Empire and the Knickerbocker, the Casino, the Comedy, the Princess, the Maxine Elliott, the Manhattan, the Thirty-ninth Street, the Broadway, the Garrick, the Herald Square, the Savoy, the Bijou, and the former homes of two celebrated stock companies, Daly's and Wallack's.

As my knowledge of dramatic literature developed, I became increasingly dissatisfied with most of what I saw in the theatre. A worshiper of Shaw, Ibsen and Galsworthy, I found the general run of plays trivial and meretricious, the writing crude, the characterization thin, the point of view banal, the content almost negligible. I was so enamored of the theatre, wanted it so much to be good, that I became unduly indignant when it did not measure up to my standards. It took me many years to accept the fact that greatness is rare, and to recognize that any theatre is better than no theatre.

4

In the spring of 1912 I was graduated from New York Law School with the degree of LL.B. *cum laude,* evidence of the slight demand made upon the student's attention and intelligence. Its importance to me may be deduced from the fact that I remember nothing about the graduation exercises, not even where they were held.

Over the summer, I prepared perfunctorily for the bar examination, leafing through textbooks, testing myself with sample questions. The examinations were reputedly stiff; about half the applicants failed on the first try. I approached the ordeal nonchalantly, not because of self-confidence, but because I contemplated using possible failure as a plausible excuse for not pursuing a legal career. I even toyed with the notion of purposely flunking; but I had ethical misgivings.

The examination was in two parts; substantive law and legal procedure. It was not uncommon for brilliant students to bog down completely on the second part because of insufficient office training in the complex, arbitrary procedural routines. A glance at the questions assured me that they were not nearly as hard as they were cracked up to be. The procedural section dealt with matters with which I had been occupied for years. Nor was the substantive paper beyond the scope of a moderately retentive mind. I simply could not bring myself to give deliberately wrong answers. Like the vaudeville knife thrower who wanted to kill his partner, I was restrained by pride. I think I saw the humor of the situation even then. However, I did gratify myself by showing my indifference to the whole thing. I am sure that my papers were unique in the annals of bar examinations, not for their scholarship, but for their form. Some of my answers were in blank verse; others included jokes, limericks, quotations from Shakespeare, the Bible, Omar Khayyám and Lewis Carroll. I left the hall feeling that, whatever the outcome, I had had a good time.

After some weeks of curious, rather than anxious, waiting, I learned that I had passed. Perhaps the examiners wanted to avoid coping with another of my papers. My friend James Watson passed, too. Another of my fellow clerks failed but passed on a second try. A fourth continued to fail on successive attempts. He gave up at last and worked as a law clerk for the rest of his life. I saw him once twenty years later. Dried out and beaten, he was still doing the same office chores we had all done as boys.

Since I was barely twenty, I had to wait a whole year before I could be admitted to the bar. I was back in the office now, full time, but with a very different status, for I was made managing clerk. This was a big step upward in the office hierarchy. With it went a raise from nine dollars to fifteen: very gratifying, for all things are relative. It did not benefit me personally, for I simply added the six dollars to the three I was already contributing to the household. That left me exactly where I had been for the past three years: with six dollars to cover carfares, lunches, clothing, medical care, theatre tickets, gifts and summer vacations. Every Saturday night I brought my mother a little present—a magazine, a bag of candy, a few flowers. And I kept adding a little bit at a time to my savings account.

The post of managing clerk in a large law office is arduous and responsible. My duties fell into two main categories. The first was supervising the work assignments of the clerical staff—the preparation, service and filing of documents, the answering of court calendars. On opening day of a new term the coverage of perhaps twenty courts was a logistical problem. Under my direct command were some fifteen office boys, law clerks and process servers. Sometimes recent Yale, Harvard or Columbia law graduates who were willing to work for nothing to get their required year's office experience were magnanimously taken on by M.H.G. Their training was left to me. Sometimes a youth who could discourse brilliantly on the philosophy of law had trouble finding his way from the office to the County Courthouse.

The other part of my job was keeping the case docket. From the preparation of the complaint to the filing of the final judgment, every court case runs a procedural course that may include answers, demurrers, bills of particulars, notices of trial, notices of appearance, notices of appeal, motions, stipulations, briefs, and numerous other documents and devices. Because of congested calendars and delaying tactics, cases may drag on for years. Each type of case and each court has its own peculiar routine, governed by arbitrary time schedules that must be rigidly adhered to. These requirements, which have no basis in logic, are prescribed in an encyclopedic volume, *The Code of Civil Procedure*. It was my responsibility to apply the code's provisions to the conduct of every pending case, keep a record of each action's progress, notify the attorney in charge when a paper had to be drawn, see to it that it was duly served. A default could seriously affect the development of a case, or even result in its dismissal. Most of this paperwork had nothing to do with the merits or the subject matter of the litigation; it was entirely tactical and procedural.

I was qualified for the job by experience and by an orderly turn of mind. My relations with the clerical staff were good; there was little friction. I took great pains not to show favoritism, and to avoid pulling rank on the clerks who had been in line for the post. Some assignments allowed for a good deal of leisure; others were burdensome and tedious. Apportionment of the work required care.

In spite of my relative independence and the authority with which I was vested, I was not happy. My work made no demands upon my mental or psychic energy; there was nothing creative or constructive about it. Of course, that is true of most jobs at any level. I long ago came to the conclusion that that is what is basically wrong with the world we live in.

With my admission to the bar imminent, contemplation of my future obsessed me. I had never really wanted to be a lawyer, but had simply followed the course along which my employment directed me. Faced now with the prospect of spending my life in the practice of law, I was filled with misgiving. In the abstract, I conceived the law as a majestic instrument for the impartial administration of justice, the protection of the wronged, the reparation of injuries. Yet in practice I saw it used for the avoidance of debt by shady bankruptcy proceedings, the collection of damages by trickery and coercion, the breach of contractual obligations by dubious technicalities, the manipulation of divorces by cynical collusion. Of course, not every case was tainted by jobbery or specious pleading; many were properly concerned with redress or defense. But there seemed to be no principle of selectivity; whatever came along was grist for the mill. As a single example, on one exciting occasion a notorious bucket-shop operator evaded the police by hiding in our office. I had to stay late to attend the switchboard and divert inquiring calls. It was like taking part in a melodrama. It disturbed me greatly; nor was I appeased by the eventual surrender of the fugitive.

My qualms led me to conduct a rather absurd little experiment. The trial of Police Lieutenant Charles Becker, to which I have referred, was one of the most sensational cases of the period. District Attorney Charles S. Whitman, who had political ambitions and was later elected to the governorship, charged Becker with employing four gunmen—unforgettably named Lefty Louie, Whitey Lewis, Dago Frank and Gyp the Blood—to murder Herman Rosenthal. Becker was convicted; the conviction was reversed on appeal; he was tried and convicted again, and finally executed. The case occupied public attention for years.

Always curious about legal ethics, I put this question to every attorney in the office: "Suppose you were Becker's lawyer and, though convinced of his guilt, found you could get him off by taking advantage of a technical flaw in the indictment. Would you do it?" All but one answered yes. I suppose they were right: a lawyer's first obligation is to his client. As Lord Brougham put it so eloquently when he was defending Queen Caroline in her trial for adultery before the House of Lords: "An advocate by the sacred duty which he owes his client knows, in the charge of that office, but one person in the world, the client and none other. To save that client by all expedient means, to protect that client at all hazards and costs to all others, and among others to himself, is the highest and most unquestioned of his duties. And he must not regard the alarm, the suffering, the torment, the destruction that he may bring upon any other."

It was an attitude I could not bring myself to adopt. My quiz went far toward building up my antipathy to a legal career. Further, it had become apparent to me that law could be successfully practiced without much legal knowledge. Trial work consisted largely in influencing juries; office work, in procedural maneuvering and in the negotiation of settlements and compromises. The prospect of a lifetime of such activities was dismal. Of course, one could devote oneself to legal scholarship. We had a legal scholar in the office: Charles Goldzier, an old fellow with untidy gray hair, untidy clothes, and a pince-nez on a gold chain. He never saw a client. He sat all day in the library or in his untidy little office, preparing briefs and answering the legal questions of the staff members. His legal knowledge was highly respected, but personally he was looked upon as eccentric and slightly comic, not a figure to inspire a youth who wanted to make something of his life.

I am not suggesting that the law offers nothing better. It has been my good fortune to know intimately many lawyers who are men and women of high intelligence, erudition, integrity and social vision, and who devote much of their time to human betterment. But in my youth I was inevitably conditioned by my environment. Had my associates been more stimulating or admirable, my response might have been different. Yet I doubt that I would ever have developed a real enthusiasm for the practice of law.

So I sat chained to my desk, seeing nothing ahead but a lifetime of uncongenial tasks and spiritual isolation. For a time Frank Harris shared my office, so at least I had someone to talk to. We laughed at the foibles of our superiors, discussed books, plays and ideas, especially those of Shaw, Chesterton and H. L. Mencken, whose contributions to *Smart Set* appealed to young dissenters. But Frank made a better connection, so I was left alone.

It was a real effort each morning to get to the office; the hours I spent there seemed endless. I had organized my docket work so that it occupied less than half the day; the rest of the time hung heavily. Concentrated reading was difficult, for there were frequent interruptions; besides, I did not want to appear to be shirking. Sometimes I had a malted milk at a soda fountain and spent the rest of my lunch hour reading. Once as I sat with my feet up, absorbed in a book, the door was flung open my M.H.G., who was showing an important client around the office. "And this," he said, "is our m-m-m-managing clerk." When he closed the door I laughed aloud, aware that he would never recognize my right to spend my lunch hour as I chose.

5

To help pass the time, I took to memorizing poetry. That could be done in snatches, without an apparent infraction of office discipline. In the course of a year I ingested a formidable amount of verse: all of the *Rubaiyat;* large sections of Gray's "Elegy," "The Rime of the Ancient Mariner" and *The Idylls of the King;* Shakespearean soliloquies and sonnets; and a variey of other poems, long and short, by Keats, Milton, Shelley, Wordsworth, Browning, Arnold, Jonson, Lovelace, Herrick, Hood, Gilbert, Lear, Carroll, Henley, Kipling and Blake. I still can recite much of what I learned.

Home life had little to offer now. I was still sleeping on the folding bed in the living room, wondering if I would ever have a room of my own, a place of privacy where I could keep my books and other belongings. I went to the theatre as often as I could afford, and now pursued a new interest: music. Organ recitals at City College were free. I did not have the price of a seat at the Metropolitan Opera House, but thought nothing of standing through four or five hours of *Tristan* or *Die Meistersinger,* conducted by Alfred Hertz or Arturo Toscanini. Besides the incomparable Caruso, I heard Scotti, Farrar, Amato, Fremstad, Schumann-Heink, Gadski, Goritz and Eames. One year Frank Harris and I subscribed to a season of the Aborn Opera Company. It was perhaps not first-class, but for a dollar we heard most of the standard repertory and a few new works, like *The Jewels of the Madonna.* Occasionally, at Carnegie Hall, I heard great soloists and symphony orchestras. In the vastnesses of the top balcony I spent some of the most aesthetically satisfying hours of my life. I was relieved when, not long ago, the old building was saved from being engulfed in the march of progress.

My only form of physical recreation, in fact the only form I ever enjoyed, was walking. Often on Sunday six or eight of us, boys and girls, would go hiking in suburban New York, on secluded roads where there was little or no traffic. We made excursions to Staten Island, the old Morris Canal in New Jersey, the Palisades and Westchester County. Our favorite walk was along the right of way of the old Croton Aqueduct system, a grassy path, forbidden to vehicles, winding through woods and fields and often through large private estates. Sometimes a friend and I went to Nyack for dinner and walked back by moonlight as far as the Fort Lee ferry, a hike of twenty-five miles or so.

Conscious of my educational shortcomings, I took evening extension courses in literature and sociology at Columbia University. Elementary though they were, I found them stimulating after a day spent in posting my office docket.

6

More and more, I became interested in trying to write. I cannot say just what it was that got me started. One influence was, undoubtedly, the example of my friends Bert Bloch and Leonard Hess, who were collaborating in the writing of short plays, which they read to me, seemingly finding my comments helpful. I began to think of attempting a play.

I had been experimenting with other types of writing. Fascinated by the French verse forms, I emulated Austin Dobson and Swinburne, turning out rondeaus, villanelles, triolets and even such difficult constructions as *chants royals* and sestinas. I had nothing to say, and no gift of poetic expression, but I enjoyed solving the technical problems. I wrote a few short stories too, one of which I actually sold to *Argosy*, an all-fiction Frank Munsey pulp-paper magazine. Called "The Fires of Thespis," it was in theme and style a bad imitation of O. Henry. An actor, long unemployed, gets a good part in a Broadway production. On the opening night, in the big scene of the play, his wife, anxious to have him find a missing document, shouts to him from her balcony seat that the paper is hidden in the fireplace. He rejoins the ranks of the unemployed. The appearance of the story in the May 1913 *Argosy* marked my professional debut. Not only was I printed, I was paid twenty dollars.

Doubtful of my ability to write a play alone, I persuaded Frank Harris to collaborate with me. Of course it had to be a problem play, so we chose as our theme the conflict between a woman's domestic life and her career—a troublesome question even fifty years ago. A small-town wife and mother, outraged by civic corruption, runs for mayor, is elected, but is forced by the deterioration of her marriage to relinquish office. The play was called *A Defection from Grace*, a pun upon the heroine's name, after the manner of *The Importance of Being Earnest*. A prize contest announcement by the Century Theatre Club spurred us on to its completion. We had only evenings free and were not too fresh after the long day's work. Frank's home offered even less privacy than mine, so our working quarters were my dining room, after the family retired. Somehow, we finished the play in time.

Expecting nothing from the competition, we were astonished several months later, to learn that we had won second prize. We were invited to the presentation ceremony, at an afternoon meeting in the Hotel Astor ballroom. In view of the rather unusual nature of the event, the office gave us the afternoon off. The only males in the crowded ballroom, we felt a little self-conscious as we sat on the dais through the reading of minutes, reports of committees, the passage of resolutions, the introduction of guests and numerous speeches. At length came the presentation. First prize, fifty dollars in cash, went to a young woman from the Middle West, whose name, I am ashamed to say, I have forgotten. Second prize, which was ours, was honorable mention. A certificate probably went with it, but it seems to have disappeared. We were roundly applauded, and were congratulated by everyone within handshaking reach. We left feeling that it had been a satisfactory afternoon, a novel change from office routine. It was flattering, too, to be beamed upon by expensively dressed ladies with orchids on their ample bosoms; and, of course, gratifying to be mentioned honorably. We even acquired a little prestige in the office, where prize-winning playwrights were a rarity.

Encouraged, Frank and I pushed ahead with another play. Its theme is suggested by its title, *The Seventh Commandment*. Again it was a feminist play, this time an attack upon the double standard of morality, the social code that condemns in a woman what it condones in a man. The heroine, trapped in a loveless marriage, leaves her brutish husband for a more compatible mate. Refused a divorce, she chooses to live openly with her lover. But the social pressures are too great; at length they are driven apart. Not long ago I glanced at a surviving copy of this work. The characters are stereotyped and the dialogue is bookish, but the play is moderately well constructed and not altogether unreadable. Nothing ever came of it, though years later the producer Harrison Grey Fiske considered acquiring it as a vehicle for his wife, the celebrated Minnie Maddern Fiske.

The only interesting thing about this juvenile effort is that while we were working on it John Galsworthy was writing *The Fugitive*, which closely resembled our play in subject matter, though not, I need hardly add, in literary quality. It was performed by Emily Stevens, who was Mrs. Fiske's niece. I thought it a fine play, but it ran only a few weeks.

7

As soon as I was twenty-one I applied for admission to the bar, submitting to the scrutiny of the Character Committee of the Bar Association, which passes upon the ethical fitness of candidates. (I have sometimes suspected that its standards are not too exacting.) In December 1913 I was sworn in, one of a crowd of eligibles, as a member of the bar of the State of New York, a designation to which I can still lay claim.

I was now a "full-fledged" lawyer, the goal I had been moving toward for more than five years. Presumably I would now be relieved of my duties as managing clerk and entrusted with the handling of minor cases. I might even get a five-dollar raise! The prospect was dismal, but I saw no alternative. As often happens, an unforeseen occurrence speedily provided one.

A few weeks after my admission to the bar, I discovered that I had failed to notify one of the attorneys that a certain document was due. Luckily, it was a minor lapse of which the opposing attorney would hardly be likely to take advantage. I went immediately to Jerry Rosenheim, the attorney in charge, and apologized for my negligence. Instead of taking the matter lightly, Rosenheim, a bumptious, bullnecked egotist whom everyone disliked, stormed and fumed. It was obvious that he intended to make an issue of it, so I was prepared for the summons to M.H.G.'s office, and for the inevitable sermon.

But in traversing the fifteen yards that lay between my cubbyhole and the sumptuous front office I made what was probably the most important decision of my life. As M.H.G. prepared to go into his full windup, I anticipated him. I said that the fault was entirely mine, that I had no excuse, that it was evident I was not paying proper attention to my work, a state of affairs attributable to my disinclination for the law. It seemed fitting, therefore, that I resign.

M.H.G., about to deliver a homily calculated to fill me with remorse for a display of carelessness that was in effect a betrayal of his confidence in me, was really bowled over. When, after a speechless moment, he reminded me of all my years of preparation, I said I saw no reason for spending more years in a distasteful occupation. He asked what my plans were. I said I had none, but would probably try to be a writer. That was the last straw. "Oh, well, of course!" he said, with what was intended to be withering scorn. "If you want to b-b-b-be a d-d-d-dilettante and a l-l-l-litterateur . . . !" Tense though I was, I could hardly contain my laughter. A dilettante and a litterateur! Where had the little man picked up such words? From Elbert Hubbard, perhaps.

Soon afterward I departed. I think my office mates meant it when they said they were sorry I was going. Bidding them farewell, I felt a slight pang. But dominant was a sense of relief and of liberation. I knew that, whatever lay ahead, I would never look ruefully back.

CHAPTER

VII

The Jackpot

1

Viewed objectively, my resignation must have seemed a quixotic act of youthful folly. My future had been assured. Competent performance of my duties would have led to a junior and, eventually, a senior partnership. Professionally and economically, I had been in the enviable position of being fixed for life. All this I had recklessly flung aside, with nothing else in view.

My choice of an occupation was narrowly limited. I had rejected a business career; now I had ruled out law too. I lacked the aptitude and the educational requirements for most professions. I wanted to become a writer, but my attempts had given me little reason to hope that I would succeed. It was not a promising outlook.

What made it worse was that I felt an inescapable financial obligation to my family. My father was no longer capable of regular employment; the few dollars he picked up from his box trade in cigars did not go far. Uncle Will, the family's mainstay, now spent most of his time in brokers' offices, one of those stolid, stoutish, cigar-chewing middle-aged men who sit hour after hour, day after day, trying to outguess the erratic fluctuations of the quotation board. Further, he had persuaded Grandpa to sell his Brooklyn flathouses and to play the market with the proceeds. Both men, I suspected, were drawing more and more heavily upon capital. That made it even more imperative for me to be prepared to assume the burden.

I was neither so impractical nor so self-absorbed as to ignore the realities of the situation. I intended to find some form of stopgap employment that would keep me going while I gave myself a fair chance to test out my potentialities as a writer. Meanwhile, out of the three hundred dollars I had painfully accumulated in the savings bank I could continue to pay my mother the accustomed nine dollars weekly. I estimated that that gave me six months in which to discover some dependable source of income. *100589*

Though I had quit my job without consulting my family, there were no complaints or reproaches, no reminders of my duties and obligations. I am sure they were all shocked and bewildered, not only because of the economic situation, but because of their genuine concern for my future. Except for my morbid addiction to reading, I had always been normal enough: a steady fellow, conscientiously progressing toward occupational stability and financial security. In their view, a man's proper occupation was some form of business. Still acceptable were medicine and the law. Writing as a career was not even within the range of their comprehension; they simply took no cognizance of the practice of the arts. But they had the decency to keep their thoughts and feelings to themselves. If I was not grateful to them then, I am now.

Others were undoubtedly less tolerant. My irresponsibility, callous disregard of my family's need, and ingratitude to M.H.G. must have provided a continuing and agreeable conversational topic for my uncles, aunts and cousins. I suspect that my mother was subjected to much commiseration and to pointed comments that were hard to cope with. That she defended me as best she could I am certain.

I began immediately to look for a job. William Grossman, M.H.G.'s brother, had given me a note of introduction to the editor of the *Morning Telegraph,* a racing daily that carried a great deal of theatrical news. An assiduous reader of O. Henry and Richard Harding Davis, I knew that the essence of a newspaperman is breeziness, so when the editor asked what he could do for me I replied breezily, "I'm tired of the law and I think I'd like to try the newspaper game." He replied coldly, "Young man, this is a business, not a game." That was the beginning and the end of my newspaper career.

Since I had no connections, I wrote to numerous individuals whose names were in the news or whose books I had read, asking for advice about getting a job, particularly in the theatrical field. Most of those to whom I wrote never answered. They were not to be blamed, I suppose; answering letters of this sort can become burdensome. However, remembering my own disappointment, I have made it a practice to reply to all personal letters except those obviously written by crackpots.

One of the replies I received was from Felix Adler, leader of the Ethical Culture Society, whose lectures on philosophical, social and literary topics I had often attended. I assumed that a man with such affirmative ideas about ethical living could assist a youth who wanted to live ethically. But Adler wrote that he had no connection with the theatrical world, which he had antagonized by opposing the appearance of children on the stage. He advised me to be courageous or hopeful or moral or something.

Another reply was from Charles Edward Russell, a well-known journalist who had several times run for office on the Socialist ticket. His letter was sympathetic but offered no practical suggestion. I saw that I would have to depend upon my own efforts.

Accordingly, I tried out for two public jobs for which competitive examinations were given. The first was to teach English to foreigners under the public-school system. Immigrants, mostly from southern and eastern Europe, were pouring in at the rate of over a million a year; hundreds of thousands settled in New York. Only about one New York inhabitant in three was native-born of two native-born parents. The schools were doing their best to instruct the newcomers in English. Many regular teachers conducted evening classes; but more teachers were needed. Since applicants were not required to have an academic background, I decided to take the examination.

The other examination, given by the State Civil Service Commission, was for the job of proofreader. I was as ill-qualified for proofreading as for teaching, my experience having consisted in holding copy when law briefs were read for errors. I did not know how to prepare myself, except by learning the arbitrary proofreading marks, which took little effort. Fortunately the examination laid much stress upon grammar, punctuation and spelling, of which I had some knowledge.

While awaiting results, I put aside job hunting to concentrate on writing, for my cash reserves still gave me a thin cushion of security. My situation was far from happy. It is exhilarating to strike out for the distant headland, but once beyond your depth you face the danger of being engulfed or the humiliation of turning back. Looking at it cold-bloodedly, here I was, at twenty-one, hanging about the house or going off on long walks when I should have been bringing home a Saturday-night pay envelope. Since I could do my writing uninterruptedly only late at night, I was likely to sleep on into the morning hours, another evidence of sloth in a household where everybody was up before eight.

2

I was further distracted by an emotional problem for which my giving up my job was responsible. During my employment I had spent most of my vacations in a summer boardinghouse at White Sulphur Springs, in the Catskill Mountains. The resort's chief attraction was the reputedly curative sulphur water—of little value to me, for I had no ailment. There was a lake several miles away, but I could neither swim nor row. I took walks, read a lot and slept late. Just being away from the office and in the country was enough to satisfy me and to justify the expenditure of twelve dollars per week for board, plus railroad fare and incidentals.

The guests were mostly middle-aged women whose husbands came up on weekends, but there were a few young people. When I was about nineteen I met there a vivacious, pretty girl of sixteen, with high natural color and silky black hair, to whom I was instantly attracted. Back in New York, we began seeing each other frequently. Appointments were usually made by mail, for she had no telephone.

It was my first female acquaintanceship that was more than just casual. In fact, I had known few girls; there were none of my age in my family circle, most of my friends had no sisters. Now and then I participated in birthday parties, May parties, outings, but without forming feminine friendships. During all my years as a jobholder my nonworking hours had been spent in studying, reading, or writing plays with Frank Harris. Besides, I could not afford to take girls out. Even paying the carfare on Sunday expeditions was a hardship; I had to cut the following week's lunches down to a ten-cent bag of candy, or perhaps omit lunch altogether. An awkward, inexperienced introvert, I did not find it easy to make feminine contacts. It was heartening, therefore, to meet a girl who was warmhearted and outgiving, as well as physically attractive. We soon developed an easygoing and intimate relationship, though not, of course, in a sexual sense, standards in those days being what they were. The girls I knew did not use cosmetics; their hair was uncut and innocent of the coiffeur's arts; dresses were ankle-long and neck-high. No "respectable" girl drank or smoked; neither did her mother, except perhaps for a glass of wine at a birthday dinner, or a bottle of beer at a picnic. Necking, petting, smooching and pitching woo may have been indulged in by some, but were certainly not generally practiced. Even a good-night kiss was likely to be taboo, unless matrimony was envisaged. I am not suggesting that human desires or impulses were different; it is the mores that have changed. Though I had the most advanced views about sexual freedom in general, I was personally puritanical; I could not have brought myself to make advances to a "nice girl."

Consequently, though our relationship was basically emotional, our behavior was on a high intellectual and cultural plane. We made walking trips, and Sunday excursions on the Hudson River Day Line; attended Central Park concerts (free) and extension courses at Columbia; or just sat and talked. After two years of companionship, we decided to get married. No date was set; there was no formal engagement. There could not have been. She had a secretarial job that paid a little better than mine; I had passed the bar examination and my future seemed secure, but my obligation to my family precluded any possibility of setting up a household of my own. We were young and could wait.

However, when I gave up my job my fiancée terminated the engagement. A sensible girl could hardly have been blamed. To wait for predictable solvency was one thing, to wait for the wildly improbable quite another. I was emotionally incapable of seeing it that way, for I was under great tension and very much on the defensive. My rebellion grew out of my belief that the social structure was polluted by greed and corruption, that most human behavior was mercenary and self-seeking. Now it seemed that even love could not escape the taint. Shocked and embittered, I wrote impassioned, highflown letters breaking off all contact.

3

Psychologically, I was in bad shape. Though I had no intention of deviating from my course, I saw myself condemned to a life of loneliness. This frame of mind, combined with my practical problems, was not conducive to creative effort. However, the very desperateness of my situation forced me to concentrate on getting started on some literary project.

The first step, of course, was to decide what to write. Frank Harris and I had been talking about writing another play, but he was building a law practice and had no real interest in becoming a writer. As for myself, I had found collaboration time-consuming and restrictive. So I decided to go ahead with a play of my own.

But what play? For weeks I wrestled with this problem. Then I happened to remember an article in *The Bookman* by its dramatic critic, Clayton Hamilton, who was a disciple of the famous Columbia University drama professor, Brander Matthews. Hamilton too lectured on the theatre at Columbia. A stout, rubicund, prematurely white-haired man, he had a free flow of words and a platform manner that won the admiration of culturally minded young women. In collaboration with A. E. Thomas (not to be confused with Augustus Thomas, the then "dean of American playwrights") he wrote several plays, ingenious exercises in dramatic technique but not notably stageworthy.

In his article he suggested writing a play that went backward in time—that is, in which each successive act antedated the preceding one. I found it an idea worth exploring. But I soon concluded that any play that, so to speak, ended before it began must inevitably be anticlimactic, a difficulty that Hamilton, for all his technical knowledge, had ignored. Further examination of the formula convinced me that it could be effective only if the play *gave the appearance* of moving backward, while actually it moved forward. For the resolution of a situation, which is the essence of drama, must be achieved progressively, not retrogressively.

Having reached this point, I plunged ahead. I had been mooning about for two months, with no work done, nothing in prospect, and my savings steadily dribbling away. It seemed better to be doing something than to be doing nothing. The first problem was to create a structure that would accommodate the technical device of time transposition: the play would have to carry the action to a conclusion to which the preceding sequences had contributed, regardless of their chronological order. Since this suggested a framework of some sort, it was not surprising that I should think of a courtroom. Trial scenes are usually theatrically interesting; furthermore, it was familiar material.

So then it was to be a trial, preferably a criminal trial, with a beginning and an end, and a middle in which time seemed to be reversed. Technically, this was not difficult: it required only a series of witnesses whose testimony would depict events in the inverse order of their occurrence.

A pattern was quickly developed. A man charged with the deliberate murder of his best friend refuses to defend himself. The law does not permit a plea of guilt of a capital offense, so the trial must proceed. As an eyewitness of the murder begins to testify, the scene changes and the substance of his testimony is acted out. It supports the prosecution's charge of an unjustifiable crime. There is a return to the courtroom. Now a defense witness is called whose enacted testimony, dealing with events *preceding* the crime, appears to diminish the defendant's guilt. Again the courtroom and again the enactment of testimony, this time to an event that happened *years ago*, an occurrence that justifies the defendant's act and explains his reason for refusing to exculpate himself. A final courtroom scene in which the accused man is acquitted.

That was how I conceived the plot from the beginning. In all the play's incredible metamorphoses there was no deviation from it. It has often been said that I borrowed the "flashback" technique from the movies. If I did, my borrowing was unconscious. I had worked out the device by logical processes. As Poe puts it in his essay on the writing of The Raven: "It is my intention to render it manifest that no point in its composition is referable either to accident or intuition—that the work proceeded, step by step, to its completion, with the precision and rigid consequence of a mathematical problem."

Having constructed the framework, I was faced with the necessity of finding something to put in it—not a simple matter, for I had nothing to say. After some reflection, I hit upon a plot based on a Kentucky feud. No subject could have been further outside the range of my experience and knowledge. Without pretense to reality or meaning, I assembled a set of characters and involved them in situations designed to make effective use of the structure. The play was called *According to the Evidence*. I wish I could recall the story or even some of the characters and incidents. But I have been unable to locate a script, and I have racked my brains in vain.

During the two months it took to construct, plot and write the play, I was notified that I had passed both my examinations. That meant the likelihood of a teachership in September, less than six months off. As for the proofreading examination, I was amazed to learn that I was seventh on a list of some two hundred—evidence, if any were needed, that civil-service standards are not very high! In that favored position, an assignment was certain to be forthcoming soon. I seemed reasonably sure now of a job that would keep me going.

The play, painfully typed on a broken-down machine I had picked up somewhere—I still type wretchedly even on a good machine—was now ready for market. I knew no one in the theatre and had no notion how one goes about selling a play; I was even unaware of the existence of authors' agents. Since the names of some Broadway producers were known to me, I thought I might as well begin by taking the script to their offices. For very specific reasons, I began my rounds with Selwyn and Company, and with Arthur Hopkins. The Selwyns were producers of *Within the Law*, a highly successful melodrama; Hopkins, a relative newcomer, had produced *The Poor Little Rich Girl*, one of the first plays to use dream symbolism, though hardly in Freudian terms.

On a Tuesday early in May I left a copy of the play at each office, simply depositing the scripts with the receptionist. I had heard that it usually took producers six months to get around to reading a play, so I was prepared to wait a while for rejections. On Thursday, there was a typed note in the mail from Crosby Gaige, the Selwyn's play reader; and a handwritten one from Hopkins. Both merely asked me to come in. Incensed, I said to my mother, "Instead of waiting six months to turn down a play, they turn it down without reading it." She nodded sympathetically; it was all part of the footless business to which I had irrationally committed myself.

Anxious to retrieve my scripts, I went down to Times Square that very morning. Gaige was out to lunch; I was asked to come back later. I then went to Hopkins' office in the ramshackle six-story Putnam Building, on the site of the present Paramount Theatre. It had two rooms, a small outer office and a somewhat larger private one. The staff consisted of a young scenic designer who was office boy, receptionist and secretary. He ushered me immediately into the private office.

At a desk heaped high with play scripts sat a little round man with large round eyes and a benign expression. He motioned me to a chair. With the laconism for which he became famous, he went straight to the point.

"Is this play original with you?" he asked.

I replied that it was.

His next question nearly knocked me off my chair: "What are your terms?"

I mumbled something to the effect that I had no terms. Indeed, I had not—I did not even know what "terms" were.

Hopkins nodded and suggested that I return in two days to sign the contract he would have drawn. With that, he rose to indicate that the interview was over. Not ten minutes had elapsed since I entered the office.

Memory of the next two days is lost in the clouds that enveloped me. I could not believe that Hopkins had serious intentions of producing the play; yet why else had he sent for me and talked about a contract? I returned on Saturday to his office, and, sure enough, there was the contract! This was long before the days of the Dramatists' Guild and its minimum basic agreement. The contract, as was customary, had been drawn by Hopkins' attorney. I thumbed uncomprehendingly through the document's eight or ten pages. Common sense warned me to seek advice before signing. Hopkins, far from taking offense, as I had feared he might, readily agreed. He told me to come back when I was ready.

When I mentioned that I had a script at the Selwyns', Hopkins advised me to get it back at once. Gaige greeted me cordially, but when I asked for the script he was furious. "We're not here to read plays for people who don't want us to produce them!" he shouted. He never forgot the episode and was fond of giving his version of it. According to his story, he was an industrious man who arrived at the office early and lunched at the usual hour, thereby missing my first call and losing the opportunity to acquire the play; whereas Hopkins, an indolent fellow, breakfasted late and reached his office at noon, so that he was there when I came in. Anyhow, the outcome was fortunate for me.

I took the contract to the theatrical specialist at my old office, who suggested some minor changes, to which Hopkins made no objection. The eminent fairness of the contract was testimony to his integrity. Many managers would not have hesitated to take advantage of an inexperienced youth. The five per cent royalty was less than what established dramatists received, but quite sufficient for a beginner. (Some producers offered young writers as little as two per cent or even bought plays outright for a few hundred dollars, practices no longer permissible.) There was also an advance payment of five hundred dollars, half down, the balance to be paid in a month. Production was scheduled for October. At that moment the two hundred and fifty dollars meant more to me than the promised production, in which I still only half believed. My skepticism would have been greater had I known that Hopkins was insolvent and that every other producer from whom he had tried to get financial backing had turned the play down.

Some weeks after the signing of the contract, he sent for me. Without mentioning his difficulties, he told me that though he was enthusiastic about the play's form he felt that the Kentucky-feud story had little appeal. He thought it advisable to find a new story to fit the novel framework. I had no objection; my allegiance to Kentucky was weak. Accordingly, I searched for a substitute story. Every day, I spent hours with Hopkins, analyzing various suggestions and rejecting them. He wanted me to use a thinly disguised version of the Harry Thaw murder trial as basis for a plot. From my high-school days, I remembered the trial well. The New York *World*, a leader in the field of yellow journalism, made the most of the sensational testimony of the glamorous Evelyn Nesbit Thaw. We schoolboys gobbled up the explicit physiological details of her seduction by the famous architect Stanford White. To me there was something distasteful about exploiting this sordid story, still fresh in many people's memory. I refused to let Hopkins talk me into it. I tried out this idea and that, wrote and rewrote. At last, I hit upon a plot that satisfied us both. I went off to White Sulphur Springs to put it into dialogue. The strain was beginning to tell. Late in June I wrote to Frank Harris: "I have worked on my play every day and have finished it at last, thank Heaven! I have grown quite sick of the thing, especially in these peaceful surroundings, and devoutly hope I won't have to do any more writing on it."

To my great relief, Hopkins was pleased with the script. Years later, in an article entitled "Playwrights I Have Known," he wrote:

Elmer had a splendid idea and a confused story. After I bought the play, I told him we would have to begin by throwing away the story. He had no objection. Then we discussed various stories—finally one definite story began to take shape. From that moment, Elmer ground out copy like a printing press. Every morning he would come to the office with reams of stuff. We would go over it together, finally agreeing on which was all right and which was bad. In two weeks the play was finished and Elmer had written every line, contrary to the belief at the time that I had written part of the play. There was never a moment that working with him was not a lot of fun and all through rehearsals we had more laughs than find their way to Broadway in a season.

The original story had indeed been thrown away! Kentucky and the feud had disappeared, and so had every character, situation and line of dialogue in the original play. Only the framework remained intact. It was still a murder trial, and within the encompassing courtroom scenes the plot elements were still disclosed in an inverted time sequence.

On the due date of the second installment, Hopkins gave me a hundred dollars, with the assurance that the balance would be paid soon. Still doubtful that the play would ever be produced, I was faced with a problem, for I had now been offered two jobs: one as a night-school teacher of English to foreigners, the other as a proofreader in the State Hospital for the Insane in Albany. If I turned them down and the play was not produced, I would soon be worse off than before, for I would have used up the advance and thrown away my prospects of employment. After much reflection, I decided to hold off as long as possible on the teaching job, then, if pressed, to accept. The other job, which required immediate acceptance, I turned down. I did not want to go to Albany; besides, though the pay was ten dollars per week more than I had been getting in the law office, it was evident that the cost of living away from home would consume most of it. It was a sensible decision, but I shall always regret that I did not learn what a proofreader does in an insane asylum.

Hopkins now asked me to consent to an assignment of the contract to the producing firm of Cohan and Harris (who, I learned later, had turned down the original version of the play). The papers were signed next day in the Cohan and Harris offices. Hopkins was handed a check for five hundred dollars to cover his advance to me, and he in turn gave me his check for the balance due me, which I deposited on my way home. Two days later the check came back marked "Insufficient funds." This well-known Broadway producer did not have a hundred and fifty dollars in the bank! Knowing that he had received five hundred dollars, I redeposited the check; this time it cleared. It was a revealing introduction to the economics of show business. Anyone with a few hundred dollars can set himself up as a producer, option a play and then look for financial backing and a theatre booking. The author can be sure of nothing but his advance royalty. Even if the play goes into rehearsal, it may be dropped at any time.

Cohan and Harris ranked with Charles Frohman and David Belasco as Broadway's foremost producers. George M. Cohan, the Yankee Doodle Boy, was the most popular figure in the American theatre, as well as the most versatile. He was a song-and-dance man, an actor, a composer, a lyric writer, a playwright, a stage director, a producer and a theatre owner. His successes included the musicals *Little Johnny Jones, George Washington, Jr.,* and *Forty-five Minutes from Broadway,* and the plays *Get-Rich-Quick Wallingford* and *Seven Keys to Baldpate.* He lived wholly in the theatre, where he strove only to provide "wholesome" entertainment: tuneful, simple-minded musical shows and skillfully constructed farces and melodramas. His mentality and his philosophy may be gauged by two of his slogans: "Always have them laughing when you say goodbye" and "The American flag has saved many a bum show." He ceased to be the idol of the acting profession when, in 1919, he bitterly opposed the formation of the Actors' Equity Association, and his popularity as a playwright declined with the rise of a new generation of writers in the 1920s. But he continued to make some notable stage appearances, in *I'd Rather Be Right*—as the President of the United States—and in Eugene O'Neill's *Ah, Wilderness!* His memory is perpetuated by a statue at the northern end of Times Square.

Cohan's partner, Sam H. Harris, who, like him, was an untutored man, had been a prize-fight manager and a producer of what were known from their admission prices as "ten-twenty-thirty melodramas." Though he looked and talked like a gangster, he was amiable, kindhearted and a man of great integrity. Besides, he had a flair for the theatre and an instinctive sense of showmanship. When things went wrong, as they so often do in the course of a production, Harris always said, "Don't worry; on opening night that curtain is going to go up."

I had hoped that Hopkins would direct the play, for it was his ingenious staging of *The Poor Little Rich Girl* that had led me to him. But, though he retained a one-third interest, the direction was entrusted to Sam Forrest of the Cohan and Harris production staff. At that time the author had no control over the choice of director and cast, so even had I wanted to I could not have objected. I shared the general feeling that *According to the Evidence* was a clumsy title. When someone suggested *On Trial*, I heartily approved.

Though Hopkins did not direct, he made a technical contribution whose value was inestimable. I had been puzzled and worried about the mechanics of making the transition from the courtroom to the interior flashback scenes. The long waits required for shifting the heavy scenery back and forth, several times in each act, were certain to diminish the audience's attentiveness. I thought of playing most of the courtroom scenes in darkness, relying upon the actors' voices to sustain the suspense; but that would have been far from satisfactory.

Hopkins found an exciting solution. On a recent trip to Europe he had studied the machinery of the Continental stages, then as now far in advance of ours. He proposed a device that was simple and effective. It consisted of two platforms placed just outside the proscenium arch and at right angles to it, arranged so that they could be pivoted on stage. On one the courtroom scene was set permanently. While it was in use there was ample time to change the setting on the other platform. The change of locale was then merely a matter of lowering the curtain briefly while one platform swung back and the other moved into the onstage position. Called a jackknife stage, because the platforms moved like the blades of a knife, this contrivance had its first American use in *On Trial*.

4

Rehearsals were to begin in September, with an opening in October at the Candler Theatre, Cohan and Harris' fine new playhouse, then being used for motion pictures. *On Trial* was to inaugurate it as a home for the drama. (The Candler, alas, has long since reverted to its original use. Like seven or eight other theatres in Forty-second Street, it is now a shabby, malodorous "grind" house given over to the continuous performance of old movies.)

Suddenly there was a drastic change in plans. It was rumored that A. H. Woods, a very successful showman, was planning a September production of a play called *Innocent* which also used the flashback technique. Fearful of having the edge taken off the novelty of *On Trial*, my producers advanced the opening to mid-August—less than six weeks off.

Hopkins and Sam Forrest began at once to select a cast. I was not consulted, nor could I have been helpful, for I knew nothing about casting. Anyhow, I was busy writing again. It had occurred to me that the play would be strengthened by the addition of a jury-room scene. I wrote a long one depicting the jurors as confused about the facts and the law, swayed by prejudice and eager to dispose of the case so that they could get back to their businesses. It was the play's only realistic scene. But Hopkins pointed out that it would hardly be helpful, for I could not expect an audience to be interested in the outcome of a trial in which the jurors took no interest. I recognized the force of his argument, tore up the scene and wrote a new one. This time the jurors were all at a high pitch of excitement, pacing the floor, wrangling, arguing cogently. It proved to be one of the most effective scenes of the play.

Things had moved fast. Here I was, with a play in rehearsal, barely six months after I had announced my intention of becoming a dilettante and a litterateur, not ten weeks since Hopkins had asked me what my terms were. Things were moving in the outside world too. At the end of June there had been quite a flurry in the press over the assassination of an Austrian archduke somewhere in the Balkans. Alarmists even talked of the possibility of a European war, an absurd manifestation of hysteria, for, as every literate person knew, Norman Angell, in his book *The Great Illusion,* had proved conclusively that the high cost of modern warfare made war economically impossible. Part-time students of politics like myself knew, too, that, let the German Kaiser rattle his sword as he would, when it came down to cases the Social Democratic Party in the Reichstag would refuse to vote war credits. That took care of the war talk.

In the cast of thirty, the only actors known to me, even by name, were the two principals: Frederick Perry, a popular leading man, and Mary Ryan, who was Forrest's wife. It was a company of experienced players, none particularly brilliant. However, brilliance was hardly called for. The plot had been manufactured to fit the dramaturgic formula. The characters had been invented to fit the plot; they were acceptable theatrical figures, without depth or individuality. The dialogue merely carried forward the action; it was workmanlike, but lacked color and distinction. The play depended upon continuous movement and incident: an accused man refusing to defend himself; a widow reconstructing the murder of her husband; a distraught ten-year-old girl recalling a domestic quarrel; a wife leaving her sickbed to reveal sobbingly her girlhood seduction; a seething jury room; the hysterical confession of an exposed thief. All that the actors had to do was keep the ball rolling—simulate primary emotions and maintain an atmosphere of tension. This, under Forrest's expert direction, they did very well.

Attending rehearsals was an exciting experience. There is something thrilling about sitting alone in the darkness of a theatre auditorium day after day, watching a play take shape from the first fumbling reading to the smooth, well-timed performance. I have been through it many, many times—more often as a director than as an observer—but the fascination has never worn off. When the elements are right, there is a unity of effort, a concentration of energy, a sense of dedication that make a production a little self-contained world. That is why those concerned in it are so stunned and bewildered when, as so often happens, the finished presentation is ridiculed or contemptuously dismissed.

The actors must have thought me unfriendly, for I spoke hardly a word to any of them. It was diffidence, not indifference, that deterred me—I was afraid of intruding, of getting in their way. Nor would I have known what to say to them. It was my first relation with people connected in any way with the arts; they seemed unlike anyone I had known. Sam Forrest, in particular, amazed me. He was a sort of modern counterpart of Mr. Vincent Crummles, though of course far more prosperous and respected. His life had been spent in the theatre, most of it as an actor. He had long hair that curled over his collar, a mellow, resonant voice and a propensity for striking attitudes. He lived entirely in the theatre, spoke and thought wholly in its terms. I have a book of his writings, printed at his expense, which he presented to me. Engagingly entitled *Variety of Miscellanea*, it is a collection of theatrical anecdotes, eulogies of his wife and random reflections about nothing. Such characters are still to be found in the theatre, but they have become increasingly rare. Nowadays actors, after graduating from college, where they have majored in Russian literature or home economics, spend much of their time at union meetings or hearings of legislative investigating committees, in tax accountants' offices, on psychoanalysts' couches, on the air praising cigarettes and deodorants or in the White House giving elocution lessons.

An actor who becomes a stage director is usually not content merely to tell his charges what to do; he feels impelled to show them. Forrest was no exception. Regardless of age or sex, he demonstrated how each part should be played. When he showed the little ten-year-old how to express emotion, Hopkins and I, safe from observation in the dark recesses of the theatre, shook with laughter. All the same, Forrest knew what he was doing; his ranting and gesticulation guided the actors in finding the tone and temper of their performances.

In the midst of rehearsals, the smoldering fires of European belligerence burst into flame. Serbia, backed by Russia, refused compliance with Austria's ultimatum; mobilization followed mobilization; Germany declared war upon Russia, then upon France; Britain declared war upon Germany. In the words of Viscount Grey, the lights were going out all over Europe. The green-gray German hordes swept into Belgium and northern France. World War I had begun, though as yet no need was seen for the distinguishing Roman numeral.

Absorbed though I was in my play, and remote as Europe was to me—as it was to most Americans—I could hardly ignore a catastrophe of such magnitude. I read the newspapers with incredulity and horror. One evening Frank Harris and I took the familiar walk around Central Park, trying to grasp the war's reality and significance. We concluded that it was a showdown between autocracy and freedom, conveniently overlooking the fact that Russia, most autocratic of all, was allied with the Western democracies. It was also obvious to us that military operations on such a scale could not long continue. Clearly, the war would be over by the time the snow flew.

On Trial was to open at the Candler on August 19 after a week-end tryout at Stamford, Connecticut—a performance on Friday night and two on Saturday. Accompanied by my mother and Bert Bloch, I put up at a hotel in Stamford. It was my first visit to Connecticut, though Stamford is less than forty miles from New York.

Oddly enough, we were opening a new theatre there too, an event of great local importance. Under the heading "*On Trial* Will Inaugurate Stamford's Splendid Future Home of Disciples of Thespis," the *Morning News* said (in part): "Tonight sees the long-looked-for opening of the Stamford Theatre . . . Following appropriate dedication exercises at which prominent citizens of city and state will speak, will come the performance of *On Trial* . . . Those who are fortunate enough to have seats for this evening's performance will see a production whose novelty of settings, fascination of story and brilliancy of acting has never before been equalled on a Stamford stage." (The theatre is still there, though Stamford has long since ceased to be a tryout town, and the building no longer houses the disciples of Thespis. A resident of Stamford since 1942, I occasionally see a movie in the old theatre.)

My mother, Bert and I sat in a stage box, from which we had a good view of the audience—and of Cohan, Harris and Hopkins, impatiently pacing the rear of the auditorium while the prominent citizens of city and state participated in the appropriate but seemingly endless dedication exercises. The *Morning News* did full justice to the occasion. Under the seven-column banner head "Atlantic Street Turned into a Broadway," the four-column story said: "The Stamford Theatre was 'On Trial' last evening before a jury composed of the Stamford public, and to say that the jury was unanimous in agreeing that the city of Stamford had a theatre of which they had abundant reason to be proud would be putting the case rather mildly. . . . The town looked like Broadway last night. . . . There was the lineup of automobiles, the dress suits of the men providing the background for the stunning dresses of the Stamford women."

When, as Sam Harris had predicted, the curtain finally did go up, the courtroom setting won a round of applause. The audience quickly became interested in the proceedings: the empaneling of the jury, the opening addresses of the opposing lawyers, the appearance on the witness stand of the murdered man's widow. But when, just as she had finished saying, "As I entered my home, the telephone in the library rang," the lights went out and the curtain was lowered, the spectators leaned back resignedly. They knew that they were the "dogs" on whom the play was being tried, and that this was the sort of thing they had to expect. Their disgust gave way to amazement when, in thirty seconds, the curtain rose again upon a library scene, with the telephone ringing and the witness, now in an evening gown, entering to answer it. There was delighted applause and a buzz of excited comment. Hopkins' jackknife stage had worked swiftly and smoothly. The successive changes of scene were eagerly awaited and received with mounting appreciation.

The second act went even better. By now the audience was interested in the story, as well as in the stage mechanics. In the second intermission I went to the lobby to find out how my producers felt about the play's reception. There was no danger of my being recognized, for nobody knew me or knew that I was there. The first person I saw was Cohan. He came over, put his hand on my shoulder and said, "Kid, if you want to sell your rights in the play, I'll give you thirty thousand dollars for them."

This was indeed a bolt from the blue. Forced to think quickly, I concluded that the offer was not serious. In my six and a half years of jobholding, my total earnings had been less than three thousand dollars. If Cohan had offered me five thousand, I might have taken it. But thirty thousand! I could not believe that anyone had that much money, much less that he would offer it for the rights of a play that had not yet opened. Obviously, Cohan was pulling my leg, taking advantage of my naïveté and inexperience. I visualized him addressing an appreciative circle at the Lambs' Club: "I offered that kid thirty thousand and he fell for it and said he'd take it." So, with a pallid smile and assumed nonchalance, I said, "I guess I'll take my chance." Cohan merely nodded and walked away.

The response at the final curtain was heartening; we were all delighted. Even the *Morning News,* in the midst of its rhapsodies about the splendors of the playhouse, did not entirely ignore the play. "Well acted, with fine beginnings, fine endings, fine climaxes and keen interest . . . A mystery play with a novel idea in the switching of the time of action . . . A number of people say they are going to enjoy the pleasure of seeing the performance over again." I don't know whether any actually did, but there were good houses at both Saturday performances.

5

Mid-August in New York is not a popular theatregoing season. Nor was a new play by an unknown author likely to be an immediate attraction. So I was offered a liberal allotment of first-night seats, even more for the second night—a hundred, if I could use them. I could not; my circle of acquaintances was small. Accordingly, my invitations were confined to relatives and a few close friends.

Dressing for the occasion was a problem. Of course I had never owned a dress suit or had occasion to rent one. Why I felt that evening dress was obligatory I do not know. Anyhow, Uncle Albert sent me a suit that no longer fit him. Having it altered and acquiring the necessary accessories occupied a good deal of my time between the Stamford closing and the New York opening.

The night of the nineteenth finally arrived. The date may also be remembered for President Wilson's neutrality proclamation: "The United States must be neutral in fact as well as in name during these days that are to try men's souls. We must be impartial in thought as well as in action, must put a curb upon our sentiments, as well as any transaction that might be construed as a preference of one party to the struggle before another."

At the Candler too I had a stage box, into which were crowded my parents, Grandpa, Uncle Will, and Uncle Albert and Aunt Emma, who had come up from Baltimore. There was neither elbow room nor knee room; I sweltered in the heavy winter suit, stiff shirt and high collar. Throughout the performance my dominant feeling was one of extreme physical discomfort. Luckily there were no dedication ceremonies. But there was no favorably predisposed audience either. Unlike the elite of Stamford, the regular New York first-nighters had come merely to see the opening of another play, willing but not eager to be impressed.

The animated courtroom scene upon which the curtain rose captured attention. There was even a ripple of applause, though that may have been for some of the actors, who were better known to the first-nighters than to me. The scene went well enough until the moment came for the first scene change. Then, as the lights went out and the curtain fell, there were murmurs of impatience and of commiseration. Something had evidently gone amiss: a wrong cue given, a wrong switch pulled. Such things are expected in tryout performances; on a New York opening night they are likely to be fatal.

When, in less than a minute, the curtain rose upon the new scene, the applause was loud and prolonged. The audience was really captivated now, and it remained so until the end of the play. As one paper put it: "During the intermission, the sidewalk was crowded with men from the audience, smoking and talking. [Note: no women!] The carriage starter called 'Curtain up, gentlemen.' Usually when this call is heard, the smokers saunter back leisurely to their seats. Last night there was a rush to get back into the theatre, every man seeming to fear that he would miss the rise of the curtain."

I was not among those on the sidewalk. I stayed in the box, to which all the people I had invited streamed to tell me that the play was going well. Dazed and uncomfortable, I just sat there, breathing with difficulty, sweating profusely, wishing it were all over. When it finally was, there was a hearty demonstration of approval, even cries of "Author!"—a practice happily obsolete in New York, though it survives in London. Someone jerked me to my feet. I stood at the edge of the box, perspiring, blinking, opening and shutting my mouth. Here is a newspaper account: "When a first-night audience is pleased it is the custom to call for the author at the end of the act before the last. At the final curtain, the audience, with a little perfunctory applause, hurries out. Last night when the curtain fell at the end, hardly anyone left his or her seat. There were cheers and there were shouts of 'Author!' The women even made no move to put on their hats, but sat and applauded until Mr. Reizen-stein, a tall, slender, eye-glassed young man, stood up in an upper box and mumbled a few words of thanks that could not be heard. It was a scene that has not been witnessed in a New York theatre in a long time." Other comments were in the same vein.

When the audience went home at last, I was ready to do the same, for I was hot and tired. But Bert Feibleman, business manager for Cohan and Harris, invited me to go out with him; evidently he felt that some gesture of managerial recognition was required. Though I would much rather have gone uptown with my family, I accom-panied him to Churchill's, then one of New York's fashionable after-theatre resorts. Feibleman suggested a drink. I had never had any-thing stronger than a glass of wine, so I ordered ginger ale and a chicken sandwich. The conversation went haltingly. After we had agreed that the play had been well received, there seemed little to say. When I had finished my sandwich I asked to be excused and took the subway uptown. My mother, still up, greeted me with evi-dent relief. Her elation at the play's reception had been exceeded by fears about my exposure to the corrupting night life of Broadway. Too tired for conversation, I retired to my folding bed in the living room and was soon sound asleep.

The reviews were what are known in theatrical circles as "raves." New York's population then was half today's, but there were more than twice as many newspapers as now—about fifteen. Almost with-out exception, their praise of the play was unrestrained: "A play which upsets all rules and precedent and is cheered by first-night audience"; " 'On Trial,' by an unknown, strong and gripping play"; "All that is melodramatic in the criminal courts is in this new play"; "The dramatic sensation of the season"; "A sensational success at the Candler"; "The first 'retroactive' melodrama inspires an ex-cited audience to arise in its seats and cheer the author"; "A re-markable example of dramatic construction"; "Has novelty, thrills and suspense"; "Thrills from start to finish; unique in stage effects."

Now a curious thing happened. Second nights are usually bad, particularly in midsummer. To guard against the probability of an empty house the management had given away nearly all the seats for the second performance. But when the reviews appeared peo-ple lined up to buy tickets for the evening showing. Since no seats were available, hundreds were turned away. It was the best advertisement the play could have had. Nothing drives an audience to a box office like the news that tickets are unobtainable. For many months there was not an empty seat.

Of course the effect upon me was bewildering. Physically and emotionally exhausted, I decided to go away for a short time, to recover my perspective. My bank account was running low, so I hesitantly asked Feibleman for an additional small advance. He immediately gave me a check for five hundred dollars—eight months' law-office pay! In less than two weeks my total advance was paid off. Eventually my earnings from the play came to a hundred thousand dollars. I had made no mistake in turning down Cohan's offer.

VIII

A New Life : 1

1

Before leaving on my holiday, I took my mother apartment hunting, for nothing seemed more important than getting into a proper bed in a room of my own. We soon found a place on Claremont Avenue, near Barnard College. Though the building had an elevator and the apartment was far more spacious than any we had ever occupied, it was not luxurious, nor was the neighborhood fashionable. Nevertheless, my mother was worried by what seemed my reckless extravagance. She simply could not grasp the magnitude of the change in our economic status. Neither could I, but a little simple arithmetic convinced me that I could afford the new apartment. Shopping expeditions followed, for many new furnishings were needed. It all went so quickly that it was only a matter of days before we were installed in the new home. Then I went off to White Sulphur Springs with Bert Bloch. The summer season was about over and the place half empty, which suited me very well, for I needed rest and a little quiet reflection.

Elated though I was, the exceptional praise that the play had received puzzled me. The critic I respected most, Louis Sherwin of the *Globe*, wrote: "Can you imagine the wickedness of a play that has the sheer audacity to be original? A play that breaks well-nigh every rule of construction that has been dinned into our ears by the professors? A play that has the impertinence to be a good play instead of a well-made play? . . . 'On Trial' contains the most radical innovation in play construction, the most striking novelty that has been seen for years. Undoubtedly it will bring about important changes in the technique of the theatre." Another critic, the caustic Samuel Hoffenstein, called the play "purely and simply a triumph of dramatic construction, . . . a remarkable piece of stage craftsmanship." Others referred to its "human interest" and "the big human note which throbs through all its acts."

Steeped in the drama of the Greeks and Shakespeare, of Ibsen, Shaw, Galsworthy, Hauptmann, Schnitzler, and Synge, I could not understand all this acclaim. To begin with, *On Trial* broke no rules of dramatic technique. As Brander Matthews, high priest of the drama at Columbia, pointed out, it was not "written backward" at all. On the contrary, it followed a murder trial straight through. If the witnesses had simply recited their stories in the usual manner, it would not have occurred to anyone that there was a departure from normal progression. The gimmick—as it would be called today—was that the testimony was visualized. But these enactments carried the story forward, as every scene in a well-constructed play must.

As for the "human interest," if it was there it was by sheer accident. I have described how the characters and the situations were contrived to fit the pattern. Putting it all together resembled the solution of a jigsaw puzzle. I was not ashamed of what I had wrought, nor am I ashamed of it now. There can be no doubt that the play is "good theatre," and that its construction is workmanlike. Craftsmanship is essential to every art, to the drama most of all. The best work of all great dramatists displays high technical proficiency.

But a good theatrical craftsman is not necessarily a worthy dramatist, a distinction that the reviewers had failed to make. There were even allusions to Byron, who, in his early twenties, "awoke one morning to find himself famous." As an admirer of Byron, I found the analogy ludicrous. I saw that, for my own salvation as a person and as a potential writer, I must not let myself be carried away. I had stumbled upon an effective device, had manipulated it into something presentable, had been aided in its realization by fortuitous association with a persevering, ingenious producer. The odds against such a happy combination of circumstances were vast;

against its repetition they were incalculable. Obviously if I was to be more than a one-shot playwright—a common figure—I not only must have something to write about, but must also learn to write.

These conclusions were not arrived at all at once, with the precision with which I have stated them. But I was aware of the pitfalls that beset a writer's path, and of the danger of complacency. I knew that to conduct my life intelligently and constructively I must try to view my situation objectively. In my new-found state of elation, it was not easy.

While I was striving to recover my balance, I was suddenly confronted with another situation that was almost as unexpected and as bewildering as the success of *On Trial*. At White Sulphur Springs I received a letter from my former fiancée. It was a fervent declaration of love, and an urgent request that our engagement be renewed.

I read the letter with astonishment and consternation. The breaking of the engagement had made me desperately unhappy, but as I became absorbed in the writing of my play my anguish had lessened; by the time the play was accepted, it had diminished to the vanishing point, particularly since I had had no communication with the young woman in all those months. As a friendly gesture I had sent opening-night tickets to her and her family, but the resumption of our former relationship had not even remotely suggested itself to me.

Consequently, I was thrown into a state of utter confusion, torn by conflicting emotions and impulses. I wanted to enjoy my sudden independence—to study, to travel, to revel in the privacy of that room of mine, to write plays that had meaning. I wanted to look about, in a leisurely way, at what the world had to offer; to try to design a pattern for my life. At the same time, the idea of marriage made a strong appeal. I was discontented with celibacy, strongly desired sexual experience. Mercenary love did not attract me. I had no compunction about nonmarital relationships, but no opportunity to form one had presented itself. Also, since life with my family provided neither stimulation nor companionship, the prospect of a home of my own was enticing. After years of solitary living, it was agreeable to visualize sharing an establishment with a sympathetic companion, a place to receive friends, to raise a family perhaps. I wavered, hesitated, weighed one set of considerations against another.

Had I been deeply in love, there would have been no indecision. But I was not. There was physical attraction, there was affection, but no compulsive emotion that sweeps aside logic and practicality. Still another factor added to my uncertainty. I knew that many women seek in marriage not only emotional but economic security. Could my changed status have prompted the letter I received? I pondered the question, then dismissed the suspicion as unjust and cynical.

Strangely enough, it was the economic factor that determined my decision. I had resolved not to let sudden prosperity worsen character and behavior, as it so often does. Yet how would I appear, in the eyes of others and in my own, if I now rejected a girl I was willing to marry when my fortunes were at their lowest ebb? Since it was not I who had broken the engagement, I was perhaps leaning backward a little too far. However, I wrote a responsive letter, and, having done so, easily persuaded myself that I was very much in love—not consciously, of course, but in self-protective justification of a difficult decision. On my return to New York, there was a joyous reconciliation, if that is the right word. But I wanted time to find my equilibrium, so I was firm about putting off marriage until June, nearly a year away.

2

I now tasted the delights of occupying a private room. Besides a bedstead, with a box spring and a mattress that was too thick to roll up, I had a desk, a chest of drawers, an armchair with accompanying floor lamp and bookrack, and a row of bookshelves, which I filled with the works of my favorite authors. I had not yet discovered the pleasure of living with paintings, but the books, in their bold, broad ranks, added warmth and color to the room. I could now go to bed and get up whenever I felt like it without incommoding anyone or being late to work. Late to bed and late to rise may not be conducive to health, wealth and wisdom, but it is a practice I have never abandoned. Greatest joy of all was to shut my door, settle back in my armchair and occupy myself with a book, a work project or nothing at all. I have lived an active domestic, professional, social and civic life, and have enjoyed most of it. But the solitary hours are best: the hours of reading, letter writing, introspection and retrospection, roving thoughts, or solid creative work. Then one is truly self-contained, self-sufficient, self-critical, self-expressive.

All my time was not spent in my room. There was, after all, the play at the Candler—still a nine-day wonder. I often stood at the back to enjoy the spectacle of the audience enjoying itself. Though my picture had appeared in many newspapers and magazines, I was never recognized. Years later I learned the trick of sitting in a box and watching the audience rather than the play. It is fascinating to observe the shifting emotions, the gradations in attentiveness, the excitement, the laughter, the tears. It is literally true that when people are tense they sit on the edge of their seats; that they cough only when their interest flags; and that, while hilarity does not actually make them roll in the aisles, it does induce exaggerated bodily contortions. I never fail to marvel at the drama's power to make people surrender to its fictions and illusions.

Still afraid of being intrusive, I went backstage very little. I had yet to learn that actors thrive upon attention and that a friendly visitor is always welcome. But I did often spend an hour in the box office, not merely to see the money roll in—though that was far from unpleasant—but also to observe the behavior of the ticket buyers. A box office is an excellent place to study human conduct: a diversity of individuals displaying varying degrees of truculence, timidity, suspicion, cajolery and confusion. Sometimes as I stood beside the window, plainly visible, a customer would demand special attention, claiming to be an old friend of the author's. "Is that so?" the box-office man would say, as he handed out the tickets. "Well, the author will be sitting right next to you tonight." What the resultant misunderstandings were, I do not know.

There were, of course, the usual publicity activities: newspaper interviews, articles to be written. I took a young woman from the New York *Times* to lunch at Shanley's, the Sardi's of its day. Lunch was sixty-five cents, martinis two for a quarter. It was my first martini. I have had many since, but have never learned to like them. One day a representative of a cigarette company asked me for a testimonial. When I told him I did not smoke, he said, "That's all right. We'll prepare a testimonial that a nonsmoker can sign." The opinion I formed of the advertising business was not high. It has declined steadily ever since.

I was dined too. Hostesses are on the alert for new faces; my freakish success made a good conversation piece. I received invitations from leaders of the Drama League: Mrs. James Harvey Robinson, wife of Columbia's celebrated history professor; and Kate Oglaby, who had a knack for giving small, lively dinner parties, at which one met, for example, Alexander Woollcott; from the beautiful Eleanor Robson, whose stage performances I had admired before she became Mrs. August Belmont; from Edith J. R. Isaacs, for many years editor of *Theatre Arts;* from Annie Nathan Meyer, an incredibly dynamic woman, at whose table I met her nephew Robert Nathan, as well as Waldo Frank. It was the opening of a whole new world of experience and associations.

In due course, I became acquainted with some of the notables in the English department at Columbia: John Erskine, Carl Van Doren and Henry Wadsworth Longfellow Dana, who, as his name indicates, was a grandson both of Longfellow and of Richard Henry Dana. He later became custodian of the Longfellow House in Cambridge. Whenever I went to Boston for a tryout, he was sure to show up at the theatre.

A closer association was with Brander Matthews' assistant, Hatcher Hughes, a handsome young North Carolinian. He conducted a course in playwriting and was interested in organizing a campus production unit. A one-act-play contest was announced. Technically a student, I submitted a short play, *The Passing of Chow-Chow,* an inconsequential trifle about a young couple's quarrel over a pet dog, written while I was still a law clerk. Since the competition was not keen, I won a silver cup—a step up from honorable mention. This playlet, written in 1913, is still occasionally performed by amateurs. Recently it had a television performance in West Germany. Each succeeding year I find the ways of the theatre more incomprehensible.

But I was puzzled from the very beginning. Since I felt a moral obligation to give the producers of *On Trial* the first refusal of my next play—if and when I wrote one!—I paid little attention to the requests from various managers and agents. However, I did accept an invitation from the highly successful producer William A. Brady to accompany him to the office of Lee Shubert, for many decades a dominant figure in the theatre. When Shubert said to me, "Next time you get an idea for a play, just bring in an outline and we'll give you a contract in advance," I thought he must be joking. In fact, though I have spent my whole professional life in the commercial theatre, I have never been quite able to reconcile the art of the drama with the realities of show business.

Another incident was even more confusing. Someone took me to see Mrs. Nash, the mother of two popular actresses: Mary, a skillful leading woman, and Florence, an excellent comedienne. The sisters wanted to costar, said Mrs. Nash, but had been unable to find a suitable play. In view of the promise I had shown, she was offering me the opportunity to write one. She then outlined what was required. One of the girls could do a Cockney accent, the other an Irish brogue. To utilize these assets, they would appear, at the beginning, to be ill-educated; poor too, so that their shabby clothes would be in contrast to the finery they would display when their circumstances improved. With wealth, of course, would come sophistication, and the use of elegant English. The rest she would leave to me. When I declined, as politely as I could, she was quite offended; obviously she regarded me as a callow youth whose head had been turned by success. There would have been no point in trying to explain how I felt about the art of the drama.

My conception of authorship was so exalted that I was amazed by an invitation to join the Authors' League of America, then only in the second or third year of its existence. I felt that I should explain that I was not really an author, but just a novice whose random shot had happened to hit the bull's-eye. Of course I did nothing of the sort, but accepted with alacrity. I was certainly the League's youngest member then, as today I am its oldest in terms of continuous membership.

When *On Trial* had been running a few months, a Chicago company was organized. I attended most of the rehearsals, feeling like an old theatre hand now. I had even lost some of my awe of the actors, talked to them, and found them responsive. With eagerness I accepted the management's invitation to go to Chicago. Baltimore was as far away as I had ever been; Chicago sounded remote and romantic. The sleeper and the diner were novel and interesting experiences.

We spent a week in Detroit to get the production running smoothly. All I remember of Detroit is a visit to the Ford plant, whose famous assembly line had just been established. As I

watched the cars moving along the belt, each worker performing
the same operation over and over, the whole process struck me as
inhuman and demoralizing. I had the same feeling nearly twenty
years later when I saw the Ford-installed assembly line in the tractor factory at Stalingrad.

In Chicago *On Trial* was an instantaneous success. It no longer
provided the same shock of novelty, but it now bore the stamp of
New York approval. It played in Chicago until the end of the
theatrical season. With two companies running, I was making over
a thousand dollars a week—not much in terms of today's theatrical
figures, but a very handsome sum then.

Continuing my industrial exploration, I visited the stockyards—a
revolting experience. I shall never forget those frightened, lowing
animals, hoisted by their hind feet to a moving trolley, stunned by
wooden mallets preparatory to having their throats slit, spurting
blood over the aprons and beards of their executioners. It was long
before I could eat meat again. In the canning section a young man
sat beside a vat through which sealed cans of beef stew moved on a
belt. Open-eyed and open-mouthed, he watched for air bubbles,
snatching out the imperfectly sealed cans, a horrible picture of im-
becility. I felt strongly about the stultifying effects of industrialism;
that moronic boy personified for me the evils of the machine age.
Like everyone else, I use, and am served by, innumerable mechanical devices, but I have always disliked them and the system
that produces them, on psychological, moral and aesthetic grounds.

3

Of the numerous invitations to speak in public which I received, the
most formidable—only because it was the first—came from the University Settlement, located in the heart of the ghetto. The prospect
of standing up before an audience was rather alarming. Afraid of
stammering or drying up completely, I laboriously composed a paper dealing with the drama as a medium for the expression of ideas,
particularly social ideas. Much of it was devoted to a discussion of
Galsworthy's plays.

Some fifteen years later I was delighted and somewhat awed to
be invited to a London luncheon at which Galsworthy was present.
Spontaneously I told him how deeply I felt indebted to him both for

his craftsmanship and for his social thinking. To my consternation, he reacted coldly, almost hostilely. Apparently he thought I was just buttering him up, plying him with insincere flattery. As he went on to speak, with bitterness, of his inability to write a play that was a popular success, I saw that he regarded himself as a failure and took my praise to be hypocritical. Attempted reassurance would have made matters worse, so I lamely changed the subject. It was for me a most unhappy occasion.

My talk at the University Settlement was the beginning of a long association with that institution. It also taught me that public speaking is not the ordeal I had expected it to be. After a few more speeches, I came to the conclusion that if a speaker is audible and keeps things moving his listeners will go along with him, since most of them come to see him perform as much as to hear what he has to say. I discovered, too, that if you are familiar with your subject—and some familiarity is desirable—it is better to speak without a prepared paper, without notes even.

Two other speaking engagements turned out to be important for me. Percy Stickney Grant, rector of the Church of the Ascension, on lower Fifth Avenue, asked me to speak at his Sunday-night forum. A brief nonsectarian service was followed by the guest speaker's address, usually on some political or sociological topic; afterward, in the parish house around the corner, there was general discussion. The audience was a strange mixture of members of the fashionable congregation, mostly conservative, Greenwich Village intellectuals, mostly radical, proponents of various causes, always seeking a chance to be heard, and miscellaneous crackpots. Since the subject was usually controversial, there was a good bit of heckling and acrimonious backchat. I found it stimulating and instructive, and went back frequently. It was probably this exposure to the rough-and-tumble give-and-take of an open forum that made me a lifelong free-speech advocate.

Important in a different way was a dinner of the Socialist Press Club at which I was one of the speakers. This association of leftist writers, which had from time to time presented an evening of unconventional one-act plays in a hired hall, was now establishing a more organized group, the Washington Square Players. The dinner was chaired by Edward Goodman, general director of the enterprise. Others who were actively engaged were Lawrence Langner,

Philip Moeller and Lee Simonson. It was a co-operative undertaking; actors, directors, scene-builders, stagehands, ushers were
all amateurs. The opening performance, at a tiny playhouse in the
East Fifties appropriately called the Bandbox, was a significant
event in the history of the American theatre. In a sense, it sounded
the first note of the movement that was to vitalize the American
drama in the 1920s. The plays, while in the main not especially noteworthy, were in refreshing contrast to the stale, predigested fare
of the commercial theatre. The whole undertaking was a step toward the establishment of a much-needed adult theatre. Out of
the amateurish Washington Square Players grew the highly professional Theatre Guild. Many of the Bandbox apprentices made
notable contributions to the development of the stage in America.

4

My fiancée and I were planning to spend our honeymoon in England. I had been reading about the old Roman road which could
still be followed from the southern coastline to Hadrian's Wall in
the north. We thought it would be both romantic and instructive
to walk the length of it. The fact that England was at war did not
disturb us. The fighting was all in Belgium and northern France
and in the marshes of East Prussia. The war as a whole still
seemed very remote.

I was under pressure from several friends not to go through with
the marriage. They thought I was too young and too inexperienced,
and that my fiancée and I were not well mated. One of my dis-
suaders was my old fourth-grade teacher, Ella McNair, with whom
I had never completely lost touch. A forthright woman, she told
me quite bluntly that I did not know what I was doing. But I was
wholly committed now to marriage and looked forward to it eagerly.
My fiancée was charming, gay and amorous. Such reservations
as I had had were swept away by my desire for intimate companionship and a home of my own.

What did worry me a little was the possibility that my father's
epilepsy was transmissible. He had not been stricken until he was
in his thirties; I was only in my early twenties. And what if I escaped, only to have my children affected? Ibsen's *Ghosts* had not
failed to impress me! The doctors I consulted assured me that the

possibility was so remote as to be almost negligible. Fortunately they were right: neither I nor any of my five children has ever been nervously or mentally disordered.

5

In that busy time, playgoing was a major activity. Between the opening of *On Trial* in mid-August 1914 and my marriage in mid-June 1915, I went to the theatre no less than seventy times. Nowadays I am hard put to find a dozen plays a year that I want to see. Though the number of Broadway productions has declined sharply, there has been a corresponding increase in the area now known as "off Broadway," so lack of opportunity cannot account for my infrequent attendance. I suppose that, as one ages, what offers itself with an air of apparent novelty seems only too often wearisomely familiar. As Shaw's Caesar says, "I grow older, but the crowd in the Appian Way is always the same age." At twenty-two, suddenly possessed with the wherewithal, I steeped myself in theatre, eager to see "anything with a curtain in front of it."

The New York theatre was certainly not better then. In spite of the feebleness of many of today's plays, the general level of writing and production is higher than it was fifty years ago. There were many excellent craftsmen, but almost no plays of literary quality. My avidity for playgoing did not blind me to the fatuities of the native drama. My program books crinkle with scornful commentaries on the crude melodramas and mechanical farces that constituted the bulk of theatrical fare. A few titles suggest the general tone and flavor: *What Happened at 22, Under Cover, Big Jim Garrity, Mr. Wu, Twin Beds, Kick In, Sinners.*

The only American play of fine texture I saw that season was *Children of Earth*. Written by a New England poet, Alice Brown, it had won the ten-thousand-dollar prize offered by Winthrop Ames for the play best suited to inaugurate his beautiful little Booth Theatre. The payment of such a sum to an unknown writer aroused expectations that the quiet, sensitive chronicle of New England life did not fulfill. It was soon withdrawn, another "proof" that art in the theatre does not pay. I never met the author, but she once wrote me a gracious note about a play of mine, accompanied by a volume of her poems, with an inscription in a stiff, aged hand.

In spite of its general banality, the season had many attractions for me. Even trivial plays often provided good acting opportunities for such stars as William Gillette, Blanche Bates, Elsie Ferguson, Leo Ditrichstein, Emily Stevens, Holbrook Blinn, Mary Boland and the various members of the Drew-Barrymore clan. It was often possible for an alert theatregoer to see interesting productions at special matinees or in out-of-the-way theatres.

Shortly after the inauguration of the Bandbox, the Neighborhood Playhouse opened, in Grand Street on the lower East Side. Built and managed by Irene and Alice Lewisohn, nieces of Adolph Lewisohn, donor of the Lewisohn Stadium, the theatre was intended to bring the drama to the people of the ghetto; as at the Bandbox, all tickets were fifty cents. On the opening night everyone was in evening dress. My friend Annie Nathan Meyer said to me, "It's a lovely little theatre, and it attracts such a nice class of people." Eventually the local people did come in. The material presented and the productions were always of high quality. The opening bill included a playlet by Lord Dunsany, the first of his works I had seen. Others were done later, as were such unusual plays as *The Dybbuk* and *The Little Clay Cart*, and a series of sophisticated revues called *The Grand Street Follies*.

It was a fine season for Shaw too: *Pygmalion, Candida, Arms and the Man, You Never Can Tell, Captain Brassbound's Conversion*, all with star performers. Particularly notable was the appearance of Granville-Barker's London company in *The Doctor's Dilemma* and *Androcles and the Lion*. On the bill with *Androcles* was Anatole France's *The Man Who Married a Dumb Wife*, an amusing trifle made noteworthy by its introduction of Robert Edmond Jones to the American theatre. His setting was a sensational innovation in a theatre in which scene designing was little more than a branch of stage carpentry. The effect was revolutionary. Other designers followed Jones's lead; scenery became an increasingly important element in play production, sometimes even overwhelming author, director and actors.

In the Lewisohn Stadium the Granville-Barker company performed magnificently two plays of Euripedes, *Iphigenia in Tauris* and *The Trojan Women*, my first experience of the acted Greek drama. To an ardent pacifist *The Trojan Women*, portraying so poignantly what Goya called "the disasters of war," seemed almost topical in its modernity.

6

About six weeks before the date set for my marriage, the liner *Lusitania* was sunk by a German submarine, with a loss of some twelve hundred lives. Among the American victims were Elbert Hubbard and two great theatrical personalities: Charles Frohman, the foremost theatrical producer, and Charles Klein, author of *The Auctioneer* and *The Music Master,* both performed with enormous success by David Warfield and characterized by *The Oxford Companion to the Theatre* as "quite trivial and worthless."

The disaster made us hesitate, of course, about crossing the Atlantic, but I think we would have risked it had it not been for the urgent pleas of our families. Reluctantly we called the trip off. I have always regretted that decision—as I have regretted almost every negative decision—for it delayed my discovery of Europe for a full ten years.

As an alternative we agreed on a trip to the Great Lakes and eastern Canada. No comprehensive tour was available, so I worked out one on my own: another jigsaw puzzle, involving the synchronizing of numerous railroad and steamship connections. I spent many happy hours poring over maps, timetables, travel folders and guidebooks, an occupation that is still a major pleasure.

We had vetoed a formal wedding, partly because of a dislike for rituals and ceremonies, mainly to avoid the problem of either inviting a horde of uncles, aunts and cousins who meant nothing to us or offending them by not inviting them. On our way to the Hudson River Line nightboat we stopped off at the Church of the Ascension, where our friend Harold Lynch, the assistant rector, rounded up two or three casual witnesses and pronounced the brief, nonreligious formula required by propriety and the law for the recognizable union of a man and a woman.

We traversed all the Great Lakes, then went down the St. Lawrence to Montreal and Quebec and up the Saguenay to Chicoutimi. French Canada was my first taste of a foreign culture; it whetted my appetite for more. We returned briefly to New York, then set out on a hike through the Berkshires—an odd honeymoon excursion!

It was late August when we finally got back to New York, ready to begin setting up a home. For me it was the beginning of forty years of marriage.

IX

Peace and War

1

We moved into a light, airy corner apartment on Morningside Drive —then one of the most attractive residential sites on Manhattan— a block or two from the Columbia campus. We did not stint ourselves, but our scale of living was relatively modest; neither of us had expensive tastes. The income from *On Trial* was still pouring in, but I knew it could not go on forever; nor could I expect another such stroke of fortune. I had heavy economic responsibilities, and I wanted to be free to experiment and to find my way without being harassed by money worries. I remembered Mr. Micawber's dictum, "Annual income twenty pounds, annual expenditure twenty pounds ought and six, result misery." I had before me, too, the image of my father, sitting night after night, covering sheets of paper with columns of tiny figures, trying to solve the daily problem of making ends meet.

Luckily it was not difficult to make provision for the future. The income tax came to less than two per cent of gross income; the dollar was worth four or five times what it is today; the general standard of living was far lower. Consequently I was able to save the greater part of my earnings from *On Trial*. It was well that I did, for there were indeed lean periods to follow, and the number of my dependents never diminished. I have always lived within my means, if not within my income, reducing expenses and drawing upon reserves when necessary, making replacement when things improved. I have never been in debt, have never borrowed a penny, have never bought anything on credit.

After the completion of the New York and Chicago engagements, the two *On Trial* companies went on tour; one played the large Eastern cities, the other worked its way to the Pacific Coast. A third company was organized to cover the Middle West. It was headed by Pauline Lord, one of the finest actresses I have ever seen. I used to tease her about having given her a start in the theatre. The itineraries of these tours seem incredible today: a company of twenty-five, in a play requiring five sets, appearing sometimes in six towns in a single week! One week, for example, the Central Company played Streator, Joliet, Elgin, Beloit, Janesville and Madison. Another week, in the Carolinas, the homeward-bound Western company visited Columbia, Anderson, Greenville, Spartanburg, Charlotte and Greensboro. It must be twenty-five years since a touring company has played any of these towns; I am sure most of their inhabitants have never seen a play performed by professionals.

I continued to attend Columbia, sitting in as an auditor in the graduate courses of some of its celebrated professors: John Dewey and William P. Montague in philosophy, Henry R. Seager in economics, Franklin H. Giddings in sociology, Charles A. Beard in American history, James T. Shotwell in European history. It is hard for me to evaluate the benefits I derived from this heavy diet. It would have been impossible not to have learned something from each of these eminent scholars. Yet I found that much of the material had already become familiar to me through years of heterogeneous reading, and that much seemed arid and useful only to specialists. It was the personalities of the men that interested me most: their attitudes, their bias, the operation of their minds. At one extreme was Montague, a superior popularizer with a fluent classroom manner, lucid, engaging, as easy to listen to as a Haydn symphony. At the other, John Dewey, without grace or emphasis, laboriously expounded his theories. His spoken words were as hard to follow as his written ones, but one always sensed that his maddening deliberation was due to the fact that he created as he went along. Giddings, vigorous and authoritative, was interesting in the development of his "consciousness of kind" hypothesis as a key to human behavior, but I could not accept his uncritical mili-

tant espousal of the Anglo-French cause. Most stimulating of all
was Beard, who discussed with cool satire the economic motives
behind the adoption and ratification of the American Constitution.
He once remarked, "The seat of the American government was
first established at the corner of Broad and Wall streets; it has remained there ever since."

I was amazed by the immaturity of my fellow students—if I
could properly have been called a student—though most of them
were my age, or even older. Like the law-school graduates who had
been under my supervision, these young men and women seemed
to have no awareness of the practicalities of daily life in the non-
academic world. I was able to interpret much of the lecture material in terms of my own experience as a wage earner and a writer.
Yet most of the students seemed to see no connection between
their studies and themselves as individuals, citizens or breadwinners.
Like so many sponges, they automatically absorbed whatever they
were exposed to; I wondered what happened when the saturation
point was reached. It slowly dawned upon me that if I had spent
my adolescent years in school, instead of being obliged to cope at
an early age with the economic facts of life, I could never have
written a play that, whatever its defects, had given me independence and opportunity. I still regretted my lack of formal education, but less wistfully now.

My Columbia attendance did not interfere with my work on a
new play. Like my two collaborations with Frank Harris, it had a
feminist theme: war as seen from a woman's point of view. An
ardent advocate of women's rights, I had been one of a small
male contingent that had marched up Fifth Avenue in a woman-
suffrage parade headed by the beautiful Inez Milholland astride a
white horse. I had felt a little sheepish, but the jeers were tempered
by cheers, and I had the virtuous feeling of having made a minute
contribution to a good cause.

Like many other Americans, I was disturbed by the increasing
vociferousness of the militarists. The war, since the sinking of the
Lusitania, had ceased to be remote. Not only the U-boat campaign
but also the German atrocities in Belgium were played up to the
limit. Ignored was the fact that war itself is the most monstrous of
atrocities, by its very nature bringing out the bestiality in men.
Every army has its vandals, looters and rapists.

To make the point that not this or that belligerent but war itself is to be condemned, I set the play on a farm in East Prussia. While the farmer, full of fervor for the Fatherland, is fighting in France, his wife is raped by an invading Cossack. As the war drags on she keeps the farm going, tends the sick and the hungry. Her husband, covered with medals, returns, learns that she has borne a child, rails at her for dishonoring him, and goes off, confident that the Fatherland will provide for him. In the end, he creeps back, disillusioned, glad to find the shelter that his wife has preserved for him. The play was called *The Iron Cross*—a "symbolic" title, of course.

It wrote itself quickly, for this time I was absorbed by the theme and the characters. I took it at once to Arthur Hopkins, who promised to read it promptly. Shortly after I reached home, he telephoned: he was enthusiastic about the play, wanted to produce it at once, for a flood of war plays was on the way. It had taken two days to place *On Trial; The Iron Cross* was placed in two hours! This time Hopkins suggested no revisions. We agreed that Bertha Kalich, a star of the Yiddish theatre, would be splendid in the leading part. She expressed great interest. I looked forward to getting into production again, this time with a play that attempted to express things I felt strongly about.

But my luck had deserted me. I now had my first—but by no means last—experience of the hazards that wreck so many promising theatrical ventures. Bertha Kalich's business affairs were managed by her husband (not an unusual situation, though it may be an agent, attorney or lover), a shrewd little entrepreneur who believed in playing off one bidder against another. He blew hot and cold, never coming to the point of a definite commitment. Hopkins made some attempt to find another actress, but as the season wore on, and the war plays began coming in, his enthusiasm waned.

2

While I waited with dwindling hopes, I occupied myself with other activities. I had agreed to take charge of dramatic activities at the University Settlement, a time-consuming task. I was also editing the little weekly bulletin of the Church of the Ascension Sunday-night forum. Rector Percy Stickney Grant, handsome, sophisticated, rather foppish, a smooth speaker, maintained a skillful balance between his aristocratic congregation and the turbulent, heterodox forum. Like most clergymen, he had a good bit of the actor in him; he was, I believe, actually a graduate of the Sargent School of Acting. In the pulpit, as on the stage, the manner often counts for more than the matter. A commanding presence, a trained voice, an air of plausibility—these are more likely to sway an audience than loftiness of thought or depth of feeling. I believe that ministers of religion, like actors, are frequently motivated in their choice of a career by the desire to perform in public. (The same may be said of legislators, trial lawyers, surgeons, lecturers, policemen and athletes.) Most clergymen are either fascinated by the theatre or violently hostile to it; either attitude may be attributed to a deep sense of kinship.

I took an active part in the forum's social and political discussions, always on the radical side, for I became a left-winger early. I was converted to socialism in my teens, mainly through reading Bernard Shaw and H. G. Wells. My contact with the legal and business world made me receptive to a philosophy that envisaged the substitution of an enlightened regard for human welfare for the prevalent greed and ruthless competition. Shaw led me to the writings of the Fabian Society, organized to "reconstruct society in accordance with the highest moral principles." I read eagerly the essays of Beatrice and Sidney Webb, Annie Besant and Graham Wallas, as well as everything by Shaw and Wells. I met Wells once, near the end of his life, at a party given in his honor by Hendrik Willem Van Loon. But he was old, tired and far gone in drink. I had no opportunity to tell him how much his books had meant to me.

Indeed, what convinced me of the evils of the capitalist system and its concomitant institutions was literature rather than economics: the plays of Ibsen (particularly *Pillars of Society* and *An Enemy of the People*), Hauptmann, Galsworthy, Gorki, Brieux; the novels of Dickens, Charles Reade, Zola, Upton Sinclair, Frank Norris. These exposures of the inequities, cruelties, hypocrisies and corruptness of the existing social order persuaded me of the need for revolutionary changes in human institutions and attitudes, and won me over to what may generically be called socialism.

I say "generically," for there were many varieties of socialists, whose divergent aims, approaches and techniques often led to factional squabbles in which more acrimony was directed toward the dissident ally than toward the common foe. I took little interest in these disputes, for I was never a member of the Socialist or any other political party. The only Socialist candidate I ever voted for was Morris Hillquit, when he ran for mayor of New York on an antiwar platform and polled 150,000 votes, though had I been old enough in 1912 I would have voted for Eugene V. Debs.

Nor was I ever a Marxist. My attempts to read Marx have always bogged down. While I believe there is much validity in the theory of the economic interpretation of history, my socialism has always been of the utopian variety. In my youth I was a great reader of utopian literature: More's *Utopia*, Bacon's *New Atlantis*, Campanella's *City in the Sun*, Swift's *Voyage to the Houyhnhms*, Bellamy's *Looking Backward*, Morris' *News from Nowhere*, Butler's *Erewhon*, Wells's *A Modern Utopia*, Hudson's *The Crystal Age*. It would be hard to find a common denominator for this miscellany, except that all spring from the premise that the existing order of things does not express the best that mankind is capable of. The concept of a human community based upon principles of truth and justice interested me more than the establishment of any rigid system.

Nevertheless, I was not so lost in the clouds as to be oblivious to the need for drastic social and economic reforms. The fifty-year period of industrial expansion that followed the Civil War had been an era of unrestricted greed and "free enterprise" whose flagrant excesses inevitably induced a wave of revulsion. In the *Metropolitan* magazine, *McClure's* and *Pearson's*, Lincoln Steffens, Ida Tarbell and Charles Edward Russell were laying bare the ugly facts of political rottenness and economic immorality. Outrageous, too, were the gross violations of human rights. Starvation wages and abominable working conditions were the rule. Sweatshops, the company store and the checkoff system reduced workers to a state of peonage. Contract laborers brought over in the steerage of transatlantic liners were offered up as living sacrifices to the Moloch of the smelteries and the blast furnaces. Attempts at organization were ruthlessly suppressed; strikers were shot down in cold blood by hired thugs.

These exposures led all believers in the rights of man to demand curbs upon capitalism run wild; organizations were formed to at-

tack this or that specific evil. The labor movement grew, ranging
from the American Federation of Labor, which aimed for craft
unionism and immediate economic gains, to the Industrial Workers
of the World, commonly known as the Wobblies—or, to its enemies,
as the I-Won't-Works—whose organizational song was "Hallelu-
jah, I'm a Bum" and whose objective was industrial unionism, the
"one big union."

At the same time, Congressional leaders like Robert M. La Follette of Wisconsin and George W. Norris of Nebraska were making
names for themselves as what might be called "people's advocates."
Theodore Roosevelt, while President, had denounced "malefactors
of great wealth," thereby becoming known as a traitor to his class,
as was his remote cousin some three decades later. Woodrow Wilson not only spoke out against "privileged big business" but appointed a Commission on Industrial Relations to inquire into the
practices of the economic barons.

I happened to attend a session of this commission, in New York's
City Hall, at which John D. Rockefeller, Jr., was the principal witness. During a strike against the Colorado Fuel and Iron Company, a Rockefeller subsidiary, armed guards had fired upon a
tent colony, killing a number of women and children, an incident
that aroused nationwide indignation. The origins of the Rockefeller
fortune had been scrutinized by Ida Tarbell in her *History of the
Standard Oil Company*. Now the crown prince of the Rockefeller
dynasty was called to public account. It was a dramatic moment.

Rockefeller, faultlessly attired and seemingly completely self-
possessed, gave polite, suave answers, even when the questions
were sharp and almost personal. His testimony amounted to a total
disclaimer of any knowledge of what had happened in Colorado,
and of any responsibility for it. Over and over again he stated that
the practical management of the company's operations was entirely
outside his scope.

No doubt he was telling the truth. It is impossible to believe that
he had connived at the shooting down of workers and their families.
I think that beneath his imperturbability he was deeply shocked by
the revelations. The appalling thing about his testimony was the
tacit admission that in the management of his financial interests
the human factors were not even taken into account.

It was a typical attitude. When J. P. Morgan was asked by the commission if he thought ten dollars a week was enough for a longshoreman to earn, he replied, "If that is all he can get and he takes it, I should think it was enough." Commenting on this general position, the commission in its final report said: "The lives of millions of wage earners are therefore subject to the dictation of a relatively small number of men. These industrial dictators for the most part are totally unconcerned with the working and living conditions of the employees in those industries. Even if they were deeply concerned, the position of the employees would be merely that of the subjects of benevolent industrial despots."

3

One of the most outrageous aspects of greed and callousness was the prevalence of child labor. In 1910 the census showed nearly two million "gainfully occupied children ten to fifteen." In mines, sweatshops, cotton mills, cigar factories and glass-blowing establishments, on the streets and in the fields and orchards, children were working fifty or sixty hours a week for as little as forty cents a day. Advocates of reform were denounced by the employers as "paid agitators" and "drawing-room faddists." Remedial legislation was opposed in the name of free enterprise, and on the Pharisaical ground that provision of work for children was an economic boon to their parents.

The most effective agency in the fight against this evil was the National Child Labor Committee. Its director, Owen R. Lovejoy, a descendant of the martyred abolitionist Elijah Lovejoy, was an admirable human being, one of the many I have known who at great personal sacrifice have devoted their lives to redressing the wrongs of mankind. At Lovejoy's suggestion I went to a convention of the organization held in the elegant Battery Park Hotel in Asheville, North Carolina, the first gathering of the sort I had ever attended.

To get a firsthand impression of children at work, I stopped off, on the way home, at Salisbury, North Carolina, where I visited a few cotton mills. What I saw was distressing enough: pale, emaciated children of ten and twelve at work in the lint-laden air of the ill-lighted spinning rooms. On the way back to town I fell in with some homeward-bound workers, with whom I discussed the efforts that were being made to abolish child labor. One man thought it only right that children should share the economic burden of the family; another, who had himself been a child laborer, hoped for something better for his children.

Deeply stirred by what I had seen, I wrote a play on the subject, though I knew it was not likely to have wide acceptance. *The House in Blind Alley*, as I called it, was a dream fantasy about two coupon-clipping giants, Janfirst and Julfirst, who enslave Mother Goose's children. Jack Horner sits in a corner over a glassblower's mold; Mary, Mary, Quite Contrary makes artificial flowers; Little Boy Blue is a messenger boy; and so on. Eventually they are set free by a lad in the guise of Jack the Giant Killer.

The play was admired by friends, particularly those who were fighting child labor. But, as I had expected, the response of the producers was not encouraging. Winthrop Ames, for whose taste and intelligence I had great respect, liked the play but saw little hope for its success in the commercial theatre. Another producer who professed enthusiasm for the script was that old fraud David Belasco. But he could not produce it, he said, because it required a cast of children, an impossibility under the stringent laws against child labor! I soon gave up trying to find a producer. The play, published some fifteen years later, is still selling. In fact, in thirty years it has sold well over three hundred copies. The campaign against child labor fared better. By 1920 the number of children "gainfully occupied" had been reduced to a million; subsequently legislation abolished the evil almost entirely.

I turned back to technical experimentation, developing a formula that was far more intricate than that of *On Trial:* each act of the play set in a different location—several rooms in the same house, for example—and synchronous with the others. The interweaving of incident and the gradual clearing up of the seemingly inexplicable had the fascination of a chess problem. I wrote no fewer than three plays employing this device; wasted effort, for none of them ever aroused the slightest interest. Yet perhaps not altogether wasted, for failure can be instructive. In later years I was able to make more successful experiments. I have never lost my interest in technical innovation, partly to counteract the constricting effect that Ibsen has had upon the drama, partly because I enjoy setting myself puzzles.

4

Since we were expecting a baby in November, we spent the summer quietly in a cottage on a little lake in New Hampshire. It was a rather primitive place, but delightfully located, in a pinewood four miles from the nearest town. I bought a canoe and taught myself to paddle and to swim, developing a taste for country living that I was unable to gratify fully until many years later.

I made no attempt to work, for it seemed time to review and to try to evaluate the sweeping changes that my life had undergone in the past two years. From complete obscurity I had been catapulted into the dazzle of the theatrical world. Overnight I had gone from poverty to undreamed of affluence. I had made numerous social and professional contacts, taken part in public affairs, assumed heavy financial responsibilities, married and set up housekeeping, and was an expectant father. The preparation of a tentative balance sheet was clearly in order.

However, I had neither the perspective nor the objectivity to appraise the effect of my complex experiences. Nor was I aware then that I was the fortunate possessor, thanks to no effort or ingenuity of my own, of two sources of inner security. One was that I had been imbued from infancy with the belief that life is potentially good, that people are potentially trustworthy and that if love does not conquer all it at least points the way to conquest. Illusory or not, this belief has sustained me through many bleak hours and helped me to emerge from depths of frustration and despair.

Second was the accident of being a product of the nineteenth century. I am convinced that there is a sharp cleavage between individuals who attained adulthood prior to World War I and those who matured later. Though this theory is not susceptible of objective proof, I think it offers a clue to much of what is wrong with the world today.

The nineteenth century was probably the most revolutionary in all history, not because of its numerous political upheavals, but because of the rise of industrialism. The factory system supplanted agrarianism; the entrepreneurs supplanted the landed gentry; urban centers mushroomed; the artisan was swallowed up by the anonymous proletariat. Mass production of "cheap and nasty" articles altered habits and living standards; the search for new sources of raw materials and new markets led to the annexation and exploitation of "backward" regions.

There was an accompanying revolution in the physical, natural and political sciences. The new order called for new inquiries into man's relation to his natural and social environment. Two explosive theories, Marxism and Darwinism, revolutionized the thinking of mankind, as the machine had revolutionized his mode of life. (Freudianism was to play its part, too, but that came later.)

The findings of evolutionary biology discredited the cosmology and chronology of the Bible. A thinking person could no longer believe that man had been specially created by an anthropomorphic deity, or that his earthly sojourn was a mere preparation for an eternity of celestial bliss. Likewise, examination of human history in the light of economic determinism destroyed any lingering belief in the divine right of a hereditary ruling class. The concept of a static, stratified society gave way to the more dynamic belief that man has the capacity to ameliorate his own lot and to create a society in which want and disease are reduced to a minimum, the causes of war eliminated and all men made free and equal. That was what the idealists envisioned—universal peace, universal education, universal suffrage. As some British peer observed, "We are all socialists nowadays." A slight exaggeration, no doubt, but indicative of the intellectual and emotional climate of the time.

The events of the twentieth century have made this belief in the creation of an earthly paradise seem incredibly naïve. Yet it engendered a faith in human progress and an inner security that must, I think, be unknown to anyone who was not already emotionally and philosophically conditioned at the outbreak of World War I. Though the war was a denial of the confident prognostications, it could not uproot the deeply implanted belief in the purposefulness of life and in the eventual triumph of good over evil. I would not want it uprooted, for it has served me well.

The war's very betrayal of utopian ideals actually strengthened my belief in those ideals. What came out of my New Hampshire summer of rumination was the resolve to combat destructive impulses, not only in the wide world but within myself as well. I believed, and still believe, that social evils are the accumulation of individual acts of aggression and malice, and that social betterment can be achieved only through individual affirmation and creativeness. Since to be creative one must be free, I was determined to speak out for freedom, both in my work and by whatever other means were available.

5

Though I had had no luck with any of my new plays, *On Trial* was still active. In spite of the war there were several European productions, and now there were performances by many of the 150 stock companies operating in the United States and Canada. Helen Hayes, who began her career young, played the part of the little girl in a Washington production. I went to see a Yiddish-language performance at David Kessler's Second Avenue Theatre. Kessler, who played the lead, did not underemphasize the play's emotional content; the audience, male and female, sobbed and bellowed. I have never seen anything quite like it in the theatre.

Unfortunately neither the foreign-language theatre nor the small-town stock company has survived. In the first decades of the century thousands to whom English was still a second tongue flocked to the foreign-language performances. In New York eight or ten Yiddish theatres presented world classics, folk plays and musical extravaganzas; among their performers were Paul Muni, Francine Larrimore, Bertha Kalich, Luther and Stella Adler. There was a German theatre under the direction of that fine actor Rudolf Christians, several Italian and Chinese theatres, occasional productions in Hungarian and French. In the aggregate they contributed to the color and variety of the New York theatrical scene. The disappearance of the stock companies, many of which were excellent training schools for actors, is deplorable, too; but they could not compete with low-priced movies and free broadcasting.

Several months after the sale of the motion picture rights to *On Trial*, the movie's director, James Young, husband of the famous silent-picture star Clara Kimball Young, called me up. He wanted my opinion of the scenario he had written. Flattered to be consulted by this august personage, for I was still a little in awe of actors, writers and producers, I went to see Young in his room at the Lambs' Club—my first visit to that celebrated gathering place of male actors. I listened to his reading in utter astonishment: he had made the crucial revelatory scene of the play into a prologue! When he asked me, with obvious self-satisfaction, what I thought of the scenario, I hardly knew how to answer. I asked if he had seen the play and was not surprised when he said no. Not wanting to come right out and say that he had completely destroyed the suspense, I discoursed, as tactfully as I could, upon the importance of the play's structure. He followed my exposition in sheer amazement. At its conclusion he crossed the room, put his hand on my shoulder and said, "Say, kid, you had a great idea there!" It was my first contact with the motion picture industry.

My contacts with the other arts gave me more satisfaction. I remember vividly John Barrymore's performance of the fumbling little clerk who is crushed beneath the "chariot wheels of justice" in Galsworthy's searing indictment of the legal system. Another unforgettable performance was a piano recital by Ignace Paderewski. He played Chopin, of course, expressing Poland's aspiration for liberation. His emotion communicated itself to the audience; many listeners were in tears.

Similar emotion was evinced at an Isadora Duncan dance recital, the only time I saw the great Isadora. She was a heavy woman who at first glance seemed almost clumsy, but when she began to dance one was suddenly aware of being in the presence of a great spirit and a great artist. Dancing to the "Marseillaise," she stripped off her white robe, beneath which she was draped in the tricolor, one breast completely exposed: an outrageous bit of chauvinism and showmanship that evoked a riotous demonstration.

Second only to Isadora, though of a very different genre, was that lovely exponent of the classical ballet Anna Pavlova, whom I saw many times. But for me the greatest aesthetic experience of all was the first appearance here of Diaghilev's Ballet Russe. In all its aspects it was a shocking and stimulating revelation. The violent reds and purples of Bakst's décors were startling. So was the unfamiliar music, particularly that of Stravinsky. *L'Oiseau de Feu*, now genially accepted by the old ladies who attend symphony concerts, seemed, on first hearing, revolutionary and orgiastic. The splendid company included Massine, Fokine and Fokina, Bolm and the charming Lydia Lopokova. Nijinsky must be mentioned separately, for I have never seen his equal. It was hard to believe that the human body could execute such convolutions and inform them with such grace and fervor. Later I saw the Ballet Russe in Paris, London and Monte Carlo. They did many exciting things, but nothing ever topped those first New York performances.

During my close association with Hatcher Hughes in the organization of an acting group called the Morningside Players, we collaborated on a play based on an idea of his. The leading part seemed well suited to David Warfield, so we went to see David Belasco, under whose management Warfield had become one of the most popular actors of the day. Belasco received us in the duplex apartment on the top floor of the theatre that bore his name. Though it was midafternoon, he wore pajamas and an imperial-purple dressing gown. (Like many men with power complexes, he had a Napoleonic fixation, though on opening nights—when he invariably took a curtain call—he wore black and, heaven knows why, the reversed collar of a priest.) His studio was cluttered with knickknacks that he believed to be works of art. His desk was so placed that the light from a bull's-eye window fell full upon our faces, while he was in shadow, an obvious, irritating bit of stage management. I have often wondered which of us would have been more incredulous if we had been told that one day I would be the owner of this very theatre!

When we mentioned Warfield, he leaned forward and said almost inaudibly, "For Warfield, you must run the gamut: a tear and a laugh, a laugh and a tear." We managed to keep straight faces and proceeded to outline the plot. He gave us enough encouragement to warrant our going ahead. When we completed the play he held it a long time, but finally rejected it.

Hopkins had dropped *The Iron Cross;* there had been too many war plays, he said! I began to wonder if I would ever get another play produced. As yet I did not know what I learned only too well later: if the author of a hit attempts a different vein, he is certain to meet resistance, even from those who mistakenly rejected the earlier work. The most successful authors are often those who write the same play or novel over and over. Nonrepetitiveness is often a handicap.

6

The war was now entering its third dreadful winter, with no end to the stalemate visible. At the outset most people were indifferent to what they regarded as an Old World quarrel that did not concern them. Wilson's pleas for neutrality were approved by all except the most ardent partisans. Even the fire-eating Theodore Roosevelt at first advocated our noninterference.

Bit by bit, the climate changed. There were several contributing factors. One was the skill of the Allied propagandists. Another was Germany's stupid persistence in its submarine campaign. Far-reaching economic forces were at work, too. The Allies' need for supplies had made American industry boom; but if they lost the war, the chances of payment would be slight.

There was a mounting clamor for "preparedness," the building up of a great military establishment, a movement led now by Theodore Roosevelt, who, like many theatrical stars, could not endure second billing. In terms more appropriate for an editor of a scandal sheet than for an ex-President, he denounced Wilson as a spineless, craven, stargazing academician and demanded that America preserve its national honor by arming to the teeth.

Seconding T.R. was General Leonard Wood, a man of inordinate vanity and insatiable political ambition, who stormed up and down the country shouting for preparedness. One of his saber-rattling speeches was delivered at the Church of the Ascension forum. I was among those who were ready to challenge him in the ensuing discussion period. We were stunned when Percy Stickney Grant announced that the meeting was over. In private Grant told me that he had not wanted the General to be subjected to hostile remarks! Outraged and disillusioned, I severed my connection with the forum. Yet what else could have been expected? According to Walter Millis, "that fall a questionnaire sent out to ministers of a score of denominations in the East came back 151 to 14 for preparedness." So it is always: the surpliced men of God blessing the cannon and the battle flags in the name of the Prince of Peace; praying for bloody victory for our side and for annihilation of the enemy, whether at the moment he be British, Mexican, Spanish, German, Japanese, Russian or Chinese; shouting exultantly, "Praise the Lord and pass the ammunition!"

Gradually Wilson came around to the acceptance of the militaristic program, even marched at the head of a preparedness parade, though he still insisted that he did not favor armed intervention. At the Democratic convention in St. Louis, where Wilson's renomination was a foregone conclusion, Martin H. Glynn sounded the keynote of the forthcoming campaign: "He kept us out of war!" It was wildly acclaimed.

At the Republican convention in Chicago, Roosevelt's proposal that the reactionary Senator Henry Cabot Lodge be nominated stunned the credulous souls who had hailed T.R. as a great liberal leader. But the mighty Bull Moose was no longer standing at Armageddon and battling for the Lord; he was merely out after Wilson's scalp. The convention chose Supreme Court Justice Charles Evans Hughes, whom I remembered well as Pink Whiskers, archenemy of my old race track friends the Allenbergs.

The closely contested campaign hinged largely upon the war issue. In spite of Allied propagandists, munition makers and militarists—lay and clerical—there was general resistance to the armament program and even greater opposition to our entrance into the war. The popular slogan was "He kept us out of war," the popular song "I Didn't Raise My Boy to Be a Soldier." In a campaign speech Wilson said, "The certain prospect of the success of the Republican Party is that we shall be drawn, in one form or another, into the embroilments of the European war."

A few days before the election my wife gave birth to a son, whom we named Robert. On my first introduction to him, I was rather startled to see him wearing a large Hughes campaign button. The doctor, knowing my political views, had pinned it on him. I rejoiced in his arrival, as I have in that of my four other children. Of all life's experiences, fatherhood is the one I would have least wanted to forgo.

On election night I went to a big ball given by the Woman Suffrage Party, at Grand Central Palace. The women were against Wilson, because he favored granting them the vote by state action rather than by the proposed Constitutional amendment. As the returns kept coming in, Wilson's early lead declined; by midnight it appeared that he had been defeated. The early edition of the *Tribune* announced a Republican triumph. As with the Chicago *Tribune* in the 1948 Truman-Dewey campaign, the announcement was a bit premature. Next day it was learned that California, credited to Hughes, had been carried by Wilson. Its electoral votes gave Wilson a narrow margin of victory: 277 to 254.

Though it did not silence the proponents of war, Wilson's election seemed to ensure our continued neutrality. I was in contact with

several pacifist groups, some Socialistic, some nonpolitical, though
I never became a member of any of them. Hatcher Hughes now
suggested the production of my antiwar play, *The Iron Cross*, with
a company composed of Columbia students and a few professional
actors, under the auspices of the Morningside Players. With great
reluctance I agreed to direct. I did not feel qualified, nor was I.
In the end I thought it advisable to call upon one of the actors
for help. The plan was to give a few special performances, with the
possibility of a longer run if the response was encouraging.

In January, Wilson, addressing the outgoing Congress, urged
that the war end in "peace without victory" and proposed the establishment of an international League of Peace for the prevention of
future wars. A few days later came Germany's shocking declaration
of unrestricted submarine warfare, perhaps the most colossal of all
the stupidities of the German high command. Wilson immediately
severed diplomatic relations; Ambassador von Bernstorff departed.
It became grimly evident that we were being drawn into the
maelstrom.

The Iron Cross opened shortly after the break with Germany: not
the most auspicious moment for an anti-war play that blamed
equally all belligerents, and had for its heroine a German woman!
The reception did not warrant giving more than the few scheduled
performances. Yet as I re-read the reviews, for the first time in
more than forty years, I am amazed by their tolerance. Along with
complaints about the surfeit of war plays, criticism of the acting
and direction, and objections to the play's philosophy, there is recognition of its earnestness, its structural soundness, and its literary
superiority to *On Trial*. It might have fared better, if it had been
produced before people had wearied of war plays, and when the
public temper was less belligerent.

7

Normally the new Congress would not have met until December,
but a few days after his March 4 inauguration Wilson called a
special session, to convene on April 16. Shortly afterward mounting
tension caused the date to be advanced to April 2. There was little
doubt now that Wilson intended to ask for a declaration of war. In
mid-March, the world was electrified by the news of Czar Nicholas

II's abdication and the establishment of a Russian people's government.

On the first day of the new session, pacifists from all over the country converged upon Washington, under the leadership of David Starr Jordan, chancellor of Leland Stanford University and director of the World Peace Federation. Horrified by the imminence of war, I went down with one of the New York groups. The police refused to permit the protestants to parade; a request to see the President was denied; access to the State Department was barred by armed guards. These rebuffed men and women were American citizens attempting to exercise their constitutional right to assemble peaceably and petition the government.

Forbidden to confer with the man they had elected because he kept us out of war, little groups of delegates called upon their representatives in Congress. I went along with some New Yorkers to see Senator James W. Wadsworth, who listened politely to the demand that he vote against war. He expressed respect for the opinions of his petitioners, but left no doubt that his mind was made up. I was distressed by the contrast between his urbanity and the vehemence of his challengers. His easy air of assumed tolerance put his emotional, untidy antagonists at a great disadvantage. It is the sort of thing I have seen happen all too often: the worse cause made to appear the better when it is associated with a gracious manner, cultivated speech and a well-tailored coat.

Since I had come to Washington in the hope of hearing the President deliver his message, I applied at my Congressman's office for a ticket to the visitor's gallery of the House of Representatives. The speech, I learned, had been put off until next day, to give the House time to organize. No more tickets were available for tomorrow's session, but I accepted one for the current sitting; it was mid-afternoon, and I had nothing else to do.

The House gallery was almost empty. In progress was the election of various staff members, usually a routine matter decided by a voice vote of the majority party. The Democrats lacked an absolute majority, but the handful of Socialists and independents who held the balance of power had announced their intention of voting for the Democratic nominees. Nevertheless, as each nomination for sergeant at arms or other petty post was made, Representative Mann, the Republican leader, insisted upon a roll call of the entire

membership of four hundred. As the clerk of the House droned on
and on, the gallery became even emptier. Just as I was about to
leave, it was suddenly announced from the floor that the President
had decided to deliver his message at eight-thirty that evening.
The House, buzzing with excitement, immediately voted a recess.

It was then only about six, but of course I stayed, almost alone
in the gallery now. I was sure someone would ask for my ticket, but
no one did. I moved down to the front row, directly above the
rostrum. Since I had no reading matter and there was no way of
getting anything to eat, I just sat and waited. At about eight
the gallery began to fill with holders of tickets for the next day. The
members of the House arrived and took places at the rear of the
chamber, the front rows having been reserved for the senators.
Extra chairs had been provided for Cabinet officers, Supreme Court
justices and the diplomatic corps. When all these dignitaries were
seated, the senators filed in, two by two, like the peers in *Iolanthe*.
It was an impressive spectacle; I forgot hunger and fatigue.

At precisely eight-thirty the President entered and received a
standing ovation. As he stood on the rostrum, I could look directly
down on him. When I read later that he had had a cavalry escort
from the White House, presumably to protect him from the blood-
thirsty pacifists, and that elaborate measures had been taken to
keep "troublemakers" out of the House galleries, I had to laugh at
the idiocy of it all. In the four hours or more that I had been in the
gallery, no one had questioned me or even come near me. From
my front seat I could have dropped a bomb on Wilson or shot him
through the head before anyone could have intervened.

Though everyone knew what was to come, the issues were so
grave, the occasion so momentous, that the tension was almost unendurable. Says that industrious chronicler Mark Sullivan: "To
every person present, from members of the Cabinet and Justices of
the Supreme Court in the front row to observers in the remote seats
of the gallery, that evening was the most-to-be-remembered of their
lives." The welcoming applause was followed by a moment of silence as Wilson arranged the pages of his speech on the lectern. I
kept looking at Bob La Follette, a stocky man with a bristling
pompadour, who sat in one of the first rows, staring ahead with
grim impassivity.

Wilson's speech, which has become a classic, began with a rapid survey of German-American relations, familiar material to most of those present. Then, from the lips of the leader who had been acclaimed for saying that there is such a thing as being too proud to fight, came the famous utterance, "We will not choose the path of submission." It was the signal gun, the awaited cue. Wild applause swept the chamber. As if by magic, silken American flags were drawn from the breast pockets of the legislators and waved frantically, to the accompaniment of shouts and stamping feet. It needed only a few beautiful cheerleaders in abbreviated skirts to make one believe that the demonstration had been evoked by a brilliant end run rather than by an invitation to plunge the nation into war. In the midst of all that uproar La Follette sat motionless, arms folded across his chest, lips slightly parted in a bitter, sardonic smile. For me that is the most vivid of all the images of that memorable night.

With each new, skillfully devised appeal to belligerence, the tumult mounted. I was both hot and cold—chilled by the prospect of what lay ahead, enraged by the sophistry of the man who had proclaimed himself a bulwark against the warlike intentions of his opponents. There was hypocrisy too. "The world must be made safe for democracy!" There was a clear-cut alignment of the autocracies against the democracies, including Russia. Yet the call for the war session had gone out *before* the Russian autocracy —perhaps the worst of all—had been overthrown. Could it be doubted that if there had been no Russian Revolution Wilson would still have asked for a declaration of war? "We have no quarrel with the German people." Yet against whom would our guns be trained: the Kaiser, the Crown Prince, Tirpitz, Bethmann-Hollweg, or those enslaved nonentities whom, in our enlightened humanitarianism, we were going to "liberate"? In a fine peroration we were told to be proud that "America is privileged to spend her blood." The end, of course, was an invocation of the Deity: "God helping her, she can do no other." It was to be a holy war, too, it seemed.

Sick at heart, I left while the demonstration was still in full swing. The pacifists were holding a mass meeting on the other side of Washington, in a hall that, ironically enough, adjoined an armory. As I entered, a brawny, shirt-sleeved young man on the platform was pounding his chest and shouting, "Here's one who won't fight!" It was John Reed, who wrote that striking account of the Bolshevik revolution, *Ten Days That Shook the World,* and whose remains are interred in the wall of the Kremlin. The scene was a remarkable contrast to the one I had just left.

Unable to get a hotel room, I took the sleeper back to New York. I sat for a while in the club car, listening to the talk of its other occupants, their eyes alight with the glint of battle. There was no mention of democracy or of the unhappy German people for whom, in Wilson's words, we had no feeling but "one of sympathy and friendship." The consensus was that it was about time we showed those dirty bastards where they got off.

In the Senate only a few voices were raised against the enactment of the war resolution. Vardaman of Mississippi objected to sacrificing a million men in the liberation of Germany "without first consulting the people who are to be sacrificed for the deliverance." Norris of Nebraska said that war was being forced upon us by the servile press and the propaganda agencies "to increase the enormous profits of munition makers, stockbrokers and bond dealers." "I feel," he said, "that we are committing a sin against humanity and against our countrymen." In a four-hour speech, La Follette declared that "the espionage bills, the conscription bills and other forcible military measures" which were being prepared were "complete proof that those responsible for this war fear that it has no popular support." The resolution was passed by a vote of eighty-two to six.

In the House it was much the same story, though there the vote was 373 to fifty. Many people believe that if the vote had been by secret ballot the resolution would have been defeated. Said Britten of Illinois, "There is something in the air, gentlemen, and I do not know what it is, . . . that seems to be picking us up bodily and literally forcing us to vote for this declaration of war, when 'way down deep in our hearts we are just as opposed to it as are our people back home." Jeannette Rankin, first woman to be elected to Congress, did not answer when her name was first called. Urged to vote, she said, "I want to stand by my country, but I cannot vote for war." As she sat down she burst into tears, an emotional display that was seized upon as proof that women are unsuited to political life. The northeastern states produced one antiwar vote, that of Meyer London, New York City's Socialist Representative.

8

The next number on the Wilson program was conscription. Even before he addressed Congress, he and his advisers, including the "pacifist" Secretary of War, Newton D. Baker, had decided that the best way to win a war for democracy was to compel the young men of America to fight it, though Americans had always counted freedom from compulsory military service as one of their blessings. Champ Clark, Speaker of the House, said, "In the estimation of Missourians, there is precious little difference between a conscript and a convict." Chairman Dent of the House Military Affairs Committee refused to introduce the bill. But there was no stopping the war juggernaut; less than six weeks after the declaration of war, conscription was adopted.

My opposition to war in general and to American participation in the current war was based upon emotional, ideological and moral considerations. I did not believe that wrongs could be righted by force of arms, that questions of principle or issues of justice could be decided by superiority of fire power. The concepts of revenge, retaliation, punishment, hatred were repugnant to me. I rejected the doctrine that good can come out of evil, or that the end justifies the means. With Benjamin Franklin, I believed that there never was a good war or a bad peace.

The moral standards that condemn the petty malefactor but applaud the grand one had always puzzled me. The psychopathic, maladjusted youth who kills a service station attendant is railroaded to the electric chair. The general who, in the security of staff headquarters, decides that a certain position is worth a certain number of lives, and cold-bloodedly sends out his young subordinates to be killed or maimed, or who orders an air raid on a city where hundreds of thousands of his fellow men huddle hopelessly, is covered with decorations and showered with ticker tape as he proceeds along a route that may lead to the White House.

War is murder. That is how I feel about it now, and how I felt about it then. Unwilling to be either a murderer or an accessory to murder, I resolved that I would never put on a soldier's uniform. I was in my twenty-fifth year, so of course subject to the draft. My first impulse was to inform my draft board that, on conscientious

grounds, I refused to register, an action which would have resulted
in immediate imprisonment. For, while there was tolerance of members of religious sects like the Quakers and the Mennonites who
were traditionally opposed to war, objectors on moral, ethical or intellectual grounds were regarded as traitors—"slackers" was the
fashionable word—and summarily clapped into jail. But I had no
desire for martyrdom, particularly since my refusal to register
would in no way have impeded the operation of the draft. Its only
effect would have been to impose hardship upon my family. My
compliance with the formality of registration in no way weakened
my determination not to be drawn into the Army. Having registered,
I applied for deferred classification, since I was solely responsible
for the support of my wife, infant son, parents and grandfather. The
deferment was granted without my even being called before the
draft board. I was prepared, if eventually called up, to take the consequences of a refusal to serve. Fortunately for me, the war ended
before my class was reached.

There were acquaintances who challenged my opposition to military service. "What would you do if a German tried to rape your
sister?" they asked. The answer, of course, is that if a German,
Eskimo or American threatened anyone dear to me with bodily
harm, I would do what I could to prevent it, even to the extreme of
killing the assailant. But there seems to me no relation between this
and putting on a uniform and submitting to military discipline in
preparation for eviscerating or blowing the heads off unknown
youths who have done me no harm.

I may be a coward, though I do not recall ever having been afraid
of anyone; nor can I think of any situation in which my physical
courage has been put to the test. I have always disliked physical
violence. Except for schoolyard scuffles, I have never had occasion
to use my fists. I am opposed to corporal punishment for children.
In the rare instances when I have struck one of my own, it has been
a sudden angry reflex, never a calculated measure of discipline, and
I have always felt sorry afterward. But the new psychology has
taught us to be suspicious of our motives, especially when they are
seemingly idealistic. Perhaps I have instinctively avoided dangerous situations. Perhaps my pacifism is indeed a manifestation of
cowardice. But whether or no, nothing could ever diminish my ab-
horrence of war.

9

While my draft status was being determined, we spent another long summer in New Hampshire. The lakeside cottage in the pinewood afforded a welcome refuge from the ever-mounting war frenzy. I found keen pleasure in watching the day-to-day progress of my young son. In a world dedicated to hatred and destruction, it was solacing to have daily reminders of the richness and beauty of nature, and of the continuity and growth of human life.

Upon resuming work at the University Settlement, I expanded my activities. In addition to the acting group I had a drama study class and a smaller one in playwriting. Finding it hard to work at home, I did my writing at the settlement house, often taking my meals with the residents, an interesting lot—graduate students, social workers, researchers in various fields. Among them was New York City's Park Commissioner, Charles Stover, a colorful, eccentric individual. Every so often he disappeared, leaving no clue to his whereabouts. A few weeks later he would show up and inform us that, feeling the need for a spell of solitude, he had gone off to Mexico or San Francisco. Another resident with whom I became particularly friendly was Jean Toomer, a young Negro writer, who later had considerable success.

The settlement houses gave important community service. There were tens of thousands of recent immigrants for whom assimilation had hardly begun. Living conditions were unspeakable. The Italian, Jewish and Irish slums were as overcrowded and insanitary as are today's Negro and Puerto Rican quarters. When I visited the homes of some of the young people, I was appalled. The settlement houses provided gymnasiums, libraries, game rooms, dramatic and musical activities, lectures, study classes, social dances. There was something for anybody who preferred self-improvement and healthful activity to frequenting poolrooms or hanging about the malodorous streets.

Yet there was a certain air of condescension and paternalism about the settlement houses, founded as they were by well-to-do individuals, whose well-intentioned ministration to the needs of the underprivileged had the aspect of a gracious bounty. Shortly before my association with the University Settlement, the head worker, Robbins Gilman, had been dismissed for permitting a band of un-

employed Wobblies to sleep in the gymnasium. The new head workers, a young couple named Crosby, were earnest, intelligent graduates of a school of social work. They tried hard to do a good job,
but could not quite solve the human equation. Well-bred New
Englanders, they could not overcome their repugnance to the untidiness, the bad manners and speech habits, the bumptiousness of
their alien charges. Many of the youngsters, on the other hand, resented what they regarded as the coldness and aloofness of the
administrators.

To enable some of the young people to break through the enforced clannishness of the ghetto and become acquainted with contemporaries with different backgrounds and ethnic origins, I established an interchange of dramatic activities among the settlement
houses. In spite of the usual inertia and administrative resistance,
I got five or six houses to form an Inter-Settlement Dramatic Association that comprised Jewish, Italian and Irish groups. Among my
associates was Henry Moskowitz, of Madison House, who later
became one of the chief architects of Governor Al Smith's social-
welfare program. Another was the dynamic, engaging head worker
of Greenwich House, Mary Kingsbury Simkhovitch, whose husband
was an economics professor at Columbia. She told me that one day
he asked plaintively, "Mary, must we choose between a world that
is run by the Germans and one that is run by the Y.M.C.A.?"

Groups from the several houses were invited to attend each
other's productions, and competitions were arranged at which each
house presented a one-act play. The scheme worked out well; on a
small scale it helped break down insularity and acquainted the participants with behavior patterns that differed from their own.

Though all this took a lot of doing, I also devoted some time to
the Morningside Players, and gave a series of lectures on the drama
at the Socialist Rand School. I found time, too, to attend some lectures of Thorstein Veblen's at the New School for Social Research. I
had enjoyed several of his books, notably *The Theory of the Leisure
Class,* that brilliant and devastating critique of capitalist society,
which would probably have landed him in jail if the heresy hunters
had been capable of understanding it. The lectures were disappointing, because I could not hear half of what he said. From his giant
frame there emerged a barely audible mumble. What I did hear interested and amused me for its cryptic expression of a point of view
that any legislative investigating committee would label subversive.

10

I was one of the original members of the Civic Club, established in Greenwich Village with a membership of liberal and radical intellectuals: artists, teachers, doctors, lawyers, journalists, labor leaders, social workers. It excluded no one because of race, religion, color or sex. Most of the leaders of left-wing movements were members or participated in the frequent debates and general discussion. During my membership I became acquainted with hundreds of men and women who were doing creative work or laboring for human betterment. It was there I first met two of my later associates in the American Civil Liberties Union, Roger Baldwin and Norman Thomas; Dr. Ira Wile, onetime New York City commissioner of education; J. Salwyn Schapiro, the well-known historian; Freda Kirchwey and Mark and Dorothy Van Doren of *The Nation;* George Soule and Bruce Bliven of *The New Republic;* Charles Ervin, editor of the Socialist daily the New York *Call,* with whom I kept in contact until the end of his long life; McAllister Coleman, who, in his sober moments, was one of the wittiest and most entertaining men I have ever met; James Weldon Johnson, poet, diplomat and at that time executive head of the National Association for the Advancement of Colored People, a truly gracious and cultivated man. There were many distinguished foreign visitors. In particular I remember Jim Larkin, the fiery Irish laborite, and Lajpat Rai, a leader in the Indian nationalist movement. Coleman and I were in charge of entertainment; we put on some one-act plays and organized some lively evenings.

I spent much time in Greenwich Village during World War I. My favorite haunts, then and for many years later, were the Café Lafayette and the basement dining room of the Hotel Brevoort, both operated by Raymond Orteig, donor of the $25,000 prize that spurred Lindbergh's transatlantic flight. At both places the cuisine was superb, the service excellent, the atmosphere charming. On Sunday nights at the Brevoort one was always sure to run into acquaintances: writers, painters, actors, newspapermen. These delightful centers of degustation and social intercourse have long since vanished. Nothing has replaced them; their leisurely rhythm is outmoded.

11

In November 1917 a new Russian revolution overthrew the Kerensky government and put the Bolshevik Party, led by Lenin and Trotsky, in power, an occurrence whose world-wide effect has probably been greater than that of any other single event in human history. Its immediate consequence was a separate peace between Russia and Germany, which released the German armies on the eastern front for service in the west. There was consternation among the Allies. American opinion, on the whole, had been sympathetic to the overthrow of the Romanovs, but Russia's withdrawal from the war was looked upon as a dastardly act of betrayal; the new regime was bitterly denounced.

From the Russian point of view, the surrender was merely a response to the demand of their war-weary armies for a cessation of hostilities. In the 1940s, in the course of a panel discussion on international relations, I happened to say that the Kerensky government fell because the soldiers were sick of the war. Kerensky, who was a member of the panel, got up, crossed the stage, shook his fist under my nose and, to my astonishment, accused me of being a Communist. I thought I had merely stated an historic fact.

Shortly after the Bolshevik uprising, I wrote a one-act play called *A Diadem of Snow;* as far as I know it was the first American attempt to use the revolution as dramatic material. It was a satiric comedy, in which the ex-Czar, happily shoveling snow in Siberia, resists the efforts of the Czarina and Count von Bernstorff to restore him to the throne. (Of course it was written before the shocking execution of the imperial family.) The play was published in *The Liberator,* of which Max Eastman was editor. Shortly afterward I was invited to attend a performance given by a church group in White Plains. The part of the Czar was played by Harry A. Overstreet, then a professor of philosophy at City College.

The Liberator was successor to *The Masses,* which prior to its suppression for opposition to the war had been the delight of left-wing intellectuals. Its credo sounds a bit sophomoric today: "A revolutionary and not a reform magazine; a magazine with a sense of humor and no respect for the respectables; frank, arrogant, impertinent; searching for the true causes; a magazine directed against rigidity and dogma, wherever it is found, printing what is too naked and true for a money-making press; a magazine whose final policy is to do what it pleases and conciliate nobody, not even its readers." With an emphasis that was literary rather than political, it offered some of the liveliest writing and drawing of the day. I remember particularly the brilliant reporting of John Reed, and the Heavenly Discourses of Charles Erskine Scott Wood. One unforgettable drawing—by George Bellows, I think—depicted an avid crowd in which a woman with a little girl perched on her shoulder is saying, "It's her first lynching."

Because of opposition to the war, Eastman and several of his associates were indicted under the Espionage Act. I attended the trial in the old Federal Courthouse. The courtroom was packed with the intellectual elite. Through the open windows came the uproar of a war bond rally in City Hall Park. At frequent intervals, a military band played "The Star-Spangled Banner," whereupon everyone in the courtroom, including the judge and the defendants, stood at attention. It was not an atmosphere conducive to an impartial trial; nevertheless the jury disagreed and the case was eventually dropped. During the district attorney's denunciation of the defendants, Art Young, who was one of them, fell asleep. He celebrated this incident in a comic drawing entitled "Art Young on Trial for His Life."

Young was one of the most lovable men I have ever known. A relentless and fearless enemy of injustice, he was personally gentle, charming and self-effacing. His dingy, disorderly studio in a ramshackle Village building was almost a caricature of the traditional artist's garret. Every now and then, word would go around that Art was up against it once again, and his friends would contribute to a fund to keep him going for a while. I have a copy of his book *Art Young's Inferno*, inscribed: "To Elmer Rice and it wasn't all fun— from the Hell explorer himself, your friend, Art Young." The hell he explored, in words and pictures, was his conception of the capitalist world.

12

All the human, industrial and ideological resources of the nation were now devoted to the prosecution of the war. The factories poured forth instruments of destruction in unheard-of quantities.

Soon camouflaged troopships were carrying the young conscripts to the blood-soaked terrain of Flanders and northern France.

Though we had no quarrel with the German people, every American of German extraction, regardless of his length of residence, was suspect. Many were subjected to ostracism, abuse, persecution, and even physical maltreatment. Hysteria and hatred were epidemic; spy scares and rumors of sabotage proliferated. Nor were non-Germans who did not succumb to the war fever immune from attack, particularly in the smaller communities. Lillian Symes and Clement Travers in *Rebel America* survey what went on:

I.W.W. organizers, Non-Partisan Leaguers, Socialists, lashed, tarred and feathered; . . . a woman indicted under the Espionage Act for a discourteous reception to a Red Cross solicitor; Kate Richards O'Hare, a Socialist lecturer, sentenced to five years in prison for an indictment of war; . . . Rose Pastor Stokes sentenced to ten years for a letter on war profiteering; a pastor of a Mount Vernon, New York, church arrested for refusing to ring his church bells to celebrate an Allied victory; . . . an I.W.W. organizer in New Jersey hanged to a tree by the chief of police and local businessmen and cut down only after he had lost consciousness.

The pulpit did its bit in fanning the flames of hate. The Reverend Newell Dwight Hilles said that German soldiers were "sneaking, sniveling cowards." The Reverend William W. Bustard said succinctly, "To hell with the Kaiser." The Reverend S. Parkes Cadman said that the German Lutheran Church was "not the bride of Christ but the paramour of Kaiserism." The Reverend Henry Van Dyke, much admired for his genteel essays on the loveliness of field and stream, characterized the Kaiser as "the werewolf of Potsdam" and said he would "hang everyone who lifts his voice against America's entering the war."

The philologists helped, too. Viennese pastry maintained its sapidity by being rechristened Danish. Sauerkraut became liberty cabbage, dachshunds liberty pups, and German measles liberty measles, though one might have thought it more patriotic to ascribe the ailment to the enemy rather than to the cause for which we were fighting. The problem of German opera called for much soul-searching and head-scratching. It was finally agreed that Wagner in English offered no serious threat to national security or to the prospects of military victory. At the Metropolitan Opera House I was edified when an obese dying Tristan sang lugubriously, as he looked out to sea, "I see a sheep!" It was inspiring; I came away confident that the sheep would not fall into the clutches of the werewolf of Potsdam.

On November 7, 1918, while I was at work at the University Settlement, someone telephoned to say that an armistice had been signed (it was before the days of radio). I went over to the office of Frank Harris in the Woolworth Building, on lower Broadway. We joined the thousands of celebrants who had poured out of the skyscrapers. Broadway was so densely packed that progress was slow. As we inched along in the frenzied, cheering throng, I saw a newsvendor holding up an afternoon paper whose banner headline announced that the armistice rumor was false. Seemingly no one in the crowd paid any attention to it.

I said to Frank, "If the rumor is really a fake, somebody ought to step on the press."

A moment later I was punched in the back, then seized roughly by the shoulder. I turned to find myself confronted by a burly executive type, far gone in drink.

"What's that about stepping on the President?" he asked menacingly.

I assured him that I had not mentioned the President. Nevertheless he told the knot of paraders who had gathered around us that I had said someone should step on the President, and that I was probably a German spy. There were angry looks and muttered threats; it would not have taken much to trigger an assault. Luckily Frank, a big man and a persuasive talker, addressed a long conciliatory discourse to my assailant while I managed to slip into an office building. The incident did not lessen my antipathy to mobs.

The armistice rumor *had*, of course, been false. Four days later the true report prompted a demonstration that exceeded even the first. There was cause for celebration: the war was over at last. Some ten million had died on the battlefields and in the devastated cities. Other millions had been gassed, maimed or mentally warped. More millions yet were homeless, destitute and bereaved. Priceless monuments had been destroyed, forests reduced to matchwood, fertile fields sown with unexploded shells. Five hundred young Americans had paid with their lives for every American victim of the submarines. But we were victorious. We had won the war to end war. We had made the world safe for democracy.

CHAPTER

X

To Hollywood and Back

1

My father's condition grew steadily worse; the doctors agreed that he was entering the last stage of the disease, the *status epilepticus.* Summoned hastily one day, I found him in a state of dementia and almost uncontrollable violence. I sat beside him, restraining him forcibly from leaping out of bed, until at length an ambulance removed him to Bellevue Hospital. There it was decided that he could not safely be discharged; accordingly he was transferred to Ward's Island, in the East River off upper Manhattan. I went there next day to see him. It was my first visit to an insane asylum; I shall never forget it. As I crossed the courtyard, I could see and hear the maniacs at the barred windows high above. Even worse was the social hall, filled with inmates in various stages of derangement: muttering, humming, vociferating, twitching, staring vacantly.

Though it was a public institution, it was permissible to pay for special treatment, so I had obtained a little private room for my father. I found him there, momentarily lucid. He said piteously, "Why did you send me to a place like this?" I tried to explain that I had had no alternative, that it was impossible to oppose the doctors' recommendations. He did not believe me; I can still see the reproach in his eyes. I came away saddened. Determined to spare my mother the pain of seeing him in those surroundings, I invented excuses for deferring her visits, meanwhile forcing myself to go back every few days. Fortunately the end came very soon, for I could not have put her off much longer.

Of course my father left nothing. For over thirty years he had made regular payments to a fraternal society, known as a "lodge," contributions that presumably ensured death benefits. I found that because of the lodge's inability to attract young members its reserve funds had been depleted to the point of complete exhaustion. Over all the years, those payments would have helped ease the ever oppressive financial burden.

2

Shortly before my father's death, I obtained a court order changing my name from Reizenstein to Rice, a step I had long contemplated. Not only was Reizenstein an awkward name for a writer, but it was a nuisance to have a name that was continually misspelled and mispronounced and almost impossible to make understandable on the telephone. Further, as an American born of American parents, I saw no reason for hanging on to a foreign-looking name with which I had no associations or emotional ties. I suppose that while I was about it I could have found a substitute for Elmer too! But somehow that had personal connotations, whereas my family name did not.

There were those who charged me with wanting to conceal my Jewish antecedents. No such consideration entered my mind. I have never paraded my origin, but I have never tried to deny it, either. It is a matter to which I have paid no attention. Ludwig Lewisohn once told me that while enjoying himself at a large party he suddenly realized that he was the only Jew present; panic seized him and he fled! I found it hard to believe that he was serious; his feeling of isolation was incomprehensible to me. In my personal contacts I have never been influenced by race, nationality or religion. My first wife was Jewish, my second was not. Among my friends and associates there have been Catholics, Episcopalians, Unitarians, Congregationalists, Quakers, Christian Scientists, Mormons, Theosophists, Ethical Culturists, Moslems, Hindus, Shintoists, agnostics, atheists and, of course, Jews.

I have taken an active part in combating anti-Semitism in many of its ugly manifestations, but it has been my good fortune never to have been personally affected by it. In my school days everybody was a sheenie, a wop, a nigger, a Chink, a Polack or a mick. The standard response was "Sticks and stones may break my bones, but names will never hurt me." (What really bothered me was being twitted about my red hair.) From time to time I have received scurrilous postcards, usually anonymous, but there was always a wastebasket handy. Once my children were rejected by the "progressive" Lincoln School because the "Jewish quota" was complete. This quota, I was informed, had been established at the instigation of the Jewish members of the school board, who did not want their children to go to a preponderantly Jewish school. So my children went to the Horace Mann School, where they acquitted themselves very well.

Apart from such minor incidents, I have never been incommoded. In the theatrical and literary worlds, in numerous professional, cultural and civic organizations with which I have been associated, there is no discrimination. If people have refrained from asking me to dinner, they have not told me so, hence I have no sense of injury. I have not had occasion to apply for a job in the aviation or oil industries; I have no interest in staying at fashionable resort hotels, in joining Westchester County country clubs, or the University Club in New York, for which I would not be academically eligible anyhow.

There can be no doubt that anti-Semitism is a shameful blot upon a land in which it is held that all men are created free and equal, and are endowed by their Creator with certain unalienable rights. But religious bigotry and race prejudice are by no means directed solely against Jews. In many respects Jews are better off than Negroes, Puerto Ricans, Mexicans, Spanish Americans, Asians and American Indians. I do not believe that a Jew could be elected to the Presidency—though prior to 1960 I would have said the same of a Catholic—but there are few high elective or appointive posts that have not been occupied by Jews. Further, they have won recognition and have prospered in the arts, in science, in sports, in the learned professions, in industry and commerce. On the whole, they are relatively immune from the indignities and handicaps to which Negroes are subjected every day of their lives. I do not mean, of course, that anti-Semitism is to be lightly dismissed because other forms of prejudice are more virulent, nor that we should fail to recognize its prevalence among those who most loudly extol the American way of life. We might be more effective in tidying up the world if our own hands were cleaner.

3

I had written a mystery melodrama, called *Find the Woman,* which my agent, Alice Kauser, a shrewd, intelligent woman of Hungarian birth, was trying to place. I knew I should be working on something I could put my heart into, but I had no heart to put into anything. My spirits and my morale were low, partly because of my failure to make any discernible progress as a writer, mainly because of despair and disillusionment engendered by the war and its aftermath.

At the war's end, the only hope for the salvation of a ravaged, bleeding world seemed to lie in the establishment of a new universal order based upon the principles of Wilson's famous Fourteen Points: freedom of the seas, lowering of economic barriers, disarmament, recognition of the rights of colonial peoples, the creation of an association of nations. But at the Versailles Peace Conference it soon became apparent that Wilson was no match for those practical politicians Lloyd George, Clemenceau and Orlando. He sacrificed point after point in order to ensure the establishment of the League of Nations. The bitter irony of it was that the treaty he brought home was rejected by the United States Senate.

Another tragic aspect of the peace conference was its failure to deal constructively with the Russian situation. Wilson, who was disposed to bring the Bolsheviks to the council table, sent a mission to Russia, headed by Lincoln Steffens and William Bullitt. The Russians, however, enraged by the intervention of English, French and American military forces in support of the counterrevolutionary generals, were suspicious of the envoys. On their side, the European diplomats declined to extend an invitation to the Russians, so nothing came of Wilson's gesture.

It is not likely that Russian participation in the Versailles Conference would have resulted in the establishment of a democratic regime in the Soviet Union. But a realistic recognition of Russia's place in the society of nations, and the sending of food instead of troops, might have eased the mutual distrust and prevented the

building up of the tension which today threatens the future of all
humanity.

News from Russia was scarce, contradictory and unreliable. However, I did hear two firsthand accounts from returned Americans.
One was a talk, at a luncheon meeting of the Foreign Policy Association, by Colonel Raymond Robins, who had been on a Red
Cross mission. He spoke enthusiastically of the revival of industry
under the control of the workers, the distribution of land to the
peasants, the establishment of schools, the administration of government along democratic lines by the local soviets, and said that
in spite of food and fuel shortages there was a general atmosphere
of elation and hope. The other report was a public address by Lincoln Steffens, author of *The Shame of the Cities* (a series of sensational articles about the corruption in American municipal government). Just back from Russia, via the Versailles Conference, his
account was even more glowing than Robins'. With his shrewd
sense of the dramatic, he began by saying, "I have seen the future
and it works!" It was a somewhat premature announcement, but it
thrilled the large, sympathetic audience. He too spoke eulogisti-
cally of political and economic developments. He said that at several meetings he had attended returned emigrants had told tales of
slums, unemployment and police brutality in America. "They told
many terrible stories," said Steffens. Then, after a well-timed pause:
"But I did not hear one of them tell a lie." His sanguine account of
Russia fostered the hope that from the shambles of war there
might arise a society based upon the principles of justice and humanitarianism.

This sympathetic attitude was hardly universal. The course of
events in Russia and the threat of uprisings in Hungary, Germany
and Italy led the American business community to fear that the
contagion might spread. Frederick Lewis Allen, in his authoritative
account of the postwar decade *Only Yesterday,* puts it this way:

> The American businessman . . . had come out of the war with his fight-
> ing blood up, ready to lick the next thing that stood in his way. . . . He
> had come to distrust anything and everything that was foreign, and this
> radicalism he saw as the spawn of longhaired Slavs and unwashed East
> Side Jews. . . . He was quite ready to believe that a struggle of American
> workingmen for better wages was the beginning of an armed revolution
> directed by Lenin and Trotsky, and that behind every innocent profes-

sor who taught that there were arguments for as well as against socialism there was a bearded rascal from eastern Europe with a money bag
in one hand and a smoking bomb in the other.

As Allen suggests, the war ended too soon to exhaust the reser-
voirs of hatred and violence that the propaganda machine had built
up. There were widespread manifestations of savage hostility, not
only to everything Russian but to anyone who did not whole-
heartedly accept the newly formed American Legion's concept of
"one hundred per cent Americanism." The revitalized Ku Klux
Klan aimed "to unite white male persons, native born Gentile citizens," and to shield "the sanctity of the home and the chastity of
American womanhood." Imperial Kleagles and Grand Goblins led
cohorts of sheeted heroes in campaigns of terrorization and violence. At one time the membership of the Klan exceeded four million.

Governmental agencies took part in the persecution. The "red
raids" conducted by Wilson's Attorney General, A. Mitchell Palmer,
known as the "Fighting Quaker," savored more of a police state than
of a constitutional democracy. Meetings were broken up, homes
searched, people arrested without warrants. In one series of nationwide raids, six thousand men and women were held incommuni-
cado for days or weeks, without even being informed of the nature
of the charges against them. The New York State Legislature distinguished itself by expelling five of its members who had been
duly elected on the Socialist ticket, a device employed by Hitler a
dozen years later. It also set up the famous—or infamous—Lusk
Committee, first of a long series of legislative investigating committees that have been plaguing the nation ever since.

It was not an atmosphere that was conducive to creative work or
creative thinking. My feeling of futility and frustration was shared
by many who, in their respective fields, had worked hopefully for
justice, tolerance, enlightenment and peace, and who now saw the
whole world convulsed by strife, hatred and persecution. Inwardly
I had not lost faith in human potentialities, but in the climate of the
day effort directed toward their realization seemed useless.

4

A curious little personal incident underscored my general feeling.
My old employer Moses H. Grossman, who for years had been

angling through his Tammany Hall connections for a Federal judge-
ship, had received a temporary appointment to the City Magistrates'
Court, lowest rung on the judicial ladder. As a matter of courtesy I
wrote a congratulatory note. In it I suggested that before sending
culprits to prison he inquire into their antecedents and the reasons
for their antisocial behavior. I may even have made a reference to
the Sermon on the Mount.

To my amazement, his reply invited me to sit on the bench with
him and help him administer justice! To decline seemed a little
rude; besides, I had some curiosity about the proposed experience.
So in due course I found myself perched beside the robed M.H.G.
on the judgment seat, feeling a little conspicuous and out of place.
Of course, I was quite familiar with the procedures and the general atmosphere, but viewed from this Olympian height the jumble
of prisoners, witnesses, attorneys and officers seemed more like
pieces in a complicated game than sentient individuals.

As usual, some minor offenders pleaded guilty and were fined a
few dollars or sentenced to a few days in the workhouse. Others
were discharged for failure of prosecuting witnesses to appear, or
were sent back to detention cells as postponements were granted. It
was all standardized and impersonal, like selling tickets at a box
office. When a more serious case came along, there was an innovation that puzzled the courtroom habitués. The prisoner and I accompanied M.H.G. to his chambers, where he questioned the accused man about his environment and his mental processes. It was,
of course, an utterly futile approach to a task that called for ex-
haustive probing by sociologists and psychologists, not a hurried
fifteen-minute inquiry, with the questioner conscious of his congested calendar and the prisoner bewildered and inarticulate, sus-
pecting perhaps that this was some new and subtle form of the
third degree. After three or four of these abortive episodes, I
pleaded pressure of business and departed.

This brief experience in a petty courtroom seemed to me to il-
lustrate in miniature not only the fallacies and inadequacies of the
whole judicial system, but the errors of social behavior upon every
level, up to and including international relationships: behavior
based upon antiquated, sterile and destructive concepts of guilt and
punishment, sin and atonement, affront and vengeance, of meeting
injury with injury, threat with threat, force with force, violence with
violence. Neither the imprisonment of felons nor the clash of armies

has ever contributed to the improvement of society or betterment of
the human lot.

5

For the fourth successive year I went to New Hampshire, hopeful
that a summer by the quiet waters of the lake would free me from
my negativism and enable me to develop a constructive work program. I had hardly arrived there when I was asked to come to New
York to discuss with Samuel Goldwyn the possibility of joining his
scenario department. Goldwyn told me he felt that the rapidly ex-
panding motion picture industry was relying too much on the personality of actors and not enough on story material. He had acquired exclusive rights in the works of a group of well-known
novelists. To adapt these books for the screen, he wanted writers
skilled in dramatic construction and not conditioned by Hollywood
routines. I listened with considerable skepticism, but he meant what
he said; throughout his long, highly successful career he has given
greater recognition to the writer's contribution than has any other
Hollywood producer.

Some weeks later, he offered me a five-year contract, which I accepted mainly because I felt that a complete change of scene and a
wholly new activity might pull me out of the bog in which I was
floundering. If Goldwyn really wanted new ideas and fresh material
there might be opportunities to use the motion picture medium
creatively. I was curious, too, about the workings of this strange new
industry that was beginning to compete with the theatre. Moreover,
the prospect of seeing the Far West appealed strongly to my appetite for travel. Finally, there was the economic situation. Another
baby was expected and I wanted to avoid drawing too heavily upon
reserves. The starting salary of one hundred and fifty dollars was
not lavish in Hollywood terms even then, but it was substantial in
terms of purchasing power, and it advanced by stages to six hundred. I was reluctant to bind myself for so long, but I was sure that
if I wanted a release I could get it, since no producer would want to
go on paying an unwilling writer.

Goldwyn insisted that I report for work in mid-August, only four
weeks off. We had to hurry back to New York, make arrangements
for storage of our belongings, wind up personal and business mat-

ters, work out travel plans. I decided to take along my mother, who was still keeping house for Grandpa and Uncle Will. I felt that after thirty years of devotion to my father and his family she should be released from responsibility. I told my wealthy widowed Aunt Fannie that it was about time she looked after her father. An indolent, pampered woman, she was not pleased, but she could not very well refuse.

We set off at last on the four-day journey, exhausted but eager. It was our first trip beyond the Mississippi; we spent most of it on the platform of the observation car, gazing at the spectacular Western scenery. As soon as we reached Los Angeles, I called the studio. Goldwyn took the announcement of my arrival calmly; he told me to report next day. When I asked him how to get out there, he replied, "Well, listen, find out how you get out here." It was not a heartwarming welcome. As I soon discovered, it would have made no difference if I had arrived a month or two later.

Next day I did find out how to get to the studio. Goldwyn, a little more cordial now, turned me over to the scenario department, with the suggestion that I take my time about looking around and getting acquainted. Jack Hawks, head of the department, made the same recommendation. When I told him that I had to find a place to live, he assured me that I need not worry about getting down to work until I was comfortably settled.

Very quickly we found a house on Crenshaw Boulevard, then on the outskirts of the city but now in its very heart. A trolley line at the corner took me right to the gates of the studio. To my relief, the rental was not excessive. I was determined not to adopt the extravagant scale of living characteristic of Hollywood. I did not intend to become a permanent resident and hoped to add to my savings. We were pleased with the house. The front lawn and the back yard were safe playgrounds for Bobby, now nearly three. There were a lemon, an orange and a fig tree, rose hedges, fuchsias and bougainvillaea, Palm trees shaded the quiet street, beyond whose distant end rose the wooded hills behind Hollywood. It was all new and strange and interesting, quite unlike the sidewalks of New York or the pinewoods of New Hampshire.

I had wanted to avoid buying a car. But the trolley service turned out to be infrequent and irregular; further, without a car we could not go anywhere on the long weekends. So after a few weeks I re-

luctantly bought one. Never having attempted to drive and con-
spicuously lacking in mechanical aptitude, I took two or three lessons from the car dealer, applied for a license, and obtained one
without being asked to pass a test. How I managed to preserve my
life and the lives of others, I do not know, but except for a few
crumpled fenders there were no mishaps. In time I learned to drive
competently enough, but I have never learned to enjoy it. Living in
the country, I find a car a necessity, but I also find it and everything
connected with motoring a great bore.

Compared to the Metro-Goldwyn-Mayer plant which superseded
it, the Goldwyn studio in Culver City was a modest establishment.
There were, of course, none of the great soundproof stages that
came in with the talkies. The administration building, the commissary and the dressing rooms were jerry-built wooden structures,
shabby by comparison with the elegant temples that replaced them.
The greater part of the "lot" was vacant land, on which outdoor
sets—those Western frontier streets!—were sometimes erected. The
industry, as its apologists were fond of saying, was still in its infancy, though it was an infancy not unlike Gargantua's.

The studio, of course, had its galaxy of stars, only two of whom,
Pauline Frederick and Madge Kennedy, had, as far as I know, been
exposed to dramatic training. The others included Mary Pickford's
brother Jack; her former husband's brother, Tom Moore; Olive
Thomas, a great beauty; and Mabel Normand, who had graduated
from Mack Sennett's slapstick comedies. Most important of all, perhaps, was Will Rogers, the gum-chewing, rope-twirling, wisecrack-
ing cowboy, who had made a great reputation in the Ziegfeld Follies. He never pretended to be an actor, but relied upon his engaging personality. Personality, looks, sex appeal: these have always been the chief Hollywood assets. A skillful, patient director
can extract a passable performance from almost any well-built boy
or girl, however innocent of talent.

Goldwyn, in pursuit of his new policy, had challenged Jesse
Lasky's Famous Players by organizing his Eminent Authors: Basil
King, Gertrude Atherton, Rupert Hughes, Gouverneur Morris and
Rex Beach. To adapt their works, he had made an even greater
break with tradition by engaging a group of writers from the East,
all of whom had had some connection with the theatre. The newcomers were Clayton Hamilton, to whom I have referred in con-

nection with *On Trial;* Louis Sherwin, able dramatic critic of the New York *Evening Globe;* and the playwrights Charles Kenyon, Cleves Kinkead and Thompson Buchanan. Kenyon's crude but forceful *Kindling* was one of the first American plays with a "social" theme: a poverty-stricken woman turns thief to provide for her new-born child. Kinkead, the year after *On Trial,* had written *Common Clay,* a courtroom melodrama in which Jane Cowl made a great hit. Buchanan was the author of several successful melodramas and sentimental comedies.

The new contingent did not supplant the existing staff; it merely augmented it. Jack Hawks, head of the department and a veteran of the infant industry, was an energetic, unlettered, likable, alco-holic extrovert, well versed in all the routines and clichés of film making, and not without a certain instinct for dramatic construc-tion. The other six or eight members of the old staff were former newspapermen, or youngsters who had "grown up" in pictures and had had no other writing experience.

Learning the ropes was not too difficult. Apart from its photo-graphic technology, in which I took no interest and which will for-ever be a mystery to me, I found that picturemaking was merely a greatly simplified form of playmaking. The absence of dialogue and the rather limited aesthetic and intellectual capacity of the mass audience for whose entertainment films were designed necessi-tated a concentration upon scenes of action: melodramatic, comic, erotic. Wit and poetry were, of course, excluded; nuances of char-acterization and subtleties of motivation were not attempted; ideo-logical conflicts were rarely and warily presented, and always with strictly orthodox resolutions.

Scenario writing, therefore, was an exercise in dramatic crafts-manship rather than a literary art, the writers often working in pairs. First came the story outline, a straight narrative based more or less upon a book or play, seldom upon original material. After much discussion and revision, the outline was turned over to a continuity writer, who broke it up into "camera angles" or "action shots"—in other words, detailed stage directions. Since the camera was still stationary, the movement had none of its present-day fluidity; each scene was rather static and self-contained. The director often used the continuity merely as a sort of general guide, impro-vising as he went along.

The third element in the development of the scenario was the writing of subtitles, those informative bits flashed on the screen to indicate locales and time lapses, to identify characters and establish relationships, and to supply snatches of dialogue whenever the action was not self-explanatory. The early Chaplin films are brilliant examples of kinetic storytelling that requires no verbal amplification. In most pictures, however, considerable visible dialogue was required. Sometimes the actors spoke the lines that appeared on the screen. More frequently they just improvised, or ad-libbed; or, if their spirits were high, they spoke words that were wholly at variance with the emotions they were portraying. Theatregoers who had mastered the art of lip reading discovered to their horror or delight that what was being said was not always fit for home consumption. Protests poured in and the exuberance of the players was checked.

After the filming was completed, subtitles often had to be substantially revised to make them conform to changes in action, or even in story line, made in the course of production. These revisions were made by a specialist called a title writer, whose contribution was sometimes the most important writing element. The whole impact of a picture could be changed if, at a crucial moment, a character said "Yes" instead of "No." Yet this drastic alteration could be effected merely by substituting one title card for another.

I had a hand in one of these title-writing metamorphoses. The studio made a picture based upon Wallace Irwin's *Trimmed with Red*, a heavy-handed "satire" on "parlor Bolshevism," a fashionable term that implied that any intellectual—particularly a Greenwich Villager—who was sympathetic to the Russian experiment was either a hireling or a dupe of the Kremlin. The picture was so bad that Goldwyn asked me to try to find a way to make it distributable so that some of the production cost could be recouped. In running the cuts, which amounted to more footage than had survived, I found that many of the castoff scenes dealt with the silly heroine's hobby of collecting animals. There were lovebirds, canaries and cockatoos, white mice and chameleons, fish and frogs, even a baby alligator in the bathtub. Brooding over this zoological abundance, I threw out parlor Bolshevism entirely and invented a new religion, Neo-Pythagoreanism, which posited the transmigration of human souls into the bodies of animals. The story now dealt with the excesses into which the lady's adherence to this exotic creed led her. I recut the whole picture, eliminating all political scenes and restoring all scenes in which animals appeared. Then I wrote a series of explanatory introductions and appropriate bits of dialogue, none of which bore any relation to the original story, but which managed to suggest the new plot. It was still a bad picture, but was now releasable. It must have brought in many times my total earnings at the Goldwyn studio.

6

Just before we left New York, my agent, Alice Kauser, had found a producer for my mystery melodrama, for which I had almost given up hope. I should have remained in the East, to be available for rewriting and to keep in touch with the production. But I had scruples about breaking my contract; besides, our arrangements for leaving had been almost completed. When my agent informed me that the play was about to go into rehearsal, with Richard Bennett (father of Joan, Constance and Barbara of the movies) as its star, I applied for a four-week leave of absence, which was refused. Sherwin and Buchanan advised me to go anyhow, pointing out that a successful play meant much more than a studio job. However, I had just transported my family across the continent, rented a house, bought a car; my wife was in the sixth month of pregnancy. So I decided not to go and reluctantly granted the producer the right to make revisions.

For a time I found the new environment and the new associations stimulating. A writer leads a lonely life; I took pleasure in the daily contact with keen-minded, worldly-wise men, most of whom were many years older than I. There was plenty of time for conversation. There was a large table reserved for the scenario department in the commissary. Sometimes a star, a director or a visiting writer from New York joined us. The talk was always lively, occasionally controversial or informative, frequently witty and invariably bawdy.

The commissary was an amusing place. At the lunch hour it had the look of a fancy-dress ball: a melange of crusaders, pirates, dance-hall girls, doughboys, circus performers, Indians in war paint, and, of course, innumerable cowboys and deputy sheriffs. The directors, as became their importance, wore jodhpurs or puttees—a fashion introduced, I believe, by Cecil B. De Mille. Cameramen and mechanics appeared in coveralls or blue jeans. Only the writers wore mufti, and even they affected vivid shirts and loud sport jackets.

A frequent visitor at the writers' table was Will Rogers, probably the most colorful figure in the studio. Refreshingly free of movie-star airs and mannerisms, he established his importance by skillfully underplaying it. He knew he was no actor, so he depended upon his gaucherie and his engagingly sheepish smile. Whenever he was wanted for a scene someone would say, "He's probably out on the back lot roping goats." He usually was.

He was always welcome at our table, though his appearance put an end to organized conversation. Like most professional comedians—like every professional comedian I have ever known, I may say—he looked upon his table companions as so many stooges and sat back waiting for them to give him cues for his quips. His gags often fell flat, but he did say many shrewd and amusing things. Most of his humor, like much of Mark Twain's, was provincial and anticultural. When he said, "All I know is what I read in the papers," he was not only telling the truth but enabling most of his auditors to identify themselves with him. His homespun know-nothingism deflated pomposity but did not contribute to an intelligent understanding of current events.

Another studio celebrity was Maurice Maeterlinck, probably the first Nobel Prize winner to be employed by a Hollywood studio. He moved uneasily about the lot, making no contact with the other writers, perhaps because he spoke little English, perhaps because he did not think himself one of us. He had brought with him a young actress for whom he had deserted Georgette Le Blanc, creator of the female leads in *Monna Vanna* and *Pelléas et Mélisande*. The young woman, a scrawny, not very pretty little thing, was turned over to the casting department with instructions to find work for her. I am sure she was very unhappy. Her faulty English and apparent lack of talent subjected her to open ridicule.

Maeterlinck's engagement had produced a great flurry of publicity, not to Goldwyn's surprise, I am sure. It is related that when the contract formalities were concluded Goldwyn put his hand on the poet's shoulder and said, "Mr. Maeterlinck, I expect big things of you." Like so many Goldwyn stories, this one may be apocryphal. But if he did say it, his expectations were destined to be unfulfilled. There is another tale to the effect that Goldwyn had complained that Maeterlinck had turned in a story whose hero was a bee. That at least would have had the merit of originality.

One day Jack Hawks handed me a story Maeterlinck *had* written, saying, "See what you can do with this." It concerned a kindly farmer to whose blissful domain comes a touring banker, seeking a night's shelter. Next morning the banker sees a telltale film upon a pool. Oil! He contrives to dispossess the farmer and take over the land. Disaster descends upon the bucolic family; the wife dies of consumption or of a broken heart (I forget which); the son becomes a criminal, the daughter—need it be said?—a harlot. The farmer takes to the hills, brooding over his wrongs and vowing vengeance. Years later, his moment comes. The banker, now a great oil magnate, goes hunting in the mountains, where he encounters his victim. The avenger levels his gun, but as he is about to pull the trigger love enters his heart; he lowers his weapon and extends his hand in token of forgiveness.

I read this concoction with amazement, unable to believe that a man of Maeterlinck's stature could have produced it. I had some reservations about his plays and philosophical writings, but there could be no doubt about his world-wide eminence. Shocked by this evidence of the corrupting influence of Hollywood, I was determined not to assist the process of degradation. So I told Hawks I could do nothing with the story—a truthful statement. Happily, the story was never filmed.

7

Learning that my play was to be tried out in the Middle West, I managed to get two weeks' leave and hurried to Ann Arbor, Michigan. It was a fruitless trip. The star, Richard Bennett, in order to fatten his part, had rewritten the play in a way that destroyed what little meaning it had ever had. I protested, but there was nothing I could do. By giving the management the right to revise the script, I had left myself unprotected. Bennett had even changed the title of the play and had had the audacity to copyright it in his own name! I went on to New York to discuss my legal position with

Frank Harris, then returned to California, sick of the whole thing. The play eventually opened in New York, where it received indifferent notices and had an indifferent run of ten weeks or so. A compromise with Bennett had been worked out, so my earnings were substantial. But the play meant nothing to me, and the money did not compensate me for the attendant unpleasantness.

In the annals of the theatre the play is memorable only for one thing. During its Broadway run, Bennett appeared at special matinees in *Beyond the Horizon,* the first of Eugene O'Neill's plays to be professionally performed. It was so well received that, when my play closed, it was put on for a run and was awarded the Pulitzer Prize. Thus, unwittingly and indirectly, I was associated with the birth of the new American drama and with the beginning of the brilliant career of the most gifted dramatist America has yet produced.

Shortly after my trip East, my wife gave birth to a girl, whom we named Margaret. Peggy, as she is generally known, was a fine child who has become an honest, courageous, high-minded woman, a daughter of whom any father could be proud. My son Robert, now three, showed signs of such high intelligence that I painstakingly compiled his vocabulary and sent it to Professor Lewis Terman of Leland Stanford, who was making a study of gifted children. A test made at Terman's suggestion produced an I.Q. of 161, which warranted Robert's inclusion in the group whose careers Terman intended to follow. Nearly thirty years later he sent me his book *The Gifted Child Grows Up,* a comprehensive survey whose conclusions are that high intelligence is a constant characteristic and that those who display it in childhood attain a level of achievement far above the average—good to know in an America in which anti-intellectualism is widespread and "egghead" has become a term of ridicule, even opprobrium.

My interest in my new surroundings, acquaintances and occupation soon diminished; familiarity bred boredom, if not contempt. As in my law-office days, I found myself caught up in a routine. My associates were more sophisticated and the pay was better, but the day-by-day performance of more or less mechanical duties absorbed only a small part of my energies. I could have done five times as much work; but excessive diligence would have been a reflection upon my colleagues, so I learned to make haste slowly.

Most of my day was spent in reading, letter writing and desultory conversation. Time hung heavily.

I had accepted Goldwyn's offer largely on the strength of his promise of free creative scope. But he had reckoned without the scenario department's entrenched bureaucracy. The practitioners of the established patterns of picturemaking saw in the invasion from the East a threat to their security. Beneath the surface affability there was a sort of struggle for power, whose chief protagonists were Jack Hawks and Thompson Buchanan. Though Buchanan was a shrewd, ambitious and unscrupulous politician, he was no match for Hawks, who, like a Tammany leader, had the advantage of status and a supporting organization.

Nor did the stars and the directors take kindly to Goldwyn's concept of the writer's importance. Even today the Hollywood writer, unless he happens also to be a producer or director, plays a secondary role. (One still hears Hollywood directors speak of "my writer.") In silent-picture days the writer was decidedly subordinate. Goldwyn's Eastern recruits, received with something less than enthusiasm, did not enhance their popularity by frequent affectionate references to the world of the theatre. There was general unfriendliness, amounting sometimes to open hostility. Once Mabel Normand, in the midde of a scene, announced in salty language that she would stop performing until two writers who were looking on left the set. Though the writers had been instructed to move freely about the studio, they had to go. There were profuse apologies from Abraham Lehr, Goldwyn's right-hand man and his former partner in the glove-manufacturing business, but the incident aggravated the general ill-will.

The proposed revolution in writing came to nothing. All story material was channeled through Hawks, who vetoed every innovation with the comment that it was "not pictures." Everything went into the old sausage machine and it all came out looking and tasting alike. I once sat beside Gertrude Atherton during the screening of a film made from one of her novels. When I asked her opinion she said, "What I like most about it is that there is still a picture to be made out of my book."

Since I had never intended to become a permanent inhabitant of the motion picture world, I had no reason to become involved in its organizational policies and problems. I had seen enough to convince me that the writer could never have complete freedom of expression. What concerned me was a problem of my own: When and how was I going to resume my efforts to become a creative writer?

Soon after my melodrama closed in New York, I learned from Hatcher Hughes that he had found a producer for our collaboration, *The Homecoming*, which I had long since written off as another wasted effort. The producer was Harrison Grey Fiske, who intended the play for his wife, Minnie Maddern Fiske—strange indeed, since it had been written for David Warfield! Hughes said, and I could well believe him, that radical alterations were required. I was more than willing to leave the making of them to him. However, when Hughes came to Los Angeles to consult me, I found even this remote contact with the drama a welcome relief from the tedium of studio life and motion picture making.

During my second year at the Goldwyn studio I took a quick trip to San Francisco, the first of many visits to that beautiful, exciting metropolis. It was a refreshing contrast to the monotonous soupiness of Los Angeles. On the way back, I met Will Rogers in the club car. He complained about the poor quality of his story material and asked me to try to write something suitable for him. I turned out a story built upon the formula of *A Connecticut Yankee in King Arthur's Court*. A cowboy, reproached by the young lady of his affections for his clumsiness as a lover, gets a copy of *Romeo and Juliet*, falls asleep over it and in his dreams re-enacts the play with himself as the hero. It gave Rogers a good opportunity to display his gaucherie amid the trappings of the Renaissance.

Rogers urged the studio to buy the story. I was anxious to make the sale, because I intended to make it conditional on the cancellation of my employment contract; the prospect of another three years of it was unbearable. But I encountered an unforeseen stumbling block. My immediate superior, Thompson Buchanan, agreed that the story was a good vehicle for Rogers, but he made his approval subject to my investing half the purchase price in an oil company he was organizing. I had no interest in speculating in oil, and I resented the coercion. But my desire to be released prevailed. The sale and the release were concluded, though not without some unpleasantness. Goldwyn pointed out that he had had no satisfactory results from his importation of Eastern writers. I refrained from quoting Saint Matthew on the subject of new wine and old bottles.

Rogers made the story into a successful picture called *Doubling for Romeo*. I saw a screening of it, not long ago, at the Museum of Modern Art. The audience was much amused, mainly by the funny subtitles Rogers had written. Buchanan's oil lands, of course, produced only dry holes, so my net profit was small. But I was happily out of my employment contract. Except for my brief service with the Federal Theatre Project, I have never signed another.

8

Free again, I went to New York to attend the opening of *The Home-coming*, rechristened *Wake Up, Jonathan*. Hatcher Hughes had done a workmanlike job in adapting the play to the talents of Mrs. Fiske. It was a routine piece of theatre, but she was a favorite of the critics—though not, I must say, of mine—and was able to carry it off. It limped along for the better part of the season and for some months on tour. Except for keeping my name alive in the theatre, it gave me little satisfaction.

In New York I had an experience that greatly altered my outlook and my behavior. I was staying with a married couple, old friends. Awakening late one morning, I found my hostess in bed beside me. I was not too surprised, for there had long been a latent amorousness. What did surprise me, upon reflection, was the readiness with which I responded to the situation, and the complete absence of any sense of guilt.

Indeed, it was the very casualness and brevity of the episode that made me feel it was imperative for me to undertake a long-deferred critical examination of my marriage. My early misgivings about it had diminished with the establishment of a home and the birth of children. I had convinced myself that it was exceptionally happy and successful. Now my easy acceptance of an extramarital relationship, based not upon passion but merely upon propinquity and physical attraction, gave me a psychological jolt that forced me to consider the possibility that I had been deluding myself. The more I thought about it, the more I saw that I had been shutting my eyes to what I did not want to see, talking myself into believing what I wanted to believe.

I do not mean that I came to the conclusion that my marriage was a complete failure. Far from it. It had many affirmative aspects: mutual affection, the pleasures and burdens of parenthood, the enjoyment of common tastes. What was lacking, I now began to realize, was the kind of creative ferment that makes for the spiritual and emotional growth of the parties to a relationship. At the time, I only sensed this; later experience convinced me of it.

Who was to blame? Neither of us, I should say. When something is amiss it is not always necessary to find a villain or a scapegoat. The trouble was that we were basically unsuited to each other: our temperaments, rhythms, behavior patterns, emotional attitudes simply did not match up; other inharmonies are too intimate to be referred to. If we had been more experienced or had lived together for a while, I am sure we would never have married. We had rushed into something for which we were unprepared; it never struck deep roots or provided meaningful satisfactions. We lived amiably enough, quarreling sometimes, but less, I think, than most married couples do. But surface living is not enough. Even in our quarrels there was a difference of tempo. My wife was hot-tempered; her anger flared high but subsided quickly. I tended to turn cold and remain so for a long time. It was only one of many discrepancies that hindered true rapport.

It was evident that my emotional and my intellectual elements were not in step. At twenty-eight, I was a relatively independent thinker, relatively free of prejudice and superstition, ready to examine any idea objectively. Yet I was still quite repressed and inhibited, not only sexually but also in my capacity to enter into enriching and fructifying relationships. I was aware that an emotional strait jacket can be even more restrictive than a mental one. Since I had not found within my marriage the satisfactions I sought, I had to either forgo them, terminate my marriage or seek to supply its deficiencies elsewhere. The third course seemed the best. I valued family life and was reluctant to break it off. Resignation to an incomplete marriage I rejected, for I have never believed that repression and frustration are compatible with psychic health.

I had no moral compulsion to monogamy. It is my belief that man is not by nature a monogamous animal. Polygamy is common both among primitive peoples and in many of the most highly developed civilizations. Even in the United States it was an avowed principle of the devout Mormons and the idealistic utopian communities. In general, statutes making adultery a crime are seldom enforced; the Scriptural injunction is perhaps the least heeded of all the Decalogue's negations. Any listener to male conversation or observer of male behavior did not need the Kinsey Reports as proof that among men monogamy is exceptional. To a lesser degree, among women too—lesser not because of lack of desire, I am inclined to think, as because of lack of opportunity, the danger of pregnancy, and fear of the social consequences of discovery. Women, too, are more likely to seek an emotional component in their relationships, though this is by no means a clear-cut sexual differentiation.

These beliefs did not make me a militant advocate of what was popularly known as "free love." To me sexual fidelity seemed a personal, pragmatic matter, like a belief in God or in life after death. Its validity depended upon whether or not it worked for you. I think that when a man and a woman find complete emotional satisfaction in each other fidelity becomes a matter of course. That was certainly true of my second marriage. But on that basis the first would never have survived.

It did survive for another twenty years, during which I always had outside attachments. I did not flaunt these relationships, nor did I discuss them with my wife; but I was not furtive about them, either. Indeed, she was often inclined to suspect intimacy where none existed. The fact that she did not seek a divorce is evidence, I think, that for her too the maintenance of a home and the pleasures of family life outweighed other considerations. Of course I conceded to her the same freedom I demanded for myself; nor did I protest when she availed herself of it. Fortunately for myself and for others, my many grave faults do not include possessiveness and sexual jealousy. I have been hurt and angered by spiritual betrayal, but physical infidelity has never disturbed me.

Since I am no Casanova eager to parade his conquests, I shall have little more to say on this subject. In fact, my love relationships were not "conquests" at all. I did not go about seeking adventures; but neither did I reject opportunities when they offered themselves. I never made advances unless I had reason to believe they would be welcome; if I found I was mistaken, I desisted. Some of these relationships were transitory, the spontaneous expression of mutual attraction. Others, deeply charged with emotion, went on for years. None, however casual, was sordid, tawdry or mercenary. Some of my partners were married, others not; almost without exception they were women of superior intelligence, talent, sensitivity and character. Over the years these attachments were a source of stimulation and contributed immeasurably to my understanding of myself and of other people. I shall refer to them again only in so far as they directly affected the events of my life.

9

Not wanting to be idle, I sought employment. There were financial problems, too. My Goldwyn salary had risen to two hundred and fifty dollars a week, but I had saved little. It was the familiar Hollywood pattern: mounting expenditure keeping pace with mounting income. I was unwilling to tie myself to another employment contract, so I looked around for free-lance jobs.

Fortunately, I had good connections. Thompson Buchanan had moved over to an executive job at Famous Players. The scenario head of that studio was Frank E. Woods, with whom I had become quite friendly through working with him and several other writers in the organization of the Screen Writers' Guild. Like the Authors' League of America, with which it soon affiliated, its objectives were the setting up of contractual standards and general protection of its members' rights. It eventually became a tough collective-bargaining agency, but in its inception membership was voluntary and the activities largely social.

Through Woods and Buchanan I obtained assignments from Famous Players and from a subsidiary somewhat hyperbolically named Real Art Films, a unit specializing in light comedies—that is to say farces—written to order for five or six young actresses. I remember only Bebe Daniels, who was not without talent. Sometimes I worked on titles, sometimes on a continuity. On one of my occasional visits to the studio I had my first glimpse of Cecil B. De Mille in action. The film, based on a quiet little story of Leonard Merrick's, was somehow being enacted in the vast courtyard of an Oriental palace. At the brink of a large pool swarming with crocodiles, a troop of lightly clad young ladies was responding to the microphonic instructions of De Mille, who stood a hundred yards away, dressed in a Byronic shirt, moiré breeches and puttees. I was better acquainted with his brother William, a quiet, well-read man, generally known as a highbrow—another way of saying that his attempts at originality in film making were not great box-office successes. William's daughter Agnes has become famous as a choreographer.

As on the Goldwyn lot, any suggestion that partook of novelty was met with the standard inquiry "Yes, but will Lizzie like it?" Lizzie was the hypothetical Midwestern small-town waitress who represented the norm of the motion picture audience. I had nothing against Lizzie or her craving for satisfaction of her simple tastes, but I did not want to spend any considerable part of my life catering to them. When I mentioned my discontent to Jeanie MacPherson, Cecil B. De Mille's script writer, she said, "Maybe you just haven't found your place in pictures." I felt not only that she was right but that I would never find it. I was now averaging four hundred dollars per week, with good prospects of a steady increase. I saw, as I had seen at House, Grossman and Vorhaus, that the longer I stayed the more deeply I would become involved, and the harder it would be to break away.

Breaking away meant going back East, a welcome prospect for my wife and my mother as well as myself. We were all thoroughly bored with life in Los Angeles. I have been back many times, for periods ranging from a week to six months, but I have never found it a livable place. It has the provincialism of a small town and the discomforts of a metropolis, yet it lacks the intimacy of one and the excitements of the other. The body is enervated by the soupy climate; the eye is offended by the nightmarish rows of juxtaposed Swiss chalets, ranch houses, Cape Cod cottages, Norman farmhouses, Spanish-Moorish villas, bastardized, jerry-built and fronted by patches of lawn that struggle perpetually against drought and crab grass; the intelligence is outraged by the antics of boosters and crackpots; the spirit is depressed by the cultural inertia.

We had been hard put to find activities. Neither my wife nor I was interested in sports or gambling. After we had seen the missions, Coronado Beach and Tia Juana, there was nothing to do except drive along endless roads that led nowhere in particular. Our chief stimulus came from quick trips to New York or San Francisco. We went to parties now and then, but did not enjoy them. The trouble was, I think, that we never identified ourselves with the motion picture community. The conversation centered on the gossip, politics and mechanics of the studios: shoptalk in which I took little interest, and to which I had nothing to contribute. Second in importance was alcohol. With prohibition in force, everyone was concerned with the problems of buying or manufacturing liquor and of increasing one's consumption of it. Since we hardly drank at all, this was a closed subject, too. All in all, we were looked upon, and we looked upon ourselves, as outsiders.

When, upon the expiration of my lease, my landlord told me that he wanted to repossess, I had to decide whether to look for another house or to pull up stakes. There was not much doubt in my mind, but the actual decision was precipitated, as had been the termination of my law-office employment, by an irrelevant accident. One day, on my way to the Famous Players studio, I ran my car into a standing streetcar. I was not going fast, and except for crumpled fenders and a smashed radiator there was no damage, but it does not take a Freudian scholar to recognize that this easily avoidable mishap was an expression of my wish to have done with everything: the car, the studio, Los Angeles. In a few weeks we were on our way East.

In a sense, those two years were wasted. Creatively I had accomplished nothing. Yet in other ways it had been a valuable experience: a new environment, new acquaintances, new perspectives, ample leisure for reflection and self-examination, which fortified my belief that nothing is more important than independence of thought and freedom of action.

CHAPTER

XI

The Nineteen-Twenties

1

The Screen Writers' Guild had asked me to represent it on the council of the Authors' League of America. (In the succeeding forty years, I have always served, in one capacity or another, on the League's governing bodies.) The literary generation of the 1920s was just coming in. On the League council the prewar notables were still in command. I found it a little odd to be sitting in with urbane middle-aged writers whom I had read in my adolescence. Most of them had three names: Ellis Parker Butler, Jesse Lynch Williams, Inez Haynes Gillmore, Louis Joseph Vance, Alice Duer Miller, Louis Kaufman Anspacher. An exception was Rex Beach, a more rugged individual, whose four-in-hand was slipped through an enormous diamond ring—symbolic of the Klondike, perhaps. The League has lost much of its early gentility, thanks largely to the rise of the Dramatists' Guild.

Shortly after my return to New York, I was asked to call on Douglas Fairbanks and Mary Pickford at the Ritz-Carlton—my only meeting with America's Sweetheart. Gracious and friendly, she seemed to wear her honors lightly. Fairbanks, whom I had known slightly, was still, in his late thirties, a handsome, likable adolescent, cavorting about the room, addressing the telephone operator as "Miss Ritz." At the recommendation of my old friend Frank Woods, the couple invited me to head their scenario department. The weekly wage was seven hundred dollars, with good prospects of advancement. In Hollywood terms the job carried with it considerable prestige; in the light of my unpromising economic outlook, the money was tempting. But acceptance meant a kind of surrender to which I knew I would never reconcile myself. Though I asked for time to think it over, my lack of enthusiasm was apparent. I came away feeling virtuous, but doubtful about the soundness of my judgment.

In fact, I was doubtful about everything, ridden by uncertainty, discontent and self-dissatisfaction. I felt I was getting nowhere, accomplishing nothing. I wanted knowledge, experience, understanding. I was disheartened about my work, wondering whether I really had a future as a writer. After two years in Hollywood, I found it hard to get back to playwriting. I toyed with one idea after another, but found none that fired me. The trouble was that everything was mentally contrived; what I wanted was something charged with emotion. But there was an emotional barrier that I seemed unable to break through.

While in this deep turmoil, I accepted an invitation from Walter Jordan, a well-known theatrical agent, to dramatize an unpublished novel, *It Is the Law,* by Hayden Talbot, a newspaperman. A crime story turning upon the legal doctrine of double jeopardy, it had interesting possibilities. Though not eager to write another crime melodrama, I felt it was better to be working than just churning about. Besides, if the play was a success I might be able to get to Europe at last.

When the dramatization was done, I went house hunting, for we had been planning to move away from New York, preferably to some small New England town where the children would be less confined and where I might find more favorable working conditions than a New York apartment afforded. I soon found a place in such a town—East Hampton, Connecticut, known as the Bell Town because of its factories that made sleigh bells, dinner bells, cowbells and the like. The town's activities were controlled by the three or four prolific families who for generations had been the factory owners—a typical New England setup, not without certain aspects of the feudal system.

Our house, situated on the crest of a hill half a mile from the business center, was a big, rambling place with a fine "summer kitchen" and an extra parlor off in one corner that made a secluded study. The grounds were large, and in back were many acres of abandoned apple orchards divided by dilapidated stone fences, a delightful area for reading, meditation, bird watching. The town's streets were lined with magnificent chestnuts (which have since succumbed to blight). Within the town limits was little Lake Pocotopaug, to which I often took the children, carrying Peggy papoose-fashion in a knapsack. In the cool water of the lake, in the privacy of my study, in the solitude of the orchards, I began to relax a little. I even began work on a play about marriage.

2

A few months after we moved to East Hampton, I had an experience which still puzzles and amazes me. One night, long after everyone else had gone to bed, I sat wide awake on the front porch, trying to concentrate on the marriage play. Suddenly, as though a switch had been turned or a curtain raised, a new play flashed into my mind, wholly unrelated to anything I had ever consciously thought about. When I say "flashed into my mind," I mean that quite literally, for in that sudden instant I saw the whole thing complete: characters, plot, incidents, even the title and some of the dialogue. Nothing like it ever happened to me before or since. I was actually possessed, my brain in a whirl, my whole being alive. I sat for a while trembling with excitement, almost gasping for breath. Then, hardly knowing what I was doing, I went to my study and began to write!

I wrote until dawn, spent a few sleepless hours in bed, breakfasted, and immediately went back to work. I kept at it day after day, scarcely speaking, sometimes leaving in the middle of a meal to hurry to my desk. My family must have thought me demented. In a sense I was: moving about in a semitrance, driven by an irresistible compulsion. It was as close to automatic writing as anything I have known. At the end of seventeen days the play was finished—finished, at any rate, as far as I am concerned, for except for cuts and typographical corrections I never changed any of it. I have just been looking at the original manuscript. It is written in pencil, on *both sides* of sheets of yellow paper of different sizes, some ruled, some unruled, whatever came to hand, I suppose. Obviously I had no very clear idea of what I was about.

I can best convey the effect that this extraordinary experience had upon me by quoting from a letter I wrote to Frank Harris, made available to me by his widow:

> I've just finished a job that has left me rather limp. About a month ago, a hurricane in the form of a new play swept me out to sea, and before I could struggle back to shore I had a first draft completed. Seventeen days and an average of eight or ten hours' work a day. I think I've stated that it left me rather limp. It was grand, though!—the best time I've had in years and years. I'm hugging myself for coming up here, where my silly nerves have had a chance to iron themselves out and my thoughts to place themselves end to end. Such a work jag would have been utterly impossible in the city. Of course, it is pertinent to inquire whether the result is worth while. Frankly, I don't know. It's very different from anything I've ever done. It's new—a radical departure in technique and subject matter (for me, at any rate). And what's more, it's the most spontaneous, the most deeply felt thing I've ever done. Of course, novelty does not connote merit and neither does sincerity (despite the sentimental belief to the contrary). But whether or not it's good, I think it's as good as I'm capable of doing, at this stage of my development. . . .
>
> For the moment, then, I'm out of the bog in which I've been floundering. The sense of frustration which has been choking me for four years has abated. I actually feel a consciousness of liberation, a relief from a state of psychic congestion which I cannot help believing strangely akin to that physical congestion which the psychologists tell us finds relief in a sexual orgasm. That may strike you as farfetched, but it comes nearer to conveying my present condition than anything else that occurs to me.

The play was called *The Adding Machine*. It was the case history of one of the slave souls who are both the raw material and the product of a mechanized society. In eight scenes it told the story of Mr. Zero, a white-collar worker tied to a monotonous job and a shrewish wife. Replaced by a machine, he murders his boss in an access of resentment and panic, and he is condemned to die by a jury of his peers. His fears and frustrations make him reject an eternity of happiness and self-expression; he returns to earth to begin another treadmill existence, sustained only by the mirage of hope. The play was written in the stylized, intensified form loosely known as expressionism, though I had hardly heard the term at the time. It was a compound of comedy, melodrama, fantasy, satire and polemics. The dialogue was unlike any I had written before: an attempt to reproduce authentic human speech.

Not the least puzzling part of the cathartic effect that the writing of the play had upon me was the purging of my lingering antagonism toward my father. I had never really hated him, but I had always resented his failure to measure up to my standards of fatherhood. Now my animosity was washed away and replaced, not by love certainly, but by a kind of pity. I cannot explain the connection between this abatement and the writing of *The Adding Machine*. It was not as though I had vented my ill-will by portraying my father in an unfavorable light. For, though he had many of Mr. Zero's prejudices and malevolences, he was proud, self-assertive and anything but a conformist. My release is part of the mystery that enshrouds the whole creation of the play.

My new-found elation did not blind me to the fact that, both in theme and in treatment, the play was not exactly what the Broadway producers were looking for. My agent, Alice Kauser, took the same view. We agreed that the Theatre Guild, a postwar reincarnation of the Washington Square Players, offered about the only hope for a production. The Guild's board of directors included Philip Moeller, Lee Simonson, Helen Westley and Lawrence Langner, members of the earlier organization; and Theresa Helburn and Maurice Wertheim. The Guild, which, unlike its predecessor, was conducted on a professional basis, had leased the Garrick, an obsolescent Broadway theatre. It had built up a subscription list sufficiently large to ensure any of its productions a five-week run, a great help to a play that had to struggle for its existence. Nevertheless, the Guild's first productions resulted in substantial losses. It was saved from oblivion only by the success of St. John Ervine's *John Ferguson*, which kept it going until the production of Sidney Howard's *They Knew What They Wanted* established it on a firm financial basis. Though the Guild's standards today are not what they were, its forty-year contribution to the American theatre is undoubtedly greater than that of any single producing organization. Its numerous presentations of plays by Shaw and O'Neill is in itself sufficient proof of that.

While I awaited, not very hopefully, the Guild's decision, plans were being made for the production of *It Is the Law*. On one of my visits to New York to confer with the producers and the director, I was dining at my old haunt, the Civic Club, when the waitress told me that one of the other diners would like me to join him. Rather puzzled, I moved over to the table of a fat, bespectacled stranger, who identified himself as Courtenay Lemon, the Theatre Guild's play reader. He said that he had enthusiastically recommended *The Adding Machine* for production and that he thought the chances of acceptance were good. Soon afterward, the Guild offered me a production contract which reserved the right to present the play at special performances instead of in their subscription series. That troubled me, but, since I had despaired of any production, I accepted. I was far more excited than I had been by the sale of *On Trial*, perhaps because *The Adding Machine* meant so much more to me, or perhaps because I had become painfully aware of how hard it is to get any play produced.

I accompanied the *It Is the Law* company on its three-week tryout. No longer shy with actors, I had a good enough time as we traveled about from one upstate New York town to another, but I felt no excitement about the play or the production. It was all just so-so: the script, the acting, the direction, the reviews, the audience response. In New York it was the same. The play was neither good enough to evoke enthusiasm nor bad enough to be dismissed. How many such plays open and close every season! They all go through the complicated process of financing, casting, rehearsing, trying out; they run their brief course and are forgotten. The aggregate expenditure of time, effort and money is enormous. Does it all serve any useful purpose? In certain ways, yes. The productions help keep the theatres open, provide employment for many capable theatre people, entertain many undemanding theatregoers. Beyond that they contribute something to the body of dramatic art. An art cannot consist solely of masterpieces, any more than an army can consist solely of generals. It must have a broad base to give it support and scope; otherwise it tends to become esoteric and precious. The need for nourishment is constant, but every day cannot be a feast day.

Though *It Is the Law* ran for fifteen weeks, and the motion picture rights were sold for a substantial sum, I benefited little, for most of the money was pocketed by Walter Jordan. The defalcation was a criminal offense, since he had acted as a trustee in collecting the money. Frank Harris went to the district attorney, who agreed to prosecute. However, Jordan came to me in tears and begged me not to send him to prison. He did not have to beg very hard, for prisons have always been repugnant to me; so I withdrew the charge. Jordan overwhelmed me with gratitude and with promises of restitution; of course the promises were not fulfilled.

3

Shortly after the opening of It Is the Law, I received the good news that The Adding Machine was to be included in the Theatre Guild's subscription series. Philip Moeller was to direct, Lee Simonson to do the settings. After a good deal of discussion I dropped one of the play's eight scenes, because some of it was repetitious. That was a mistake; I should have cut the redundancies and retained the scene. (In the Phoenix Theatre revival a few years ago, I included a condensed version, which played very well.) Except for this major excision and a few minor ones, the play was presented exactly as it was first written.

The Guild spared nothing in its efforts to make a fine production. It was a pleasure to work with people of taste, who were interested primarily in the drama as an art, rather than as a business. Simonson's settings were original and elaborate. Deems Taylor was engaged to write incidental music. A splendid cast was assembled. Mr. Zero was Dudley Digges, who had come to America from Dublin's famous Abbey Theatre. Mrs. Zero was to be played by Helen Westley, a choice that delighted me. When the young woman who had been cast as Zero's office mate, Daisy Diana Dorothea Devore, was found not quite up to the part, she was replaced by that fine actress Margaret Wycherley. Lieutenant Charles, Zero's custodian in the afterlife, was Louis Calvert, known for decades on the British and American stages. Shrdlu, another murderer, was Edward G. Robinson, not yet Hollywood-bound. Judy O'Grady, the young prostitute, was Elise Bartlett, recent bride of that fantastic character, publisher Horace Liveright. In retrospect it seems odd that in this typically American play two of the principal actors were English and one Irish; but their skill transcended linguistics.

The Guild's directors were unlike the general run of theatrical personalities. Phil Moeller, suave and outwardly dilettantish, was well read, widely traveled. A playwright as well as a director, he had contributed some sophisticated one-act comedies to the Washington Square Players and had had several Broadway productions. I had attended the opening of his play *Madame Sand*, starring Mrs. Fiske. At the end of the second act, as the heroine began her big love scene with Chopin—or it may have been Alfred de Musset —someone gave a wrong cue and the curtain came down. Poor Moeller, in tails and a white tie, appeared flutteringly before the curtain and tried to describe the curtailed scene. But the play was already dead and the corpse could not be revived. Such are the hazards of the theatre.

Lee Simonson, one of America's ablest stage designers, was, like Moeller, an intellectual, well versed in art, music and literature. But he was aggressively egotistical, contentious and sometimes downright rude. I had several clashes with him during rehearsals, but we always respected each other, and still do. Lawrence Langner, the only active survivor of the original directorate, is the personification of the Theatre Guild. His early success as a patent lawyer has enabled him to devote most of his life to the theatre. He too is a playwright, but is best known as director of the artistic and business policies of the Guild. In spite of the Guild's decline, he is still an important force in the American theatre. The establishment of the Shakespeare Theatre at Stratford, Connecticut, is due largely to his initiative.

Helen Westley was decidedly not an intellectual, but behind her façade of outlandish dress, raucousness and eccentric behavior there was great common sense and extraordinary talent. She was a source of constant amusement and the butt of her colleagues' witticisms; I think she enjoyed the roles of *enfant terrible* and palace buffoon.

The two directors whom I had not known previously were Maurice Wertheim and Theresa Helburn. Wertheim was a banker who had already multiplied his large inheritance, and he went on doing so. But he was interested in the arts, and his financial genius was useful to the Guild. Adding money to money, he had married Alma Morgenthau, daughter of the real-estate baron Henry Morgenthau and sister of Franklin D. Roosevelt's Secretary of the Treasury. Alma was a woman of exceptional taste and sensitivity; we became close friends.

Theresa Helburn, a product of Bryn Mawr, Radcliffe and the Sorbonne, was perhaps the most intellectual of them all. She had keen judgment and executive ability too; during most of the Guild's existence she shared managerial responsibility with Langner. One day at rehearsals I was surprised to see John B. Opdycke, my High School of Commerce English teacher, and even more surprised to learn that he was Terry's husband. I always enjoyed Terry's company; she was witty and stimulating. It saddened me to see her turn slowly into a little old lady, and I mourned her death.

An out-of-town tryout of *The Adding Machine*, with its large cast and elaborate settings, would certainly have entailed losses that the Guild could not afford. The play therefore was to "open cold," which put a great strain upon everyone. It was not easy, for example, to know to what extent the acting and the staging should be stylized. The actors were not sure about the interpretation of their parts. At the request of Dudley Digges, I prepared a long memorandum on the psychology of Mr. Zero, and shorter notes on the other characters. A practical problem was presented by Louis Calvert. Nearing the end of his career, he had trouble remembering his lines. I was reluctant to cut his speeches, but it was evident that if I did not he would be unable to give a performance.

Deems Taylor had composed some bits of incidental music for the Elysian Fields scene. A few days before the opening, Moeller decided he wanted music throughout the scene, which ran for half an hour, putting upon Taylor the task of producing quickly a great amount of additional material. I supplied him with a bottle of whiskey and left him alone in my hotel room to work against time. He did the job, but Moeller changed his mind again and most of the new music was never used. Taylor had reason to be resentful, but he took it all in good part.

The dress rehearsal was agonizing. Under union regulations, scenery, properties and scene lighting cannot be used unless a full stage crew is in attendance, a prohibitive expense. Hence there is no opportunity until the dress rehearsal for the actors to accustom themselves to the settings, the furniture and the hand props, nor for the director to co-ordinate lights, sound effects, scene changes and curtains. The stagehands are handling the production for the first time, too. So mistakes occur and unforseen problems arise; there are discussions, arguments, interminable delays. Hour after hour goes by; nerves tighten, bodies ache with weariness.

Simonson's settings were striking, but the very originality of their construction made them hard to handle. Even when the play was running, the long waits between scenes dissipated audience attention. Some of the mechanical devices were startling. In the murder scene the turntable on which Zero stood began to revolve slowly, picking up speed as his brain storm swept over him, while a jumble of numerals rotated on a projection screen and sound effects mounted to a crescendo. It was the first time I had seen projection used on the stage. Later I saw impressive use of it in the European theatre, particularly in Russia. Its meager employment in America is one more evidence of the technical backwardness of our theatre.

In the courtroom scene everything was askew. The immobile judge, perched up high, wore a coldly cruel mask. In the final scene, the infernal adding machine which Zero operates nearly filled the stage; the keys were as big as bar stools. When we finally got through this scene, Moeller gave orders to reset one of the earlier scenes. Fifteen minutes went by, and another fifteen. It was long after midnight; we had all been in the theatre since early afternoon. Moeller sent for the stage manager, who explained apologetically that there was a jurisdictional dispute among the stagehands. The property men contended that the adding machine was scenery and must be moved by the carpenters; the carpenters insisted that it was a prop. I do not know who won the argument, but eventually the scene change was effected.

Under Moeller's direction the cast performed brilliantly. Digges, one of the finest actors I have ever worked with, was perfection in his long, difficult role. Helen Westley's comic genius was just right for Mrs. Zero. When, at the end of a long tirade directed at her mute, motionless husband, she climbed, frowzy-haired and clad in a shapeless cotton nightgown, into bed beside Digges, the assembled Theatre Guild directorate and staff roared with laughter. Margaret Wycherley was gauchely touching, Calvert impressively orotund, Robinson—another splendid actor—properly eerie. I knew that if the play did not succeed I could not put the blame on the production.

All I seem to remember about the opening is that I sat in the balcony, as I usually do, and that the audience was attentive. Certainly I was not unduly nervous, for I am always less tense on an opening night than at the dress rehearsal, when improvements can still be made. Once the first-night audience has assembled, there is nothing to do but await the verdict.

The verdict was not as favorable as I had hoped, but better than I had expected. I once asked T. S. Eliot how often he had had a really good press. He thought about it and replied, "Twice, I should say." Then he added, with a wry smile, "But my standard of a really good press is rather high." In rereading the reviews, I find them more favorable than they seemed at the time. Perhaps long experience has taught me to lower my sights. I have learned to look upon any expression of approval as a net gain.

Since the play is still being widely studied and performed, a glance at some of the comments may be in order. Most of the influential critics had good things to say. Alexander Woollcott: "a play worth seeing"; Franklin P. Adams: "deeply interesting"; Kenneth Macgowan: "a bizarre and entertaining novelty"; Burton Rascoe: "a genuine contribution to American drama"; Heywood Broun: "For the first time in our theatrical experience, expressionism has come over the footlights to us as an effective theatrical device." Others said: ". . . the best and fairest example of the newer expressionism in the theatre that it has yet produced"; "biting social satire—a highly satirical drama"; "exactly the type of play which justifies the existence of the Theatre Guild." Later, favorable reviews appeared in many periodicals. Ludwig Lewisohn, in *The Nation*, wrote a eulogistic piece. *Theatre* magazine said it was "a play which coming from Prague would excite the townsfolk to prayer and fasting."

There were many unfavorable reviews, too. Some complained of the play's sexual allusions, which would hardly be noticed today. Alan Dale pointed out that, too indolent to think of names for my characters, I had called them Mr. One, Mr. Two and so on. Burns Mantle, in his annual compendium, failed to include the play among the year's ten best. Stark Young observed that the play brought expressionism "smartly to market." In view of the play's frenzied composition and my doubts about ever getting it produced, I was tickled by this picture of myself deliberately concocting an expressionistic play with an eye to the box office.

An allegation that has persisted is that I was influenced by the German expressionists and had even borrowed liberally from them.

The fact is that, though I had heard of expressionism, I had not read any of the German plays. It was only later that I became acquainted with the work of Georg Kaiser, Walter Hasenclever and Ernst Toller. Eventually I met Hasenclever in Paris. Toller I saw now and then in New York, where he came as a refugee from the Nazis. A few days after my last meeting with him, he was found hanging in his hotel suite, presumably a suicide, though there were dark hints that he had been murdered by Nazi agents.

In spite of the limited use of expressionism in the theatre, much has been written about it. Its origin is usually traced to Frank Wedekind and Strindberg; but its emergence in Germany and the United States after World War I can be attributed to rebellion against Ibsenism and, even more, I think, to the influence of Freudian psychology and the postwar social upheavals and psychic dislocations. Actually, though, there appeared in 1916 a work that has not received the attention it deserves: Theodore Dreiser's *Plays of the Natural and Supernatural,* which contains several remarkable expressionistic one-act plays. Besides the dramatists I have mentioned, European authors of expressionistic plays include Lenormand, Capek, O'Casey and, I suppose, Brecht. In the United States there were not more than a dozen such plays produced. Besides *The Adding Machine* and another play of mine, *The Subway,* there were John Howard Lawson's *Roger Bloomer* and *Processional,* Sophie Treadwell's *Machinal,* and O'Neill's *The Hairy Ape* (and perhaps *The Emperor Jones* and *The Great God Brown* should be included). It was a movement that arose quickly and died quickly, yet had an important influence upon the theatre. Recently it has shown signs of recurrence in the work of some of the younger playwrights. In the novel and in poetry, expressionism has been widely used; in painting, it is, of course, at the moment dominant.

I tried several times to define expressionism. In an article written for the New York *Times* I said: "The author attempts not so much to depict events faithfully as to convey to the spectator what seems to him to be their inner significance. To achieve this end the dramatist often finds it expedient to depart entirely from objective reality and to employ symbols, condensations and a dozen devices which, to the conservative, must seem arbitrarily fantastic." And in my memorandum to Digges: "What we must convey . . . is a subjective picture of a man who is at once an individual and a type. . . . In the realistic play, we look at the character from the outside. We see him in terms of action and of actuality. But in the expressionistic play we subordinate and even discard objective reality and seek to express the character in terms of his own inner life. An X-ray photograph bears no resemblance to the object as it presents itself to our vision, but it reveals the inner mechanism of the object as no mere photographic likeness can."

At the end of the Guild's five-week subscription period there was still enough public interest to warrant the play's continuance. Neither its subject matter nor its method of treatment was likely to attract large audiences; but it did attract people who were interested in new techniques. It ran for an additional four weeks; then the seasonal decline in attendance forced a closing. I had no reason to be dissatisfied. A first-rate production, substantial recognition, a nine-week run: it was all more than could have been reasonably expected. Today it would be impossible to find a Broadway producer for the play—the cost of presentation alone would be a deterrent. An off-Broadway theatre might attempt it, but the cast and production could hardly measure up to the Guild's. Thus the fate of a play often depends upon extraneous considerations over which the author has no control.

In the succeeding years *The Adding Machine* has had innumerable productions. There is hardly a community or university theatre in the English-speaking world that has not produced it at one time or another. It had successful runs in London and in Paris, and it has been performed throughout the world, in almost every country that has a modern theatre. Interest in its production seems to be constant, perhaps because of the spread of automation, with its replacement of man by machines, perhaps because the play's stylized technique offers opportunities to the director who feels limited by the narrow requirements of realistic plays. Whatever the reasons, the play's survival has been a bright spot in a career that has not been without defeats and frustrations.

4

Expressionistic plays were but part of the new drama that transformed the American theatre and won for it world-wide recognition. Actually this movement was the belated end process of a dramatic renaissance that had begun in Europe late in the nineteenth century. Ibsen's first realistic play, *The League of Youth*, antedated O'Neill's *Beyond the Horizon* by exactly fifty years.

There was no lack of native playwrights prior to World War I. Though their plays were often enlivened by shrewd representation of American speech and behavior, they were, for the most part, conventional melodramas and cut-and-dried farce comedies, on a far lower literary and intellectual level than the novels of such craftsmen as Stephen Crane, Henry James, Edith Wharton and Willa Cather, or such crusaders as Jack London, Upton Sinclair and Frank Norris. Because of my freakish early start in the theatre, I became acquainted with most of the leading lights of the prewar generation of dramatists. Clyde Fitch and Charles Klein were a little ahead of my time, but, besides George M. Cohan and David Belasco, I knew Avery Hopwood, Winchell Smith, Owen Davis, George Broadhurst, Langdon Mitchell, Eugene Walter, Augustus Thomas, Samuel Shipman and Channing Pollock. All these men were prolific and highly successful; several became millionaires. Yet how many of today's theatregoers have any familiarity with their works or even with their names?

In the 1920s a whole new generation of playwrights made its appearance, rapidly superseding the older group and bringing freshness and vitality to the American theatre. After half a century of industrial development unparalleled in history, America was beginning to pause for breath, to stop and look at what it had wrought. Self-satisfaction still prevailed, but self-criticism was beginning to intrude. Sensitive observers were revealing the cruelties, fatuousness, corruption and maladjustments that lay behind the grandiose façade. I do not mean that all the new writers were satirists or social critics—though many of them were; but they all surveyed the American scene with a sharp and skeptical eye.

The dominant figure is, of course, Eugene O'Neill, recipient of four Pulitzer Prizes in drama (one posthumously) and of the Nobel Prize in literature. The power, depth and poetic insight revealed in his plays are rare in modern drama. But acknowledgment of his pre-eminence does not diminish the importance of contributions made by his contemporaries, any more than the peerlessness of Shakespeare lessens the value of the work of Jonson, Marlowe, Kyd and Webster. I am not suggesting that American plays of the twentieth century are comparable to the masterpieces of the seventeenth, but only that O'Neill, like Shakespeare, was one of a large group of writers who collectively transformed the theatre of their day.

It has been my good fortune to know most of the new writers and to have been associated with many of them in various professional activities. Except that they were nearly all born between 1890 and 1905, and all loved the theatre, it would be hard to find a common denominator. In theme and style their work covered a wide range. I have mentioned the expressionistic plays of John Howard Lawson and Sophie Treadwell. Maxwell Anderson resuscitated the historical play and brought back verse to the theatre. S. N. Behrman, Claire Kummer, Arthur Richman, Zoe Akins and Philip Barry, each with an individual approach, wrote sophisticated or whimsical comedy. George S. Kaufman, working with various collaborators, turned out a series of hilarious commentaries on the contemporary scene. Robert E. Sherwood wrote skillful parables that became increasingly serious. Paul Green and Lynn Riggs composed regional plays of the South and the Southwest. George Kelly and Susan Glaspell made subtle psychological explorations. Marc Connelly and Thornton Wilder made excursions into fantasy. George Abbott, Philip Dunning, Ben Hecht, Charles MacArthur and Bartlett Cormack produced hard-boiled topical melodramas. Paul Osborn, Sidney Howard, Martin Flavin and Edwin Justus Mayer wrote on a variety of subjects, sometimes with psychological overtones. Howard Lindsay, Russel Crouse, Clifford Odets, Lillian Hellman, Moss Hart and Sidney Kingsley did not become active until the 1930s, but they were all part of the new movement. In the musical comedy field too there were many new and original talents.

It is too soon to attempt to evaluate the movement as a whole or to appraise individual plays. Many are no doubt dated. Others, worthy of survival, are neglected because, unlike most European countries, we have no permanent theatres, no repertory companies that present vital plays year after year, generation after generation. The young theatregoer has no opportunity to see the plays that his father and grandfather enjoyed. Anthologies keep the texts alive, and drama courses perpetuate their study; but plays are written to be acted. Except for infrequent and usually inadequate productions by amateurs, yesterday's dramas are ignored; nor are those that are

performed necessarily the best. Without theatres dedicated to the
preservation of the dramatist's art, plays become obsolescent in a
way that novels, poetry, music, painting and sculpture do not.

5

I derived little financial benefit from the Guild's production of *The
Adding Machine*. In appreciation of what the organization had done
for the play, I invested nearly all my earnings in bonds to finance
the construction of its own theatre: a bit of Maurice Wertheim's
fiscal wizardry by which the Guild was actually presented a lavish
theatre by public subscription. At the laying of the cornerstone the
principal speaker was that American Maecenas, Otto H. Kahn. In
top hat and morning coat, he delivered a polished address on the
art of the drama. He was followed by Governor Alfred E. Smith, in
a brown derby, who said, "You have just hoid about the poiposes
of this the-ayter." I told this story to Alan Bunce when he was rehearsing the part of Smith in *Sunrise at Campobello,* and he used it
as a basis for his characterization. When the Guild Theatre opened,
Alexander Woollcott, looking at the elaborate tapestries in the
lobby, said, "The Gobelins will get you if you don't watch out."
Though the Guild prospered, the theatre never paid its way, and I
lost practically all that I had invested.

While I was occupied with the production of *The Adding Machine,* Grandpa died, in his ninety-fourth year. I had been away
from New York so much that I had almost lost contact with him.
When I did see him, conversation was difficult, for he had become
stone deaf and was too stubborn to use a hearing aid. Nevertheless
I mourned him, for my affection for him had always been deep.
Now my mother was the only strong link to my childhood. I rarely
saw Uncle Will, now leading a cheerless bachelor existence; my
other relatives I did not see at all.

My wife and my mother had had a rather thin time of it in East
Hampton, particularly in the winter months; so, much to my regret,
we moved back to New York. After two years of ample country life
I found it impossible to work in a cramped, stuffy New York apartment, so I rented a little studio, where I could stay overnight if I
worked late. Night is perhaps the best work time for a writer. Noise
and distraction are at a minimum; the senses seem more acute, the

imagination more vivid. But the routine of night work is not compatible with family life.

I went to work on another expressionistic play, *The Subway*, which, like *The Adding Machine*, dealt with the maladjustments of a mechanized society, though this time the central figure was sympathetic: a bewildered young girl who is crushed to death by an onrushing subway train. It had satiric moments, but its general tone was tragic. Except that it provided a good role for a young star, I saw little likelihood of its attracting managerial interest.

While I was writing *The Subway*, Philip Goodman asked me to collaborate on a play with Dorothy Parker. Goodman, a successful advertising man, had recently made his theatrical debut by producing a musical comedy hit, *Poppy*, in which W. C. Fields, long a vaudeville headliner, was starred. I came to know Goodman very well. He was physically gross, loud, hectoring and frequently insulting. But he was well read, had taste and wit, and was an entertaining companion. He considered himself far superior to the general run of theatrical producers, attributing their failures to stupidity. He insisted that there was no mystery about achieving success in the theatre: it was just a matter of using one's intelligence.

Dorothy Parker had written a first act which Goodman felt had great promise but lacked theatrical craftsmanship. Professing great admiration for *The Adding Machine*, he urged me to work with her. The act was as long as an entire play, and completely formless. The characters, suburbanites all, just went on talking and talking. But they were sharply realized, and the dialogue was uncannily authentic and very funny. Since I have always enjoyed the technical side of playwriting, I agreed to Goodman's proposal; not without some misgiving, however, for, though I had never met Dorothy, I had heard tales about her temperament and undependability.

To my relief, everything went smoothly. She was punctual, diligent and amiable; no collaboration could have been less painful. I concentrated on plot development and scene construction, while she did most of the writing. It was a simple tale of a suburban householder who, bedeviled by a sweetly dominant wife and an insufferable brat, finds solace in the companionship of a neighbor, a former chorus girl; but habit and convention are too strong, and the spark flickers out. The play's merit lay in Dorothy's shrewd observation and pungent writing.

We had a good work routine. Every few days we went over what she had written, line by line, pruning out irrelevancies and reorganizing. Then we discussed the next scene in minute detail, and she went off to write it. She was unfailingly courteous, considerate and, of course, amusing and stimulating. It was hard to believe that this tiny creature with the big, appealing eyes and the diffident, self-effacing manner was capable of corrosive cynicism and devastating retorts. I discovered that in the granite of her misanthropy there was a vein of softish sentimentality. Our relationship was cordial and easygoing, but entirely impersonal. The finished play, called *Close Harmony*, pleased Goodman, who scheduled it for the coming season. I too felt that we had done a good job.

Two other offers now came my way. Warren Munsell, business manager of the Theatre Guild, asked me to do some work on *The Mongrel*, a play by the well-known German dramatist Hermann Bahr, in which Munsell intended to star Rudolph Schildkraut. It was a routine job, but I greatly admired Schildkraut, whom I had seen in Hauptmann's *The Weavers* and in Sholem Asch's controversial *The God of Vengeance*, so I undertook it.

Almost at the same time, Sam Harris asked me to adapt another German play, *The Blue Hawaii*, by Rudolph Lothar. The play dealt with the mysterious disappearance of a rare postage stamp, to which the title referred. I think there was a murder in it, too. It was another of those exercises in dramatic technique that I seem unable to resist, so I went to work on that too.

On top of all this, I received the astonishing news that my agent had placed *The Subway* with the Actors' Theatre, a producing organization created by the Actors' Equity Association, partly to provide work for some of its members, partly to improve the tone of the theatre. There was talk of engaging Winifred Lenihan, who, after making her Broadway debut in my play *For the Defense*, had appeared in the first American production of Shaw's *Saint Joan*. For the coming theatrical year I now had contracts and advance payments for four productions. It promised to be a busy, even a lucrative, season.

Early in the season came the first jarring note. On the opening night of *Dear Sir*, a new musical production by Philip Goodman, the misbehavior of a horse on stage completely disconcerted the performers and distracted the audience; the show was a disastrous failure. Goodman, quickly losing his belief in the infallibility of his success formula, suspended operations on *Close Harmony*, intimating that he might abandon it.

Next came *The Mongrel*, directed, oddly enough, by Winifred Lenihan. Young, inexperienced and insecure, she adopted a dictatorial manner which the actors, especially the older ones, resented. I was so embarrassed by the incessant wrangling that after the first few rehearsals I stayed away. The production, except for Schildkraut's performance, was mediocre. After a few feeble weeks the play was withdrawn.

Goodman, his self-confidence shaken, persuaded Arthur Hopkins to coproduce and stage *Close Harmony*. I was glad to be working with Hopkins again—it was ten years since *On Trial*. But his directing methods, which I now saw at work for the first time, seemed very odd. At eleven the stage manager put the company through its routines. Hopkins appeared at noon, leaned against the proscenium arch and looked on for a while. Then he led the actors aside one by one, engaged them in inaudible conversation, and departed for the day. On one of these occasions, Dorothy turned to me and said, "The American Belasco!"

Hopkins leased the Gaiety Theatre, one of New York's most desirable, at a guaranteed rental of four thousand dollars a week. I was worried about opening just before Christmas, when attendance is always poor, but Hopkins reassured me, in his usual laconic manner. "Whenever you open this play," he said, "it will run for a year."

The day before the Wilmington tryout opening, we all boarded a parlor car reserved for the company. Hopkins, Goodman, Dorothy, two of the actresses and I occupied the private compartment at the end of the car. One of the performers, a connection of the prolific Drew-Barrymore family, immediately began to regale us with detailed information about the private lives and habits of dear Jack, dear Ethel and lesser members of the clan. When she paused for breath, her companion took up the burden, describing her activities in various stock companies: the parts she had played, the notices she had received. This antiphonal performance went on uninterruptedly for the three-hour trip. No one else spoke a word; what was there to say? There was no escape, either; we were trapped, elbow to elbow, knee to knee.

In the Wilmington station, Dorothy, Goodman and I stood at the car steps, a little apart from the others. Dorothy eyed the cluster of actors waiting for taxis. Then, gazing up at us with those melting eyes, she said in that deceptively appealing voice, "*Let's* go to Baltimore!"

Without a word, Goodman and I picked up our bags and the three of us climbed back into the train, just as it started to pull out. As we settled back, Goodman and I looked in bewilderment at each other, then at Dorothy.

"I'm terribly sorry," she said, as though she meant it, "but I just couldn't look at them any more!"

It was after eight when we reached Baltimore. The train had no diner, so we were famished. Goodman called H. L. Mencken, a close friend, who invited us to his hotel suite, where he supplied food and drink, as well as entertaining talk. There was a morning rehearsal, so at midnight Dorothy and I left, Goodman having decided to spend the night in Baltimore. The train stopped at every way station; it was after three when we arrived at Wilmington. A comic, edifying and wearying expedition.

Dorothy and I were disappointed in Mencken. The Mencken cult was at its height and perhaps we expected too much. He antagonized Dorothy by telling some jokes that had an anti-Negro flavor. I found him rather coarse-grained and insensitive, an impression that later meetings confirmed. I remember a stag party at which Ernest Boyd, Burton Rascoe, Paul de Kruif and Theodore Dreiser were also present. Mencken's conversation was interspersed with sex jokes that astonished me, not because they were shocking but because they were so adolescent. He also spent considerable time trying to hang a slice of Swiss cheese on Dreiser's ear. We had all had enough to drink, but nobody else's exuberance was quite so childish.

Much that Mencken wrote is, it seems to me, outmoded. He performed a valuable critical service by ridiculing the prevalent provincialism, bigotry, pomposity, ignorance and exhibitionism. But his intellectual arrogance made him contemptuous of the common man and destructively hostile to all attempts at social betterment. I think he will be best remembered for his brilliant studies of the American language.

Like so many tryouts, the Wilmington performances served

merely as dress rehearsals that gave no indication of the New York reception. What I remember best about Wilmington is Robert Benchley's opening-night telegram to Dorothy. It simply said: "That old filling has just come out." Sophisticated American humor leans heavily upon the *non sequitur*—witness the happy career of *The New Yorker*.

Hopkins and Goodman counted—not altogether secretly—on the enthusiastic support of the circle of town wits to which Dorothy and Benchley belonged. They could not have been wider of the mark. The opening-night audience and the critics evinced no interest in the play. During its three-week run the total receipts were insufficient to pay the guaranteed rental of the theatre. Subsequently, Hopkins sublet the touring rights to another producer. It played fifteen weeks in Chicago and another ten in smaller Midwestern cities. These things are inexplicable.

Soon after the *Close Harmony* fiasco, I learned that Sam Harris did not intend to go ahead with *The Blue Hawaii*. He pleaded the heaviness of his program as an excuse: like so many active producers, he had optioned more plays than he could produce. However, I suspected that he was not satisfied with the adaptation, but did not want to offend me by saying so.

My catalogue of woes was now completed by the Actors' Theatre's abandonment of *The Subway*. Casting problems and the complexity of the setting were given as the reasons. But it was rumored that the organization was in financial difficulties; and indeed its existence came to an end soon afterward: the failure of another attempt to establish a permanent theatre for the production of plays of merit.

With all my rosy prospects faded to nothingness, I felt that I must review my past as a writer—and think about my future! In the eleven years that had elapsed since I had given up the law, I had had seven plays produced (not counting one-acters); had written eight or ten others. Also, I had spent two years as a Hollywood writer. It could not be said that I had been idle, or wholly unsuccessful. Yet it seemed to me I was not really developing as I should, either as a person or as an artist. I felt it was time to make a drastic change in my way of life, to widen my horizon, seek new experiences. The longer I waited to see the world, the harder it would be to make the break. It would be foolish to wait for that great success that would finance the trip. The time to go was now. The children were old enough to travel. My wife was as eager to go as I was. Investigation had convinced me that we could live in Europe for half what it cost us in New York, so we decided to go, as quickly as arrangements could be made.

XII

The Discovery of Europe

1

It was the time of the great exodus, when the "embattled high-brows," as Frederick Lewis Allen calls them, were flocking from the sidewalks of New York and the prairies of the Middle West to the boulevard cafés and to the sands of the Côte d'Azur. This migration was another phase of the revolt against the stodginess and insular-ity of postwar America, a revolt that found expression in satirical plays, novels of social criticism, and "free" verse, and in the ad-vocacy—and often the practice—of "progressive" education and "free" love. The participants, says Allen, were "the men and women who had heard of James Joyce, Proust, Cézanne, Jung, Bertrand Russell, John Dewey, Petronius, Eugene O'Neill and Eddington; who looked down on the movies but revered Chaplin as a great artist; could talk about relativity, even if they could not understand it; . . . and doubted the divinity of Henry Ford and Calvin Cool-idge."

For the dissidents, *The American Mercury*, edited by Mencken and George Jean Nathan, was obligatory reading; so were *Vanity Fair, The New Republic* and the newly launched *New Yorker*, which announced rather smugly that it was "not for the old lady from Dubuque," a slogan it abandoned when the subscriptions from Iowa started coming in. In 1922 a book unique in the annals of literature appeared. Called *Civilization in the United States,* it contained thirty essays by a group of specialists that included Mencken, Nathan, Van Wyck Brooks, Lewis Mumford and Deems Taylor, each of whom examined some phase of American artistic, cultural or intellectual life. Their general conclusion, as summarized by the book's editor, Harold Stearns, was that "the most amusing and pathetic fact in the social life of America today is its emotional and aesthetic starvation." Stearns, a militant emigré, eventually came back and published a revised estimate of American culture.

The Stearns book was strictly for the highbrows, but its animus was vividly expressed in Sinclair Lewis' phenomenally popular novels *Main Street* and *Babbitt,* books so cogent and timely that their titles quickly became part of the American language and still connote small-town provincialism and the anti-intellectualism of a depressingly large section of the dominant business community.

Many, if not most, of those who sought escape from the cultural poverty of American life were artists, would-be artists or what may be called artistic camp followers. Great impetus was added to the migratory movement by the decline of European currencies, the French franc in particular. There was a direct relationship between the purchasing power of the dollar and the Europeanization of the American intellectual. Another influence was prohibition—described by Herbert Hoover as that "great social and economic experiment, noble in motive and far-reaching in purpose"—which now had America in its strangulating grip. On the Continent, liquor was cheap, good and plentiful.

Though I shared the distaste for American Philistinism, I felt no compulsion to expatriate myself. I put no term upon my absence, but I never doubted that I would come back. What impelled me was my inner need for development, my awareness of the painful limitations of my knowledge, my desire for new aesthetic stimuli. I wanted to experience new modes of living, to acquaint myself with richer types of civilization, particularly in the field of art.

2

Pulling up stakes was quite simple: just a matter of storing our belongings and packing our bags. One of a writer's chief blessings is his mobility: he carries his business with him wherever he goes, and finds his raw materials everywhere. My chief concern was making suitable provision for my mother. I had qualms about leaving her, but her health was good and she had many friends in New York.

The European expedition was a success from the moment we set foot on the French Line's cabin-class steamer *De Grasse*. I have made many sea voyages since in American, British, Canadian, German, Swedish, Norwegian, Italian, Japanese and Soviet ships, but have always preferred the French. I have crossed on the *Normandie*, the *Lafayette*, the *Champlain*, the *Paris*, the *France*, and the *Île-de-France*, all of which have disappeared from the Atlantic, victims of war, fire or old age.

We put up temporarily at a little hotel-pension in the Rue de Fleurus, a few steps from the Jardin du Luxembourg. I did not know that Gertrude Stein was almost our next-door neighbor; it was not until many years later that I met her for the first time at a New York party given in her honor by Carl Van Vechten and Fania Marinoff.

I immediately felt at home in Paris. A fairly wide reading of French literature, supplemented by an intense study of guidebooks and street plans, had acquainted me with the city's history, topography and monuments. Before we even unpacked, I went for a walk through streets whose names were already familiar to me. Paris, with its boulevards, parks and quais, and with its sidewalk cafés offering rest and refreshment, is the perfect city for the walker. Eventually there was hardly a corner of it that I did not traverse on foot.

We soon found a delightful apartment in the Rue Bonaparte, near the École des Beaux-Arts, a three-minute walk from the quais in one direction and from St.-Germain-des-Prés in the other. Three flights up a magnificent spiral staircase in an eighteenth-century house, it contained six high-ceilinged rooms, amply furnished in bourgeois fashion. There was an improvised bathroom and, quaintly situated just off the imposing foyer, a water closet. The monthly rent was seventy-five dollars.

Since there were many small restaurants in the neighborhood—notably Michaud's in the Rue Jacob, known to every American denizen of the Left Bank—where an excellent meal with wine cost about sixty cents, we engaged a governess instead of a cook. A well-bred Norwegian, she had come to Paris, like so many Scandinavian girls, to further her education, taking employment to help pay her way. She was well pleased with the standard monthly wage of fifteen dollars. Everything cost less than half what it had in New York. Our entire living expense came to less than sixty dollars per week. It cost me almost that much to maintain my mother in New York. It was easy to see why the footloose and the impecunious came flocking to Paris.

3

I soon began a systematic exploration of the city's museums, churches, monuments. The French Revolution had had a fascination for me ever since an older boy had shown me his drawings of marching sans-culottes bearing dripping severed heads upon pikes. At the Place de la Bastille, white paving stones marked the perimeter of the old fortress. The Carnavalet Museum was crammed with Revolutionary relics. One could identify the site of the guillotine in the Place de la Concorde, visit Marie Antoinette's cell in the Conciergerie, note the pockmarks made by young General Bonaparte's whiff of grapeshot on the façade of the Église St.-Roch. I reread Carlyle.

For the first time, I began to have opinions about architecture: the elegant octagonal Place Vendôme; the ancient Place des Vosges; the noble dome of the Invalides; the flamboyant façade of the Opera, bathed in lavender light. My opinions were not necessarily sound, but in forming them dormant faculties came into play.

And, of course, the churches. I was overwhelmed by Notre Dame, but not immediately stirred. There is something lowering about those great square towers that at first sight keeps the spirit from soaring. Countless times I have made the slow circuit of the interior, have climbed the narrow winding staircase to the bell tower and the open gallery studded with gargoyles. At the other extreme is the tiny St.-Julien-le-Pauvre, not particularly distinguished, but invested with devoutness. For me, best-loved of all is St.-Germain-des-Prés. I have gazed at its quiet, Romanesque tower hundreds of times from a seat on the terrace of the Café des Deux Magots, just opposite.

On my first visit to the Louvre I discovered that I had never really looked at paintings either. I came away from the Grand Gallery dizzy and drunk; returned soon afterward, and went back every few days, concentrating each time on half-a-dozen pictures. Attracted at first by the bright colors and pictorial prettiness of Murillo, Raphael, Vandyke, Hals and del Sarto, I went on to Mantegna, Titian, El Greco, Antonello da Messina, Rembrandt, and, in the cabinets off the Rubens gallery, single little paintings by Vermeer, Memling and Jan van Eyck, particularly the latter's *Virgin and Chancellor Rolin*, still one of my favorite paintings. One day, as I stood before a Titian in the Grand Gallery, an elderly American woman gently tugged my sleeve. Looking at me with anxious eyes, she said, "The *Mona Lisa's* over there."

Modern painting captured my interest, too. I had missed the great Armory show in New York in 1913, for no one had suggested that I go. In the Louvre the Camondo Collection, tucked away in three or four small rooms under the roof, contained canvases by Cézanne, Degas, Manet, Monet and Sisley. Others were to be seen in the Luxembourg Museum and in the dealers' galleries on both sides of the Seine. I attended an auction sale at which more than a hundred Renoirs were sold at prices that seem incredible today. Anyone who had invested ten thousand dollars would now be a millionaire. But I had not enough self-confidence to begin collecting. What is more to the point, I did not have thousands to put into paintings. But in the course of my exploration I developed a passion for painting that has taken me far and wide and given me profound aesthetic, emotional and spiritual satisfaction.

We investigated the environs: St.-Cloud, Versailles, St.-Germain-en-Laye, St. Denis, Chantilly, Fontainebleau. Then we went farther afield, to Rouen, Beauvais, Amiens, Reims, Chartres: a lavish feast of Gothic. Reims Cathedral, which somehow had survived the German bombardment, stood in the midst of the raw newness of the rebuilt city, focusing attention upon the savagery of war and marring enjoyment of the ancient fabric's beauty. The neighboring battlegrounds were desolate fields that yielded only a harvest of unexploded shells, and blasted woods reminiscent of Doré.

For Chartres I had been somewhat prepared by Henry Adams, but there could be no preparation for the emotional effect produced by the actual viewing, an effect that each visit—and I have made many—intensifies. Of all the world's great surviving structures that I have seen, none, except the Parthenon, has moved me as has Chartres. As Henry Adams says: "Chartres expressed, besides what' ever else it meant, an ambition, the deepest man ever felt—the struggle of his own littleness to grasp the infinite." The pursuit of that struggle, not through trips to Mars, but through self-enlarge-ment and elevation, seems to me humanity's best hope.

4

We went frequently to the opera, to concerts of the Pasdeloup and Lamoureux orchestras (usually given at five, a pleasant hour between the day's occupation and *apéritifs*), and to the Diaghilev Ballet. The French theatre never attracted me, partly because of linguistic difficulties, mainly because I have never been able to accept what seems to me the artificiality of the plays and of the acting. In view of its achievements, this is manifestly an absurd prejudice; but I have never pretended to be free from prejudice.

Lighter diversions included street fairs, Petit Guignol shows in the Jardin des Tuileries, Montmartre cabarets, occasionally the Folies Bergères or the Moulin Rouge, the Cirque d'Hiver (especially when the illustrious Fratellinis were performing). I much prefer the one-ring European circuses to the distracting multi-ring American af-fairs, where one really sees nothing. We sometimes went to the jumping races at Auteuil, and to Longchamps on Grand Prix day, when the mannequins paraded in front of the flower-decked pa-vilions.

The chief diversion, the time-consuming diversion that never lost its charm, was café-sitting, outdoors when the weather permit-ted, indoors when it did not; but always we sat and drank and talked. We made the rounds of the celebrated Right Bank estab-lishments: the Café de la Paix, where one was bound to encounter American "tourists" of one's acquaintance; Weber's, on the Rue Royale, one of the few places that served a snack at almost any hour; Fouquet's, on the Champs-Élysées, rendezvous of actors; the big, crowded *brasseries* of the Boulevard de Clichy.

However, we were Left Bankers, and our regular hangouts were there. Chief and best-beloved was the Deux Magots, post-World-War-II headquarters of Sartre and Company, but in my day almost monopolized by foreign residents, natives of Central Europe, Scan-dinavia—and America. (The *magots*, by the way, are not maggots, but grotesque Chinese figures, visible in the interior.) Next in order came the cafés of the Boulevard Montparnasse, favored by the artists. On a balmy evening you had to get to the Dôme early if you wanted a sidewalk table. In summer the rows of tables extended farther and farther into the pedestrian area. When the American schools closed, more adventuresome members of the teaching profession descended upon the Dôme in swarms. It was always engaging to see the lady in a print dress at the next table smile up at the waiter as she said in unsullied South-Carolinese, "Ah'd lak a choc'late sodah, please." The Rotonde, across the boulevard, was where the north-Europeans gathered. The Select, whose clientele was largely homosexual, stocked Bass's ale, which it served with the best Welsh rarebits I have ever eaten, a wonderful combination late at night. The Coupole, biggest of all, had not yet opened.

There was good reason for the popularity of the cafés. Coffee was about three cents, brandy seven or eight, vermouth-and-soda perhaps ten. Whether you piled the saucers sky high or nursed a glass of beer for a whole evening, you were unmolested. In spite of the low cost of alcohol, drunkenness was never a serious problem. Of course, many drank excessively, particularly Americans; there was loud talk and boisterous laughter, but brawls or offensive behavior were rare.

The cafés were more than just drinking places. They were social centers and, for many who inhabited wretched little furnished rooms, an extension of living quarters. Here you could meet your friends and make new acquaintances, exchange gossip or confidences, discuss your work, your health or your financial problems, transact business or kiss your girl, meanwhile enjoying a sandwich and a beer and watching the world go by—and a very lively and amusing world it was, too.

Social life was chaotic and kaleidoscopic. It was impossible to remember everyone you met. By appointment or by chance you would join acquaintances for *apéritifs*. Soon two or three tables were combined, and in due course a company of eight or a dozen moved on to a favorite restaurant, or to a new one somebody had just heard of. After dinner, to another café for coffee, brandy and fresh encounters. A random sampling of non-Americans indicates the range of acquaintanceship. There were Eugene Jolas, editor of *transition,* best-known of the short-lived "little" magazines; Helena Rubinstein, the cosmetics magnate; Walter Hasenclever, the German expressionistic dramatist; Victor Llona, a Peruvian diplomat with a patrician manner and a deft hand for a quick touch; the distinguished Romanian-born painter Rubin, still a cherished friend, now a resident of Tel Aviv; Princess Kropotkin, whose father's *Memoirs of a Revolutionist* had stirred me in my youth; Sisley Huddleston, a Gargantuan British journalist whose velveteen jacket and imperial reminded one of *Trilby,* and whose book *Back to Montparnasse* speaks charitably of my literary work but deplores my sartorial inelegance.

Our closest friends were the painters Yasuo Kuniyoshi, a Japanese resident of the United States, and his American wife, Katherine Schmidt. Under the barbarous American laws, since amended, they were both aliens, who had to return periodically to the United States or be forever barred. Desperately poor, they lived in an appalling rookery opposite an abattoir. They had no hot water, much less facilities for bathing. They used to come to our apartment for baths, as did other friends who were in the same predicament. To avoid conflicts, we worked out a bath-night schedule. Our arrangements were interesting. The apartment had no proper bathroom, but one had been improvised in a sort of butler's pantry. It contained a tub, and a gas heater that provided hot water. The bathroom had no doors; a large screen surrounding the tub ensured the bather's privacy while the traffic flowed from dining room to kitchen.

We also knew the American painters Man Ray, Marsden Hartley and Samuel Halpert, and the young composers George Antheil and Roy Harris, who were studying with the famous Nadia Boulanger. Antheil gave some recitals of his works, whose unorthodoxy outraged the French critics. The writers were legion, most of them desperately hard up, living on small allowances from home, supplemented by borrowings, or meager income from sporadic jobs. They worked for American banks and travel agencies, staffed the "little" magazines and the Paris edition of the New York *Herald,* collected commissions for conducting American tourists to shops. Sometimes they wrote a little something that sold back home. But there were a few who later distinguished themselves. One need only mention Elliot Paul, John Dos Passos, Malcolm Cowley, e.e. cummings, Donald Ogden Stewart, Ernest Hemingway, and the latter's Canadian sparring partner, Morley Callaghan.

Some of our American acquaintances—Conrad Bercovici, William Aspenwall Bradley, Sholem Asch, Ludwig Lewisohn—had become more or less permanent residents. Lewisohn, who had given up his post of dramatic critic for *The Nation* to become a propagandist for Zionism, presided over a sort of salon in the Montparnasse quarter. A meeting was held there, at James Joyce's request, to discuss the pirating of *Ulysses* by an American publisher. We all signed a strongly worded protest, which, of course, had no effect whatever. I sometimes ran into Joyce at Les Trianons, a restaurant opposite the Gare Montparnasse that specialized in regional cookery and in a particular white wine which Joyce fancied. He told me that in *Ulysses* there was a passage of one thousand words on which he had spent a thousand hours. In general he was exasperatingly taciturn, a trait that prompted Dorothy Parker to remark, "I guess he's afraid he might drop a pearl." On another evening at Lewisohn's, I watched in fascination as Sinclair Lewis consumed an entire bottle of brandy.

Two Parisian friendships have been particularly enduring and enriching. One is with Marvin Lowenthal, bibliophile, *bon vivant* and lively conversationalist. One Thanksgiving we decided to produce an American dinner, with the aid of Madame Le Conte, proprietress of Au Rendez-vous des Mariniers, a tiny, sawdust-floored restaurant on the Île St.-Louis. The mushroom soup, the celery and olives, the turkey with chestnut stuffing presented no problem. For the mince pie we had to scour Paris to find an American grocery that had mincemeat in jars. Spiked with brandy and encased in pastry from the cunning hand of Madame Le Conte, it developed into a pie such as no American kitchen has ever produced. A few choice bottles contributed to a meal of monumental stature.

The Lowenthals lived on the Île St.-Louis (in the same building in which the Curie family had an apartment), that placid residential haven in the heart of Paris. Their windows afforded a charming view of the apse of Notre Dame, on the neighboring island. The house was easily identifiable in fair weather, for the concierge was sure to be seated on a square of carpet atop the quai's parapet, fishing with a long rod in the muddy waters of the Seine —for what, I do not know. The Lowenthals had a cook and man of all work, a eunuch named Mohammed who claimed he had seen better days in the harem of the deposed Sultan of Turkey. He had a low opinion of women and refused to take orders from Sylvia; they had to be transmitted through Marvin.

Another friend whom I met in Paris is Lewis Galantière, as well-rounded and amiable a man as I have ever known: urbane, sophisticated, erudite, witty, a brilliant linguist, a skillful translator, an able writer. Equally at home in the worlds of letters, finance and public affairs, he has been an executive of the International Chamber of Commerce, an editor of *Vanity Fair*, a foreign expert for the Federal Reserve Bank and program director of Radio Free Europe. The Galantières had a pleasant apartment on the Boulevard St.-Michel, where they gave lively parties. Lewis introduced me to Madame Léonie Jean-Proix, who undertook to translate *The Adding Machine*. It was produced by one of the foremost French directors, Gaston Baty; but I was back in America, so I did not see the production.

But what of French friendships? The sad truth is that I formed almost none in all my time in Paris. The only Frenchman whom I knew at all well was H. R. Lenormand, whose play *Les Ratés* had been produced by the Theatre Guild, under the title *The Failures*. The last time I saw Lenormand was in New York; he was on his way to the Fiji Islands to get material for a play! We got on well together; he spoke excellent English, so there was no language barrier.

For my inability to speak French properly I have only my own wrongheadedness to blame. My wife went to a school of languages and applied herself diligently. She had the advantage, too, of a predisposition to French, for her father had been born in Alsace prior to the Franco-Prussian War. Surrounded by Americans and engrossed in the appreciation of art, I did not want to take the time and the trouble to study French. I picked up enough for utilitarian purposes and let it go at that. I have paid for my irrational stubbornness, for in my extensive travels and frequent attendance at international congresses I have been seriously handicapped by my inability to carry on in any language but English.

However, language was not the only barrier. I think many Americans will agree that the French, though broad-minded enough in their reception of alien art and alien refugees, are inclined to be provincial, hidebound and reluctant to accept foreigners socially. They have rigid notions about behavior, especially in externals. Their traditional politeness, one finds, is apt to be formal and superficial. Very often a graciously turned phrase is charged with mockery or downright rudeness.

The American exiles of the 1920s constituted a tight little enclave in a society that tolerated them but did not encourage their
eager desire to become assimilated. The aloofness of the French
was aggravated by the unconventional behavior and eccentric attire of some of the visitors—a minority, but unfortunately a visible
and audible one. Deeply resented, too, was the financial advantage
that the exchange situation gave to Americans. The more the
coveted dollars flowed in, the greater became antagonism to the
spenders, who could live on a scale far beyond the range of their
French opposite numbers. Matters were not helped by the tendency
of some of the foreigners to gloat about the cheapness of everything.
Thousands of Americans enjoyed the French mode of life, the
glory of French art, the beauty of Paris, but few, I think, ever
really became acclimatized. All this became for me, in time, the
subject of a play.

5

I had little time or, for that matter, inclination for writing. That did
not disturb me very much, for I had come abroad to learn and to
savor new experiences, and I was doing both at a great rate. A
few months after my arrival in Paris, Irma Kraft, head of a new
producing organization that was planning to do *The Subway* in New
York, asked me to meet her in London. My reading had made
London even better known to me than Paris, yet I did not glide
as easily into its ambiance and rhythm. Coming from Paris, I found
London grimy, ugly and uncomfortable. It took many subsequent
visits to make me appreciate its solidity and strength, the homely
restfulness of its parks, the quiet dignity of its many residential
squares, the richness of its art treasures and historic associations.

Most of my short visit was spent in a whirl of social activity. I met
many friendly people, most of whom, I was surprised to learn, were
acquainted with *The Adding Machine.* How the myth of English
coldness and aloofness ever arose has always puzzled me. Nowhere
have I encountered more kindness and hospitality than in England.

I had arranged a meeting with David Garnett, whose novel
A Man in the Zoo had struck me as excellent play material. We
reached a tentative agreement, but when we met again in Paris

and I outlined the changes I thought were necessary to transfer the book to the stage, he seemed so distressed that, rather than have him feel I was mutilating his work, I dropped the project. But I did not lose interest in it. Twenty years later I persuaded Kurt Weill that the book would make a good musical. Again I had a session in London with Garnett—now so aged that I hardly recognized him—but again there were obstacles, so I finally gave up.

We spent the summer in Switzerland, at a small boarding school on Lac Leman, run by an Englishwoman but international in character, where our children were to remain for the school year. The swimming was good; on clear days, the gleaming panorama of the Mont Blanc massif was an added enjoyment. The school was rather faddish, with its strictly vegetarian regime and its general air of Christian Socialism. Before returning to Paris, we made a tour of Switzerland. For me it is the least interesting of all European countries. The scenery is magnificent; cleanliness and comfort prevail. But I am soon surfeited by nature's grandeur, and man does not live by soap and water alone.

In Paris, I went to work on a new play, *Life Is Real*, again a technical novelty: a man's life story, from birth to death, enacted in brief episodes, while a cynic and a sentimentalist seated at opposite sides of the proscenium interpret the action, always coming, of course, to different conclusions.

Having decided to go to New York to market the play, I booked passage from Genoa, so that we might see something of Italy before I left. We went first to Pisa, then to Florence for a first comprehensive survey of Italian painting. The Louvre has many superb examples of Renaissance masters, but almost no works by Botticelli, Fra Angelico, Masaccio, Uccello, Simone Martini or Gentile da Fabriano.

In Venice we were joined by our children, down from Switzerland for the Christmas holidays. In December the Piazza, which in August resembles Grand Central Station during the rush hours, is almost deserted. It is too chilly to sit outdoors; one takes a gondola for the experience rather than for enjoyment. But what a city for walking—a city without a wheel turning, unique in the world! We attended High Mass in San Marco on Christmas, an eye-filling display of pomp and ceremony: the solemn evolutions of the celebrants, the rich vestments and encrusted utensils, the ranked choristers, the flickering candlelight upon the gold mosaics of the low-domed ceiling. If you moved around to the side of the altar, you could see the baby spotlights concealed by the pillars. Religion and drama, the temple and the theatre: the kinship is close.

6

After nearly a year's absence, I was happy to see my mother and my friends. The New York theatre was at its all-time peak; the new generation of playwrights was in full swing. In that 1925–26 season there were about seventy Broadway theatres in operation, something like two hundred productions. With the advent of talking pictures, a year or so later, the Broadway stage began its steady decline to the present level of thirty theatres and sixty productions.

During my brief visit I saw several interesting plays by the new writers: O'Neill's *The Great God Brown*, George Kelly's *Craig's Wife*, John Van Druten's *Young Woodley*. *The Dybbuk* was at the Neighborhood Playhouse; Basil Sidney was doing *Hamlet* in modern dress; the Musical Studio of the Moscow Art Theatre was presenting *Carmencita and the Soldier*. A year earlier I had expressed to a friend my regret at leaving for Europe without having seen *Abie's Irish Rose*, then in the fourth year of its run. He suggested that I see it on my return. I now did, and found it good enough popular entertainment at the comic-strip or Hollywood level.

From a business point of view the trip was successful. The Theatre Guild offered me a contract for *Life Is Real*. When I asked that the proposed five-hundred-dollar advance be increased to a thousand, pointing out that the difference could mean little to the Guild, since a blizzard could cost them more than that at a single performance, Philip Moeller replied, "That's true, but we can't do anything about the blizzard." It was a candid statement of the typical managerial attitude, but hardly what one would expect from an organization of artists. The Guild also asked me to work on a comedy about academic life, written by Burdette Kinne, a young instructor at Columbia. Like Dorothy Parker's original script, it was full of shrewd observation and amusing dialogue but lacked form.

A crisis in the relationship between dramatists and producers delayed the signing of both my contracts. For years a standard form of dramatic contract recommended by the Authors' League of

America had been in general use. Lately, abuses had crept in: royalties were being reduced, payments were in default, rights were curtailed. With the growing importance of motion picture rights, new problems arose. Traditionally the sale of these rights had been handled by the managers, who shared the proceeds equally with the authors. It now appeared that certain managers were making collusive arrangements with motion picture companies whereby, in return for salaries, financing or other benefits, they sold the rights for less than the fair market value—to the author's detriment, of course.

When the managers refused to enter into discussions looking to the adoption of a contract that would correct these abuses, the playwrights organized the Dramatists' Guild, as a subsidiary of the Authors' League, and, following the example of the actors six or seven years earlier, called a strike. In response to an appeal from George Middleton and Arthur Richman, the guild's leaders, almost every leading American playwright pledged himself to sign no production contract until a collective agreement had been adopted. The managers, finding themselves without plays for the next season, quickly capitulated. Within a few weeks, a contract known as the Minimum Basic Agreement was ratified. It has been in effect ever since.

The agreement, which has profoundly influenced the mechanics and economics of play production, establishes the Dramatists' Guild as the collective-bargaining agency for playwrights. Whether or not the guild is a trade-union is a debatable question; but, trade-union or not, it operates a union shop. Managers may deal only with guild members, and guild members only with managers who are signatory to the basic agreement. The guild has the power to discipline playwrights or managers who violate the agreement, a power it has not infrequently exercised. The agreement, a voluminous document strengthened in its periodic renewals, deals with every aspect of play production, defines the author's rights, establishes minimum terms, provides safeguards against defaults, and puts the disposition of motion picture rights in the hands of an impartial negotiator. By providing for compulsory arbitration of disputes, it has eliminated litigation almost entirely.

The Dramatists' Guild, like the Actors' Equity Association, has been a steadying influence in an industry which is characterized

by waste and inefficiency and in which sharp practices, if not controlled, would soon become prevalent. One of the founders of the
guild, I was elected to its council when I came back to America to
live. I have served on it ever since, as well as on the contract committee and as one of the guild's representatives on the council of
the Authors' League. For four years I was the guild's president. The
countless hours I have given to guild activities I consider well
spent; the associations have been priceless. Many old colleagues
are no longer living: Sidney Howard, Robert Sherwood, Maxwell
Anderson, Owen Davis, Kurt Weill, Arthur Richman, George Kaufman, Oscar Hammerstein, Philip Barry, Rachel Crothers, Moss Hart.
But, happily, many of my contemporaries still gather about the
luncheon table at council meetings: Marc Connelly, Howard
Lindsay, Russel Crouse, Richard Rodgers, Arthur Schwartz, Lillian Hellman, Sidney Kingsley. The vacant places have been ably
filled by the younger men and women who are keeping the American theatre alive.

When the dramatists had won their fight for recognition, I completed my negotiations with the Theatre Guild. The advance payments conveniently covered the cost of my trip. As for the plays, the
familiar pattern repeated itself. In due course, the Guild dropped
both *Life Is Real* and the Kinne play. I sold *Life Is Real* twice again,
but except for a transitory production in Germany it has never been
performed. *The Subway,* dropped by the Kraft organization, was
optioned by another producer, Charles Hopkins (not related to
Arthur), who eventually dropped it, too. The flow of advance royalties was useful, but it was no compensation for my frustrated hopes.

7

After six weeks in New York, I was glad to return to Paris. I took
my mother with me. Though she had many friends in New York,
I knew that she did not enjoy living alone. Besides, her life had
been so devoid of pleasures that I wanted to give her an opportunity
to see something of the world.

My wife was not pleased. I had not expected her to be, for her
disapproval of my mother's living with us had always been evident.
I was not indifferent to her attitude; I knew that almost any woman
objects to being saddled with her husband's mother. But circum-

stances do alter cases. My mother, now in her late sixties, had no one but me to rely upon. Had she been meddlesome or domineering, I would certainly not have imposed her upon my wife. But she was undemanding, self-effacing, good-humored; the children loved her, and she was most helpful with them. From my point of view my marriage had never attained the kind of intimacy that makes the presence of a third person an intrusion. In the absence of any absorbing interests of her own, my wife was completely dependent upon me; I deliberately set up barriers to keep myself from being swamped by possessiveness. Up to a point, I made broad concessions to domesticity; beyond that I did as I pleased. Whether this was intelligent self-preservation or cold-blooded selfishness is not for me to say. Perhaps it savored of both. At any rate, the problem of my mother was a constant source of discord.

We were soon off on our wanderings again. When the children's school moved en masse to Arles for the spring holiday, we went there, too. I instantly fell in love with Provence. There are fine Roman remains everywhere. Arles itself has an arena, an amphitheatre and a Gallo-Roman cemetery; it also has my best-beloved of all small Romanesque churches, St.-Trophime, with its exquisite cloister. And everywhere one sees the canals and wind-blown poplars that van Gogh memorialized, and the little farmsteads, known as *mas,* sheltered by wattled fences from the chilling mistral that blows and blows. On Saturdays there is a vivid market in Arles; the cookery is spicy; the women, said to be descended from Greek colonists, are beautiful (the older ones sometimes wear the regional costume). On Sunday mornings, in the Place du Forum, the farm laborers gather at the cafés to line up jobs for the coming week.

We traveled and traveled, lingering here and there: Marseilles, the Riviera, and the Casino at Monte Carlo; the spectacular Route des Alpes to Grenoble; the great Gothic cathedral of Bourges and the châteaux of Touraine. Then a quiet summer in a little house on the Lac d'Annecy, in Haute-Savoie, with expeditions to Chamonix and Aix-les-Bains.

Our next major expedition was to Germany. With my childhood conditioning, I had expected to be delighted with Germany and its way of life, but everything suffered by contrast to France, though it must be said that the people were more friendly. In Munich the music was, of course, splendid. We heard *Elektra, Fidelio* and a particularly fine performance of *Die Meistersinger*. During an intermission I was enchanted by the spectacle of a frail old lady who took from her jet reticule a large sausage sandwich, which she avidly consumed. In general, though, I was repelled by the prevalent grossness and overindulgence of the appetites. At the Oktoberfest, the annual jamboree held in Viktoria Park, each of the city's numerous breweries had erected a pavilion furnished with long trestle tables and benches. At one end was a large brass band; along the sides, enormous kegs, and counters laden with food, mostly smoked meats. Beer was sold in liter jugs only. While I put down my liter others at our table consumed two or three; they were still at it when we left. At night the scene was one of reeling drunkenness and wild disorder, an unattractive Saturnalia. Unattractive in another way was the display of anti-Semitic posters, a portent of things to come. I remember one that announced a meeting to combat "Jewish-Marxism," with a warning to Jews to stay away.

Ludwig Lewisohn had given me a letter of introduction to Thomas Mann. I mailed it to him and was promptly invited to tea. A heavy, sneezing cold made me hesitate about accepting, but I risked it. We were warmly received, but I was a little taken aback to learn that Mann hardly knew Lewisohn; I had assumed they were old friends. We had a very animated conversation. I spoke English, Mann German, a basis on which we got on very well. However, I associate the visit with one of those trivial but excruciatingly embarrassing moments that haunt one for the rest of one's life. On leaving, I was puzzled by a sudden coldness in Mrs. Mann's manner. As we walked to the bus, my sneezes, which I had managed to keep under control, overcame me. I reached into my breast pocket for my handkerchief and pulled out the tea napkin! I was appalled, for I could just hear my hostess going on about those souvenir-hunting Americans. To send back the napkin with a note of apology seemed somehow too banal and absurd. The Manns either forgot the incident or did not hold it against me, for in subsequent meetings in Europe and in southern California, where they lived during the war, they were most cordial.

Nuremberg was another city that for me failed to live up to its reputation. Evidently I should have visited Germany *before* France. At Mannheim we saw one vivid reminder of the war: French soldiers guarding the bridge across the Rhine. For the rest, one could hardly believe that it was only eight years since Germany's unconditional surrender and less than five since the ruinous inflation. In contrast to victorious France, everything was booming. Industry was humming, employment was at a high level, everyone seemed well fed and well dressed. One had the impression of a strong, lusty, determined, efficient people. While France seemed decadent, Germany was patently on the march. Yet I gave my heart to France.

8

My mother now returned to New York. The European trip had been a great experience for her; she talked about it for the rest of her life. We settled down in a Paris apartment, where I wrote a novel called *Papa Looks for Something*, a fantasy written in the deliberately naïve style of a story for children. It was a psychological parable of a man's struggle to liberate himself from servitude, conformity and his own inhibitions, a theme that has obsessed me all my life and that has recurred, in one way or another, in almost everything I have written. I enjoyed working in the unfamiliar medium. Though I showed the book to several publishers, I never made a real effort to sell it.

We had an ever-widening circle of acquaintances. Ernest Gruening and his family lived for a while on the Left Bank and we saw them quite often. Ernest, a liberal, fearless newspaperman, had been managing editor of *The Nation* and then editor of the Boston *Traveler*. Later he became governor of Alaska and one of its first senators. I regret that I never availed myself of his invitations to visit Alaska during his governorship.

Another frequent caller at our apartment was Sherwood Anderson, whom I liked very much. Outwardly rugged, he had a sensitivity that I missed in Mencken and Sinclair Lewis. Anderson was another of the many writers of stature whom I have met—Galsworthy, Dreiser, Joyce, Sean O'Casey, Edgar Lee Masters, J. B. Priestley, Ford Madox Ford—who felt that they had received inadequate critical and popular recognition. Some were bitter, some rueful; to all it was a matter of vital concern. It has been so with painters and composers I have known. Do artists overestimate the importance of their work? Do they refuse to be satisfied with anything less than unqualified praise and wide popularity? Or is it that the artist in modern industrial societies, the United States and England in particular, has an inferior status? Undoubtedly both factors are contributory. A diminution of the artist's *amour-propre* is unlikely; but it is not hard to envisage a society in which artistic achievement is as highly regarded and as well rewarded as business enterprise.

Another quick trip to New York to market my wares produced no results. Among the handful of passengers on the voyage back to France were Philip Barry and his family, en route to the Riviera. The ship was slow, the weather inclement; to pass the time, Barry and I went to work on a play. Since Barry too was in the doldrums, we thought it would be a good idea to turn out a popular success that would enrich us both. The play was to be a mystery melodrama with comic overtones. The murder was to be cleverly committed in full view of the audience, without their being aware of it. There were such surefire ingredients as a spinsterish detective, a subtle villain and a Helen Hokinson clubwoman. By the time we reached Le Havre we had completed the scenario of a play that could not fail. It remained only to write it—an operation that proved to be extraordinary indeed.

The Barrys were leaving for Cannes; we were planning to go to southern Italy. I agreed to write a draft of the first act and to stop over at Cannes to discuss it with Barry. But at Marseilles we decided to take a Japanese steamer that stopped at Naples en route to the Orient. I wrote an apology to Barry, promising to send him the draft soon.

Our carefully chosen destination was the Pensione Minerva, on Capo di Sorrento, a little promontory not far from Sorrento itself. We had large airy rooms, with balconies commanding a wide view of the Bay of Naples, dominated by Vesuvius. The volcano was active that spring; at night flames blazed against the black, starry sky. Every day we went down a lava-paved lane, between lemon groves with stone walls over which little green lizards scampered, to the ruins of a Roman villa, amid whose pillars we changed to bathing suits. Sometimes we visited neighboring fishing villages or scrambled up steep hillsides set with ancient, twisted gray-green olive trees. The *pensione* itself was spotless, due undoubtedly to the fact that the proprietor's wife was Swedish. Meals were ample and delicious: hearty soups, excellent *paste*, bowls of fruit, fresh seafood from the villages, unlimited quantities of local wine and cheese. The total cost for the four of us was about fifty dollars per week.

As on my previous visit, I had been a little hesitant about going to Italy, because of my detestation of Mussolini. Like all liberals I had been outraged by the cynical murder of the Socialist leader Matteotti. But I concluded that enjoyment of the beauties of the Bay of Naples did not imply an endorsement of Fascism. If I had confined my travels to countries whose government I admired, my range would have been limited indeed. The only evidence of political activity that we saw was a dislocation in traffic due to Il Duce's promotion of automobile racing. Every few days the roads were cleared and *carabinieri* were stationed at every gate to prevent egress while, for an hour or two, the racing cars roared by.

The villa just across the road from the Pensione Minerva was occupied by Maxim Gorki, who had come to Italy to seek a cure for tuberculosis. I saw him almost every day, pacing the terrace, a heavy, gray, pensive figure. I had admired much that he had written, especially his vivid account of his childhood and youth. Though I wanted very much to make his acquaintance, my aversion to intrusiveness kept me from attempting any approach.

My desultory progress in the study of Italian was suddenly accelerated by a sensational international event: Lindbergh's New York–Paris flight. Too excited to wait for the arrival of the *Herald* from Paris, I managed with the aid of a dictionary and the *pensione's* staff to spell out the reports in the local dailies. For the first time, I was interested in the possibilities of aviation; I wondered if I would live long enough to fly the Atlantic.

We lingered on in Sorrento, making the classical excursions to Capri and Pompeii, and by carriage over the extravagantly—but not too extravagantly—praised Sorrento–Amalfi road. I sent off a first act to Barry, received from him a revised draft, and set to work on a second act. We agreed to meet during the summer, somewhere in Central Europe—vaguely Switzerland, Zurich perhaps.

In Rome we found another pleasant *pensione*—Swiss, this time— overlooking the Piazza di Spagna, not far from the Pincio Gardens. We sampled the city's wonders, until the unbearable heat sent us

fleeing to Bolzano, in the south Tirol, for a breath of air. Bolzano—
the name is an Italianization of Bozen—was part of the loot demanded by Italy as a reward for joining the Allies in World War I.
This crude act of annexation was typical of the cynical jobbery that
characterized the postwar settlement. The war, one of whose os-
tensible objectives had been the self-determination of subject
peoples, had resulted, here in the Tirol, in the incorporation of the
Austrian population into a nation with which it had no ethnic,
linguistic, cultural or psychological ties. The effect upon the inhabitants was painful; they were treated as a conquered people,
not as compatriots. Italians occupied the key jobs; Italian settlers
were being infiltrated to leaven the indigenous mass. In the little
public square, formerly the Wilhelm von der Vogelweide Platz, now
the Piazza Vittorio Emanuele, a towheaded band blared out the
Italian national anthem. At the postoffice, where Italian was the
obligatory language, the struggles of a German-speaking peasant
trying to buy a stamp from the German-speaking clerk were pitiable.

At Innsbruck we lingered for almost a month. We did not stay
in the town itself, but on the cliff called Hungerberg, by funicular
only five minutes from the central square. Our hotel was perched
on the cliff's edge; our balcony almost overhung it. We could see
the municipal band performing in the square; if the wind was right
we could hear the music, too. A mile away was the airport. The
arriving and departing planes flew on a level with our balcony, so
close that the pilots leaned out of the open cockpits and waved to
us. Lindbergh's exploit had aroused my interest in flying; now the
daily passage of the planes was irresistibly tantalizing. We were going by rail to Salzburg, for the music festival; after weighing the
risk, we decided to fly. So, not without trepidation, we made our
first flight, in a tiny single-engine biplane quite unlike the jets of
today. My younger children have no conception of a world in which
the automobile, the motion picture, the airplane, radio and television were astonishing novelties. It is hard to believe that there
could ever again be, in so short a period, so many radical changes
in the externals of life.

Salzburg again is unique: one of those places that must be seen
to be believed. Even one who does not incline toward the romantic
and the baroque cannot resist its appeal. The festival was then the
best in Europe; still is, perhaps, though it may be excelled by Edin-

burgh. We drowned ourselves in Mozart: *Don Giovanni* in the Stadttheatre; the Vienna Philharmonic in the Mozarteum; the Requiem in the cathedral, with the voices floating down from the choir loft; "Eine kleine Nachtmusik" in the courtyard of the archbishop's palace, illuminated only by the tiny candles on the music stands.

In the drama section Max Reinhardt was, of course, dominant, with a fantastic *Midsummer Night's Dream* in the Festival Hall (a converted riding school), and a spectacular open-air *Jedermann* in the cathedral square, with the cathedral's façade as a backdrop and voices calling Jedermann from all the neighboring church towers. Just across the German border, we visited Bad Reichenhall, and the not yet infamous little town of Berchtesgaden.

During all this moving about I kept up an active exchange of manuscripts with Barry, for it was apparent that the projected meeting in Switzerland would never take place. Somehow or other, we managed to get the play finished. Barry was enthusiastic, confident that it would be a great success. I thought we had done a workmanlike job, but innate skepticism and painful experience made me a little less optimistic than he. We agreed to meet in Paris, at summer's end to discuss the marketing of the play.

9

We took a steamer down the beautiful brown Danube to Vienna. I wish I had seen Vienna in the days of its imperial splendor. In 1927 it was merely a huge head attached to a diminutive body: a hydrocephalous midget. But though no longer a world capital, it still ranked among European cities with London, Paris and Rome. For me the chief of its many attractions were the masterpieces of Pieter Brueghel the Elder, a painter previously almost unknown to me.

The prevalent poverty was distressingly evident. At a large outdoor café in the Prater only a few tables were occupied, while hundreds of persons who had not even the price of a cup of coffee pressed against the railings to hear the music. No wonder there was political unrest. A few weeks before our arrival an uprising had been savagely suppressed by the antidemocratic central government. Many lives were lost; the Palace of Justice had been badly damaged by fire.

While we were in Vienna, an occurrence in Massachusetts aroused world-wide horror and anger and gave America a bad name among liberals and radicals everywhere. After seven years of legal struggle, Sacco and Vanzetti were electrocuted. In Vienna, with its large Social Democratic population, the day of the execution was a day of mourning. The left-wing papers, black-bordered, carried not only detailed stories of the celebrated case, characterized as a judicial lynching, but also recapitulations of the Chicago Haymarket Riot trials and other examples of the administration of justice under capitalism. It was not a happy day for an American who loved his country. I regretted that I had not been in Boston to participate in the demonstration against the carrying out of the death sentence.

Suddenly we decided to return to the United States. We had never thought of ourselves as expatriates; we had come over to enjoy, for a time, European life and culture. Now, after two and a half years, several considerations made it advisable for us to go back. Though the children had learned much in the course of our wanderings, we felt that their education should be stabilized. Another factor was the progress, or rather lack of progress, of my work. Continued absence was weakening my ties with the theatre and impeding my career as a writer, or at any rate as a family provider. I had been willing to pay the price for what I was getting out of my European sojourn, but I could not go on doing so forever.

When Frank Harris wrote me that the Shuberts were interested in producing my long-forgotten adaptation of *The Blue Hawaii*, I felt I should be there. A letter from Barry clinched it. In Paris he had met the well-known producer-director Guthrie McClintic—husband of Katharine Cornell—and had asked him to turn over the script of our play, *Cock Robin*, to a New York typist. On the boat McClintic had read the play and had cabled Barry an offer to produce it in the fall. It was too important a prospect to be ignored. So we decided to get back for the opening of school and the beginning of rehearsals.

This settled, I made a purchase that seemed inconsequential at the time. As a lasting souvenir of the long sojourn, nothing seemed more appropriate than paintings—modern ones, for I could not afford Old Masters. There were plenty to be had in Vienna. We finally chose two water colors: a landscape by Maurice Vlaminck and a nude by a Viennese painter, Egon Schiele, who died just after World War I, and whose work was almost unknown in America until a few

years ago. The pictures were inexpensive, but there was the homeward journey to be provided for. We solved the financial problem
by traveling back to Paris third class instead of second. Those two
water colors were the beginning of a collection that has steadily
grown and has become one of the joys of my life.

10

We stopped in Belgium long enough to savor the richness of Flemish
art, in which Antwerp, Ghent and Bruges abound; then returned
to Paris for a last taste of its delights. It was a good time to be
leaving France. The franc had been slipping and slipping; it looked
as though it might follow the course the German mark had taken
five years earlier. There were disturbing political rumblings; people
were tense and edgy. The Parisians, never particularly cordial to
foreigners, were now openly hostile. They had to stand by and
watch the aliens, especially the Americans, stock up with merchandise they themselves could no longer afford. At the banks, knots of
well-to-do Americans kept their eyes glued on bulletins that announced fluctuations in the rate of exchange, waiting for another
drop so that they could get a few more francs for their dollars.
This did not go down well with the French. Nor did the fad,
adopted by some exuberant tourists, of pasting hundred-franc notes
on the outside of their valises. I resisted the temptation to snap up
art bargains, confining my purchases to a few inexpensive prints by
Matisse, Marie Laurencin and Foujita.

Our return to Paris coincided with the arrival of hundreds of
members of the American Legion, who had come over to attend
the organization's tenth-anniversary celebration. Careful preparations for the event had been made, especially with respect to public
relations. An American friend of mine who had close connections
with the French press was asked to handle the publicity. He agreed
on condition that he was to have a million francs to use at his dis-
cretion. During the convention, the only newspapers that criticized
the Legion were the Socialist L'Oeuvre and the Communist L'Hu-
manité.

The behavior of the Legionnaires was characterized by the boor-
ishness, bad taste and rowdyism that are typical of the annual
gathering of this aggregation of professional patriots. In American

cities one endures it with resignation, knowing that the boys will soon be going home to their service stations, funeral parlors and haberdasheries. But on foreign soil, and in Paris of all places, the American who esteems his country and values its good name squirms at the antics of these ill-bred middle-aged adolescents.

An uproar in the Rue de Lille informed me that the Legionnaires were in town. Drawn to the window of my hotel room, I saw one of the visiting merrymakers on the balcony outside his room at the Hotel Palais d'Orsay, across the street. Stripped down to his underwear, he was brandishing a bottle to which he had frequent recourse. To the passing women in the street below he addressed pointed invitations; to the men he shouted, "What you make in francs I make in dollars." For almost the only time in my life, I wished that I were anything but an American. This opening note was repeated over and over, with variations. Everywhere one saw blowzy men in fatigue caps, drunk, boisterous, quarrelsome, trying to bargain with shopkeepers, drinking champagne at little bistros at eleven in the morning, lining up in the stifling heat and the stench of frying fat to buy doughnuts in the barracks which the Salvation Army had erected in the citadel of French cookery.

On the final day of the convention, the day of the big parade, there was an incident that was both hilarious and grim. We posted ourselves in the Place de la Concorde to get a good view of the proceedings. The Parisians who packed the huge square stared in amazement as the paraders, state by state, marched by, the trim drum majorettes cavorting, the men arrayed like members of the chorus in an operetta with a Ruritanian setting. In due course the Massachusetts delegation appeared, resplendent in scarlet or green or purple. Suddenly someone shouted, *"Où est la chaise électrique?"* The memory of the Sacco-Vanzetti execution was fresh; the crowd took up the cry with savage delight. Soon it filled the whole square. The men from Massachusetts, interpreting it as some special tribute, beamed and waved in grateful acknowledgment.

A few days later we left for home. It was the end of the most enriching period in my life. My days had been filled with aesthetic and sensory delights. I had widened my knowledge of history, geography, language, politics and manners—as well as food and drink. I had begun to acquire an understanding of painting, sculpture and architecture; had broken through the barrier of my introversion and become freer in my association with people. If I was not a different person, I was certainly a more developed one. Reluctant to leave Europe, I consoled myself with the promise that I would return soon. However, it was nearly three years before I saw Paris again.

XIII

The Play That Had No Chance

1

It was not easy to readjust to life in America. I wanted to live in the country, but was unwilling to impose my preference upon my wife and my mother. However, I was firm about not setting up an elaborate housekeeping establishment, for I was finding the minutiae of domestic life more and more oppressive. So we moved into a small apartment hotel, a mode of life to which we had become accustomed in Europe.

On my return, I had hurried straight to Boston, where *The Blue Hawaii*, retitled *Is He Guilty?*, was being tried out. I could have spared myself the trip. Someone in the Shubert employ had made alterations in the play, not the least confusing of which was the merger of two acts that had different locales and were separated by a considerable time interval. The whole thing was hopeless; the management wisely decided not to bring the play into New York.

More promising was the news from Barry, whom I saw for the first time since we had parted company on the dock at Le Havre. He told me that McClintic intended to produce *Cock Robin* as soon as he had put on another play of Barry's. (Called simply *John*, it was about John the Baptist.)

In spite of this financial prospect, I was unhappy about my career. I tried putting the blame for my lack of progress on the commercialism of the theatre and upon the distracting demands of domestic life; but in the end I came to the conclusion that I lacked the qualifications of a good writer. I had ideals and aspirations, good dramatic ideas too. But the ideas never seemed to develop fully; the achievement always fell far short of the goal.

What was I to do? Give up writing as a bad job? But if I did, then what? Economic considerations apart, I had to have an occupation; to live in idleness was unthinkable. A return to the practice of law had no attraction for me. Nor did any form of employment: Hollywood, civil service, teaching. I had drunk too long and too headily of freedom. The solution seemed to be to regard writing as a trade, forgoing dreams of excellence and of eminence, learning to be content with breadwinning competence. With this troublesome question settled, and with rehearsals of *Cock Robin* three months off, I began work on a new play, a tragedy with some seventy-five characters.

Some years previously, I had written a play called *The Sidewalks of New York*—a title not yet hackneyed through association with the career of Al Smith. It was another technical experiment: a play without words; not a pantomime, in which speech is indicated by gesture, but a series of situations in which there was no need for speech. It dealt with the struggles of a boy and a girl who come separately to New York to make their own way (a theme to which I returned many years later in *Two on an Island*). It contained a series of episodes illustrative of various phases of New York life, linked only by the passage of the same set of characters through them. Some of the scenes were realistic, some symbolic, some expressionistic. The intended total effect was a panoramic impression of New York. It was a very special play, and when, after long deliberation, the Theatre Guild turned it down, I made little effort to market it. Now, viewing New York with a European perspective, seeing it in a way that was new and vivid, that somehow illuminated my childhood memories, I was seized by an irresistible impulse to give it dramatic form.

One of the settings of *The Sidewalks of New York* was the exterior of a typical Manhattan brownstone-front walk-up housing ten or a dozen families. The scene depicted the awakening of the house, a few hours compressed into a few minutes of wordless action: homecoming roisterers, the milkman, the patrolling policeman, alarm clocks, radios, bedclothes put out to air, adults off to work, children off to school, an organ grinder playing "The Sidewalks of New York." This setting became the sole background for my new play; the scene I have outlined, the opening of my second act. But the house was much more than a background; it was an integral part of the play. It might almost be said that it *was* the play. I had been strongly influenced by the work of the seventeenth-century French painter Claude Lorrain, in most of whose pictures there was a dominant architectural unit, usually ornate and romanticized; in the foreground were groups of figures, seen always in relation to the pervasive structure. (It is believed that the figures were often the work of other hands than Claude's.) Though it was a far cry from the idyllic classical painting of Claude to a realistic play about modern New York, I was excited by the concept of a large number of diverse individuals whose behavior and relationships were largely conditioned by their accidental common occupancy of a looming architectural pile. In keeping with this plastic approach, I thought of calling the play "Landscape with Figures." But that seemed a little too esoteric, so I borrowed another term from painting, "Street Scene."

To some extent, the play adhered to the classical unities. The single setting was analogous to the traditional temple or palace; the elapsed time was less than a day. There even the superficial resemblance ended, for instead of unity of action there was a multitude of varied and seemingly irrelevant incidents. Blending and arranging these unrelated elements into a patterned mosaic and introducing the many characters in a seemingly natural way posed technical problems of the greatest difficulty. The play is, by all odds, the most experimental I have ever attempted, a fact not readily apparent to the reader or spectator, for its construction depends not upon novel or striking technological devices, but upon concealed architectonics. I was helped by concert-going, as well as by picture-gazing. No musician, I yet had some grasp of the structure of symphonic music: the statement, restatement and development of themes, the interplay of contrasting instruments. Unconsciously I utilized my slight knowledge of the principles of orchestration.

My characters were not epic heroes or demigods, nor did they inhabit a palace. Yet this was not Skid Row. They represented a fair cross section of what might be called the lower middle class. Of various national origins, religious faiths, political opinions and degrees of education, they included shopkeepers, clerks, artisans, students, a schoolteacher, a taxi driver, a musician, janitors, policemen. Like people at any social level, their lives comprised birth, death, love in its many aspects, economic problems, ideological conflicts, selfishness, self-sacrifice, kindness, malice, fears, hopes, aspirations. Not even a great master could expect to reproduce all of this complex tapestry. Aware of my limitations, I confined myself to a fragment of it.

2

I suspended work on *Street Scene* to attend rehearsals of *Cock Robin*. Barry's John-the-Baptist play, which I had found well written and quite moving, had closed after eleven performances. So we were both pinning our hopes on *Cock Robin*—though Barry's prospects were better than mine, for a sophisticated comedy of his, *Paris Bound*, was being produced by Arthur Hopkins.

For *Cock Robin*, McClintic, an excellent director, had assembled a good cast that included the popular monologist Beatrice Herford, who played a suburban clubwoman. Barry had written a very funny speech for her. Jo Mielziner, on the way to becoming one of the theatre's most important designers, did the settings. I had known his parents a long time: his father was a portrait painter, with a studio on Washington Square; his mother I had seen frequently in Paris. It was my first contact with Jo, the beginning of a long and happy association.

We went to Boston for a two-week tryout. The play went well enough; we told ourselves, as one always does on tryouts, that it would go better in New York. Certain changes were indicated, and here I found myself in a rather awkward position. *Paris Bound* was about to open in New York, and Barry had shifted his attention to it. I could not blame him, for it meant much more to him than *Cock Robin* did. However, he arbitrarily refused to authorize me to do the necessary rewriting, so my hands were tied. *Paris Bound* was an instantaneous success. Barry immediately set off for the Riviera, finally giving me, with what I thought very bad grace, the right to work on the play.

McClintic's wife, Katharine Cornell, was playing in Boston in Somerset Maugham's *The Letter.* I was glad to become better acquainted with her. Tryouts entail hard work, late hours and great nervous tension; it helps to have sympathetic companionship. There is a fine, heartwarming camaraderie among theatre people. I look back with pleasure upon the many hours I have spent sitting informally over a meal or a drink, gossiping, reminiscing, telling stories, discussing everything under the sun.

Cock Robin managed to survive in New York for a hundred performances; but that was far short of everybody's expectations. We had all been sure that there would be spirited bidding for the motion picture rights, yet not a single offer was ever made. For Barry, with his glittering success, the indifferent showing of *Cock Robin* meant little. As I remember it, he did not even stay for the New York opening. For me it was another setback. I had no great pride of authorship, but I had believed that the play would ease my economic pressures.

3

Though discouraged, I went back to the writing of *Street Scene*. It was fortunate that I did, for I had hardly finished the play when calamity struck. Before my departure for Europe, I had had several attacks of severe abdominal pains. I had consulted one of the leading specialists of the Rockefeller Institute, who attributed the pains to muscular spasms due to tension, a disastrously erroneous diagnosis. In Europe I had had sporadic recurrences, always obtaining relief by the administration of morphine, as prescribed by the New York specialist. Once I had an attack on a train en route from Genoa to Pisa. I could only writhe in agony until we reached our destination. A doctor, hastily summoned, obligingly gave me a dose of morphine that was so effective that I lost consciousness for twenty-four hours. My wife, terrified, thought I would never wake up.

Now the attacks became increasingly frequent and acute. Complicated and painful tests revealed a chronic organic disorder unrelated to nerves or muscles or tension. Properly diagnosed at its inception, it could have been successfully treated; now it had gone so far that immediate drastic surgery was my only hope of survival. It was apparent to me that the doctors were by no means sure that

I *would* survive. I did not want to die; but I felt as I always do just before a first-night curtain: there was nothing I could do now to affect the outcome. I remember wondering, as I dropped off under the anesthetic, whether that roaring in my ears was the last sound I would ever hear.

It was not. Things were not as bad as they might have been. Thanks to a rugged constitution and an innate stubbornness, I made a quick recovery. To everyone's amazement, I was home in twelve days. But the deep wound and the severed nerves were long in healing. For six months I was bent over and in constant pain; it was two years before I was entirely free from discomfort.

Harder to endure was the postoperative depression. For the first time in my life I experienced insomnia. Sedatives only depressed me more. Night after night I lay wide-eyed, waiting for dawn, conscious of my throbbing wound and of the open window only six feet from my bed. I have never had suicidal tendencies; my belief that this life is all there is makes me want to experience all of it that I can. But there was something curiously fascinating about lying there knowing that obliteration was only two strides and a quick heave away.

My mental state was not improved by the Theatre Guild's rejection of *Street Scene*. The comment "no content" puzzled me. I was sure the play lacked many things, but I would not have thought that content was one of them. The Guild, still not wholly given over to commercialism, had seemed the play's most likely producer. In no condition now to market it myself, I put it in the hands of Frieda Fishbein, a very capable agent.

Another situation disturbed me even more. I had been long involved in an emotional relationship that had much meaning for me. If my illness had not become critical, it is not unlikely that I would have terminated my marriage. As it was, the struggle for mere physical survival had drained me of all emotion. For the time being, I had no interest in any relationship; I wanted only to work out my own salvation in solitude. The knowledge that my apathy was mistaken for callousness added to my distress.

I now had to make up my mind whether I wanted to survive as a person, not merely as a physical organism. I decided that I did. My first affirmative measure was to attend an Easter performance at Carnegie Hall of Bach's *Saint Matthew Passion*. I could hardly walk, and sitting upright for all those hours was an ordeal, but I proved to myself that I still had interests. That was really all I needed.

Next I bought pastels, water colors and a block of paper, and began to paint, an activity I had never before attempted. My quick discovery that I have no talent for it did not deter me. I painted for hours every day, producing a body of art whose quality was in inverse ratio to its quantity. Among my varied works was a sort of street scene: a panoramic view of roofs as seen from my window. As a souvenir of that critical period, I had it framed. It hangs in my house in company with Picasso, Braque and Rouault. Puzzled guests are unable to identify the painter. The closest anyone has come yet is Grandma Moses.

As therapy the painting was a great success. I put aside sedatives and began sleeping again, for I had to be fresh for the next day's work. It followed quite naturally that I began work on a new play— one as unlike *Street Scene* as it could be, for I was not yet capable of feeling anything. So it was a farce comedy, *See Naples and Die,* set on the terrace of the Pensione Minerva on Capo di Sorrento, rechristened the Pensione di Medici. It had a cast of extravagant international characters, an absurd, complicated plot. There were even an automobile race and some digs at Mussolini; it is hard for me to keep politics out of anything I write. By the time I had finished it, a matter of two or three weeks, I was no longer floundering in the slough of despond.

My agent went on diligently peddling *Street Scene* from door to door. The response was not merely negative; it was downright hostile. Winthrop Ames, for whose judgment I had great respect, said it was not a play. My first theatre friend, Arthur Hopkins, found it unreadable. Others pronounced it sordid, depressing, clumsy, pointless, confusing, undramatic. Each successive rejection was accompanied by a new derogatory adjective. One manager turned back the cover, looked at the cast of characters and immediately put the script back into its envelope.

A windfall as unpredictable as everything else in the theatre helped me meet my medical expenses. In drawing the contract for the sale of the motion picture rights to *On Trial,* the attorney for Cohan and Harris had reserved the talking rights—a farsighted precaution in 1915, when talking pictures seemed at least a generation away. So we were able to sell the sound rights for a substantial sum. To keep the pot boiling, I began writing stories and articles for periodicals, among them *Collier's* and *The New Yorker*. I was marking time—waiting for what, I do not know, for *Street Scene's* chances were growing dimmer and dimmer, and *See Naples and Die* was faring no better.

4

At last my agent found a producer for *Street Scene*: my old acquaintance Sam Harris (no longer in partnership with George M. Cohan). My elation was tempered by caution. I knew that Harris made a practice of optioning twice as many plays as he intended to produce, giving himself a range of choice that was well worth a few thousand dollars in unrecouped advance royalties. The standard contract gave the manager six months within which to produce, with the right, upon further payment, of a six months' extension. Though no one else had shown the slightest interest in the play, I was reluctant to tie it up for a year. To my surprise, Harris agreed to limit the option to three months, with no right of renewal. So I was sure that within three months the play would either be in production or back in my hands. I deferred coping with the problem of what to do with it if it did come back.

Still far from complete recuperation, I went to Maine, where the children were at a camp, on Bailey's Island in Casco Bay. There was a good sandy beach on one side, low cliffs of eroded rock on the other; lobsters and other seafood were abundant. It was restful and healing. I swam every day and spent hours looking at the marine life left in the rock pools by the receding tide. I have seen identical creatures on the coast of Brittany.

In September I returned to New York, ready to go into rehearsal. Luckily for my morale, I was also prepared *not* to go into rehearsal. As the expiration of the option drew near, Harris told me that he could not do the play, because the young actress he had wanted for the lead was not available. I did not believe that he had ever been very serious about doing it. I had the satisfaction of knowing that there was still time to get it on during the current season, in the unlikely event that another producer could be found. There was no other reason for self-congratulation!

My agent was getting near the bottom of the roster, but she kept doggedly on. When she asked me if I would be willing to let William A. Brady do the play, I could hardly believe that I had heard aright. Long a leading producer, he had not had a success for twelve years. He had almost passed into oblivion, completely overshadowed by his wife, Grace George, and his daughter, Alice Brady, both fine actresses, and by his son, William A. Brady, Jr., who had formed a partnership with Dwight Deere Wiman, a millionaire industrialist turned producer. As Brady once put it to me, "They had me dead and buried." I had not seen him in nearly fifteen years; I had almost forgotten his existence. He was now about sixty-five—an age that, at the time, seemed to me advanced. Besides, his reputation had been built upon the production of obvious farces and melodramas.

However, I was hardly in a position to be choosy, so I went to see him. To my surprise, he saw values in the play that I had hoped were there but that no one else had detected. As a poor boy, he had known the teeming life of the New York streets. Uncouth and semi-literate, he yet had a keen sense of theatre, the quality known as showmanship. His decline had been due to his continued production of plays outmoded by the war and by the advent of the new generation of playwrights. His only hope of making a comeback was to gamble on something different. In view of the play's prospects, I felt I had little to lose by letting him do it.

Again I proposed limiting the option to three months. Brady agreed; he said he wanted to begin work at once. This, together with his willingness to pay an advance of a thousand dollars, made me think he was in earnest, for his stinginess was notorious. That reputation led me to make another demand: approval of the director. I wanted to protect myself against being saddled with some third-rate hack. At that time there was no such protective provision in the Dramatists' Guild contract; on the next revision I had it inserted, and it is now a standard clause. Again Brady agreed, though he insisted on the face-saving formula "by mutual consent." It came to the same thing, so I had no objection.

In spite of his eclipse, Brady had held on to the Playhouse, the theatre which he had built in the days of his affluence, and which had long since paid off its cost. He wanted the Playhouse for *Street Scene*, for if the play succeeded he would get the theatre profits as well as the producer's. He asked me to keep his intention confidential, because the theatre was tenanted by a Brady-and-Wiman production that would be forced to vacate. The fact that one of the producers was his son and that the play's expulsion would necessitate its closing did not disturb him. However, it happened that when we went down to look at the stage, to make sure it would meet the technological requirements of *Street Scene*, young Bill stepped out of the shadows and without preliminaries said, "What are you doing, digging my grave?"

Brady set the opening for early January, and it was already November. A director had to be found, a cast of fifty assembled, a setting designed and built. (Obviously nothing in Brady's famous warehouse would do for *Street Scene*.) As I had surmised, Brady proposed several inferior directors, from whom my veto power saved me. At length I agreed to George Cukor, who had a good record as director of an upstate stock company.

I roamed midtown Manhattan looking for a house that could serve as a model for the setting. The script described the house in minute detail; the stage business had been planned with precise relation to the architectural features. There is no shortage of brownstone fronts in New York, but none seemed to have exactly the right arrangement of windows, stoop, vestibule and cellar steps. I preferred continuing the search to changing the carefully devised business. After days of exploration and many miles of walking, I found, at 25 West Sixty-fifth Street, a house that completely answered my description. When I suggested the immediate engagement of a scene designer, Brady said none would be needed, for his stage carpenter, who was also a builder, could photograph the house and reproduce it. It was not easy to persuade Brady that stage design called for something more than a deft hand with a hammer and nails. When at last Jo Mielziner was engaged, I took him up to look at the depressingly ugly building. As we stood inspecting it the janitress appeared, eying us suspiciously.

"We're planning a house," said Jo, "and we want to use this as a model."

She beamed and said, "Yes, it *is* a beautiful house."

I did not know that Brady was having trouble financing the play. The amount needed was certainly not large, probably less than ten thousand dollars. Actors did not then get rehearsal pay; all costs were a fraction of what they are today. Now the rehearsal pay alone for a cast of fifty would be about double the entire cost of the play's original production. Brady, I learned later, had tried to find a coproducer; but, of course, every management in town had already rejected the play. At last Lee Shubert came to the rescue, perhaps to give Brady a helping hand, more likely because, as a large-scale operator, he believed in what is known in baseball parlance as playing percentages. Whatever his motives, he advanced the production cost and acquired a fifty per cent interest in the play.

Cukor immediately began casting, a trying and inefficiently managed procedure. When a play goes into production, thousands of unemployed actors make a mass attack upon the producer. Those who are not known to the producer, the director or the author, or who are not introduced by an agent, have little chance of getting past the receptionist. The few who do are more likely than not to be dismissed with a scant word or a wave of the hand. Conditions in the Brady offices, located on the top floor of the Playhouse building, were the worst I have ever seen. In an atticlike room, large enough for rehearsals, applicants assembled, hopeful of getting into Brady's private office. Each of the many hundreds who arrived was sure that in a cast of fifty there must be something for him. The teetery elevator held only six, so most of the aspirants climbed the four flights, arriving breathless, to find the large room already packed to suffocation. Brady's staff consisted of a middle-aged secretary-bookkeeper-receptionist, who could do nothing to stem the tide. Each time an applicant left Brady's office, there was a rush to get in; whoever disentangled himself from the scrimmage entered with clothes and temper in disarray, often on the verge of tears. It was hardly the ideal method for selecting artists for the performance of a play.

Though I was not happy about many of Cukor's selections, I used my veto power sparingly, for I did not want to antagonize him. I hoped he would bring out qualities in the actors that were not apparent to me. I was uneasy, too, about the nepotism that crept into the casting. All the members of Brady's family thoroughly disliked the play and had urged him not to do it; nevertheless, they put pressure upon him to engage their unemployed friends and relatives. I had an uncomfortable feeling that Cukor too was not enthusiastic about the play, and that he was doing it only because he wanted a Broadway production to his credit.

My misgivings were well grounded. One day Cukor did not come back after lunch. Next morning a telegram informed us that he had been called to Rochester on business. There was no time to spare, so Brady and I went on seeing actors. On the third day Brady said, "Cukor isn't in Rochester. He's down the block, rehearsing Maxwell Anderson's play *Gypsy.*" So he was. I never saw him again. *Gypsy* opened two days after *Street Scene* and ran seven or eight weeks. Soon afterward Cukor went to Hollywood, where he has had a successful career.

The search for a director began anew. Reluctantly Brady approached George S. Kaufman, Rouben Mamoulian and, I think, George Abbott, men who were accustomed to being well paid. They all pleaded other commitments, though I was sure it was their lack of confidence in the play that prompted their refusal. With rehearsals scheduled to begin in a few weeks, we were in trouble. In desperation I proposed that I direct the play myself. My only directorial experience had been with the amateur group at the University Settlement, but observation of Cukor had persuaded me that my understanding of the play's characters and values was better than his.

Understandably, Brady hesitated. Turning over the play to an untried director was a risky business. Yet his belief in the play made him unwilling to abandon the production. What was more, he had an irrational confidence in me, seemingly because I reminded him of the nineteenth-century Irish-American playwright Dion Boucicault, with whom he had been associated, and who had actually written a play called *The Streets of New York.* My acquaintance with Boucicault was limited to W. S. Gilbert's allusion to him in *Patience,* so I did not know whether to feel complimented or not. I clinched matters by saying that I would expect no payment for directing unless the play was a success; nothing could have appealed more to Brady. When I added, however, that if it did succeed I would feel entitled to some sort of percentage, he smiled deprecatingly and said, "You wouldn't even have needed to mention that."

I stipulated that I was to be in complete charge, for I wanted no division of authority. Brady had a reputation for making offensive remarks to actors, especially when he had been drinking. I also demanded that I have the set to work in for at least a week prior to the opening. Because of the cost, there was to be no tryout; we were to open cold after two invitation previews. Since the Actors' Equity

Association limits rehearsals to twenty-eight days, regardless of the complexity of the production, I was faced with the necessity of giving a public performance twenty-six days after the beginning of rehearsals. Brady knew that my request was reasonable, but as usual his penuriousness created obstacles. To squeeze every possible penny out of the Playhouse, he was permitting the Brady-and-Wiman production to stay on until a few days before the *Street Scene* opening. He was unwilling to incur the expense of setting up *Street Scene* in another theatre, taking it down and resetting it in the Playhouse. Luckily a solution was found. Brady was one of the proprietors of a onetime motion picture studio in Fort Lee, New Jersey, now used as a scene-building shop, in which the *Street Scene* set was being constructed. By having our technical rehearsals there, Brady saved the rental of a New York theatre and the cost of the stage crew that would have been required there. It was not an ideal arrangement, but I could hardly object.

I began my directorial work by eliminating most of the actors Cukor had tentatively engaged; fortunately, no contracts had been signed. Getting rid of the Brady pensioners was not quite so easy. But there were not too many of them, for some of the family friends, who had been accustomed to playing "ladies," did not wish to be identified with the lower-class characters of *Street Scene*. In selecting actors, I was handicapped not only by my long absence abroad, but also by Brady's unwillingness to meet the salary demands of well-known players. I was limited to performers who were unknown to the public as well as to me. One exception was Robert Kelly, who for years had played the missionary opposite Jeanne Eagels in *Rain*. When I sent for him, he asked belligerently, "Is this part another one of those goddam ministers?" "No," I said, "it's a stagehand who gets drunk and murders his wife." "All right," he replied, "I'll take it."

For Mrs. Jones, a shrewish gossip, Brady had selected a family retainer who could never, I was sure, bring out the comedy values of the part. I wanted Beulah Bondi, who had played the detective in *Cock Robin*. She was enthusiastic about the part, but did not want to work for Brady; besides, her salary was far beyond his range. However, I went to work on him. He saw no reason for a change; the part was "just a bit," which his nominee was quite capable of playing. Finally he yielded to my insistence, but was adamant about the salary. I suggested half the salary, plus a percentage if the weekly receipts exceeded nine thousand dollars. To this he agreed, for it was a dozen years since a production of his had reached that figure. Beulah accepted the arrangement, as well as my assurance that she would have no contact with Brady. It was a lucky stroke for me. On the same conditions I engaged Mary Servoss and Horace Braham, actors of considerable standing. On more modest terms I was able to get Leo Bulgakov, a former member of the Moscow Art Theatre, for the old Jewish radical, and excellent players for the Swedish janitor, the Italian musician and his German wife.

My chief casting problem was the central part of Rose. The budget precluded the engagement of an important actress, so I had to choose among the countless novices who applied. After hearing dozens of them read, I selected a beautiful girl, Erin O'Brien-Moore, whose intelligent and sympathetic approach appealed to me in spite of her lack of experience. She appealed to Brady too, because she was Irish—the colleen type, he said—and because of her willingness to take a small salary for the opportunity to be seen in a part that merited a large one. That completed the casting. Of the fifty actors, Beulah Bondi was the only one I had known personally; five or six others I had seen perform; the rest were strangers.

Meanwhile, *The Subway* was being produced by an amateur group, the Lenox Hill Players, whose director, Adele Nathan, was an old friend. The organization had taken over the Cherry Lane Theatre in Greenwich Village. I had given up hope of a Broadway presentation, so I had agreed to the amateur production with the expectation that I would take an active part in it. Once I took over the direction of *Street Scene*, I had to forget about *The Subway*—rather too bad, after waiting five years for a production.

In mid-December, exactly twenty-eight days before the scheduled opening of *Street Scene*, the cast assembled in Brady's attic. Fifty was a large cast even then; today, when the Equity minimum salary is more than a hundred dollars, its size would be prohibitive. But there was no minimum then; only five or six members of the cast were getting as much as a hundred dollars (the highest salary was two hundred and fifty), and many were getting twenty-five or less. I had an argument with Brady about the walk-ons, of whom there were a dozen or so. He wanted to pay them a dollar a performance, the standard wage for extras. I had nothing to say about salaries, but I protested so strongly against paying anyone eight dollars a week that Brady reluctantly agreed to pay fifteen.

On the first reading by the cast, the play, as I had expected, was forty minutes too long. I always overwrite, because I find it easier to cut than to pad. Besides, when an actor knows what he is required to express he can often employ a gesture or an intonation that makes words superfluous. I had marked substantial cuts in my director's script, and at the end of the reading I said, "We'll go back now and cut twenty minutes out of the first act." At this point Brady, who had been sitting at the rear of the room tilted back in a chair, chewing a dead cigar, his greasy old fedora pulled down over his eyes, arose and left. Long afterward he told me that my announcement had gone far to allay his misgivings about me. "I been in this business a long time," he said, "but I never heard an author say a thing like that before."

In writing the play I had had to overcome a very difficult dramaturgical problem. It was all very well to have all the action take place on the sidewalk; but a New York house does not stand by itself. To shut out the inhabitants of the adjoining houses would be arbitrary and unreal; to let them spill over would be to dilute the story. I solved the problem by having on one side a building in process of demolition, on the other the blank wall of a storage warehouse. This provided the required isolation and at the same time heightened the effect of the setting by the addition of two typical bits of New York topography. The absence of vehicular traffic was easily accounted for by a tar barrel at the curb bearing a "Street Closed" sign. Anyone who knew New York accepted that unquestioningly.

In rehearsal I was faced with a technological difficulty of a very different but even more troublesome nature. Since the use of scenery, properties and stage lighting entails the employment of a full stage crew, an expense no producer is willing to incur, plays are rehearsed on a bare stage, with kitchen chairs for furniture and a single, blinding light overhead. European directors, accustomed to working from the beginning with scenery, furniture and even costumes, have often expressed to me their amazement at the handicaps imposed upon American actors and directors. With a play like *Street Scene* the difficulties were almost insuperable, for the action did not take place on a flat stage, but at numerous levels: the curb, the cellar steps, the stoop, the vestibule, the windows of the two lower stories. There was constant movement, people coming and going, entering and leaving the house, appearing at the different levels. In the first act alone there were more than a hundred entrances and exits, as against perhaps fifteen in the average play. There were crowd scenes, a variety of sound effects and numerous offstage cues. All these elements had to be precisely co-ordinated, like the instruments in a symphony orchestra. To achieve all this and at the same time instruct the actors in the interpretation of their parts was a task for a beginner! I think if I had been more experienced I would not have dared undertake it. As for the actors, they could only estimate the time that each movement required. Sometimes they stood three or four deep on the flat stage to indicate the different levels they were supposed to be occupying.

Luckily I was kept too busy to become discouraged, even though I knew that word was going around that poor old Brady had been reduced to presenting a play that everybody had found hopeless, and that he was entrusting its direction to the author, who had never in his life staged a play. At a large party given by Maurice Wertheim in honor of Alfred Lunt and Lynn Fontanne, Philip Moeller said he had heard that *Street Scene* was in rehearsal and asked who was directing. When I told him that I was, he merely said, "Oh!," with a look that was half pitying, half contemptuous.

The atmosphere at rehearsals was not helpful. Grace George came almost every day, with her daughter-in-law, Katharine Alexander, also an actress. Sometimes Katharine brought her little daughter, who added her childish prattle to the incessant whisper, whisper that went on behind me. Now and then there was an adverse comment, but never a word of encouragement. Their doubts began to infect Brady. He kept his promise to refrain from talking to the actors, but he did not spare me. He was always interrupting me with scribbled notes or critical comments. Whenever Beulah Bondi appeared he would say, "I don't know what we're paying that woman all that money for. It's just a bit."

Brady kept nagging me, too, about the title. Because plays are listed alphabetically in the daily newspaper advertisements, he wanted a title that began with *A*, so that the play would head the list. I told him I would be glad to change the title if he could think

of a better one; but I declined to accept any of his numerous suggestions. A friend of mine facetiously proposed "A Street Scene"; I
did not pass it on to Brady, lest he take it seriously. One morning at
two I was awakened by a call from him. "I've got it!" he said.
" 'Atoms'!" I am afraid my response was not altogether cordial.

A week before the opening, rehearsals were transferred to the
Fort Lee studio, where the scenery had been set up. Each day we
made the long, tiring trip—which included a ferry ride—in a de-
crepit bus which Brady had hired. The return late at night, in the
hard January frost, was anything but pleasant. Nor was foraging
for food in the dismal precincts of Fort Lee. But what were the discomforts of fifty people when weighed against the several hundred
dollars it would have cost to have rehearsed in a New York
theatre?

There were few complaints, for the excitement of the actors was
mounting. The first view of Jo Mielziner's set, solid and realistic, yet
richly atmospheric, filled everyone with elation. For weeks we had
all been pretending it was there, and now it was! It remained to be
seen how all the plotted movement would accommodate itself to
the actual configuration of the set. With considerable uneasiness, I
gave the order to begin. Luckily, all those long hours of methodical
drill justified themselves. Everything fell neatly into place: in and
out, up and down and across, the action flowed. When, at the end of
the murder scene that climaxed the second act, the stage seethed
with a swirling crowd, Brady stood up and applauded. Here and
there a minor adjustment had to be made, but in the main it all
worked. The sedulous picture-gazing in Paris, Florence and Vienna
had enabled me to think of the production in terms of composition
and plasticity.

5

The opening was on a Thursday, with previews Tuesday and
Wednesday. It was not until Monday that the set was ready for use
on the Playhouse stage. That gave me less than a day and a half for
mechanical co-ordination. Checking of costumes and properties
alone took much time. Jo Mielziner said that the prop list was the
most entertaining he had ever seen. Among its items were: old baby
carriage, handcuffs, hospital stretcher, old washboiler filled with

pots and pans, ice tongs; black rosette, crepe, with streamers; nail keg filled with sand, garbage can; two racks of milk bottles—one full, one empty; cigar butt, folding paper fan, tin pail filled with soapsuds, small three-wheeled ice wagon, pair of roller skates; female dog, small, no pedigree, collar and chain.

A recording instrument set up in an open window on Times Square had provided a disk that reproduced the hum of city traffic, punctured by rumbling trucks, shrieking brakes, honking horns, even a distant steamship whistle. Two record players, started a minute apart, produced an overlapping effect that was always varied. The records kept going throughout the entire play, sometimes at a roar, sometimes at a murmur, as the mood demanded. One man was kept busy just supervising them. I do not know how many hundred disks were worn out in the course of the play's run.

During the Fort Lee rehearsals I had been troubled by the hollow wooden tread of the innumerable passages across the platform that represented the sidewalk. It was distracting and destructive of illusion. I urged Brady to put down a thin coating of cement, but he balked at the expenditure of seven hundred dollars. He finally gave in—an eloquent expression of confidence in the play! The actors were delighted by this improvement. But when the sound records were first turned on they were up in arms. It was impossible, they said, to play against that racket. I assured them they would soon become accustomed to it. So accustomed did they become that once when the sound apparatus went out of order the whole performance fell apart.

On the day of the first preview I was still working on production details. The timing of the curtains was very important, and I rehearsed it again and again, whereupon I was handed a scrap of paper on which Brady had scrawled: "Please don't forget that the curtain man gets a dollar fifty an hour."

The invited preview audience was a fair cross section of the theatregoing public: business and professional people, office workers, students, nurses, a sprinkling of personal friends. When the curtain rose, the vivid setting evoked a round of applause. Interest in the play was quickly evinced; at the end of the long first act the response was enthusiastic. The second act went even better; the melodramatic murder scene created a high pitch of excitement. At the end of the play there were nineteen curtain calls, hardly usual at a preview. I heard later from several persons that they had become so steeped in the play's atmosphere of summer heat that it was a distinct shock to step out into the January cold.

Backstage everybody was elated. Dozens of people streamed back to offer congratulations. I went home feeling that things had not gone too badly. Shortly after midnight Brady called up, to tell me gloomily that Lee Shubert's casting director—a former osteopath, known to me only as Doc Hunt—had reported that the play was a certain failure; the acclamation merely expressed a friendly audience's appreciation of the many fine performances—no one would pay to see this dismal play. I could say only that I hoped the doctor was mistaken.

I spent the whole next day with the cast, going over the copious notes I had made the night before. The second preview followed the pattern of the first, except that there were twenty curtain calls. It was encouraging, but the opening night was what counted. I had made more notes, and we worked next day almost until curtain time. The actors were tired, but not too tired, I felt, to have lost the fine performance edge that the enthusiasm of the preview audiences had given them.

Surely there are few professional situations more trying than those two or three hours that may result in the complete rejection of a work upon which a year or two of creative effort has been spent. The opening of *Street Scene* was for me far more of an ordeal than that of *On Trial* had been. With *On Trial,* I had very little to lose; even complete failure could have been put down to youthful inexperience, and at worst I would have had a Broadway production to my credit. The failure of *Street Scene* might be the end of my career as a playwright; and fifteen years' experience had made me painfully aware of the likelihood of failure. Besides, I was, for the first time, carrying directorial responsibility. I sometimes think opening night is harder on the director than on the author. He is always seeing things that might have been done better, and every faulty movement or fumbled line is a sword in his entrails.

Prominent in the first-night audience was Al Smith, who had just lost the Presidential election, his personal popularity outweighed by anti-Catholic prejudice. In inviting him, Brady had shrewdly sensed the publicity value of his presence at the opening of a play about the sidewalks of New York. Every newspaper mentioned it, stressing the fact that Smith had arrived early and made himself as inconspicuous as the circumstances permitted.

I stood through the performance, at the rear of the orchestra. When the curtain rose, the audience reaction was even more marked than it had been at the previews. As the leisurely first act unfolded, interest mounted; at its end there was warm applause. I slipped backstage to give words of encouragement to the actors: hardly necessary, for they did not have to be told that the play was going well. The tumultuous second-act ending was roundly applauded. At the final curtain there were cheers. The curtain went up and down so many times that I lost count. I went backstage to tell the stage manager not to force the calls. It was a futile errand, for I found Brady rhythmically punching the curtain man in the small of the back to accelerate the rise and fall of the curtain. As the demonstration continued, there were cries of "Author!" I did not want to appear, for I think a play should speak for itself. But, as the cries and the urging of the actors became more insistent, I went on and said a few words in praise of the cast. The curtain came down, the house lights went up; it was over at last.

The press was unanimously favorable. Some reviewers had reservations about this or that aspect of the play or of the production, but the over-all response was affirmative. The setting was praised by all; in spite of the size of the cast, almost everyone in it was favorably mentioned in one review or another. Opinions about the direction differed. Some attributed the play's effectiveness to the direction; others said I had made a mistake in directing it myself.

In the universal approbation, there were numerous doubts about the play's chances of popular success. Burns Mantle, a veteran critic, ended his review by saying: "It is a good show, but I don't believe they can sell it." Robert Garland began: "Even though it runs no longer than a fortnight, and Variety sends me to the foot of the class for enjoying it, I enjoyed the new piece at the Playhouse just the same." Variety itself, that bible of "show biz," while praising the play, said: "Whether this play which starts so interestingly will catch high public favor is questionable."

I went to Brady's office expecting to find him as elated as I was by the first-night reception and the favorable reviews. Instead he was gloomy and depressed. He had made the rounds of the ticket agencies, hoping to place large blocks of seats, but not one of them

was interested. They all said the play was a "critics' success" with
no element of box-office appeal. Their clients were not buying tickets for a play that dealt somberly with tenement-house life.

The second-night demand was disappointing. Next day, which
was Saturday, the matinee showed a little more sign of life. The
evening performance was completely sold out. But that was not decisive; a play that does not sell out on Saturday night is in a bad
way indeed. Sunday was a long day, what with the uncertainty, and
the fatigue I was beginning to feel. On Monday morning when the
Playhouse box office opened, a line formed. For the next six months
the line never broke.

CHAPTER

XIV

Work and Play·

1

Though the reviews that kept coming in were, in general, favorable, there were some interesting notes of dissent. St. John Ervine, the Anglo-Irish playwright, who was serving as guest critic for the New York *World* and who had been unable to attend the *Street Scene* opening, came out later with a scathing critique. He called the play "a drama of the garbage can." "There on the stage," he wrote, "was a garbage can, an actual and veritable garbage can"—as opposed, I assume, to a fictitious or fanciful one—"and I felt that if Mr. Rice had had his way the entire contents of the can would have been shown us, too." He overlooked the fact that, since I was in sole charge of the production, there had been nothing to prevent my making this exposure. What exasperated Ervine even more than the garbage can was my "sentimental morbidity about poor people." A stickler for the hard truth, he pointed out that "given adequate food and clothing and shelter and entertainment, the workman is happier than the person who employs him." It somehow reminded me of Mr. Dooley's remark to the effect that the poor, who are the people who need money most, never seem to have any of it.

Stark Young, in *The New Republic*, expressed the opinion that if the play merited attention it was only because it was not quite as bad as the rest of the season's wretched crop: in the country of the blind, the one-eyed man is king. He deplored, at some length, the tendency of young actresses to dress fashionably regardless of the parts they played. This amused me, because all the women in the cast had been sent to S. Klein's famous bargain dress shop on Union Square, where the price of garments averaged about fifteen dollars. Here Brady's budgetary ideas and my conception of how the characters should dress had coincided! The most expensive costumes in the play, costing about fifty dollars each, were the French uniforms worn by two Park Avenue nursemaids. Erin O'Brien-Moore, whose high spirits included a dash of Irish belligerence, wrote Young an indignant letter itemizing the cost of her wardrobe, three complete changes of costume. The whole thing—dresses, shoes, stockings, hats and accessories—came to less than seventy-five dollars. Instead of having the grace to admit his error, the silly man wrote another silly piece, in which he said that what mattered was that the clothes *looked* expensive. That was, of course, the very reason brownstone-front residents went to Klein's.

With the play firmly established, I was afraid that Brady would attempt to replace the principal actors with cheaper ones. So I urged him to give Horace Braham, Mary Servoss and Beulah Bondi run-of-the-play contracts, in order to protect himself against their being lured away. Still dazed by the incredible success, Brady was ready to listen to anything I proposed; he signed up all the important members of the cast to long-term contracts, thereby ensuring the continued integrity of the performance. For the actors who had percentage arrangements it was a bonanza: for nearly a year their weekly pay was twice what they had originally demanded. I am sure that Brady never fully forgave me or himself. To keep up the tone of the play, I called frequent rehearsals to correct little lapses that had crept in. People who see a play that has been running a while often find that it does not come up to their expectations. That is because the production has deteriorated through cast substitutions and inadequate supervision of performances.

The Subway opened at the Cherry Lane Theatre a few weeks after the opening of *Street Scene*. The production, though far below the best professional standards, was creditable enough. The reviews were surprisingly good. Brady, whose feet had not yet returned to their earthly anchorage, gave me an advance—the fourth I had received for this play—and moved the production to Broadway. But its run was short.

After waiting for Brady to broach the subject of my directorial compensation, I gently called the matter to his attention. He offered me twenty-five hundred dollars, which I declined, reminding him that he had agreed to a participation arrangement if the play was a success. He denied ever having made such an agreement. After a long and rather acrimonious correspondence, I accepted five thousand dollars. There was no open breach, though I was annoyed at Brady—and even more at myself, for having taken him at his word, an incurable weakness of mine for which I have often paid heavily. But the honeymoon was definitely over. We had been negotiating for the production of *Life Is Real* and *See Naples and Die*, but could not agree on the question of directorial participation. During the years of our joint interest in *Street Scene* we dealt at arm's length. There were sharp conflicts, but we were kept from open warfare by the curious liking we had for each other.

With the play doing capacity business, Brady instituted a second midweek matinee; for many months there were nine performances a week. In Easter Week there was a daily matinee, with standees at each of the week's twelve performances. Brady finally threw away his battered fedora and appeared in a crisp new model. But his staff, which consisted of his middle-aged secretary and two female box-office employees, was not enlarged. Incredible as it seems in the theatre's present state of organization, during the entire run of *Street Scene* at the Playhouse there was no house manager, no company manager, no press agent, not even a stage doorman. Friends who were in closer touch with Broadway doings than I informed me that Brady was selling bundles of tickets at high prices to the agents who had originally refused to buy. Legally I was entitled to a royalty on these augmented receipts, known as "ice," but I had no taste for litigation.

Shortly after the opening, I tried to persuade Brady to organize a Chicago company. He resisted the idea. He said that *Street Scene* was a New York play that would be unlikely to interest audiences elsewhere. Though he had taken up his option on the British rights, he was even more dubious about the play's chances in London. In due course, the motion picture companies sent their representatives to see the play. These scouts, viewing the performance from rear seats, which they had bought at greatly advanced prices from ticket agents, and to which they made their way through the standees, all reported that the play had no audience appeal.

My agent was now able to obtain production contracts for *Life Is Real* and *See Naples and Die*. The plays were neither better nor worse than they had been before the production of *Street Scene*, but in the American theatre, as in many other areas of American life, nothing succeeds but success. Each contract left the production entirely in my hands.

I had been looking forward to a trip to Europe, but with two plays scheduled for production it seemed unwise to leave New York. So I stayed home and wrote *A Voyage to Purilia*, a satiric novel about a space visit to an imaginary planet, the sphere of the screen —not Hollywood, but the world that is portrayed in motion pictures. Purilia is a portmanteau word: from *pure* and *puerile*. The book, in its description of the peculiar customs, beliefs and behavior of the inhabitants of this fictitious realm, is intended as a commentary upon the banalities, clichés, distortions and taboos of the screen. I had a fine time writing it. It was immediately accepted for book publication; and also by Harold Ross, for serialization in *The New Yorker*.

The casting of the leading role in *See Naples and Die* presented difficulties. I was quite ready to go ahead, as I had done in *Street Scene*, with some promising unknown, but my producer, Lewis Gensler, a songwriter with little managerial experience, felt we must have a "Broadway name." Week after week went by without our being able to agree on anyone who was available. At last I consented to the engagement of a young actress, Claudette Colbert, who had recently appeared in Eugene O'Neill's short-lived *Dynamo*. I had not shared the general enthusiasm she had aroused, but time was running out and every other possibility had been exhausted.

Meanwhile, *Street Scene* had been awarded the Pulitzer Prize, much to my gratification, of course. Brady was so pleased that he asked permission to hang the certificate in the Playhouse lobby, even going to the length of paying for the framing. The award prompted the motion picture companies to take another look at the play, and to make tentative inquiries about the rights. They saw now that it might be the basis of a picture, with the action modified to include what went on inside the house. When I made it clear that the locale would have to be limited to the exterior, the inquiries were not pursued.

2

In those late days of the 1920s, the social, economic and moral life of America was shaped, or rather distorted, by two ugly influences, the bull market and prohibition. The sensational advance in stock prices had plunged the whole nation into a frenzy of gambling. It could not even be called speculation, for most people hardly knew what they were buying. Persuaded by the irresponsible pronouncements of bankers, brokers and "expert" economists to believe in an ever-expanding economy and a continuing increase in the price of "securities," hundreds of thousands of small businessmen, housewives, taxi drivers, stenographers, clergymen, college professors, farmers and artists were using every penny they had saved or could borrow to snap up whatever was offered. It was a universal madness, destructive of morals and of morale. Tragic faces reflected a decline in the market; an upswing brought jubilation and another spending spree. All life was colored by obsessive dreams of getting something for nothing, of getting rich quick. It was the South Sea Bubble distended to gargantuan size.

So much has been written about the prohibition era that I shall record only my personal reactions. Prior to my departure for Europe in 1925, I had done very little drinking. On the Continent I learned to enjoy an *apéritif*, a bottle of wine, a liqueur; I even began to know my way around on a wine list. Drinking was a normal, moderate, leisurely practice that comprised relaxation, sociability and degustation. When I returned to New York, I found, instead of convivial drinking, a desperate determination on the part of nearly everyone I knew to obtain alcohol regardless of means, price or quality. Bootlegging had become a major industry, and gangsterism was blighting the land. It is my belief that the prohibition years were largely responsible for the growth of organized crime, corruption of public officials, and general disrespect for law.

What shocked me most was the deterioration in social behavior. At overcrowded, raucous, graceless parties everyone seemed to concentrate on swallowing the greatest possible amount of vile concoctions. It was appalling to see people of taste and sensitivity guzzling mixtures of fruit juice and raw alcohol; it was distressing to see nice young women reel and fall unconscious, or to observe the bleary eyes and simpering mouths of men one admired for their wit and character. If you asked a few friends in for an evening and supplied a bottle or two of bootleg whiskey, because it was expected of you, word got around that liquor was available, and fifteen people would show up, most of whom you had never seen before and certainly never wanted to see again. They broke glassware and ornaments, spilled liquor on the rug, ground out cigarettes on table tops.

In dining out, one tended to go to speakeasies, not so much for the liquor—which was served in coffee cups, while the coffee was served in glasses—but because the food was better than in the legal restaurants, whose cuisine had declined with the shrinkage in the epicurean patronage. The speakeasies most popular with theatre folk were Jack and Charlie's, precursor of the famous "21" and Tony's. I resented the secrecy and the general air of naughtiness. It seemed outrageous that one had to become a lawbreaker in order to enjoy a good meal and a glass of wine.

Now and then I lunched at the Round Table in the Hotel Algonquin, that celebrated rendezvous of such town wits as Robert Benchley, Marc Connelly, George Kaufman, Dorothy Parker, Harold Ross, Franklin P. Adams and Heywood Broun. The large table, set up in the middle of the dining room by Frank Case, the Algonquin's shrewd proprietor, was surrounded by smaller ones at which hero-worshipers and curiosity-seekers gathered, eager to gaze at the celebrities and hopeful of overhearing a bon mot. Actually, the conversation, like most table talk, consisted mostly of gossip, complaints about the weather, the traffic, the servant problem and taxes, and much detailed discussion about the state of everyone's health. Among those I encountered there, I particularly admired Heywood Broun, who always had the courage to say what he believed. He was an able labor leader too. In organizing the Newspaper Guild, he drew upon the experience of the Dramatists' Guild. Once he asked me to address the newly formed Newark chapter of his organization.

Woollcott I never really liked. I had no respect for his critical judgment (even though he often gave me favorable reviews!), and his persistent rudeness—cannily exploited by Kaufman and Hart in *The Man Who Came to Dinner*—I found inexcusable. Nor did I ever take to George Kaufman, whom I heard, in the many years of our acquaintanceship, say many devastatingly witty things, but never a kind one. As a contributor to *The New Yorker*, I came to know Harold Ross quite well. In later years he was a neighbor of mine in Stamford. In contrast to his rather puritanical editorial standards, his conversation was as bawdy as any I have ever heard. I liked a sign he had on the wall of his office: "Don't be famous around here."

3

When I put *See Naples and Die* into rehearsal, my misgivings about Miss Colbert were confirmed. I could not get her to play the part as I had conceived it. Matters were not helped by displays of "star" psychology: lateness at rehearsals, criticism of fellow actors, displays of "temperament." Sometimes, in dealing with an actor of note, one has to put up with such antics; in a comparative newcomer, I found them insufferable. Among the hundreds of actors I have worked with, she and Richard Bennett are the only ones with whom my relationship has not been cordial. At the dress rehearsal I was so exasperated by her calculated tardiness and discourtesy that I stopped the performance and reprimanded her sharply in the presence of the entire company and of whoever was sitting out front— something I had never done before and have never done since.

As with *Street Scene*, we were opening cold. The two previews went so well that the ticket brokers who had attended the second arranged to buy out the entire orchestra for eight weeks. It looked as though we had a smash hit. But it was not to be so. The first-night audience was lukewarm; the reviews were unfavorable. The critics seemed to resent my having followed *Street Scene* with a giddy farce comedy. One of them even said that if anyone else had written the play he would have given it a good notice! The ticket brokers revoked their oral commitments; the play struggled on for two months or so, its demise hastened by the stock market crash. Eventually Warner Brothers made a movie of it, entitled *Oh, Sailor Behave,* starring the comedians Olsen and Johnson. There were no sailors in the original play. I never saw the picture. In London the play was a success. It still has an occasional English production.

A. H. Woods dropped his option on *Life Is Real,* as I had expected he would; I had not understood what made him acquire it in the first place. *A Voyage to Purilia* was duly published. In spite of generally favorable reviews, it sold less than fifteen hundred copies. In England, again it was another story. Highly praised by Sheila Kaye-Smith, J. C. Squire and Arnold Bennett, it sold very well, was subsequently included in Victor Gollancz' *Holiday Omnibus,* and was reissued years later by Penguin Books. There were several translations too. The ways of the world of books are as inexplicable as those of the theatre.

After ten months of my urging, Brady agreed to organize a Chicago company of *Street Scene.* However, he objected to paying me for directing it, on the ground that it was a mechanical job of duplication that any stage manager could perform. I told him that in that case he had better let the stage manager do it. After a week of rehearsals, Brady sent for me, as I had expected he would. The production was a hopeless mess. The stage manager, an efficient backstage boss, had no understanding of the intricate movement and split-second timing that the play required. I could have held out for a stiff sum, but my instinct of workmanship was outraged by the sorry spectacle, so I again left the amount of payment to Brady. I began once more by dismissing some of Brady's waifs and strays. After that, everything went smoothly.

At the Chicago dress rehearsal, after the second act, in which the surly stagehand comes home drunk and brutally murders his wife and her lover, one of the backstage crew at the Apollo Theatre grasped my hand and said, "Mr. Rice, I want to thank you. You're the first author who has ever shown a stagehand as a human being."

Brady's fear that the play's appeal was limited to New York was unfounded. The Chicago critics and public seemed to have no trouble in accepting it. On New Year's Eve, by which time I was back in New York, Brady called me up jubilantly to inform me that the combined receipts of the two companies for that one night came to ten thousand dollars.

I had a fine gay time in Chicago. Ernest Byfield, proprietor of the Hotel Ambassador West, had given me his private suite, admirably adapted to entertainment. I had transferred several of my New York principals to the Chicago company (making careful replacements, of course). All old friends now, they were at the Ambassador, too, as were the Marx Brothers, who were playing in *Animal*

Crackers; Judith Anderson, then in *Strange Interlude;* Helen Menken, in *The Makropoulos Secret.* There was a party every night after the show, and much merriment. That season of 1929–30 there were fifteen theatres in Chicago, presenting about sixty-five productions. Yet the dramatic critic Charles Collins called it a "terrible season." In 1959–60, exactly thirty years later, there were four theatres and fourteen productions.

My next conflict with Brady was over the English rights. Dubious about the play's chances in London, he kept putting off a production. Besides, he contended that my right of approval of cast and director did not extend to a British presentation. A further complication was his reversion to alcohol, from which, by some miracle of will power, he had abstained during the rehearsals and early run of the play. Now he was in and out of a private sanatarium, where our business discussions took place—when he was in condition to discuss anything.

The British rights had long been sought by Maurice Browne, producer of a play whose history strikingly parallels *Street Scene's.* While my play was making the New York rounds, London managers were rejecting *Journey's End,* a play by a young man named R. C. Sherriff. As with *Street Scene,* it was obvious to everyone that the play had no audience appeal: a grim war drama, devoid of women and jokes, in which all the characters are killed. A special Sunday-night performance by the London Stage Society, to which all the West End managers were invited, aroused no interest in anyone except Maurice Browne, a struggling actor-producer identified mainly with classical plays. He took an option and managed to scrape together the modest sum needed for a West End production (the play had only one set and a cast of nine). It was an instantaneous and sensational hit. Opening in New York shortly after *Street Scene,* it duplicated its London success. Soon it was being performed throughout the world.

Browne, who was said to have made a million dollars out of *Journey's End,* bought the Globe Theatre in Shaftesbury Avenue. It was there he proposed to do *Street Scene.* Brady was determined to produce the play himself, but when the American principals, learning that he intended also to direct, refused to go to London, he entered into negotiations with the English producer. However, as I stood pat on my contractual rights, Browne, unwilling to keep his theatre dark, withdrew his offer. The upshot was that Brady's British option ran out. Browne thereupon made me an offer to direct the play and coproduce it with him and Leon M. Lion, a well-known West End manager. I agreed, though I knew that London theatres are small and that, even at capacity, a play with a cast of fifty could hardly pay for itself.

4

Though I was not needed in England until midsummer, I was eager to renew the pleasures of European living. Paris seemed a good place for working on a play that had that city as its locale. Moreover, I was chafing again under unremitting domesticity; I longed to be on my own for a while. Wearying of wrangling with Brady, I was willing to leave business matters in his hands, even at the risk of financial loss.

My ship, the *President Roosevelt,* known to its crew as Rolling Rosie, took its time waddling across the stormy North Atlantic, but I was happy to be on the move again. The ship's lively company included Anna De Mille, former wife of movie director William De Mille and daughter of Henry George, the single-tax advocate whose *Progress and Poverty* was one of the most widely read books of its time. Over cocktails and chess, we sympathetically shared socialistic opinions. Another interesting passenger was Helen Keller, with whom I had a "conversation." She enunciated very slowly, syllable by syllable, on a dead level, without tone or inflection. To understand me she placed her finger tips lightly on my lips, interpreting the vibrations: a strange experience.

The return to Paris was like a happy homecoming. I stayed at a small hotel five minutes on foot from St.-Germain-des-Prés, fifteen from the Louvre and Montparnasse. My daily routine was smooth and pleasant. First to the Deux Magots for coffee, a brioche and a look at the morning papers. If it was rainy, I stayed on until lunchtime, writing letters or reading; on fair days, I strolled along the quais and the boulevards, visited the Louvre or the dealers' galleries. Then a simple lunch, usually at Michaud's, and back to my room for an afternoon's work. Evenings there was no lack of social life. Sometimes I took a day off to revisit Chartres, Chantilly or Versailles.

Many old acquaintances had returned to America, as the pinch of the depression tightened family purse strings. But it was good to see those who were still in Paris. A vermouth at a sidewalk café, a leisurely dinner at a carefully chosen restaurant, coffee and brandy to the accompaniment of a string ensemble, a homeward stroll past shuttered houses: all quite remote from the furtiveness and frenzy of New York speakeasy life.

One day I ran into Theresa Helburn and Aline Bernstein, who were traveling together. Aline's association with the Neighborhood Playhouse and with Eva Le Gallienne's Civic Repertory Theatre established her as one of America's best designers of scenery and costumes. She was a truly remarkable woman, warmhearted, generous, gifted in many ways, and endowed with an exuberance and a zest for living such as I have rarely encountered. We arranged to meet for dinner at one of the big café-restaurants in Montmarte. Terry and Aline brought along a curly-headed young giant whom they introduced as Thomas Wolfe. His love affair with Aline is, of course, part of literary history, since they both wrote books about it. I saw Wolfe several times afterward at dinner meetings of the National Institute of Arts and Letters, to which we were elected at about the same time. He always struck me as gauche, self-conscious and morbidly self-absorbed. As for his books, I find their verbosity and turgidity insuperable obstacles; I have never been able to get through any of them.

My new play, appropriately named *The Left Bank*, examined, realistically but with a touch of satire, the behavior and psychology of a group of American expatriates. Its thesis was that revolt against America's cultural sterility was likely to be symptomatic of an inability to adjust to the conditions of American life. In the end, one of the exiles chooses to return to a land where she has roots, rather than to go on attempting assimilation to an alien environment.

The finished play did not satisfy me; nothing I have written has. I suppose that is true of any writer. Complete satisfaction would destroy incentive. It is the hope of doing better next time, of eventually achieving perfection, that is the perpetual spur. Yet I suppose *The Left Bank* came nearer accomplishing what I had intended than anything else I had written. If it is an illusion, it is a pleasant one; I have refrained these many years from rereading the play, lest I dispel it.

Before leaving Paris, I gave a party at the apartment of my friends the Lowenthals. Among the guests was John Gunther, newly arrived from Vienna. He told the horrifying story of the reactionary government's murderous attack upon the housing project of the Socialist workers. Tragic in itself, it typified the European unrest that was soon—how soon no one suspected—to produce the series of crises that culminated in World War II.

The Authors' League had asked me to attend an international congress of authors' societies in Budapest. En route, I paid my first visit to Berlin. I did not find it attractive. It seemed heavy and somber, completely lacking the grace and elegance of Paris. Yet there was a vitality and a dynamism that did not exist in France. What it foreboded I did not grasp.

Dresden I liked better than any German city I had yet seen. I had the pleasure of hearing Richard Strauss's light opera *Intermezzo,* conducted by himself. Almost anywhere in Europe there is sure to be a theatre or concert hall, usually municipally operated, where one can enjoy music or drama, in sad contrast to what is offered to the overnight visitor in all but the largest American cities. I have another reason for remembering Dresden. In a bookshop window I saw some water colors by Paul Klee. I knew instantly that I wanted to add them to my growing art collection. But I had no German money and my train for Prague was leaving in an hour. I hurried with my letter of credit to the nearest bank, where I had to wait and wait for the man ahead of me to finish some very complicated business. I dashed back to the bookstore, bought two of the paintings, and caught my train just by an eyelash. Those Klees, and others that I acquired later, are cherished possessions.

Prague, predominantly baroque, I found impressive, though rather dark and lowering. The people were dour, too, not only openly anti-German, but hostile to all foreigners. If I asked for a German menu—since I could not read Czech—it was provided grudgingly and with sullen looks, though it must have been obvious from my speech that I was not a German.

Of course I was enchanted by Budapest, as who is not? I had a corner room on the quai, with a sweeping view of the hills across the Danube. The congress was the first of many international gatherings I have attended. The pattern is always the same: a certain number of business sessions, interspersed with dinners, official receptions, organized sightseeing and divers entertainments. What I always enjoy most is meeting the delegates from all over the world. It is heartening to discover anew the like-mindedness and good will of professional people everywhere. The world would be better off if it were run by artists instead of by politicians. There might be less efficiency and mechanical progress, but there would be more idealism, imaginativeness, humaneness, mutual understanding—and humor!

5

The first step in the production of *Street Scene* in London was the application to the Lord Chamberlain for a license, a prerequisite to the public presentation of any play. A letter from that dignitary's office is, I think, worth quoting:

I am desired by the Lord Chamberlain to write to you regarding the above play and to say that before a license can be issued his Lordship will require an undertaking that the following alterations will be effected:

1. Pages 87, 91 and 105, the screams of a woman in childbirth must be omitted.

2. Page 118, Mae's undressing at the window must not take place.

3. Page 185, the stage directions regarding the appearance of Maurrant appearing after the murder smothered in blood must not be interpreted literally.

4. The word "God" on the following pages must be omitted: pages 87, 104, 205, 224. The word "Goddam" to be omitted on page 69.

5. Some other expressions for that of "dirty little tart" on page 117 should be submitted for approval—"bitch" should not be selected.

Yours faithfully . . .

I am a militant opponent of every form of censorship, but the deletions were so insignificant that I did not protest. British intellectuals have long been demanding abolition of the whole licensing system. It still persists, though there have been recent indications of modification of the Lord Chamberlain's Victorian standards.

Another governmental intervention presented more difficulties. The play had closed in New York, after a run of 601 performances, so I was planning to bring over Erin O'Brien-Moore, Mary Servoss and several other members of the cast. At first, work permits were refused, on the ground that there were unemployed English actors who could fill the parts. We finally convinced the authorities that the employment of some forty resident actors to complete the cast was contingent on bringing in the Americans. The restrictions on both sides of the Atlantic upon the employment of alien actors— restrictions for which American and British Equity are largely responsible—is deplorable. Art is international; there should be no barriers to the free interchange of artists.

My family had joined me in England. We had a comfortable service flat in Buckingham Gate where we could have friends in. Our social life was active. We made the acquaintance of Benn Levy, J. B. Priestley, John Galsworthy, J. C. Squire, Harold Brighouse, A. A. Milne and Rose Macaulay (a fragile, delightful creature, whose conversation I enjoyed to the extent that her clipped speech was intelligible). At a party given by Henry Arthur Jones's daughter Doris Thorne, who presided over a sort of literary salon, I met Max Beerbohm. He was just about what one would have expected: rosy-cheeked, urbane, immaculately turned out, with a carnation in his buttonhole. My publisher, Victor Gollancz, introduced me to a man I had long admired, the great political cartoonist David Low: a keen-eyed, keen-minded, courageous liberal. I was amused by his dogmatic rejection of all modern art.

We also met James Maxton, John Beckett and Fenner Brockway, members of Parliament who belonged to the left-wing Independent Labor Party. Maxton, universally known as Jimmy, took us on a tour of the House of Commons. Pausing before a statue of Oliver Cromwell, he said, "Now, that's the sort of man England needs today"; at which a bobby standing nearby doubled up with silent laughter. A few days after John Beckett dined with us, great headlines announced that, in a moment of exuberance, he had lifted the mace from the Speaker's table. This display of irreverence for the symbol of legislative authority, an act almost without precedent in parliamentary history, outraged the nation to such an extent that Beckett made an apology. Several years later I was distressed to see him announced as the principal speaker at a meeting of Sir Oswald Mosley's fascists. Once while I was having tea on the terrace of the House of Commons, an M.P. at the next table was entertaining Sybil Thorndike and Paul Robeson, who was not only black but red. It was a scene not likely to be duplicated in the Capitol at Washington. The British seem to be able to take nonconformity in their stride.

Among our right-wing acquaintances was Dulcy Sassoon, in whose Mayfair house one met Francis Yeats-Brown, author of *Lives of a Bengal Lancer,* who later became a Hitlerite. Then there was a countess or baroness just back from the Middle East, an Islam convert. I think it was at Dulcy's that I met Louis Golding, though he was no Tory. When he talked to me at length about his successful novel *Magnolia Street,* I said apologetically that I could not follow his references because I had not read the book. He looked at me in silence for a long moment, then said, "You don't read novels?"

With the cast of *Street Scene* completed and rehearsals still a few weeks off, we took a holiday at Dinard, on the coast of Brittany. The highlight of our sojourn was a visit to Mont St.-Michel, bracketed by Henry Adams with Chartres, and second only to Chartres in grandeur. We stayed only a few hours, but on subsequent visits I spent the night to enjoy the famous omelets of Madame Poulard and to climb the heights by moonlight.

One night, in a café at Dinard, I encountered Gelett Burgess, whom I had not seen in years. He explained why. His wife, Estelle Loomis, a successful fiction writer, had been thrown from the upper deck of a skidding Fifth Avenue bus; she was almost totally incapacitated and unable to work. Burgess had taken her from country to country in search for a cure. For want of something to say, I asked if he had read *Man's Supreme Inheritance,* by Matthias Alexander, who claimed to have perfected a new technique of physiotherapy—not at all the sort of book I usually read, but I had been attracted by John Dewey's glowing review. Several years later Burgess showed up at my New York apartment, to tell me that he owed me a debt of gratitude. He had read the book and had taken his wife to London for treatment by Alexander. Though not entirely cured, she was now able to work again. A casual remark had altered a person's life! It has always seemed to me an extraordinary coincidence.

Staging *Street Scene* was becoming a rather routine job for me now. My chief problem was getting the English members of the cast to talk American. The results did not altogether satisfy me, but I knew that London would be less sensitive to the niceties of

American pronunciation than I was. While I was giving the production its final tune-up, Hannan Swaffer, an influential dramatic critic and columnist, often likened to Walter Winchell (though he was decidedly leftist), walked into the auditorium unannounced. I had just finished rehearsing a comedy scene of two nursemaids that opens the third act, and I was about to go on to Erin's entrance and the ensuing emotional scenes. It was unthinkable to let an important critic see these scenes on the eve of the opening; yet I could not very well stop the rehearsal. So I called back the nursemaids, told them I was not quite satisfied with the scene, and had them go over it again. As they finished, Erin started to enter. Again expressing dissatisfaction, I went up on the stage to demonstrate leisurely what I wanted, which was exactly what the girls had been doing. After each repetition I waved Erin back and went at it again. At length Swaffer, complimenting me upon my attention to detail, said he was sorry he had to leave, a regret which I assured him I shared.

As in New York and in Chicago, there were opening-night cheers and innumerable curtain calls. When the audience had departed, we had a gay celebration in the lounge. The press was enthusiastic. But of course there was the usual skepticism about the play's chances of running: "It has just the same human appeal as Porgy. I only hope it may be a great deal more successful"; "Street Scene is a play to be seen, although I think it will have a limited appeal"; "I wonder how the great mass of the entertainment-seeking public will respond"; and so on!

The entertainment-seeking public responded very well. The play ran for five months, far longer than I had expected in view of the operating expense. It even paid off its production cost. I was beginning to believe that it did have some audience appeal, after all —a belief that was strengthened by subsequent authorized productions in Argentina, Denmark, Australia, France, Belgium, Holland, Germany, Mexico, Poland, New Zealand, Palestine, Norway, Scotland, South Africa, Spain and Sweden, and pirated ones in Greece, Turkey and Japan. As far as I have been able to ascertain, it failed only in France, where the translation was made by Francis Carco, an authority on life in Montmartre, who had never visited America and knew almost no English—so all the characters came out as apaches, which was, of course, wholly contrary to the spirit of the play.

6

In New York, my battle with Brady was renewed. As I had feared, the two road companies he had organized in my absence were sadly miscast and badly directed. I could not make him see that the good old days when the road towns accepted whatever was offered were over, that third-rate productions could no longer complete with star-studded, low-priced talking pictures. Upon my threat of public repudiation of the productions, he removed from the program a line that read: "As directed by Elmer Rice." The companies toured all season and fared quite well, but not nearly so well as they should have, for critical comments on the inferiority of the productions undoubtedly kept many people away.

In another department things went better. Samuel Goldwyn, my old employer, suddenly evinced a strong interest in the motion picture rights. Negotiations were conducted by Joseph P. Bickerton, Jr., a well-known theatrical lawyer, who was impartial arbiter jointly chosen by the Dramatists' Guild and the managers. An agreement was quickly reached. To preserve the integrity of the play, I asked for an assurance that its spirit and intention would not be violated and that only such changes would be made as were necessary in transferring it from one medium to another. Bickerton said he would draft the clause, though he doubted its acceptance.

When Goldwyn arrived in New York, his attorney told him the deal was off because of my impossible demands. Goldwyn asked for a meeting, at which his attorney read the restrictive clause. Goldwyn said he could not agree to it.

I said, "Sam, you're paying one of the highest prices ever paid for motion picture rights. If you have some other story in mind, why don't you hire someone to write it, instead of wasting your money on *Street Scene?*"

"What are you talking about?" said Goldwyn irritably. "I don't want to make some other story. I want to make *Street Scene.*"

"That's all I'm asking you to do," I said.

He turned to his attorney and said, "I'll sign the contract." He then engaged me to write the screenplay.

While I was at work on it, Sid Grauman, large-scale movie exhibitor and the builder of those architectural monstrosities on

Hollywood Boulevard, Grauman's Egyptian Theatre and Grauman's Chinese Theatre, asked me to make a Pacific Coast production of the play. He had not seen *Street Scene* and had probably never heard of it; but the Goldwyn organization, feeling that a Los Angeles showing would be helpful, had persuaded him to do it. Brady, for once, left the whole thing in my hands, so I worked out a deal with Grauman, undertaking to direct the play and to engage most of the principals of the original cast.

After rounding up about fifteen actors in the East, I wrote Grauman to make arrangements for me to interview applicants for the remaining parts, assuming, of course, that he would provide an office, where I could see a few people at a time. However, when I arrived at the Mayan Theatre I was appalled to see some six or seven hundred actors lined up on the sidewalk. Grauman's press agent explained that it would be a good publicity stunt to take pictures of hundreds of actors, thrown out of work by the depression, queuing up for jobs in *Street Scene*. Infuriated by this crude attempt to exploit the unemployed, I threatened to abandon the production unless the photographers were dismissed. Then I invited the actors inside. They filled almost the entire theatre. It was not a pleasant situation, but it had to be faced. I came out on the stage to explain that only minor parts were open, and that any applicant's chances were about one in twenty. I waited for an exodus, but only a handful left. Since, as usual, there were three times as many women as men, I said that I would see only men that day, thereby reducing the crowd to manageable size. Fortunately, next day most of the women did not come back.

One day, just before the opening, I saw on the wall of the theatre the painted announcement that *Street Scene* was playing there "with the original cast of seventy-five." I let this modest fifty per cent Hollywood mark-up pass. Next day, however, an electrical sign immediately below the wall proclaimed "a cast of one hundred." I hunted up Beall, the press agent, to point out that it was a mistake to have both signs on the same side of the theatre, since some keen observer might detect the discrepancy. Beall saw my point, and the numerals were accordingly reduced.

Since Grauman had not attended any of the rehearsals, I asked Beall if his employer would like to see the dress rehearsal. "Does Mr. Grauman have to be there?" he inquired rather huffily. I said

I had thought he might like to see what he was putting his money into. "No," said Beall. "He's too busy getting stars to come to the opening."

The opening-night curtain had been announced for eight-thirty. At eight-thirty-five I looked through the curtain peephole, saw that the house was almost filled, and went out to the box office to tell Grauman that I was about to ring up. Panic-stricken, he said, "You can't do that! Mary Pickford isn't here!" I agreed to wait three or four minutes. At eight-forty I said, "The audience is in and I'm not going to keep them waiting any longer." As I pressed the button to give the cue backstage for the house lights to dim, Mary Pickford swept into the lobby, arrayed like Solomon in all his glory. "Oh, my God!" said Grauman, almost in tears. "Now she won't be able to make her entrance." Nevertheless, the play went well and the notices were excellent. Everybody agreed that Grauman had scored a great triumph.

As I entered the theatre one day just after the abdication of Alfonso XIII of Spain, Grauman called me into his office, where several of his advisers were gathered. He wanted my opinion of a wireless message they were preparing. It read substantially as follows: "King Alfonso XIII, royal yacht off coast of Spain: Believe a motion picture based on the colorful history of the Bourbon family in which you appeared under my personal supervision could easily gross a million dollars. If interested please advise me of your terms. Sid Grauman." I asked if he thought the figure was high enough. "No, you're right!" he said. "Let's make it three million." A week later I asked him how his negotiations with Alfonso were faring. "What do you think?" he said. "The so-and-so never even answered my wire."

7

My *Street Scene* scenario was duly examined by Colonel Joy of the Association of Motion Picture Producers for violations of the motion picture "Code." His proposed emendations were, like the Lord Chamberlain's, so few and, with one exception, so inconsequential that I did not think it worth while to contest them. They included the elimination of "hell" and "damn" and a line here and there. For example, "I'll give you two dollars if you let me snap your garter" was characterized as containing "a suggestion which is likely to prove offensive."

Another item that amused me was: "As a matter of foreign policy, we suggest that the reference to the Prince of Wales be omitted, since the English are very prone to take offense at any flippant reference made to this personage." I did not bother to point out that the Prince of Wales had seen the play twice in London, without international repercussions. It was all too trivial to be taken seriously.

The one suggested change that did arouse me had a stormy background. In the play, a social worker who appears briefly in the first act scolds one of her "clients" for spending part of her relief money on the movies. Throughout the run of the play I was deluged with letters from various social agencies, some quite imperious in tone, alleging that I was maligning social workers and demanding that I alter the characterization. In reply, I defended the right of an author to depict life as he sees it. To William Hodson, who claimed he was "voicing the sentiments of seven hundred social agencies," I wrote:

Street Scene is not a sociological treatise and there is no intention to generalize about anything or anybody. I have simply tried to portray certain aspects of the New York scene as they have presented themselves to me. . . . I wonder what you would think if the American Federation of Labor denounced the play as unfair upon the perfectly reasonable ground that every stagehand does not murder his wife, or if all the milk companies entered a formal protest to the effect that their collectors do not make a practice of having illicit relationships with their female customers.

The battle went on and on. Every kind of cajolery and pressure was brought to bear upon me. An attempt was even made to get at me through my old friend Owen R. Lovejoy, now secretary of the Children's Aid Society. But Lovejoy wrote me: "Of course we both know that there are many social workers of an entirely different type . . . but I regret to have to agree that your picture of a certain kind is not overdrawn." An article in *The Survey*, the social workers' trade journal, stated that at an indignation meeting the "cooler heads" had prevailed and it had been decided to take no action. I have often wondered what action would have been taken if the hotter heads had prevailed!

But that did not end it. When one of the touring companies played Minneapolis, the Family Welfare Association and the Twin City Chapter of the American Association of Social Workers demanded that the characterization be modified. Brady, recognizing the implied threat of the withholding of patronage, ordered the changes made. I was in Europe and knew nothing about it until I received a letter from Erin telling me that the scene had been so garbled as to be unintelligible. Of course it was too late for me to do anything.

Now I found in Colonel Joy's memorandum the directive that Miss Simpson should not be characterized as a social worker "unless she is shown as a kindly and tolerant person." In response to my vigorous protest, which had the support of the Goldwyn organization, Colonel Joy said that while he did not find the characterization objectionable or violative of the Code, the influence of the heads of community chests and local charity organizations was so great that exhibition of the picture could be seriously curtailed by pressure brought to bear upon exhibitors and municipal censors. Even before the picture rights had been sold, the Association of Motion Picture Producers had received intimidating letters from charity organizations. No motion picture company can withstand organized boycott and organized blackmail. The investment is too large to be jeopardized for anything as insubstantial as the principle of freedom of expression.

Indignant at the tactics employed by the apostles of civic virtue, I racked my brains to find a way of circumventing them. At last I hit upon a simple and effective solution. There was only one line in the play that identified Miss Simpson as a social worker, though by her words and actions she could not have been anything else. By merely eliminating the identification, I put the social agencies in the impossible position of being obliged to say, "This unpleasant woman is obviously a social worker, and we protest her characterization as such." My suggestion was accepted, and the scene was screened exactly as I had written it, with the excision of "She's from the charities."

King Vidor, director of the picture, was in complete sympathy with the spirit of the play. The picture, almost an exact replica of the play, had enough audience appeal to make it a great financial success. Goldwyn has often told me that he considers it one of his most satisfactory productions.

The story of *Street Scene* would be incomplete if I omitted one final episode. In 1954, just twenty-five years after the first production, a television agent, fired by my suggestion that the play, with its New York setting and its great variety of characters, seemed good material for a serial, approached several leading producers of TV shows. His efforts were unsuccessful, for reasons clearly set forth in a long letter from the president of one of the companies, written in the pontifical style peculiar to important executives. The writer acknowledges that the play has merit and expresses the opinion that there is "a need for a television series which will dramatize the daily incidents of urban life." Nevertheless, he says, there are "many serious objections to the treatment of this property as presented in the existing prospectus." He proceeds:

Foremost among these objections is the squalor of the setting, the lower class social level of all the chief characters, and the utterly depressing circumstances which they all find themselves in. . . .

We know of no advertiser or advertising agency of any importance in this country who would knowingly allow the products which he is trying to advertise to the public to become associated with the squalor, depression, continuous frustration and general "down" quality of *Street Scene* week after week.

On the contrary, it is the general policy of advertisers to glamorize their products, the people who buy them, and the whole American social and economic scene. If you will glance at the advertisements in your favorite magazine, listen to radio or television, for any one night, you will see the confirmation of this. The American consuming public as presented by the Advertising Industry today is middle class, not lower class; happy in general, not miserable and frustrated; and optimistic, not depressed.

8

My failure to interest anyone in *The Left Bank* led me to consider the possibility of producing it myself. Seventeen years' contact with producers had convinced me that few of them made creative contributions to the production of a play. Mostly they were middlemen who optioned a play, engaged the required personnel, rented a theatre, even got their capital from outside sources. Since I had been casting and directing my own plays, it seemed to me that with the aid of a competent business manager I could handle the other details too. Financing was the main problem. Even if I had had fiscal connections, I would have been reluctant to solicit backing for my own plays. It came down to a question of whether or not I was willing to risk my own money.

Like everyone who had any assets at all, I had been hit by the Wall Street debacle, even though I had never bought anything on margin and had confined myself to investments whose safety was regarded by financial experts as beyond question. My losses, however, were more than made up by the continuing revenue from *Street Scene*. The production cost of *The Left Bank*, a one-set play with a cast of moderate size, could not be very great. Further, unless the play was a complete failure my royalties would help offset the production cost. All in all, it seemed to be not too harebrained a venture.

I asked Joe Bickerton, the motion picture arbiter, who had been associated with numerous Broadway productions, whether he would act as my general adviser and business manager on a profit-sharing basis. He immediately agreed, suggesting, however, that I spread my risk by producing two plays instead of one. That fell in very well with my plans, for I was intending to begin work on a new play.

When the children went off to camp, my wife and I, who had no summer plans, sought to escape the city's heat by staying for a while at the Half Moon Hotel in Seagate, at the tip of Coney Island, away from the crowded beach and boardwalk. From our windows we had a sweeping view of the sea. In fact, the view was too good, for I was driven to distraction by the sight of the ocean liners steaming to Europe almost under our noses. Unable to endure it, I booked passage, and in a few days we were on our way to France. We went straight to St.-Jean-de-Luz, on the Basque coast—which is far more attractive than the Riviera—just a few miles from the Spanish border.

There I wrote a play about a law office, undoubtedly suggested by my years of servitude but in no sense autobiographical or based upon actual individuals or incidents. Like *Street Scene*, it had many atmospheric touches, several interweaving subplots, and a large cast of diverse characters. But in *Counsellor-at-Law*, the action centered upon one character, an aggressive New York lawyer who had risen from poverty to glittering success. The play wrote itself easily, almost effortlessly, in five or six weeks.

During our stay at St.-Jean-de-Luz we visited Pamplona. Heming-

way's bulls were not running, but we enjoyed this first glimpse of
Spain none the less. We did see bullfights at San Sebastián, former
summer residence of the royal family whose colorful history Sid
Grauman had not been fated to bring to the screen. The first
fight, in which a horse was disemboweled, revolted me. But in the
other fights the horses wore protective pads, and to my shocked
surprise I found myself getting interested in the balletlike evolutions
of the participants. I detest violence and cruelty, yet here I was
becoming quickly inured to torture and suffering! It was disturbing.

On our trip back to Paris, by way of the Pyrenees, we stopped
at Lourdes, an ugly place, made uglier by the crass commercial-
ization of religion. Most distressing was the spectacle of sufferers
on litters and in wheel chairs, drawn from afar by a pathetic belief in miracles.

The casting of *The Left Bank* gave me no trouble. *Counsellor-at-
Law* was another matter. Everyone who read the play felt that its
success depended largely upon finding the right actor. I agreed,
but could think of no one suitable, nor was I enthusiastic about any
of the numerous suggestions I received. Then I happened to remember an actor named Muni Weisenfreund, who had come to Broadway from the Yiddish theatre. *Four Walls,* the play in which I had
seen him, was neither very good nor very successful; the character
he had played, a young gangster, was wholly unlike George Simon
in *Counsellor-at-Law.* Yet he had a quality I liked. Bickerton and
everyone else I consulted reacted unfavorably. The consensus was
that Weisenfreund, now become Paul Muni, besides being wrong
for the part was very hard to work with. I was temporarily dis-
suaded; but, unable to find anyone who satisfied me, I sent a script
to Muni, who was in Hollywood making a picture. When he expressed eagerness to play the part, I entered into negotiations with
him, quickly reached an agreement, and against everyone's advice
sent him a run-of-the-play contract. I was in sole charge and could
be as stubborn and arbitrary as I pleased. However, when the
signed contract came back I began to think that I had been a
little foolhardy in making this irrevocable commitment to an actor
I had never even met and had seen perform only once. Muni
was not due in New York until rehearsals began, so I could only
wait and see.

Since I had always felt that *The Left Bank's* appeal would be limited to traveled, sophisticated theatregoers, we arranged with Winthrop Ames to book his charming Little Theatre, which because of its small seating capacity was bypassed by most producers. For *Counsellor-at-Law,* which had potential mass appeal, we were lucky enough to book the Plymouth, which now was managed by Arthur Hopkins. Ames and Hopkins were old friends of mine; it was pleasant to be doing business with honorable, generous, literate men.

The opening of *The Left Bank* had been set for early October. In order to hold the Plymouth, I had to agree to bring in *Counsellor-at-Law* by mid-November. That gave me five weeks between the two openings, a tight schedule that precluded the possibility of a tryout for *Counsellor-at-Law.* A little worried, I plunged ahead, hoping everything would run smoothly.

Rehearsals of *The Left Bank* did. The only slightly jarring element was Katharine Alexander, Brady's daughter-in-law, who was playing the feminine lead. She had been a constant annoyance to me during the *Street Scene* production, but I did not hold that against her; I liked her personally and admired her as an actress. She thought as little of *The Left Bank* as she had of *Street Scene.* Anything but an intellectual, she asked constantly for explanations of her lines and wanted to cut some of her most effective speeches. But I was more amused than exasperated by her objections, for I was well satisfied with her performance. One day during a break in rehearsals, when we were all sitting about chatting, she sighed and said, "If I ever had a good part, I'd like Philip Moeller to direct me in it." When we all roared with laughter, she blushed and stammered an apology.

Bickerton and my very capable press agent, Phyllis Perlman, had advised a Saturday-night tryout in Great Neck, Long Island. The play, attuned to the intimacy of the Little Theatre, was swallowed up in the vastnesses of the suburban playhouse. Discouraged, I was inclined not to bring it into New York. Better quietly to acknowledge failure, I thought, than to go through the agonies of a New York fiasco. My associates argued that, having gone this far, I should risk the final step. So I spent the weekend steeling myself for the worst.

Things went better in New York. Raymond Sovey's amusing reproduction of a third-class French hotel room papered with one of those inexcusable designs (selected from samples I had brought back from France) immediately delighted the numerous cognoscenti in the audience, as did the familiar electrical arrangements which permitted only one light to be on at a time, and the voluble, inefficient *valet de chambre*. The cast was in fine form, the production ran smoothly, there was a friendly ripple of laughter throughout, warm applause at the end.

The notices were what are called "mixed" (defined by George Kaufman as "good and rotten"). Luckily, the best was where it counted most: Brooks Atkinson's in the *Times*. The rest ranged from the mildly commendatory to the outright denunciatory. The more down-to-earth reviewers, who connoted Paris with the Folies Bergères, dismissed the play entirely. It was generally agreed that the play had no chance of running. While still reading the reviews, I was amazed by a telephone call from George Jean Nathan, whom, at that time, I had never met. He congratulated me upon the play and urged me to keep it going in spite of the notices. Later he gave it an excellent review.

I had to turn at once to *Counsellor-at-Law*, for rehearsals were to begin within a week. My first meeting with Muni dispelled all doubts about his rightness for the part. Nor did I ever find him "difficult," either during rehearsal or in the course of my long association with him. Now and then he grumbled about the performances of some of his fellow players, but all leading actors tend to do that. Sometimes his complaints were justified. His expertness won for him the admiration of everyone who worked with him.

Halfway through rehearsals we had disquieting news. The "first-string" critics were planning to attend the opening of S. N. Behrman's *Brief Moment*, scheduled for the same night as *Counsellor-at-Law*. In those crowded years, conflicting openings were quite common. (On the night of December 26, 1927, there were eleven Broadway openings. Faced with a manpower shortage, the newspapers pressed financial editors, sportswriters and police-court reporters into service as dramatic critics.) Our only solution was to advance the opening from Monday to the preceding Friday. Muni protested vigorously, and with reason: his part was long and difficult; he had been worried from the beginning about opening cold with only one preview. But, rather than be reviewed by the assistant critics, he gave in. Things were tense now, and we really had to put on steam.

The preview went well; everything moved right along. Muni was

brilliant and received an ovation. The outlook was good. On opening night, I sat with Arthur Hopkins in the Plymouth's little gallery, from which lights are projected. There is room for four or
five chairs, and we were the sole occupants. The first scene, in which
Muni did not appear, went smoothly. But in the second scene, which
he dominated, something seemed to be going wrong. I soon discovered what it was: he had forgotten his lines—"dried up," in stage
lingo—and had to wait to be prompted. Fortunately he was helped
by his training in the Yiddish theatre, where actors depend largely
upon the prompter. Nevertheless, the performance was appreciably
slowed; all the carefully rehearsed timing went by the board. I was
in agony, sitting up there under the ceiling, inaudibly prompting,
too, reciting Muni's whole part. Hopkins did not help matters. He
paced the narrow gallery behind me, pausing now and then to say,
"He's throwing your play, Elmer. He's throwing your play."

But, fine actor that Muni is, he rode it out and was acclaimed at
the end. I hurried backstage and asked what had happened. "Well,"
he said, "when the curtain went up I suddenly remembered that
Robert Garland was out there; and all I could think of was that he
gave me a bad notice once."

The press was, on the whole, favorable. John Mason Brown said
he had spent a "completely fatiguing evening," and there were other
adverse comments, but Muni was lavishly praised and the play did
not come off badly. Several critics complained that it was too long,
meaning that they had fifteen minutes less than usual to meet
their early deadlines.

This is another of the absurdities of the Broadway theatre.
Every playwright is expected to accommodate himself to the
schedules of the morning newspapers by cutting down his play
so that it does not run more than two hours. It is as though no
novel were permitted to exceed three hundred pages, or no symphony to play more than twenty minutes. Theatregoers do not
share this demand for an arbitrary time limit; if they are interested,
they are glad to stay. I have attended European performances that
lasted five hours. During the run of *Counsellor-at-Law* I watched
the play scores of times; not once did I see anyone leave before
the final curtain.

There was never any uncertainty about the play's success. In
three weeks it paid off its production cost—which was less than

eleven thousand dollars! The perennial question "What is wrong
with the theatre?" may be partly answered by the fact that a comparable production today, some thirty years later, would cost about
$125,000. Though the theatre as a whole was sharply affected by the
depression, *Counsellor-at-Law* continued to play to capacity for
many months. Soon after the opening we put a second company into
Chicago, headed by Otto Kruger, who gave a fine performance,
though it was not up to Muni's. The play ran in Chicago for
twenty weeks.

The Left Bank, thanks in part to the low operating expenses of
the Little Theatre, ran eight months, for a total of 250 performances.
It was comfortably filled every evening by three our four hundred
people, who would have been lost in a large theatre. Some weeks
showed a slight profit, others a slight loss. So it ran on, week after
week, month after month, in spite of the gloomy prognostications of
Katharine Alexander. Almost every time I went backstage she would
say, "Are we closing Saturday? Mr. Brady says we can't possibly
run another week." A curious feature of the Little Theatre was a
corridor that ran backstage from the box office. Several times I
saw Katharine tiptoeing down the corridor to peep through the
iron grille at the ticket rack. In a spirit of mischief, I had the
grille curtained. We never discussed it, of course, but she knew I
enjoyed scoring the point.

Once I told the three principals that if they would cut their
salaries by one third I would guarantee them another six weeks.
They agreed, but smiled wanly at my promise to reimburse them if
business picked up. Of course I took a cut in my royalties, and
Winthrop Ames co-operated too. Business did pick up, so I summoned the actors again and handed them checks covering their
cuts. They were utterly dumfounded. A few days later, Horace
Braham, who was one of them, wrote me: "After years of cozening,
clipping, gypping, squeezing, nicking, grafting, paring, sniping,
skinning, scorching, flaying and blistering, on the part of most
managers, it is a novel and happy experience to do business with a
man who is generous and fair." Next came a letter from Frank
Gillmore, president of Equity: "It may seem strange that we should
write you on such a subject, but unfortunately our experience has
been that managers who are compelled to cut salaries and promise
that they will make it up, should there be a profit, generally forget

this obligation." These reactions to the simple act of a man keeping his word struck me as a sad commentary on the ethics of the theatrical business—though I think the same could be said of most businesses.

To my great surprise, Universal Pictures bought the rights to *The Left Bank*, apparently at the instigation of one of its directors. The picture was never made, which pleased me very well, for the play would have required drastic alterations to make it conform to the Code. All in all, my managerial venture showed a substantial profit. More important than that, the play's production gave me about as much satisfaction as anything in my professional life. Yet today the play would go unproduced, for instead of costing eight thousand dollars it would cost seventy-five thousand, which no one would risk, least of all myself.

During the run of *Counsellor-at-Law* we were invited by Warden Lewis E. Lawes of Sing Sing to give a Sunday-night performance at the prison. With mingled curiosity and misgivings, the cast and I accepted. We were greeted by the entertainment director of the Mutual Welfare League, a stock swindler once well known on Broadway. I made a quick survey of the production facilities. They were quite adequate: a workable stage and a battered interior stage set, the gift of some producer, which could be made to serve for both of the play's locales. I conferred with the stage crew of prisoners, one of whom was giving sharp orders which the others meekly obeyed. Upon inquiry I learned that he was a former stagehand.

As we passed through the corridors on our way to dinner, the women members of the cast were disconcerted by the frank stares of the prisoners. We ate at trestle tables, waited on by trusties. When the actors went off to dress, I accompanied Warden Lawes to the front row of the auditorium. The gray-clad prisoners, in platoons, marched in and took their places. Lawes made a few introductory remarks and then called upon me to speak. I was taken completely by surprise, but of course could not refuse. As I faced the two thousand men, I was horrified to see how young most of them were: under twenty-five, it seemed. The whole penal system had always revolted me; here was a vivid demonstration of the callousness of a society that acquiesced in the waste of all these young lives. I suppose the community must protect itself against those who prey upon it, but I believe that the aim of incarceration should be to cure, not to punish; that the millions spent on the degradation of the perpetrators of crime could be better employed in studying and removing its economic and psychological causes.

It was not easy to know what to say, so I described in some detail the New York stage settings and asked forbearance for any roughness in the performance because of mechanical problems. The play went as it had never gone before. Every member of the audience was familiar with the workings of a law office; many of the characters were recognizable types; often the situations were anticipated. Muni was at his best. The many lines that referred to crime and criminals he glided over with great tact. Throughout, the laughter and the applause were thunderous. The emotional strain left the actors limp. They all agreed that it was an experience they would not have wanted to miss, but one they would not want to go through again.

A few days later Warden Lawes sent me an anonymous critique headed "An impression by No. 81–284." A few excerpts will indicate its general tone:

> Over two thousand men in gray, prisoners doing sentences from one year to natural life, vigorously applauded the cast of *Counsellor-at-Law*. . . . Was it merely a polite gesture? Or did they witness something keenly alive and intensely human? . . . To us prisoners George Simon is not an unfamiliar figure. He fights our battles. He confirms our hates. He is sympathetic with the underdog. . . . It wasn't really George Simon we prisoners were watching. We were seeing life. . . . Prison is a grim thing. Prisoners are grim people. Yet one does hear laughter within the walls. Men smile through tears. Neither seems unnatural as we wear down the years that still separate us from all that we hold dear and vital. And so we enjoyed keenly the varying shades with which Elmer Rice portrayed the grimness of life. . . .
>
> Two thousand men in the audience. Two thousand human problems. All reflected in the struggles, the objectives, the hopes and the failures of George Simon and his company. That was the reason for the spontaneous and prolonged applause of Sing Sing's population for *Counsellor-at-Law*.

Universal Pictures bought the screen rights to *Counsellor-at-Law* as well as to *The Left Bank*. It was a lucrative deal that included my services as scenarist. With this important matter settled, the play itself prospering in New York and Chicago, and *The Left Bank* holding its own, I felt that the time had come to put into effect a long-contemplated project: an extensive trip to the Soviet Union.

XV

The Future at Work

1

Russia had always had a particular fascination for me. Years before the revolution I read widely in Russian literature: Tolstoi, Turgenev, Pushkin, Gorki, Dostoevski, Chekhov, Andreyev, Artsibashev, Gogol, Kropotkin. Though I could not hope to emulate Chekhov, I was undoubtedly influenced by the delicate tapestry of his plays. My first encounter with the Diaghilev Ballet was an aesthetic awakening. I was enchanted, too, by the New York appearances of Baliev's Chauve-Souris, the Moscow Art Theatre and the Artev Theatre. Nijinsky, Pavlova, Stanislavski, Moskvin and Chaliapin were among the most exciting performers I had ever seen. I greatly enjoyed Russian music: Moussorgski, Borodin, Stravinsky, Prokoviev, even Tchaikovsky and Rimski-Korsakov in small doses.

While admiring Russia's artistic achievements, I detested its dark, tyrannical political regime. Like all freedom lovers, I was outraged by the pogroms, the mowing down of Father Gapon's followers on Bloody Sunday, the reports of illiteracy, hunger and terror. The overthrow of the Romanovs was cheered everywhere. I was not among those who turned hostile when the Bolsheviks made a separate peace with Germany, for I sympathized with the desire of the peasant soldiers to withdraw from a war in which hundreds of thousands of their comrades were victims of cold, hunger and military incompetence. Though I was repelled by the execution of the imperial family, I did not feel that it justified the exclusion of the Russians from the Versailles Conference, or armed intervention in aid of the counterrevolutionary generals.

As a socialist, I saw in the revolution the possibility of the establishment of a truly democratic society in which there would be no extremes of wealth and poverty, no exploitation of the many by the few. It was a fervent hope shared by millions throughout the world, but a hope that could obviously not be immediately realized. The difficulties of converting an agrarian economy to an industrial one, and of setting up political institutions for an illiterate population not long removed from serfdom, were aggravated by faulty communications, a shortage of technicians, factional disputes and the threat of counterrevolution. It was not easy for the outsider to know what was going on. The more one listened to travelers' contradictory tales, the more puzzled one became.

Interest in Russia was intensified by the situation in America. Now, in the spring of 1932, the much vaunted American economy had hit the toboggan and was coasting fast. What someone grotesquely called "the peak of the depression" had been reached. Twelve, perhaps fifteen, million workers were unemployed, using up what savings they had, living on home relief, selling apples at street corners, panhandling. "Brother, can you spare a dime?" was the theme song of J. P. McEvoy's satiric revue *Americana*. Hunger, desolation and fear stalked the land. I had moved to the Hotel Ansonia, near Riverside Drive. Along the riverfront there had sprung up a wretched colony of hovels made of waste lumber and flattened gasoline tins. At night the inhabitants gathered about bonfires to cook whatever they had been able to procure, and to keep themselves warm: a hobo jungle on the fringe of one of Manhattan's more expensive residential districts. Yet these people were not derelicts, but ordinary American citizens who had been reduced to living in these "Hoovervilles," so called in honor of the apostle of laissez-faire who had declared in his 1929 inaugural address that the problem of poverty had been abolished in the United States. It seemed evident that something was wrong somewhere with the American system. I was interested in trying to find out if the Russians had devised anything better. I remembered Lincoln Steffens' vociferous "I have seen the future and it works!"

The Soviet Union's attitude toward foreign visitors has, like most of its policies, been subject to wide fluctuations. At that time tourists were welcomed because of the desperate need for foreign currency—*valuta*, the Russians called it—to pay for the importation of machine tools. I carefully planned a ten-week trip, working through the Soviet tourist agency, Intourist, and an American travel bureau that had a Moscow representative. I had numerous letters of introduction to American residents and to Russian theatrical and literary figures. My son, Robert, now fifteen, and I planned to be in Moscow for the May Day celebration. My wife and daughter were to join us in June.

On the eve of our departure, the combined casts of *The Left Bank* and *Counsellor-at-Law* gave me a surprise farewell party at Sardi's, just a few steps from the theatres that housed the plays. There were gracious speeches and the presentation of an inscribed travel clock. I was touched. It is not customary for actors to fete producers.

En route to Moscow we stopped in Berlin. Shortly after our arrival, we went for a stroll to the Lustgarten, where a meeting was in progress. Mounted on the base of a statue was a dark, ugly man, haranguing his apathetic listeners in a harsh voice. From a bystander I learned that the speaker was Dr. Paul Goebbels, chief lieutenant of Adolf Hitler. Though I was a fairly close follower of European political events, the name of Goebbels was barely known to me. Even Hitler had attracted relatively little attention in America, where there was a tendency to regard him as a demagogic crackpot with a ridiculous Charlie Chaplin mustache.

In the bar of the Hotel Bristol I ran into H. R. Knickerbocker, the well-known Hearst correspondent, who had just accompanied Hitler on a nationwide campaign tour. In Knickerbocker's opinion, Hitler had no program and knew it; therefore he did not want the chancellorship, for if he came to power his hollowness would be revealed. He preferred to go on as a sort of gadfly, exercising increasing influence upon the government without assuming responsibility. Coming from an acknowledged expert, it was a comforting analysis.

2

We took the night train from Berlin, crossing the Russo-Polish border through a gap in the barbed-wire barrier, and detraining at

Negoreloye, not only for entry formalities, but also to change trains. Under the czars, the Russian railways were constructed with a wide gauge to make military invasion more difficult.

The Red Army men at the station were still wearing their ankle-length winter coats. Customs inspection was less rigid than I had expected. But the passenger just ahead of us, a self-important German who might have been an engineer or industrialist, was incensed when an official untied a carefully wrapped package of phonograph records and examined each one on both sides. Next, heedless of the German's protests, he opened a packet of Swiss travel folders and spread them on the counter. I was sure he was just enjoying the colored pictures of Alpine scenery. When our turn came, he concentrated on our books, designating two as inadmissible. Since he obviously could read no language but Russian, I hunted up a French-speaking inspector, to whom I pointed out that the banned books were a German language manual and a guide to Berlin. Thereupon the books were passed.

The little we saw of the White Russian countryside on the overnight trip to Moscow was not attractive: swampy land, with here and there a wretched village. But there were signs of the new order: railroad tracks being laid, factories and homes under construction. Most striking was the sight of women doing work usually performed by men. I never did get quite used to seeing these stocky, brawny women, in head scarves and knee-length skirts, shoveling coal, cleaning streets, putting down railway ties, carrying heavy loads.

In Moscow we were met by the representative of our travel agency. With her was Ernest Hitzegrath, a young Intourist guide especially assigned to us. Of him I shall have much to say. A Lincoln limousine took us to the Novo Moskvaskaya Hotel, where we had a room with private bath. It was comfortably enough furnished, with brass bedsteads such as I had not seen since childhood, and a large spittoon, another reminder of my boyhood home. I discovered that the call bell was out of order and told the room clerk about it. Next morning a workman carrying a large tool kit appeared. When he had finished, I saw that he had neatly tacked up a card announcing in English, French, German and Russian that the bell was out of order. At the end of our two-week occupancy the card was still there.

From Ernest Hitzegrath, our constant companion, I learned more about Communist psychology than from any other source. A tall, broad-shouldered, handsome youth of twenty-one, with angular features, bright-blue eyes and close-cropped blond hair, he looked like one of Hitler's brown-shirted storm troopers who strutted about Berlin. In fact, he was a German. His parents, resident in Russia at the time of the revolution, had either fled or been killed. He had been reared in an orphanage, had gone to work young and at eighteen had a factory job in Baku on the Caspian Sea. He told me that when he passed the vats of caviar on his way to work he scooped up a double handful for his breakfast. When, later, he was sent to the Intourist school in Moscow where bright young people (mostly girls) were trained as guides, he elected to study English and was assigned to a class conducted by a former Oxford don. After some weeks, Ernest headed a committee which informed the head of the school that it was American they wanted to learn, not some strange English dialect. Accordingly an American teacher was substituted for the bewildered Oxonian. By the time I met Ernest he was speaking fluent New York slang, though with a marked Russian accent.

Ernest, who had come up through the youth organizations, was hoping for membership in the Communist Party, a privilege accorded to relatively few. I never doubted that he was a member of the secret police, then known as the G.P.U. (and to American correspondents as the Y.M.C.A.). But that neither affected our cordial relationship nor kept me from freely expressing my opinions. Though he detested the Germans and knew no word of the language, his Germanic traits were unmistakable. He was methodical, Calvinistically conscientious and, luckily for us, extremely efficient. A normal boy with normal appetites and a lust for life, he had imposed upon himself the asceticism that pertains to membership in a dedicated elite. What saved him from stuffiness and intolerable dogmatism was an un-Teutonic sense of humor. There is no common language like laughter; it bridged many of our differences.

Two aspects of Moscow that struck me immediately were the crowdedness and the cleanliness of its streets. From the windows of our hotel, only a few yards from the Moscow River, we could see, at any hour of the day or night, the incessant human stream that poured across the Balchug Bridge. There were almost no taxis;

buses and trolleys were crowded beyond the limits of decency and safety. We never even attempted to use them, for we were within walking distance of Red Square and of many of the theatres, museums and hotels. For longer trips, Intourist usually supplied a car. The cleanliness of Moscow as compared to New York or even to most European cities was due to the shortage of paper and the absence of dogs. Newspapers were saved for wrappings; there was no food to spare for pets.

Except for the Kremlin and its environs, Moscow was neither beautiful nor architecturally interesting. The general effect was squat heaviness: nondescript nineteenth-century buildings, many of them dilapidated, interspersed with wooden structures and here and there a log cabin. The new buildings were strictly utilitarian and often hastily constructed; some were already showing signs of deterioration. Of course, the transformation of a provincial city into a world capital had hardly begun.

The Kremlin, with its fifty-foot-high crenellated wall, studded with nineteen towers, dominates the city. The palace, now a museum for the exhibition of imperial relics, contained some objects of artistic merit, but in the main it was a display of what Thorstein Veblen called conspicuous waste. Legends affixed to the showcases contrasted the luxurious life of the Romanovs with the wretchedness of the masses. In one of the three handsome cathedrals dating from the fifteenth and sixteenth centuries, a chart detailed the expenses, seven million rubles, of the late Czar's crowning. Beside it was one of the bags of nuts and sausages distributed to the crowds on that occasion; in the struggle to obtain these trifles, hundreds of people had been trampled.

On our obligatory visit to Lenin's tomb in Red Square, hundreds of people were patiently waiting to get in, but as tourists we went to the head of the line. There were lines everywhere. If it was rumored that meat or kerosene or candy was to go on sale at a certain shop, people began to queue up hours before the place opened. Even if the rumor was not false, the supply was exhausted long before the end of the line was reached. "When a Russian sees a line," said Ernest, "he joins it." My laughter was tempered by recollections of the lines at employment agencies, relief centers and soup kitchens in prosperous, democratic America.

We dutifully shuffled past the purported remains of the great leader. Whether what we saw was actually Lenin's body, miraculously preserved, or a wax effigy, seemed of little moment. One of the grim jokes then current in Moscow concerned two citizens who meet in Red Square. "How is it with you?" asks one. "With me," says the other, "is like with Lenin. They don't bury me and they don't feed me." We heard many such jokes. When open criticism is rigorously suppressed, the human spirit finds expression in surreptitious humor.

The traditional museums were only moderately interesting. Except for classical icon painting, under Byzantine influence, Russian painting is uninspired and conventional. The prerevolutionary canvases are meticulously representational; the contemporary "socialist" art, banal beyond belief, crude depictions of revolutionary incidents, tractors and industrial activity. Throughout the city large caricatures, dealing mostly with the German situation, were on display. But it was not Hitler who was satirized. The butt was the Social Democratic leader Karl Kautsky, who was portrayed as the lackey of the German Junkers!

Tolstoi's house, tastefully preserved as a museum, had the appearance of a home that was still lived in: coats hanging in the entry, a table set for tea, toys scattered about, a workbench strewn with tools used by Tolstoi for his shoe-repairing hobby. I asked Ernest what he thought of Tolstoi. "He was a great writer," was the reply, "but he was not one of ours."

But it was the present—and the future—that we had come to see, so we devoted ourselves to inspecting the new order. It is commonly alleged that the Russians permit visitors to see only what they want them to see. (Of course, we do not go out of our way to show foreigners our Skid Rows, segregated schools, tenant farms and death houses.) The only request of mine that was denied was for permission to visit a G.P.U. prison. We did see a prison for women convicted of nonpolitical crimes. We also visited a housing project, a civil court, a night sanitarium and a marriage and divorce bureau.

In the "People's Court," all formalities were dispensed with. During our brief stay three cases were disposed of. The presiding judge, who was a lawyer, was flanked by two nonprofessional "people's representatives," women in kerchiefs. One complainant, a woman, wanted to evict a lodger; his defense was that the landlady was a "merchant." Though some private trading was permitted, those who engaged in it were not looked upon with favor, so the verdict went against her. "Class policy," said Ernest. The whole atmosphere was one of rough frontier justice.

Soviet policy with respect to marriage, divorce, contraception and abortion has undergone many changes. At that time, marriage and divorce were mere formalities, important chiefly for keeping one's identity papers in order. Marriages were terminated upon the mere request of either party; the clerk simply made an entry in the applicant's passport. If the other party was absent, a postcard notification of the divorce was sent. It was mechanical and cold-blooded, yet more realistic and honest than the collusion, perjury and legal hypocrisy that characterize American divorce procedures. In one of the cases we observed, the husband, who opposed the divorce but could do nothing to prevent it, asked what was to be done about the couple's room. The clerk directed that the wife remain there until she was able to find other quarters. I said to Ernest, "This seems unfair. The man cannot prevent the divorce, yet he must go on sharing his room with his ex-wife. What if he decides to re-marry?" "Very easy," said Ernest. "They just put up a curtain."

The apartment house we inspected, though jerry-built, was up-to-date. Each two-room unit had cooking facilities; there was at least one bathroom on each floor. On the ground floor was a large auditorium suitable for concerts, movies and meetings: an indispensable feature of any social complex in the Soviet Union. An eight-year-old tenant tagged along with us. In contrast to the dirt-floored log hut from which his family had just moved, this was an earthly paradise. He told us proudly that he could read and write, and that he was a member of the Young Pioneers, the lowest stratum in the Communist structure, roughly analogous to our Cub Scouts. He said he would like to ask a question of the "American delegation." "And what," he said, "is the condition of American children?" It was a hard question to answer.

The 250 inmates of the women's prison, called a "house of correction," included thieves, illicit distillers, carriers of venereal disease, and more than twenty murderesses. The minimum age was eighteen, the maximum sentence ten years. There was no death sentence except for political offenses. The prison was organized as a shawl manufactory. The women worked in large, airy rooms equipped with radios; they were locked up only at night. We saw the nursery and playroom for the inmates' children, the "club" where movies were shown, and the schoolroom. By the time a prisoner was discharged, she was literate, had been taught a trade, and was eligible for trade-union membership, which meant job security. Once yearly during the term of imprisonment the inmate was allowed to go home for a week or two. In short, the emphasis was upon rehabilitation rather than upon punishment, a policy for whose advocacy my friend Judge Ben Lindsey of Denver had been denounced as an impractical idealist and a softy.

The night hospital was occupied entirely by tubercular railroad workers, who returned there at the end of the workday for medication, therapy and special diet. In many cases the disease was arrested or cured. If the patient did not respond to treatment he was invalided and transferred to another hospital. By American standards, the hospital was far below par: unscreened windows, a general air of untidiness. But Ernest pointed out that what we were seeing was only a beginning: an affirmative recognition of the needs of the patients, who formerly would simply have worsened and died.

Ernest's comment taught me a lesson that might well be heeded by any American who visits Russia. The Soviet citizen did not think in terms of penthouses, station wagons and deep-freeze units. His basis for comparison was life in prerevolutionary times. The housing-project tenants were discovering the miracles of electricity and running water. The tubercular patient may have had a father who died of neglect. The woman prisoner remembered that her mother was an unskilled illiterate farm drudge. Moscow shops offered no display of luxurious footwear, but when, at last, every citizen had a pair of shoes there was rejoicing, though the shoes may have been ill-fitting. Sugar was often in short supply, but in former times most people saw it only on feast days.

Typical was the point of view of one of the hotel chambermaids. She spoke German, so we managed to communicate. When I offered to pay her for doing our laundry, she said money was no use to her, for there was so little to buy, but she would like "things." To her great joy, I gave her soap, cigarettes, chocolate and two neckties. She complained about shortages and high prices, but said she was well enough off, with an eight-hour day, adequate food and excellent maternity care. In another country, she said, she might be unemployed and starving.

3

One of the first persons I looked up was Walter Duranty, whom I had met a few times in Paris. As a front-line correspondent he had gone uninjured all through World War I, only to lose a leg in a French railroad accident shortly afterward. New York *Times* correspondent in Russia for more than ten years, he was in high favor with the Soviet government. In collaboration with Maurice Hindus he had written a play, for which I had tried without success to find a New York producer.

Duranty's private opinion of the Soviet regime was quite at variance with his dispatches. He dwelt upon the bureaucracy and favoritism. When I said that he made it sound like Tammany Hall, he replied that it was, except that there was very little graft. He dismissed as illusory Western hopes that the regime was in danger of collapse. A curious little incident marked our visit. While we were chatting informally with Duranty and his charming Russian housekeeper, with whom his relations were obviously not entirely impersonal, Ernest arrived to take us to the theatre. Duranty, who had been sharply criticizing the Soviet system, immediately launched into a eulogy of the great construction projects, the heartening success of the Five-Year Plan. It was the sort of thing that happens backstage: an actor, conversing casually in the wings, hears his cue and instantly bounces on to enact his assumed role.

The American correspondents were an alert, intelligent group. Ralph Barns of the New York *Herald Tribune*—killed not long afterward in an airplane accident in the Balkans—felt, as Duranty did, that there was no likelihood of an overthrow of the government. Another correspondent whom we saw often was W. H. Chamberlin, who represented, I believe, both the *Christian Science Monitor* and the London *Observer*. His Russian-born wife, a former New York schoolteacher, was bitterly anti-Soviet. With their little daughter they occupied uncomfortably cramped quarters. Chamberlin, a scholarly, conscientious man, wrote reports that depended upon documentation rather than upon sensationalism. In recent years he has conducted an unremittingly hostile campaign against the Soviet Union in the *New Leader*. In spite of differences of opinion, I have always respected his knowledge and his sincerity.

My opinion of Eugene Lyons, the United Press correspondent,

was somewhat less high. He and his vivacious wife, Billie, both of whom spoke Russian fluently, occupied a large, luxurious house that contrasted strangely with the wretched accommodations of the other correspondents. His glibness did not appeal to me. Like Chamberlin, he became a bitter foe of Sovietism (and of liberalism as well). The title of his book about Russia, *Assignment in Utopia,* is a giveaway. Either he was incredibly naïve in expecting to find Utopia there or he was setting up a man of straw as a target.

One of our earliest Soviet acquaintances was George Andreytchine, a Macedonian by birth, who had migrated to the United States, where he became active in the I.W.W. Charged with sedition during World War I, he jumped his bail, fled to Russia and became one of Trotsky's chief lieutenants. When Trotsky lost his struggle for power with Stalin, Andreytchine's fortunes, of course, went into decline. Now he was making a slight comeback as a greeter for the unimportant Intourist organization. Eager to talk about America, he spent much time with us. One day at lunch I suggested a bottle of wine. His eyes lighted, but then he quickly said no. Too much fraternization with foreigners was not looked upon with favor, especially if one bore the stigma of Trotskyism.

I saw an amusing illustration of the Soviet practice of rewriting history, so tellingly alluded to by George Orwell in *1984.* Among the numerous figures in a large painting in the Historical Museum depicting the signing of the Treaty of Brest Litovsk, Lenin and Stalin were prominent, but I looked in vain for Trotsky, chief architect of the treaty, until Ernest pointed him out to me: a fur-capped figure in the foreground, of whom only the back of the head was visible!

Another outsider was Rafael Rubinstein, formerly a lawyer and a member of the defeated Menshevik Party. A sensitive, self-effacing man, he never spoke of his hardships; but there was tragedy in his eyes. He made it possible for us to study the structure and operations of the Kamerny Theatre, with which he was connected. Its director, Alexander Tairov, was like Eugene Vakhtangov and Vsevold Meyerhold, a disciple of Stanislavski; but each of the three had developed his own style of production and founded a theatre of his own. I had letters to Stanislavski, but he was too ill to see anyone.

The Soviet writer I liked best was Leonid Leonov, author of the successful novel *Soviet River,* a vital, perceptive man with a keen sense of humor. Like many Russians, he was pessimistic about Western Europe but hopeful about America because it was not too deeply steeped in European tradition. Somewhat tentatively, I broached the subject of censorship. He was not evasive about it; considering the revolution and the prolonged civil war, he said, it was surprising that there was not more restriction. He regarded himself as an artist, not as a politician; in his opinion, if a writer was good enough he could succeed anywhere. When, a few years ago, I met him again in New York, he was gray-haired and paunchy, but still vigorous, forthright and bubbling over with healthful laughter. Whatever the fate of some of his contemporaries, he seemed to have come undamaged through forty years of Sovietism.

Through VOKS, the Society for Improving Cultural Relations with Foreign Countries, I met numerous writers; on one occasion, two dramatists who had had plays produced in New York. Ouspensky's *Red Rust,* which dealt with the intrigues of a Communist "cell," was an example of Soviet "self-criticism." It was permissible to criticize defects in the execution of policies, as long as the policies themselves were not questioned. Tretykov's *Roar China* was about Western imperialism in the Far East. I told him I shared his detestation of imperialism, but felt that his British villains were gross caricatures. He retorted, "Did the Chinese tell you that?"

With the head of VOKS, a bearded professor named Petrov, I had a long argument about freedom. To my comments upon the absence of opposition parties and an opposition press, he replied that since the government represented all the people there was no need for opposition. I tried to explain the concept of civil liberty, the right of the individual to express his opinions even though they might be erroneous or inimical to governmental policy. He shrugged, took a sip of tea, and said, "Well, this is one of the luxuries of a stabilized society."

However, here, as everywhere in the Soviet Union, my strictures, though sharply combated, were not resented; I spoke my mind freely but was never chided for doing so. At the same time, I was constantly put on the defensive by inquiries about the Sacco-Vanzetti case, the Scottsboro boys, the Scopes "monkey" trial, the shooting of Harlan miners by armed guards, and, of course, the depression, with its shuttered factories, its bread lines and its suicides.

One's tendency abroad is always to stand up for the homeland, but it was hard to explain situations that seemed so inconsistent with the principles of democracy and equal justice and with the superiority of the free-enterprise system.

At another meeting at VOKS, with seven or eight writers, one of them in a naval officer's uniform, I tried to explain the operation of the Dramatists' Guild; but I could not make them see that it was possible for an organization to protect the economic and professional interests of its members without taking positions on political questions. It was clearly the general belief that Americans are denied access to scientific and political writings. A great point was made of the fact that the New York *Times* had played up the hundredth anniversary of Lewis Carroll's birth, but had ignored the fiftieth anniversary of Darwin's death. My assertion that the works not only of Darwin but also of Marx and Lenin were readily available in bookshops and in public libraries was received with obvious disbelief. I was distressed, as I have often been in the United States, by a rigid dogmatism that prevented the acceptance of anything that conflicted with preconceptions.

4

We went to the theatre almost every night. It was hard to decide what to see. There were about twenty playhouses, all under state control, of course, and all operated on the repertory system, so that in a ten-day period there were about a hundred productions to choose from. The variety was bewildering. Contrary to the generally accepted belief that the Russian theatre is given over entirely to propaganda plays, the classics not only of Russian but of world drama were well represented. In the course of a year there is more Shakespeare to be seen in Moscow than in New York. Ibsen, Schiller, Strindberg, Sophocles and Molière are also performed. A few contemporary American and European plays are presented, chosen usually for political reasons, just as foreign plays done in America are usually chosen for economic reasons. Then there is the standard repertory of world opera and ballet. Since we could not see everything, we concentrated on the most important theatres and on plays of the new order. Getting tickets was a major problem, for many of the theatres were sold out far in advance.

It was thrilling just to enter the doors of the Moscow Art Theatre, and to see on the curtain the great sea gull that identified the playhouse with Chekhov. Unfortunately, none of his plays was being done at the moment. I asked Ernest if he knew Chekhov's work. He said, "I saw a play called *The Three Sisters.* It was all about three women who lived in the country and wanted to go to Moscow. Why didn't they get on a train and go?"

We saw three postrevolutionary plays at the Moscow Art, all acted superbly and produced with the meticulous care for which the theatre is noted. *Bread,* dealing with the collective-farm problem, had a certain topical interest and offered a colorful display of peasant types, but it was little more than an illustrated lecture. One scene, however, could not fail to impress any playwright or stage director. A party official made a fifteen-minute speech to twenty or more peasants, not one of whom spoke—yet each actor, by the way he stood, listened and reacted, managed to create a characterization, without destroying the unity of the scene.

Another play, *Fear,* was concerned with the adjustment of intellectuals to the new society: their confusion, conflicts, backsliding and, of course, eventual wholehearted acceptance. One story element was a child's struggle to overcome her reluctance to inform on her counterrevolutionary father. There were effective moments, but on the whole the play was talky and loosely constructed.

The third play, *Days of the Turbins,* is the only Soviet drama known to me that has literary quality and dramaturgic force. The Turbins are a distinguished family of Ukrainian nationalists, one of the several factions who bitterly resisted Bolshevik control. The play deals with their defeat and conversion, but throughout they are honestly portrayed, without a trace of caricature or animosity. I was told that this sympathetic treatment had caused the withdrawal of the play, and that it was revived only because Stalin wanted to see it. To my surprise, the family, during a birthday celebration, sang the Czarist national anthem. When I remarked upon this, I was told that at first the censor had objected, but the director had pointed out that it was an authentic bit, just what these people would do, especially when they had been drinking. The censor finally gave his assent, but only on condition that the singing be off key! The idiocies of censorship are universal.

Ostrovsky's *The Storm,* one of the old stand-bys of Russian

drama, was well done at the Kamerny Theatre, though I thought
the romanticism of the production a little too self-conscious and
tongue-in-cheek. Technically, the Kamerny was fifty years ahead of
any theatre in America. I was overwhelmed by the backstage facilities: the roominess, the scene-changing equipment, the complex
switchboard (purchased in Germany with the proceeds of a successful tour). The theatre's organization too was in striking contrast
to the sporadic, hit-or-miss American system. The Kamerny had a
permanent staff of four hundred, including actors and apprentices,
musicians, stagehands and technicians, scene designers and build-
ers, a wardrobe department, a business and managerial staff,
ushers, cleaners, cooks, waitresses, laundresses. Employment was
permanent; among the perquisites was a month's vacation at the
theatre's rest home in the Crimea.

At the Vakhtangov we saw *Tempo,* a half-serious, half-comic
depiction of a construction project. Fun was poked at the mistakes
and inefficiency of the new labor corps, but happily the bricklayers,
lagging far behind their American counterparts, not only closed the
gap but finished far out in front. Humorously and sympathetically
portrayed was an American engineer, who spoke a kind of pidgin
English, to the audience's delight. (One of the heroes of the day
was Colonel Hugh Cooper, who was helping build the great
Dnieprostroi Dam. We met him at a party—a brisk, forceful personality.) I liked the Vakhtangov's stylized, slightly satirical production technique.

We saw an antireligious play at the Theatre of the Young Spectators. It was the story of the conflict between science and religion:
Giordano Bruno versus the Church. It was a cleverly conceived,
cunningly executed hodgepodge of ballet, historical documentation,
scientific exposition, knockabout comedy, lurid melodrama and
song-and-dance that enchanted the youthful audience. When I
commented upon the absurdity of a caricature of the Pope, Ernest
said that for young people "simplification" was necessary.

On our first visit to the Bolshoi Theatre, the great opera house—
built in the traditional style, red and gold, with tiers of boxes and
baconies—we saw the popular Soviet ballet *Red Poppy,* a lugubri-
ous tale of a Chinese dancer who gives her life to save her lover, a
Soviet sea captain; the red poppy symbolizes the ever continuing
fight for liberation. Everywhere I found great interest in China

and confidence in the uprising of the Chinese against their Japanese oppressors. An American Y.W.C.A. worker who was visiting Moscow told me that in the Chinese district where she was stationed possessors of Communist literature were likely to be beheaded. (Duranty had remarked contemptuously, "Communism is a system for Asiatics.")

The ballet was disappointing, except for the colorful first act, which portrayed the loading of a ship in a Chinese port. The second was standard French ballet; the third, in which the dead heroine is wrapped in a red flag to the strains of the "Internationale," was like a stage show at the Radio City Music Hall. For me the high spot of the evening was a peep, during an intermission, into the former imperial box, where I saw the revolution epitomized. Seated alone on a red damask sofa was a young woman in tam and sweater, munching an apple.

Far more exciting was a second visit to the Bolshoi, in company with George Andreytchine, to attend a gala performance in honor of the official Turkish delegation that had come to Moscow for May Day. It was a brilliant assemblage. In the imperial box were the Turkish chiefs and the Kremlin bigwigs, headed by Maxim Litvinov, Commissar for Foreign Affairs. The diplomatic corps, in tails or dress uniform, was out in force. So was the elite of the Bolshevik regime: party functionaries, top-ranking military men, G.P.U. officials, artists, engineers, scientists. There was a pervasive atmosphere of power and achievement. Andreytchine looked up nostalgically at the official box, where he had often sat in the days of Trotsky's glory.

The ballet performance was magnificent: an act each from *Don Quixote, Sadko* and *Prince Igor.* I had been thrilled in New York by the Diaghilev Ballet's interpretation of the wild Polovtsian dances from *Prince Igor,* but the Bolshoi presentation surpassed it. The vast stage swirled with the frenzied evolutions of a hundred dancers, to the accompaniment not only of a large orchestra, but also of a chorus of equal size. In the presence of that glittering audience, the executants were at the top of their form.

I noticed that in an apparently unoccupied stage box a familiar-looking head appeared now and then from behind the drapery. I asked Andreytchine if it could be Stalin. He said it might well be, for Stalin was a great ballet lover. "But why isn't he up there with the big shots?" I asked. Andreytchine looked at me in amazement. "He's not a member of the government," he said. "He's only the secretary of the Communist Party."

5

From the moment of our arrival we had been trying to get places in Red Square for May Day, but we had about given up hope, for the permissible number was limited and Moscow was full of foreigners. On the eve of the event, we were delighted to learn that we were among a favored fifty. Due to the lateness of Easter and the thirteen days' disparity between the religious and the secular calendars, May Day, for once, fell on Easter Sunday. The government decreed that the church services, which traditionally began at midnight and went on most of next day, must terminate at dawn in order to avoid conflict with preparations for the May Day parade. With Ralph Barns and Fay Gillis, an American aviatrix, we rented a car for a tour of the churches.

Moscow was no longer the city of "forty times forty" churches; but scores, perhaps hundreds, survived. We went first to the Church of the Redeemer, an ugly eighteenth-century edifice said to accommodate ten thousand. After all I had heard about the suppression of religion, I was amazed to find the church packed to the point of suffocation. We joined the throng that moved slowly toward the entrance. Bearded priests in gaudy vestments were intoning a litany; the people chanted responses. Once inside, one could only inch along with the tightly packed mass. The air was stifling, the stench almost unbearable. Since many of the peasants who carried lighted candles were drunk, the fire hazard was great. There was no feeling of devoutness or religious exaltation; the whole atmosphere was crass and sordid.

But at a church of the Old Believers, a sect that had broken away from the Orthodox Church in the seventeenth century, the atmosphere was serene and lofty. The whole congregation joined in a kind of plain chant, reminiscent of Palestrina or the early Spanish composers. In the church of another sect of Old Believers, which had no priesthood, a woman at the lectern read the Scriptures while bearded elders swung censers. In the low-ceilinged gallery, women on benches rocked or breast-fed their children. There was a touching sense of simple, quiet devotion. It was three when we returned to the hotel. The expedition had made Ernest very unhappy. "How can any contemporary person believe such things?" he asked.

Shortly after six, we went bleary-eyed to the Intourist office to join the rest of the lucky fifty. Ernest placed us at the head of a column that marched through half a dozen police lines into Red Square, to positions in front of the large GUM department store. Directly opposite was Lenin's tomb, flanked by bleachers erected to accommodate the dignitaries. All the buildings were draped with large red banners bearing, in five languages, the legend LONG LIVE THE VICTORIOUS ADVANCE OF THE WORLD-WIDE PROLETARIAN REVOLUTION. In front of us, along the whole length of the square, were Red Army units. Shortly before nine, Stalin—forgetful, apparently, of his nonofficial status—appeared on the roof of the tomb, which serves as a reviewing stand. With him were the members of the Politburo. Promptly at nine a Kremlin gate opened and out came Klimenti Voroshilov, Commissar for Defense, at the gallop. His pronouncement of an oath of allegiance, which the massed troops repeated, was followed by an address. Then the soldiers began to sing, unit by unit, so that the singing seemed to move in rippling waves—very effective. At ten the parade through the square commenced: infantry, cavalry, artillery, tanks, ambulance corps, interspersed with many bands, one mounted; then veterans, the G.P.U., Komsomols, Pioneers. After two hours of this, the people: men, women and children, thousands upon thousands, in solid masses, carrying slogans, flags, cartoons, graphs, industrial symbols, effigies of silk-hatted capitalists and of the Pope. Throughout, Stalin stood at attention, saluting each unit.

At one-thirty, after standing for nearly six hours, we had had enough; the problem was how to get out. Egress was at the far end of the square, which meant a circuitous three-mile walk to get back across the river. Footsore, we groaned at the prospect. Since the parade was moving in the direction of our hotel, I suggested to Robert that we join one of the marching groups. So we fell in with a passing delegation and were soon at our door. The parade went on until after five. The number of participants was estimated at a million.

The sudden arrival of spring wrought a wondrous change: the ice in the river disappeared, the muddy streets dried. Boots, heavy jackets and fur hats were discarded. The women appeared in gay bandannas and unfashionable but bright print dresses, the men in high-collared smocks and little embroidered skullcaps from Bokhara. On the "day of rest"—Sunday had been abolished, but there was a day off for everybody at the end of the work week—people flocked to the Park of Culture and Rest to patronize amusement devices, sit at little restaurants, or just stroll about. There were several small arenas for singing games and group dancing. As anywhere, the people seemed to enjoy their day off.

Ernest thought it advisable to take food with us on the long tour of the Soviet Union that we had planned. It was no secret that there were grave shortages. In Moscow, paying in precious dollars, we were, of course, well provided for. We had the best of the excellent Russian cuisine: shashlik, borsht, fresh sturgeon, chicken cutlets, delicious little pancakes with sour cream, caviar as often as we asked for it, and the good sour black bread. (Russian wines are good, too, and the beer quite drinkable.) But there was no certainty how we would fare in the provinces. We had brought with us a good supply of chocolate and dried fruit. This we supplemented at the Torgsin store, which accepted only *valuta* and stocked merchandise unobtainable elsewhere. We had difficulty getting to the food counters; the art counters were neglected. We bought canned vegetables, fish and meat; boxes of biscuits; drinking cups and a few cooking utensils.

On our last evening in Moscow, we went to a workers' club, a large, new building. People were milling about confusedly; there was much shouting and jostling. Except for the exhibits of industrial products and antireligious material, it all reminded me of the University Settlement. In the large auditorium a group game was in progress. To the question "What is the difference between Christianity and socialism?" numerous answers were given, most of them extremely childish. At length the leader awarded one of the contestants a plaster bust of Lenin. He said, however, that no one had given the correct answer, which was that socialism concerned itself with the welfare of the individual, which Christianity ignored. He advised the audience to read their Marx and Lenin, so that they could give better answers next time.

Ernest turned to me happily. "Well, what do you think?" he asked. I said it was like a Sunday-night parish house meeting in the

Middle West. The clergyman asks what the difference is between Christianity and socialism. A contestant is awarded a colored lithograph of Jesus. But no one has given the correct answer, which is that Christianity cares for the individual, while socialism ignores him. They had better read the Scriptures, so that next time they will be better prepared.

Ernest shook his head. "Oh, Mr. Rice," he said, "you never want to take anything seriously."

He was mistaken; I had been quite serious. The more I saw of the Soviet system, the more I inclined to the ecclesiastical analogy. It had its supreme, infallible potentate, who issued edicts and pronunciamentos; its synod and ecumenical councils; its minutely graded hierachy; its sacred, irrefutable texts; its holy days, anthems, litanies, rituals and processions; its office of propaganda; its world-wide corps of missionaries; its official press; its censorship and *index expurgatorius;* its writs of excommunication; its inquisition, purges and heresy trials; its punitive executions, though shooting in the back of the head had been substituted for burning at the stake. Finally, it was as indifferent to the true principles of socialism as many religious bodies were to the true principles of Christianity.

On the evening of our departure, we went to the station expecting to take the seven-thirty train, only to be told by the gateman that our tickets were for the ten-thirty. Rather than struggle back to the hotel, we decided to wait. As we passed through the third- and fourth-class waiting rooms, where peasants lay on the floor surrounded by bedding, bundles and babies, I asked Ernest if all railroad stations were as bad. He said, "This is a good one. We consider it bad when people are lying a mile around the station." The first-class room was almost empty. When I asked Ernest how he reconciled the concept of a classless society with this stratification of accommodations, he grinned. "There are no classes," he said, "only different carriages and waiting rooms."

We had a compartment for four, and we wondered who the other occupant would be, for in Russian sleeping compartments there is no segregation of the sexes. Our companion turned out to be a male technician bound for Gorki, which was our destination. In the next compartment were three American men and a middle-aged American woman. They met the situation by sitting up all night, to the bewilderment of the car attendant. On the other hand, the

Russian passengers were shocked by the American girls who paraded the corridor in their pajamas. *Autres pays, autres moeurs.*

This mingling of the sexes in sleeping compartments was, I began to see, just one of the aspects of Russian life that had no logical connection with Communism, but had simply carried over from the old order. Others were the terroristic methods of the secret police, the excellence of the ballet, nude bathing, the fondness for vodka, and the capacity for delivering and for listening to interminable speeches. So to "Am I seeing this through American or Russian eyes?" I added a second criterion: "Is this Communistic or just Russian?"

Flood waters covered the lower part of Gorki, formerly Nizhni Novgorod, situated at the confluence of the Oka and Volga rivers, one brown, one gray. Nizhni Novgorod had romantic associations for me, perhaps because of something I had read in childhood. But the unattractive girl guide who took us on a perfunctory tour wanted to talk only about the new automobile factory. Like most young Communists we met, she could not understand an interest in the past.

We embarked on the Volga River steamer *Karl Liebknecht,* named for the German Spartacist leader who was brutally murdered in the disorders that followed World War I. Our cabins were comfortable, there was a promenade deck, and the combination dining room–lounge afforded a sweeping view ahead. But we made good use of our packaged rations and of the blankets that Ernest had had the foresight to bring. (The more I saw of the overwrought, humorless Intourist girls, the more grateful I was for Ernest.) I refused to drink the disgusting grayish-green water, though we were assured it had been boiled. Whenever the boat docked, we foraged for beer or for bottled Narzan, an excellent sparkling water from the Caucasus.

There were only a few first- or second-class passengers, mostly small Dutch or English groups. Red Army officers kept getting on and off. They changed to bedroom slippers and paraded the deck at all hours, singing loudly. The third and fourth classes were inhumanly crowded. We could look down at the tightly packed masses on the lower decks, eating, sleeping, tending innumerable babies. Many of the women were delousing each other. "It is forbidden to kill livestock," said Ernest, "but they do it anyhow."

After Moscow, the leisurely four-day trip was a welcome change. We observed the river life, read, wrote letters and had many political arguments. Ernest asked permission to read some of my plays, which I had brought along as gifts. *The Left Bank* meant nothing to him; he understood neither the people nor their problems. But *Street Scene* and *Counsellor-at-Law*, written in the New York vernacular, interested him greatly, because, he said, they were the first books in English he had read that showed "the way people really talk." When the English tourists spoke to him he called upon me to translate, much to their annoyance.

We enjoyed guessing when meals would be served. When Ernest told me he had ordered breakfast for eight so that we could have it at nine-thirty, I told him he should have more confidence in the cook. "I do have confidence," he said, "or I'd have ordered it for six." One time he returned from an inquiry into the progress of an omelet, some hours overdue, with the report that it was "under construction," a phrase one heard applied twenty times a day to every phase of Soviet activity.

Many of the villages we passed were half under water. The villages themselves were squalid, for the Volga region had always been the most backward in Russia. The striking exception was the Volga German Republic, inhabited by descendants of German peasants brought in by Catherine the Great in the hope of improving Russian agriculture. They had preserved their language and national characteristics; their villages were neat, their farms well tended.

Stalingrad, formerly Tsaritsyn (now Volgograd!), where we debarked, was being transformed from a provincial town to a great industrial complex. Five distinct suburbs were being created, each with a special focus: metallurgical, chemical, lumber, tractor-building, administrative. Along the rough, improvised roads, wagons were hauled by camels. A whole city was rising on the bare steppes, not haphazardly but as a carefully planned, integrated community providing for all the needs of its inhabitants: workers' homes, bakeries and community kitchens, clubs, schools, hospitals, a theatre, a circus. The plans called for boulevards, parks and trolley lines. The housing projects were, for once, attractive—small brick buildings, separated by garden plots. The over-all scheme was characterized by imagination and forethought.

Tractors were already coming off the assembly belt in the Detroit-like factory, at the rate of 150 per day. The machine tools mostly bore American name plates. Everything was humming. But in the yard thousands of tractors were rusting away because of insufficient rail transport. I was surprised to see numerous old church bells, some inscribed in Old Russian characters. The guide hesitantly explained that they had been collected from the villages because of the shortage of nonferrous metals.

In my discussions with Ernest and other Russians, in plays and films, in newspaper articles and public addresses, there were frequent references to the "war danger," the threat of invasion by one of the Western powers or a coalition of them. It seemed that the whole nation was obsessed by this fear, almost to the point of hysteria. But the day was not far distant when Hitler was to bring death and devastation to half the land. During the long months of the Stalingrad siege, which began almost exactly ten years after our visit, I often thought of all that amazing work of construction, now senselessly and savagely reduced to rubble. However justifiable suspicions of the Soviet Union's intentions may be, it should not be forgotten that bitter experience has taught them to be suspicious, too.

On the overnight trip from Stalingrad to Rostov-on-Don, in the heart of the Cossack country, there was no "soft" carriage, so we traveled in a candlelit third-class car, sleeping on wooden benches covered with thin mattresses. There were no doors or curtains; the lavatory was unusable. We did not get undressed, for the woman guard had stationed herself just outside our compartment. At Ernest's suggestion, I locked up my camera and binoculars, and double-knotted my shoelaces to prevent my shoes from being removed. The 340-mile journey took twenty-two hours, ample time for observing the countryside, which with its plastered houses and blossoming orchards was far superior to the Volga region. Everywhere collectivization, chief cause of the food crisis, was in process.

Rostov was rather like a provincial town in Central Europe. The tension of Moscow was noticeably absent. There was as much difference in the atmosphere as there is between Paris and Arles, or New York and Iowa City. After the usual mixups, we got places on the Moscow–Baku express. The north-Caucasus countryside was charming, reminiscent of the Tirol. The villages, with whitewashed houses and new brick schools, were inhabited by Armenians, Georgians and the varied peoples of the Caucasus. The fields were alive with birds and bright with spring flowers. At one stop, Ernest bought lilacs and tulips. The Russians love flowers. Our rooms sometimes lacked towels, curtains or even sheets, but never a gay bouquet.

At Mineralye Vodi we took a branch line through lovely alpine country to Kislovodsk. The fragrant mountaineers who were our fellow passengers were fascinated by our baggage, particularly my oversized valise with its bright stripes and heavy brass trimmings. They crowded about it, examining everything, asking where it came from, how much it cost.

Kislovodsk ("sour water"), the source of sparkling Narzan, was like a small French spa, with a park, a bathing establishment, a theatre, a bandstand and refreshment booths. There were differences, however: workers' clubs, a school for the "liquidation" of illiteracy, sanatoria that had been aristocratic villas. Somewhat to Ernest's disappointment we declined an invitation to bathe in Narzan water. Instead we took a two-mile walk. Children were gathering violets and lilies-of-the-valley; Robert captured some lizards. The attire of the holiday crowds was bewilderingly varied: white cotton suits, riding breeches, smocks, fleece hats, sombreros. Young Pioneers paraded and sang; there were guided tours of workers' groups. Everyone seemed to be having a good time.

On the way back to the main line, one of the passengers aired his grievances to me in German. He said that his brother and his seventy-year-old father, farmers in a German village, had been condemned as kulaks—that is, wealthy peasants—because they owned three horses and had a hired hand. Sixty or seventy families had been sent north, where many had died. He was now in a collective with five hundred Russians and Armenians. To buy shoes he had sold his cow. If you questioned a hundred peasants, not one would be in favor of collectivization. As for himself, he would walk barefoot to get to America. "You, an educated man," he said, "speak to me as an equal. Here, where everyone is supposed to be equal, an educated man would look down on me." Ernest, unable to understand the man but aware that he was complaining, listened frowningly. When he tried to pump me, I merely said that the man was a farmer who had been having family troubles. "He's no farmer," said Ernest. "Did you look at his hands?" It was the only time I saw him display ill-temper.

In the dining car, en route to Baku, we were offered bread and a choice of salt fish or cold roast grouse; there was absolutely nothing else. The grouse was good, though full of birdshot. Ernest was of the opinion that it had been shot during the revolution. We now traversed the autonomous republics of Dagestan and Azerbaijan, non-Russian regions annexed by the czars, inhabited by an exotic mixture of Caucasian and Turkish peoples: Avars, Lezghians, Tabasaranians, Kumiks and Nagoyans. Interspersed with meadowlands on which goats and sheep grazed were semiarid plains dotted with water buffaloes, pack horses and camel caravans. On the telegraph wires unfamiliar birds roosted, some a metallic green-blue with red backs, others crowlike with white neckbands; hawks and eagles soared overhead. We went past adobe villages reminiscent of Arizona, and clustered moundlike tents of nomadic tribes. The station signs were in Turkish, Arabic and unidentifiable characters. Many of the people had an Asiatic aspect. The men wore fleece hats and sheepskin coats, the women long shawls.

At Baku we were met by a prettified blonde Intourist girl. I was not surprised that Ernest took an instant dislike to her. "A piece of Paris," he muttered. Once when I had commented on the general absence of make-up, he said, "For a Komsomol girl to use lipstick is just as bad as for a boy to get drunk." I suspect that this is no longer true.

We hurried dinner to be in time for a performance of *Othello*. It was in Turkish, so for once I had the advantage over Ernest and had to outline the plot for him. I was amazed to see Turkish women not only on the stage but also, unveiled and unaccompanied, in the audience: striking evidence of the changes the revolution had wrought. The actresses were obviously novices, but the men in the cast were very good. It was an athletic performance: Othello raged and stormed, striding the stage, seizing Iago by the throat and hurling him about. I tried to keep Ernest's interest alive by promising him that Othello would strangle Desdemona. But he grew increasingly restive and said reproachfully, "Mr. Rice, he is never going to kill her." I counselled patience, and at last he was appeased.

Along the waterfront there was a fine new park, where hundreds of Persians in conical caps squatted to wait, perhaps for days, for a steamer that would take them across the Caspian to their homeland. A few older women were veiled, but the dress was mostly

Western. Ernest said that Central Asians sometimes killed a Komsomol who put off the veil; since they were backward people, the penalty was limited to five years. "But if kulaks kill a schoolteacher, at least three are shot." He said that Islam was harder to uproot than Russian Orthodoxy. I suggested it might be because it had a greater ethical content. Ernest shrugged and said, "It's just the old people, and they don't count. Only the young who work in factories are important."

The effects of industrialization were already evident. I looked, as I do everywhere, for handicrafts, but found little of interest. Like national costumes and customs, they were rapidly being submerged in the rising wave of colorless uniformity—a phenomenon not peculiar, of course, to the Soviet Union. Undoubtedly the factories have provided for millions a welcome improvement in the standard of living, but everything has its price; the disappearance of craftsmanship and traditional usages unquestionably entails a loss in emotional, spiritual and aesthetic values.

From Baku we doubled back south of the Caucasus to Tiflis, capital of Georgia and home town of Stalin, a charming, colorful city with tree-lined avenues and with flat-roofed houses rising in terraces. The population is half Georgian, half Armenian; there is a constant influx of wild-looking Caucasian tribesmen wearing shaggy hats, and belted coats to which long knives are attached. As we approached the Tatar market in the course of a stroll, one of these mountaineers was thrusting his knife into its sheath. In the middle of the square a crowd was gathering about the body of a man. The killing had merely been an incident in a tribal feud, apparently a common occurrence.

Our local Intourist guide, a beautiful Armenian with dark skin, glossy black hair and liquid eyes, spoke neither Armenian nor Georgian, only Russian and American. She had guided an American engineer for two months and was an enthusiastic Los Angeles booster. She took us shopping, for there was more uncontrolled trading in Tiflis than anywhere we had been. I bought a handsome hand-woven rug. Carrying it about was a nuisance, but it was worth the trouble. As we were about to leave a shop where I had bought some tribal jewelry and a Georgian costume for my daughter, the Russian proprietor showed me a parchment manuscript of the four Gospels in exquisite Armenian script and adorned with full-page illuminations, naïve in conception but beautifully executed. The dealer named a figure that was obviously an invitation to a bargaining contest. My offer of about one tenth elicited a long harangue. I asked Ernest whether the man was saying that I was taking the bread out of the mouths of his children. Ernest, knowing I understood no Russian, said in astonishment, "That's exactly what he's saying." "Good," I said. "He wants to do business with us." I raised my figure slightly, he lowered his. So the game went on, to the enjoyment of the crowd that had gathered. At last we shook hands on a price that was very satisfactory to us both. But our little Armenian guide was profoundly shocked. "I am so ashamed for him," she said. "How could he ask so much when he was willing to take so little?"

We found the regime in Tiflis far less rigorous than elsewhere. The Georgians seemed to lack the zeal and the steeliness of their awesome compatriot in the Kremlin. Two jokes expressed the sentiments of at least some of the inhabitants. A man who saves Stalin from drowning is asked how he can be rewarded. Says the rescuer, "By not telling anyone I saved you." Again, a worker who is heard cursing Columbus is asked why. "Well," he says, "if Columbus hadn't discovered America, we wouldn't always have to be overtaking and outdistancing."

Ernest told us that because floods had washed out a railroad bridge we would have to leave our train for Batum and walk across an improvised trestle to a connecting train. The prospect of crossing a makeshift bridge at night, laden with luggage, did not appeal to me, so we arranged to go by car to Mtzkhet, ancient capital of Georgia.

The car was on time, our baggage was crammed into it, but the chauffeur was presiding at a meeting, so we had to wait until a substitute chairman was elected. We proceeded along the wet, slippery Georgian Military Highway, dodging buffalo carts and mountaineers on burros. At Mtzkhet I saw our sleeping car on a siding, waiting to be picked up. I asked if we could get on, but the attendant said no. Our chauffeur excused himself and returned in a few minutes with the bowing, smiling stationmaster, who ordered the attendant to open the car and conduct us to our compartment. When we asked the chauffeur how he had accomplished this miracle, he replied, to Ernest's dismay, that he had told the stationmaster I was the American consul general! I thus became, unofficially, the first American diplomatic representative in the Soviet Union. Incidentally, the question of diplomatic representation was one that gave me trouble throughout my entire visit. I was constantly asked why, fifteen years after the revolution, the United States still withheld recognition. Since I was puzzled, too, I could give no satisfactory answer.

Our route lay through the autonomous republic of Adzharistan, in whose miserable villages wooden plows were still in use and pigs of every size and color abounded. This was the ancient Colchis, home of Medea and destination of the Argonauts in their quest for the Golden Fleece. At Batum we boarded a Black Sea steamer for Yalta, stopping here and there along the mountainous coastline, whose luxurious villas and fashionable hotels were rest homes for workers.

One of our fellow passengers was a brash Californian of Russian extraction who was now a Soviet citizen. His account of the effects of the depression in America was grossly exaggerated, but sufficiently based upon fact to make complete refutation impossible. Ernest was contemptuous of him. Like many Russians, he had a low opinion of American Communists; he thought them naïve, politically illiterate, and ill-mannered.

Ernest and I had a sharp argument about war. I criticized the military expenditures, when people needed bread and shoes. Ernest stressed the war danger and said that the Soviet Union would fight to the last man to keep what had been so hard to win. I retorted that if there were a war it would be the proletarians that the Russians would be shooting, not the capitalists. He expressed his fervent belief in a world revolution. I tried vainly to convince him that universal suffrage, intelligently exercised, could bring about any desired reform. By the time we broke off, we were both rather heated. At breakfast he apologized for his vehemence. I reassured him by saying I felt we had merely had an honest disagreement. Actually, we were in many respects quite like-minded. We both ardently wanted a world in which peace, equal justice and security for the individual prevailed. It was about methods that we disagreed. The same may be said today of millions on both sides of the Iron Curtain.

The hotel manager at Yalta, who wore striped trousers that did not quite reach the top of his high shoes, informed us in carefully enunciated phrasebook English that the chef had been in the employ of a grand duke. Later we came to the conclusion that either the grand duke had been no epicure or the revolution had destroyed the chef's touch.

We idled on the pebbly beach crowded with sunbathers, many of them nude. The countryside was bright with mimosa, lilacs and flowering plum trees; swallows darted everywhere. On an obligatory visit to a modest waterfall, we saw a teacher haranguing a group of schoolchildren. "He's probably explaining the waterfall's historical importance," said Ernest. "What it was before the revolution and what it is now."

Ernest kept reverting to our political discussion, obviously worried by his inability to convert me to Sovietism. I told him that after twenty-five years of search I was convinced that there was no "system" that could cure humanity's ills. The hope for betterment lay in the voluntary co-operation of integrated individuals, not in the parroting of slogans or in blind allegiance to demagogic leaders. Deeply troubled, Ernest said, "I have been able to answer every American's criticisms except yours. But if you come back next year I will have the answers."

At the time of the revolution, the valuables from Yalta's villas and palaces were hidden to prevent looting. Now they were being unearthed and offered to tourists for *valuta*. Among stacks of trashy modern icons I was able to find a few fine old ones, some from the seventeenth century. The Intourist staff could not understand why anyone wanted to buy such things. I also found a faïence wine pitcher with a handle in the shape of the imperial crown, property of the late Czar. When I told the manager his prices were too high, he said that if he reduced them he would be sent to prison. I said that considering how good conditions were in Soviet prisons, that would be a privilege. He laughed and cut his prices substantially.

We made a delightful excursion to the famous wine cellars at Massandra. Crimean wines are excellent, reproducing almost every European type. We saw the great casks, the bottling works and the "wine library" where rare vintages were stored. Then came the wine tasting: a dry white wine, three muscats—white, pink and black— Tokay, Madeira, port and Château Yquem. After that we inscribed our compliments in the guest book, which contained many celebrated names, and tributes in every language, including Chinese, Arabic, Greek and Hebrew. A Frenchman had written: "The only place in the Soviet Union where it is possible to hesitate between the reds and the whites."

At Livadia we saw the great palace built by the Czar for his ailing son (later the scene of the historic meeting of Stalin, Roosevelt and Churchill), now a rest home. A thousand workers and peasants were at table in the vast courtyard and at the imperial board, at least fifty feet long, made from a single oak plank. It was not a pretty spectacle. The diners, unkempt, unshaven, untidy, many barefoot, were guzzling amid a din of conversation and a clatter of dishes. But here again was the revolution epitomized: serfs and slum dwellers regaling themselves at the Czar's table.

On the boat to Odessa the congestion was the worst yet. If you had to move about, nobody budged an inch; you simply had to step over whoever was lying or sitting in your path. At Odessa, the chief point of interest for me was the famous staircase of two hundred steps down which, in the 1905 uprising, the Cossacks had driven the rebellious population, an incident immortalized in Serge Eisenstein's motion picture *Potemkin*.

The long northward journey took us through the Ukraine, Russia's granary. As the well-constructed white-plastered, red-tiled houses attested, it was the most prosperous and most advanced region of the Soviet Union. Somewhere along the road we passed a train of flatcars loaded with trucks of Soviet manufacture. Ernest, continually brooding over my criticism of Soviet standardization, pointed to the train and said, "There is our poetry."

6

During our trip we had been out of touch with world events, and I was anxious to get caught up. The news was not good. In Germany, the Brüning government had fallen; the advance of fascism was ominous. In the United States, bread lines were lengthening, people were sleeping in the parks, but laissez-faire was still the order of the day. The Russian food situation was alarming. The collectivization program had set quotas for every village, whose fulfillment was insisted upon by zealous local officials. Since the resistant peasants had underplanted, their seed reserve was insufficient for the new sowing. The result was near-famine. Even Stalin admitted that the rigid enforcement had been a serious mistake.

I had long discussions with the Soviet Union's two foremost film directors: Serge Eisentein, whose *Potemkin* and *Ten Days That Shook the World,* based on John Reed's book, had won him an international reputation, and Vsevolod Pudovkin, esteemed in the Soviet Union for *Storm over Asia* and *The Fall of St. Petersburg.* Eisenstein, a sensitive, suave, sophisticated cosmopolite, invited us to his home, a single room about fifteen by fifteen where he had lived for twelve years. Bookcases defined the "library," "bedroom," "study" and "dining room." He was enthusiastic about Mexico, showing us some dressed fleas he had brought back and some fine stills he had made there. He talked at length about the Soviet film industry's technical researches; a new social approach, he said, demanded new techniques.

Pudovkin's quarters were in the building that housed a "cinema college" which gave a three-year course in every phase of film making—including, of course, political ideology. Of all the Russians I met, Pudovkin, I think, impressed me most. He had a mobile face with roughhewn, irregular features, and gnarled hands with long fingers. In contrast to Eisenstein, he was simple, forceful and earnest. He had spent most of World War I in a prison camp, where he had learned German, French and English.

We talked for three hours, discussing the thematic differences between American and Soviet movies. "This ideal of the little home, love, success and so on," he said, "this is a dream to make the worker forget his problems." And again: "Sex is a powerful opiate used by the owning class to drug the senses of the workers." Though I could not altogether disagree with him, I had not found the Soviet pictures I had seen superior to the Hollywood product. There was always something interesting in them—unfamiliar locales, amusing little episodes, good performances—but they were as rigid in their political orientation as were the American movies in their escapism and false eroticism. I pointed this out to both Eisenstein and Pudovkin; the answer was always the same: "Consciously or unconsciously, all art is political." Pudovkin asked me about the reception of Soviet films in America. I said they were admired by intellectuals, but that workers had little interest in them. He shook his head. "You intellectuals do wrong," he said. "It is your duty not only to praise these films but to bring them to the workers, explaining the philosophy behind them."

He invited us to the film studio, once the famous artistocratic night club Yar. The dance floor was the stage, the big lights were in the musicians' gallery, where there were still traces of gilt paint on the rails. I watched Pudovkin film a scene depicting a workers' meeting, almost obligatory in any Soviet movie. There were a platform with a table, for the speaker, and about a hundred kitchen chairs for the listeners. Pudovkin divided the actors into three groups. On cue, he told them, each group was to make a different type of gesture. He rehearsed this three or four times, then told the group to scatter among the seats. Now all gesticulated at once, but, since no two persons moved in exactly the same way, it looked as though everyone were responding individually and spontaneously. After a few more quick rehearsals, the cameras turned. I was astounded. The whole thing had not taken half an hour; in Hollywood, an entire day would have been required. One of the American correspondents told me that Pudovkin had made a fine picture about agriculture that would never be released. "Too much poetry and not enough tractors," he said. I thought of Ernest's remark about the trucks.

A granddaughter of Tolstoi, a tall, broad-shouldered woman who bore a striking resemblance to her grandfather, showed us an exhibit of books published by the Federation of Soviet Writers. A chart tabulated the books by subject matter: history, politics, agriculture, industry, social problems, technology. Not included were biography, sex, bridge, golf, personality development, beauty culture and hints on how to succeed.

Another interesting personality was Ivy Low Litvinov, a forthright English intellectual, who had married the Commissar for Foreign Affairs in his prerevolutionary days of exile. I was told that her hospitality to foreigners was frowned upon in official circles. Litvinov was in Geneva, attending a League of Nations session, so to my regret we were unable to meet him.

With several correspondents, we attended an "exhibition" trial of some gypsies, held in the barrackslike clubhouse of a ball-bearing factory. As we drove up, we were surrounded by gypsies—wild-looking people and very handsome too, the men with sleek round heads and silky black beards, the women wearing orange, purple and yellow bandannas over their braided hair. Most of them were smoking little silver pipes. The police, assuming from our Lincoln limousines that we were important officials, opened a lane through the shouting, gesticulating crowd. The courtroom was empty except for the front bench, on which the defendants, sixteen gypsy elders and a Russian doctor, sat. The gypsies were charged with killing a violator of tribal law, the doctor with signing a false death certificate. They were not being tried for murder, however, but for holding an illegal court. The purpose of this public trial was to show the gypsies that they must conform to Soviet law. When the doors were opened, the crowd swarmed in, scrambling wildly over the benches. At sight of the prisoners, their families, who had not seen them in months, sobbed and wailed. Many of the women began to nurse their babies. As Billie Lyons peered about, one of the women asked her not to look at her baby, for she might have the evil eye. We did not stay long, for the howling of the babies was deafening and the proceedings promised to be long drawn out. Besides, the verdict was a foregone conclusion.

Robert and I went to Negoreloye to meet my wife and daughter. On the trip back to Moscow, I had a strange psychological reaction. My wife was, of course, full of news about the activities and personal problems of our friends in America, in which, ordinarily, I would have been greatly interested. Yet now it all seemed remote, alien and unimportant. Then it dawned upon me that during the seven weeks I had been in the Soviet Union my attention, thoughts and conversation had centered almost entirely upon social, political and cultural matters. Personalities and the private concerns of individuals had been completely overshadowed by broad social movements and conflicting philosophies. It took a great effort to get back into the old orbit.

In Moscow we resumed our round of social activities and of theatregoing. My reaction to the Meyerhold Theatre, then very much in vogue, was most unfavorable. At the end of one of the plays, which dealt with the familiar subject of intervention, the leading actor asked how many of the members of the Communist Party in the audience would resist invasion with their lives. People stood up all over the auditorium. In turn, he put the same question to Red Army men, trade-union members, intellectuals, until the whole audience was on its feet. It was rather like an American revival meeting. After the performance, Eisenstein introduced me to Meyerhold, who had a world-weary air that struck me as a pose. Since I could not honestly praise the banal play and the tricky production, we had little to say to each other.

The most exciting production I saw in Russia, in fact one of the most exciting I have ever seen anywhere, was the Vakhtangov *Hamlet*, a Marxist interpretation so original in conception and so fascinating in execution that it had all Moscow buzzing. In preparation for what was to come, there was a big lobby display illustrative of productions of the play over the centuries, demonstrating that each had reflected the prevailing mood of its era: philosophical, romantic, psychological. Why not, then, in the Soviet Union, a political interpretation?

So the play became a struggle for the throne of Denmark, between Hamlet and Claudius, who, made up to look like Henry VIII and brilliantly played, for once almost equaled Hamlet in importance. Hamlet was neither philosopher, romantic lover nor madman, but a canny politician, a tubby little man with a pointed beard— "fat and scant of breath," as Shakespeare describes him. The lack of poetry was atoned for by the dynamism and vividness of the whole production: the plastic beauty of the settings, the splendid costumes, the startling innovations, the incisive acting, all enhanced by Shostakovich's incidental music.

Two examples will indicate the unorthodoxy of the whole approach. The king, to divert attention from the murder of Polonius, gives a party, at which Ophelia gets drunk and is carried off to a bedroom by some young men. Her suicide is prompted by shame and remorse, not by standardized Elizabethan madness. Again, Polonius, bearing Hamlet's letter to Ophelia, finds the king standing upon a dais in all his royal panoply, posing majestically for his portrait. As he hears Polonius' report, he steps down from the platform, a skinny man in tights, leaving behind the robe, the scepter and the crown, all of which, we now see, are held up by lackeys: a stunning commentary upon monarchy that even a non-Marxist could applaud. At one point, Ernest gripped my arm and said, "You know, the man who wrote this play was a great dramatist!" I am sure that Shakespeare was never paid a more sincere compliment.

A little episode involving Ernest had touched me. On our long tour, he had advanced the money for certain minor expenses. When he gave me a bill which, translated into *valuta*, came to forty or fifty dollars, I could see that he was going through some great inner conflict. At last he confessed that he had set his heart on a fine camera at the Torgsin store. As a Soviet citizen, he could not trade there; and for a dedicated Communist the acquisition of the camera was deplorable self-indulgence. But he was a healthy human being and the temptation was too strong. His state when I handed over the camera to him can only be described as ecstatic. He asked to be excused for an hour so that he could dash home and exhibit the treasure to his roommate.

On the eve of our departure for Leningrad, our friends gave us a farewell party at the Hotel Metropole. Ernest seemed preoccupied and left the room several times. When it was time to leave I discovered why: Intourist had obtained tickets for the wrong train. It took two hours to straighten things out. I was annoyed by the inconvenience, but more concerned by Ernest's unhappiness. He was so anxious that we should take with us a good impression of the Soviet Union. It was not easy to say goodbye to him. I had developed a paternal fondness, and he had become attached to all of us, too. What made the parting harder was the premonition that I would never see him again. Nor have I. I wrote to him several times, but never got an answer. Perhaps my letters never reached him, perhaps he was warned against maintaining contact with bourgeois foreigners. I have wondered many, many times what became of that clear-eyed, high-spirited, vital youth. Was he killed in the war, or "liquidated" for some "deviation"? Or has he risen to a position of power? I wish I knew.

7

Compared to Moscow, Leningrad seemed sophisticated and cosmopolitan; the people too had a more urban look. The Hotel Astoria was first-rate, both in accommodations and in service. The manager, a gracious, elderly man, was a former diplomat; the headwaiter, an Italian-American once employed at a New York night club, had been wiped out by the stock market crash. He said he liked his present job, but had trouble teaching the Russians to be efficient. Our guide, a sensitive young woman fluent in five or six languages, had obviously been reared in an atmosphere of wealth and culture. Once she let slip that her father had been a prosperous merchant, but she hastened to add that her grandfather had been a serf on the Volga—a very unlikely story.

The famous art collection in the Hermitage contained many fine Italian, Dutch, Flemish and French paintings, but on the whole it was not comparable to the great collections of Western Europe. When I asked about the Rembrandts, of which I had heard so much, my guide hesitated, then said, "I think they are turning factory wheels in the Urals." I believe they were bought by Andrew Mellon and are now in the National Gallery in Washington.

Fifteen miles from Leningrad was Detskoe Selo, the Children's Village (now Pushkin), formerly Tsarskoe Selo, the Czar's Village. It contains the elegant eighteenth-century palace of Catherine the Great, richly decorated in the *chinoiserie* style of the period. In shocking contrast was the modern palace where we saw the depressingly ugly quarters of the late imperial family, rooms crammed with unsightly, useless objects, the walls covered with frightful paintings, mostly of religious subjects, and with photographs, including some of Rasputin. In the room of one of the princesses, magazine pictures of movie stars were tacked up. The imperial bedchamber contained a washstand with bowl and pitcher, such as one might find in an old-fashioned summer hotel in the Catskills. The Czar's study adjoined a swimming pool which was surrounded by cabinets filled with state documents.

At the Children's Theatre in Leningrad we saw a play whose name, as I spelled it out painfully, was "The Small Hut of Uncle Thomas." I knew that Mrs. Stowe was highly regarded in Russia, but it might have surprised her a little could she have learned that her major work had been made into a simple revolutionary object lesson that any child could grasp: one slave defers meekly to his master, only to come to an unhappy end; another rebels, kills his oppressor and lives happily ever after. The play, performed in an arena theatre, had a unit set of several levels, which could be used as a whole or broken up into small locales by the focusing of lights. There was no patronizing of the children or giving them shoddy goods. Everything was professionally expert: acting, scenery, direction, music. There were lively scenes of plantation life, and a charming little one of Uncle Tom rocking a baby and crooning, *"Nichevo! Nichevo!"* When Eliza jumped through a window to flee across the ice, she was pursued by two handsome Russian wolfhounds.

I talked to the stage director and the scenic artist, elderly men obviously less interested in Communism than in providing fine theatrical entertainment adapted to the emotional and intellectual age of their audience. Trained psychologists' reports on the attention span, responsiveness and comprehension of the children were used as bases in planning new productions. In view of the almost complete lack of good children's theatres in the United States, I was impressed by the creativeness of this enterprise. The emphasis upon propaganda may have been deplorable, but the application of theatrical skills was worthy of emulation.

The Intourist manager had assured me repeatedly that our tickets for Finland were in order. But on the day of our departure I was told that no places were available. It was really the last straw. I stormed and fumed; at length places were found. It was not until our train had pulled out that I made the appalling discovery that our places had been snatched away from some Finnish consular officials who had been waiting for weeks to get them.

It was not far to the border. We had expected customs difficulties because of our many acquisitions, but I had letters from the right sources and we were whisked through. However, I had to surrender the two worthless rubles I had left. At the Finnish station across the border there was a little buffet, where oranges and chocolate bars were available; even more amazing, there was no queue. We made small purchases, enjoying the novelty. After ten weeks in the future, it took a little while to readjust to the present.

8

After a lively tour of Scandinavia, we re-entered Germany at Hamburg. In three months the political situation had worsened. Hitler was more and more strident; his following was growing. A coalition of Communists and Social Democrats might have held him in check, but the left-wing parties preferred fratricidal strife to union against the common enemy. Among the three major dissident factions there was provocation, even armed conflict. One Sunday night we had dinner at a big beer hall in the Reeperbahn, Hamburg's Broadway. We lingered on to watch some Bavarian dancers, then walked back to our hotel through quiet streets. Next morning we learned that while we were in the restaurant there had been bloody street fighting not half a mile away, in the working-class quarter of Altona. Many Nazis and Communists had been killed or wounded. One of Hitler's first acts upon assuming power was to avenge the fallen Nazis by executing Communist leaders in Hamburg.

Berlin was tense, in the last stages of another electoral campaign. There were political slogans everywhere, and banners displaying the swastika, the hammer and sickle, and the three bars of the Social Democrats. One day there was a commotion at the Prussian Ministry of the Interior, just across from the Hotel Bristol, where we were staying. A crowd gathered, cars came and went, then the police dispersed the onlookers. A lieutenant and two privates had taken the Social Democratic Minister into custody on some trumped-up charge. He had submitted meekly. It was the end of the Weimar Republic, for it gave notice that it would not resist attacks upon it. Years later in New York a refugee Social Democratic leader told me that everything had been in readiness for a general strike that would have paralyzed all the city's activities. The pressing of a button would have cut off water, gas and electricity. I asked why no one had pressed the button. "Oh, we couldn't!" he said. "Think of the condition the toilets would have been in."

A few days before the election there was a Hitler rally at the Deutsches Stadion, a big sports arena in the suburb of Grunewald. For a few marks we obtained reserved seats in a field box. The Stadion, which seated thirty thousand, was filled to capacity; another twenty thousand packed the adjoining race track, where loudspeakers had been rigged up. It was a predominantly young crowd —mostly under twenty-five, I should say. The proceedings began with the appearance of several hundred storm troopers, tall, brawny youths, very smart in brown uniforms and swastika armbands. With German military precision they performed mass evolutions, while the crowd sang the Horst Wessel song and other Nazi anthems. Then Goebbels mounted the speaker's stand: a graceless man, with a discordant voice. It was his function to whet the audience's appetite for the master.

As the crowd began to grow restless, a small airplane circled the arena and landed on the race track, amid welcoming roars. A few minutes later a touring car entered the stadium. On the collapsed top, his feet on the back seat, sat Hitler, hatless, wearing a storm trooper's uniform. As the car crept around the field, he held up his arm in the Nazi salute, the wrist flipping in acknowledgment of the frenzied ovation. It was growing dark now. While Hitler made his way to the rostrum, the storm troopers, carrying flambeaux, formed a great circle, ringing the arena with fire. It was a spectacle that exceeded anything ever attempted by Max Reinhardt. The state of the crowd bordered upon madness.

Hitler spoke for half an hour or more: all rant and bombast, frenetic denunciations of the Versailles Treaty and the Western Powers, exhortations to his hearers to throw off the yoke of slavery, to be free again, to be men again. But he could have recited the alphabet with equal effect. The singing, the manuevers, the flaming torches, above all, that throaty voice with the heartbreak in it, had swept away reason and normality. When, at the end, Hitler shouted, "*Deutschland!*," fifty thousand fanatics roared, "*Erwache!*" Again and once again the hoarse cry and the maniacal response: a frightening display of mass hysteria. If he had commanded that crowd to burn, pillage and kill, obedience would have been automatic. I had never believed that Hitler was just a Mack Sennett character; now I was convinced that he was a menace to all humanity. No one who kept his head at that meeting could think otherwise.

Next day I lunched at the home of Alfred Flechtheim, the noted art dealer, from whom I had bought some Paul Klees and a Kokoschka landscape. When I mentioned casually that we had attended the Hitler rally, he turned so pale that I thought he was going to faint. In a shaking voice he said it was inconceivable that we could have taken such a risk. It had never occurred to me that we were in any personal danger!

On election night Edgar Ansel Mowrer, the Chicago *Daily News* correspondent, invited us to his office to hear the returns. About a dozen people were there, including several German journalists and Professor Harper of the University of Chicago, an expert in Central European politics. It was like an election night in the United States: we sat around, talking and drinking, as the returns came in over the radio. It was soon apparent that Hitler would poll about a third of the vote, as he had done in the last previous election.

Mowrer and most of the others present saw this as a setback. In their opinion, the success of the Nazi movement depended upon a snowball-like accretion; once it lost its momentum, it would begin to recede.

"I'll call Putzi and see how he feels," said Mowrer. Putzi was Dr. Ernst Hanfstaengel, son of a German father and an American mother, a Harvard graduate and formerly a successful New York art dealer. Now he was Hitler's piano player and court jester. Mowrer called the Brown House, Hitler's Munich headquarters, and got Hanfstaengel on the wire. "Hello, Putzi," he said. "How does the Führer feel about the election?" As he listened to Hanfstaengel's reply, he smiled and winked at the rest of us. When he hung up he said, "Putzi says that Hitler is well satisfied with the way things are going. But of course that's just conversation; he knows he's on the downgrade." There was a general feeling of elation. Less than six months later, Hitler became Chancellor. This is no animadversion upon Mowrer or the others who were there that night. Hitler's accession was unpredictable and incredible.

On our way to Bremen we stopped for a few days in Hanover. The town was plastered with anti-Semitic posters, mostly denouncing the F. W. Woolworth Company, which was opening a branch store, as a Jewish organization whose activities spelled ruin to the German small businessman.

It had been an illuminating trip. I had seen Stalinism at work and Hitlerism in the making. In future discussions of either, I could at least make reference to a little firsthand experience.

XVI

A Time of Turmoil

1

It seemed time to pay a little attention to my professional life. Since I had no new play ready, I produced an old one, *Black Sheep*, written a good many years previously. I quickly assembled a cast and put the play into rehearsal. But I had lost interest in it; my mind was too much on the state of the world, particularly on the state of America. We opened cold, and though the press was unfavorable there were indications of audience interest. I did not care enough about the play to make a fight for it, so I closed it and immediately set to work writing a new one.

Franklin D. Roosevelt was running for the Presidency against the incumbent Herbert Hoover. I was asked to join a group of non-Communists who were supporting William Z. Foster, the Communist Party leader, and his running mate, the Negro trade-unionist James W. Ford. After some reflection, I agreed. I felt that everyone who had the welfare of America at heart should take part in the campaign. To vote for do-nothing Hoover was impossible. There was nothing in Roosevelt's record to suggest that his glittering promises were more than electoral bait, or that he would really come to grips with the desperate situation. I inclined toward the Socialist Party, led by Norman Thomas, but felt it had failed to take the strong affirmative position that the crisis demanded. Like the German Social Democratic Party, it had dissipated its energies in quarrels with the Communists. I had no respect for the Communist Party. If I had believed it could win, I would have opposed it. But observation of European politics had convinced me of the value of a protest vote. I thought that if the Communists could pile up a big vote it might galvanize the apathetic Congressional leaders and the new President—probably Roosevelt—into adopting strong remedial measures.

I was not alone in taking this position. The League of Professional Groups for Foster and Ford issued a pamphlet, *Culture and the Crisis*, among whose fifty-odd signatories (of whom I was not one) were Sherwood Anderson, Sidney Howard, Waldo Frank, John Dos Passos, Edmund Wilson, Malcolm Cowley, Erskine Caldwell, Sidney Hook, Lincoln Steffens and Langston Hughes. A typical paragraph was subtitled "Serfs and Vagabonds":

After three years, the flag is still at halfmast, the economic activities of the country are at a rate of approximately 50% of capacity. . . . The giant steel plants, the magnificent motor factories, such as those of Ford, are shut down in great part. Our means of production, sufficient to sustain all of us in comfort, function at half pressure or rust away. . . . The farming population, the largest and most conservative section of the country, has been driven to violence, after deepening poverty of many years' standing. They have too much food to sell in a country whose masses are hungry. In addition to 12,000,000 or 15,000,000 unemployed workers, other millions are employed only part time. One of the most tragic aspects of the capitalist-made depression are the 300,000 children who, according to government reports, are completely homeless, wandering to and fro.

The plight of the intellectuals was set forth in detail: eight thousand unemployed teachers in New York City alone; librarians, chemists, engineers, architects, musicians, actors desperately seeking jobs; Ph.D.s glad to work in department stores at twelve dollars per week; writers and painters finding no market for their creations; students by the thousand compelled to leave school.

James Rorty, secretary of the organization, asked me to speak at a Cooper Union mass meeting. He assured me that since I was an "independent" there would be no objection to my making "some criticism of Communism." In accepting the invitation, I wrote:

I have very little sympathy with the Communist Party. My interest in this thing is to try to inject a little intelligence into the revolutionary movement, so that if a revolutionary change does come it will not be guided by hysteria and mob spirit. . . . I think that the dictatorship of the proletariat is nonsense. . . . Furthermore, I am unequivocally opposed to violence as a means of effecting social change. . . . I shall probably say all of these things and maybe more . . . , so if you think my remarks will embarrass you, you can still call me off.

Of course the invitation was withdrawn. In an apologetic letter Rorty explained that the committee was afraid my remarks might be used by the anti-Communist press to stigmatize the party. So my participation in the campaign was limited to an endorsement of the candidates and a small monetary contribution. My expectation of a huge protest vote was completely unrealized. As I recall it, the total Communist vote was less than 100,000, and even the Socialist poll was only about a million—figures that would have been greatly augmented, of course, if the millions of aliens and homeless migrants had been able to vote. Even so, it was evident that, no matter what their grievances, the American people were unwilling to support parties that challenged the existing economic order.

By the time the election was over, I had finished my new play, *We, the People*. It dealt with the fortunes, or rather the misfortunes, of a typical skilled workman and his family, helplessly engulfed in the tide of national adversity. Their story is told against a kaleidoscopic background that shows the industrialist, the banker, the university president, the United States senator, the high-court judge tacitly united in an alliance for the preservation of the status quo.

The play required a cast of fifty. In view of the appalling unemployment situation, I interviewed personally everyone who applied. I wanted to make even those who were not selected feel that their need was not unrecognized. When my secretary informed me that the thousandth applicant had been reached, I called a halt, for I was nearing the point of exhaustion, both physically and from the cumulative effect of the pitiable stories I had heard.

As designer of the production, which called for fifteen sets, I engaged Aline Bernstein, who not only did a splendid job but heartened everyone with her vitality and enthusiasm. All the members of my fine cast were excited about the play. I had never seen actors approach a play with such fervor. Their elevation of spirit was apparent even to those spectators who disliked the play. In fact, one hostile critic said that the cast played with "a sense of dedication."

The play opened at the Empire Theatre, that plush-and-gilt temple of the drama where the late Charles Frohman had paraded the talents of Maude Adams, John Drew, William Gillette, Ethel Barrymore and Francis Wilson. The opening night was unlike anything I had ever seen in the theatre. The performance was frequently interrupted by mingled expressions of approval and disapproval. At the end there was a demonstration: cheers and bravos, mainly from the balcony; boos and hisses, mainly from the orchestra.

The notices were agitated, emphatic, confused and confusing. Everybody praised the acting, the direction and the scenery, but as to the play itself a few voted yes, some vehemently no, the majority both yes and no. Brooks Atkinson, obviously troubled, called it "a rude, grim, lumbering drama that can stimulate a mixed audience into choosing sides" and "an angry, headlong and disturbing attack upon social complacence." Burns Mantle said: "No presentment of the sins of the community and of humanity in general has been so completely and so movingly set forth before." John Anderson, strongly against, said: "*We, the People* would be interesting if untrue. It is, as Mr. Shaw puts it, too true to be good." *Variety*, its eye, as ever, focused on the box office, remarked concisely: "Indications against lower-floor drawing power, which limits its chances." One critic saw in the production "a showman's thrifty attempt to capitalize on the depression." Another called it, somewhat more accurately, "a quixotic gesture" that would probably cost me many thousands of dollars.

The political orientation of the play was variously appraised: "It takes a keen-minded Communist to pay attention to him." ". . . would undoubtedly win the approval of Socialists and liberals, not to mention many capitalists." "Liberals will see it and approve; conservatives and radicals will alike object." "Mr. Rice's treatment of his theme is thoroughly bourgeois." "With one eye closed, and the other seeing red, Mr. Rice looks at present-day America."

The public response was satisfying spiritually, but not economically. Every night there was an enthusiastic demonstration—from the packed gallery, where the seats were a dollar. The three-dollar orchestra seats had, as *Variety* had predicted, few occupants. Unfortunately, in terms of dollars and cents every orchestra patron was worth three in the gallery. The problem was how to meet the payroll of fifty-four actors and twenty-four stagehands. I had financed the production myself; there was a limit to what I was willing to lose. I was deluged with letters urging me to keep the play on; nothing else I had written had evoked such a flood of mail. The letter that pleased me most was a long, warm, amusing one from William Allen White, who said that the points the play made were all in the 1912 platform of the Progressive Party.

I wrote letters and articles, made speeches, invited influential people to see the play; but the orchestra remained empty, while the gallery bulged. I urged the theatre manager to price the whole house at a dollar. If we could fill it, even at that price both the theatre and the production could meet expenses. But he was unwilling to bring the illustrious Empire down to that lowly level.

At the end of the third week I told the cast we would have to close. They replied that they refused to quit, that the play must be kept on, even if they had to go without pay. Here was something new in the history of the world: fifty actors clamoring to be permitted to work for nothing, because they believed in the play! So I agreed to turn over to them whatever was left after I had paid the theatre expenses, the advertising costs and the stagehands, who in accordance with the policy of their union refused to make any concession.

We staggered along for another three weeks, the cast reveling in those nightly cheers from above; but the net proceeds hardly provided carfares and cigarette money. When I called the actors on stage, to thank them and to say goodbye, they presented me a testimonial signed by the whole cast. It hangs on the wall of my study as I write this. One sentence reads: "We consider it a splendid achievement in the modern theatre and we are proud and happy to have been associated with you in setting it before the public." They ended with a line from *As You Like It:* "You have deserved high commendation, true applause and love." So ended *We, the People,* after a tempestuous run of six weeks.

Luckily, my losses were offset by the returns from the touring company of *Counsellor-at-Law.* The company's business manager insisted upon getting in cash the producer's share of the receipts.

He spent every Sunday traveling to New York, where we put the money in a safe-deposit box, rather than deposit it in a bank that might suspend business any day. It was indicative of the country's state, and state of mind.

2

Physically and emotionally exhausted, I felt the need of a temporary escape from the theatre; so with my daughter Peggy, now thirteen, I took a trip to Spain. In Madrid, for the first time I encountered Velázquez, one of those experiences that nourish the soul and enlarge the inner life. I was prepared for *The Maids of Honor*, but not for *Vulcan's Forge, The Triumph of Bacchus* and, above all, *The Surrender at Breda*, whose sweet graciousness is unmatched in any painting I have ever seen.

Many painters can be fully appreciated only if one sees a concentration of their works in a particular locality. Titian, Rubens, Raphael, Cézanne, Picasso and many others are widely distributed, but as one goes to Madrid for Velázquez and Goya, so one must go to Venice for Tintoretto, Vienna for Brueghel, Florence for Botticelli and Fra Angelico, Padua and Assisi for Giotto, Chantilly for Fouquet, Rome for Michelangelo, Amsterdam for van Gogh, London for Turner, Albi for Toulouse-Lautrec.

Another high spot of our Spanish tour was Toledo. There are certain small cities—Salzburg, Arles, Bruges, Dubrovnik—that have a style, a color, a personality all their own. Toledo is one of them. I had looked often at El Greco's view of it in the Metropolitan Museum of Art, assuming it to be the fevered vision of a distraught man. Yet as we approached the city I saw it before us just as El Greco had painted it: the dramatic, clustered towers, the twisting gorge of the Tagus River. In fact, the Greco seemed almost photographic. I had a similar experience sailing into the harbor of Marseilles. There was the suburb of L'Estaque, needing only a frame around it to make it a Cézanne. This is greatness in any art: to express the quintessence of a place, a character, a situation, an emotion, in symbols that not only reproduce reality but illuminate and transcend it.

Spain was a good prelude to Mexico, where we all spent the summer as members of a sort of seminar organized by the Committee on Cultural Relations with Latin America. Many special events had been arranged, and we were able to meet some leading figures in Mexican cultural and civic life. Even more fortunately, one of the group's leaders was Count René d'Harnoncourt, an Austrian descended, as his name indicates, from French *émigrés*. René, now director of New York's Museum of Modern Art, is not only a man of great erudition, wit and charm, but an outstanding authority on the ancient and modern Indian cultures of the Americas.

Besides the Aztec remains, we saw the vast creations of the great trio of contemporary Mexican painters, Diego Rivera, José Clemente Orozco and David Alfaro Siqueiros, all of whom were active in the Communist movement. Rivera told me that as secretary general of the Mexican Communist Party he had called a meeting of the executive committee at which he demanded the expulsion of a member who was guilty of deviations. The culprit, he said, was named Diego Rivera.

In Mexico we encountered an agrarian, handicraft culture relatively unaffected by industrialism. Almost every village had its own style of workmanship. René knew which village made the most interesting pots, baskets or serapes, and which villager was the best workman. He conducted us straight to the peasant's hut, where we could watch the operations of the loom or of the potter's great toe. It was all very unlike the Soviet Union.

3

An urgent telegram from Carl Laemmle, Jr., asked me to come to Hollywood to assist in the casting of the picture of *Counsellor-at-Law*. While I was thinking it over, William Wyler, who was to direct the picture—his first major assignment—arrived in Mexico. We all went to Hollywood together.

Laemmle, a diminutive, highstrung young man, was in a state of nervous tension. Paul Muni had flatly refused to appear in the picture. (I suspect he felt that his Hollywood future would suffer if he became "typed" in a Jewish part.) After much turmoil, John Barrymore was engaged. I admired him as an actor, but had doubts about his rightness for the part; moreover, he was definitely on the decline. But, in view of his great talents and great name, I could hardly have objected to him even if I had had the veto power.

As for the other parts, Laemmle said, there were simply no actors to be found. I pointed out that nearly a year before I had sent him the names of the actors who had been in the play and had urged him to engage them. Laemmle asked frantically if I thought they were still available. It took only a telephone call to Jane Broder, the New York agent who represented most of them, to set the wheels in motion. Soon, to my great satisfaction, nearly all my New York cast was reassembled. The picture was a great popular success. Barrymore was quite wrong for the part and had many shaky moments, but his magnetic quality mitigated his deficiences.

While I was in Hollywood I was plagued again by a recurrent annoyance. From time to time I had received clippings from small-town newspapers, mostly in upstate New York, reporting that I had called on the mayor or the town librarian, or had been entertained by the local women's club. I wrote to several of the editors, who confirmed my conjecture that someone was impersonating me; their own suspicions had been aroused by the impostor's strange behavior. I tried to track him down, but he was constantly on the move. Sometimes I would receive a letter reproaching me for failing to send opening-night tickets as I had promised to do on the Albany night boat or in a Buffalo bar. In Hollywood an indignant landlady who had read of my arrival in some gossip column called to demand payment of the six weeks' room rent I allegedly owed her. This sort of thing went on intermittently for years. Once I received a letter from a young Canadian woman informing me that she had decided to leave home and was awaiting my arrival in Toronto. I have often wondered how long she waited. Eventually the incidents ceased; perhaps my alter ego found a new outlet for his talents, or maybe his wanderings came to an end in some jail.

Another persistent annoyance that has always had its amusing side has been the confusion of my identity with that of Elmer Davis. How this mistake arises I do not know, for Davis and Rice neither look nor sound alike. Yet it has been made hundreds of times, a nuisance to us both. After a while, we made a sort of running gag of it. Once Davis wrote me: "That was a wonderful Phi Beta Kappa oration you delivered at Harvard. At least, I assume it was you, since one of the customers came up to the speaker afterward and said: 'That was a splendid address, Mr. Rice!'" Again he wrote: "Do you or we still consider *Street Scene* our best work or do we prefer

Dream Girl? This question, in abeyance during the war years, has recently come up again, and I want to know on which work to take the enthusiastic compliments of the lady who sits next to me."

Again and again, on the lecture platform, the chairman, after reciting the usual biographical data, has presented me to the audience as Mr. Davis. When I received an acknowledgment of a charitable contribution, made out to Davis, I sent it to him with the suggestion that he deduct it on our income tax return. He replied: "The deduction will have to be split three ways. The last time I was in New York, Elmer Harris was staying at the Algonquin too; and when I was checking out, a bellboy said briskly: 'Leaving us, Mr. Harris?' " Strangest of all was the slip of a German refugee doctor in London whom I had occasion to consult. As I was leaving, he said, "It was pleasure to meet you, Mr. Davis." Then, profusely apologetic, he explained that during the war he had looked forward every evening to Davis' incisive broadcasts from America. Though Davis has been dead for some years, the confusion persists in private and public introductions. Sometimes a telephone caller asks for Mr. Davis. The fact that my telephone exchange happens to be Davis probably does not help matters.

4

My wanderings temporarily at a halt, I wrote three plays. I thought it would be interesting to commemorate the twentieth anniversary of *On Trial* by writing another courtroom melodrama, particularly since I had at hand a subject very much to my liking: the Reichstag fire trial. I had followed closely the accounts of the burning of the Reichstag, engineered by the Nazis and imputed by them to the Communists, a stratagem that had accelerated Hitler's accession. Even more sensational was the staged Leipzig "trial" of certain Communist leaders. Not wanting to present a mere documentary transcription, I changed the trial's locale to an unspecified Balkan country and made the plot turn on the attempted assassination of a fascist leader. Some of the characters were suggested by actual participants in the Reichstag affair: Goering, its prime mover; Hitler, who appeared briefly in a crucial scene; Marinus van der Lubbe, the psychotic young Dutchman employed by Goering to set the fire; and Georgi Dimitrov, the Bulgarian Communist whose bold resourcefulness had done much to discredit the proceedings.

All the other characters were fictitious. The entire action of the play, which I called *Judgment Day*, took place in a courtroom. The material lent itself to melodramatic treatment; I packed the play with tense situations and highly colored incidents. Afraid I might have overdone it, I sent the script to my friend Arthur Garfield Hays, one of an international panel of lawyers who had courageously attended the Leipzig trial. He complimented me upon capturing the atmosphere of a European courtroom and said that, if anything, I had understated the extravagance of the actual proceedings.

The play almost wrote itself. In fact, at its completion I felt so fresh and exuberant that I went on to write another, dealing with the shipboard romance of a tough-minded Soviet commissar and a wealthy American girl. The title, *Between Two Worlds*, suggested the possibility of a compromise between the apparently irreconcilable extremes typified by these two characters, a theme perhaps even more pertinent today than it was then.

Still in a working mood, I attacked a third project, *Not for Children*, a rewriting, or rather a re-creation, of an earlier play, *Life Is Real*. I retained the formula of two commentators analyzing the incidents of an inner play; but for the two males, a cynic and a sentimentalist, I substituted a man and a woman whose observations turned upon differences between the male and the female outlook.

When I told my business associate, Joe Bickerton, that I had three plays ready, he made the startling suggestion that I buy the Belasco Theatre. Since Belasco's death the theatre had been unsuccessfully operated by his former business manager. Interest payments on the mortgage were in default, foreclosure was threatened. Bickerton, besides wanting to protect the equity of the Belasco estate, for which he was attorney, thought that it might be advisable for me to acquire a theatre.

At first I rejected the suggestion as fantastic. I was a playwright who had become a director and a producer by accident; I did not think of myself as a businessman, least of all a real-estate speculator. But Bickerton pointed out the advantages of controlling a theatre. If only one of the three plays succeeded, the theatre's profits, added to the producer's, would establish a reserve for the financing of future productions. The Belasco estate, hard pressed, was willing to accept a surprisingly small amount of cash.

Half persuaded by these arguments, I made a tour of the dark, dusty theatre, guided by the one-eyed property man Matty Purcell, who had worked most of his life for Belasco. What I saw impressed me. The theatre had many features not usually found in New York theatres: a fine, roomy stage, a scenery dock, a large rehearsal room, a suite of offices, a duplex apartment with a large studio (where I had several times visited Belasco). Most of the "art treasures" which shrewd dealers had foisted upon Belasco had been sold or thrown away, but there was still some trashy bric-a-brac about: Japanese decorations in the apartment bedroom; a model of a medieval fortress, whose portcullis, when lowered, revealed a telephone; and other curiosities. Puzzled by a large iron stand, I asked Matty what it was for. "Well, Mr. Rice," he said, clearing his throat, "that's where the old man used to keep his halberds."

The upshot was that I bought the theatre. Besides the sound business reasons, I had a secret one. My marriage had slowly deteriorated. Now that the children were growing up, their care no longer provided a strong common interest for my wife and me. Mutual affection, friends and some similarities in taste were still ties, but not strong enough for a creative relationship. It occurred to me that if my wife became active in the management of the theatre—a task for which she was suited by intelligence and ability —we might, through participation in a joint enterprise, be drawn closer together. I do not know how much I really believed that the breach could be narrowed, but it was a possibility that substantially influenced my decision.

My acquisition of the theatre amused me. It had been incongruous enough to thrust the rude *We, the People* into the hallowed Victorian precincts of the Empire; for me to become the owner of the great David Belasco's temple struck me as comic indeed. Belasco was the embodiment of everything I detested in the theatre: meretriciousness; pretentiousness; *Kitsch;* fake "glamour"; synthetic romanticism; heavy-handed artiness; theatricality parading as creativeness, stage carpentry as dramaturgy, cunning as integrity—in a word, phoniness. However, the purchase of the theatre entailed no oath of loyalty to its builder.

5

I made other purchases far more modest, but more enduring and satisfactory. The theatre was not the only art severely affected by the depression; in times of adversity, expenditures for cultural goods are the first to be curtailed. Many dealers in paintings, particularly modern paintings, were compelled to dispose of their wares at forced sales. I attended these auctions mainly out of curiosity, but when I found that the pictures were going begging, I acquired, at absurdly low prices, works by Picasso, Braque, Dufy, Metzinger, Rouault, di Chirico, Friesz, Léger, Modigliani, Pascin, Derain and others.

It was a time of momentous happenings. The excesses that followed Hitler's rise to power foreshadowed the years ahead. The bloody purge of some of his closest associates was an ominous revelation of his bestial, maniacal nature. I felt that *Judgment Day* indeed understated the truth.

On the domestic front things were happening, too. Like most left-wing liberals, I had expected little of Franklin Roosevelt. Nothing in his record indicated that he was prepared to take the steps required to pull the country out of the morass. It was gratifying, therefore, to find him initiating sweeping measures designed to bring order out of chaos and to assist the millions of innocent victims of the collapse.

Supplementing the social and economic reforms was the repeal of prohibition, the most absurd and futile restriction ever foisted upon a free people by a fanatical minority. Unfortunately, corruption, racketeering, organized crime and general disrespect for law had become so deeply embedded in the social order that it has been impossible to extirpate them.

Another constructive measure was official recognition of the fact that, whether we liked it or not, the Soviet government had been very much in existence for some sixteen years. I attended a dinner given in honor of William C. Bullitt, our first ambassador to the Soviet Union, and Alexander Troyanovsky, the newly arrived Russian envoy. I had a chance to talk to Bullitt, who was very optimistic about his mission. He invited me to look him up if I ever returned to Moscow. But by the time I did get there, in 1936, he had become discouraged about Soviet-American relations and had given up his post. Bad as those relations have been, there can be no doubt that they would have been worse had there been no diplomatic channels of communication—a fact to which the opponents of recognition of Communist China seem oblivious.

6

After a quick trip to London to see *Counsellor-at-Law*, which had opened at the Piccadilly under the auspices of Sir Barry Jackson, I began work on the production of *Judgment Day*. Many excellent actors were unemployed; it was not hard to assemble a fine cast. The direction presented technical problems, since, except for one scene, almost the entire cast of thirty-five was on stage throughout. To keep this large group mobile and yet unobtrusive was difficult. What I had seen of the handling of crowds on the Soviet stage was very helpful.

To emphasize the extravagant and sinister character of the proceedings, I pitched the performances high, aiming at an emotional response from the audience. That was exactly what I got. There were cheers and applause throughout the opening-night performance, and a demonstration at the end. But there was still the press to be reckoned with, so I did not allow myself to become too jubilant.

As with *We, the People*, the reviews were bewilderingly contradictory. Some called the play "hysterical hokum," "a wild phantasmagoria of theatrical hysteria," "almost as funny and as old-fashioned as *The Drunkard*," "sophomoric fireworks," "fantastic and inflammable folderol, over-written and overplayed." Others said: "There is a power behind *Judgment Day*, and a power in it too, which will not be denied"; ". . . the play actually stays way behind the mad extravagance of the actual trial"; ". . . a play to make your hair and sympathies stand on end. The audience paid it the deserved tribute of the season's first excited yells." Most confusing of all was this comment from Burns Mantle: "It matters very little that Mr. Rice can prove that he has not overstated the case of Hitler. The audience still does not believe it possible for so vicious and brazen a travesty of justice to have taken place in any civilized state."

There is one point upon which theatre people agree in their perennial discussions of the function and influence of dramatic criticism: the critic's effect upon the play's reception depends less upon his capability than upon what paper he writes for. In New York, almost the sole American center of play production, nearly all theatregoers, especially those who buy orchestra seats, read either the *Times* or the *Herald Tribune.* Good reviews in these papers do not necessarily ensure a play's success, but they invariably create a flurry of immediate interest. On the other hand, unless it has a large advance sale or a popular star a play can hardly survive bad notices in these two papers, even though the others praise it. One often hears somebody say of a play, "The papers say it's very bad," a statement usually based upon one man's critique in one newspaper. Thus the fate of a play often hinges upon two men, invested with the authority of the press, whose opinions may be determined by a variety of limitations and prejudices. This nightmarish prospect of the total waste of vast expenditures of time, effort, talent and money by the unpredictable pronouncements of a few fallible individuals forever haunts those who live in the theatre.

I had expected a disparaging review from the witty but shallow Percy Hammond of the *Herald Tribune,* but had hoped for something more from Brooks Atkinson of the *Times.* While he did not condemn the play outright, the general tone of his notice was unfavorable. He disliked its storminess and charged me with being "intemperate." In an article in the *Times,* I cited examples from the Greeks onward to suggest that temperateness was not essential to dramatic excellence. I had a long correspondence with Atkinson, whose integrity and earnestness I respected and whom I liked personally. When I sent him a copy of Douglas Reed's factual report, *The Burning of the Reichstag,* by contrast to which *Judgment Day* seemed restrained indeed, Atkinson said he found the book hard to read. I concluded that, like so many other Americans, he was unwilling to face the realities of the world we were living in. In later years he took a broader view, both as a war correspondent and as a supporter of liberal causes.

So again I had to fight to keep a play running. Again I was flooded with letters commending the play, denouncing the critics. Every night at the final curtain there was a demonstration. But again it was the balconies that were crowded, while the orchestra was almost empty. As at the Empire, I wanted to price all seats at a dollar, but my business advisers urged me not to. They said that, once lowered, the prices could not be raised again, and that the theatre could not be operated on a cut-price basis. Besides, they felt that *Between Two Worlds,* already in rehearsal, had an excellent chance of success, so that I would benefit by having it in my own theatre. I was reluctant to close *Judgment Day;* the cast, keen about the play and elated by the audience reactions, wanted to go on, too. So I moved the production to a theatre that had a cut-rate policy, waiving all royalties or other financial return. By this means the play was kept running for a total of one hundred performances, not too bad considering the adverse notices, the size of the cast and the dismal state of theatrical business. Nor did the Broadway closing mark, by any means, the end of the play's history.

Between Two Worlds, with a cast of fifty headed by Joseph Schildkraut, came to nothing. It was dismissed with a kind of patronizing condescension that was worse than outright condemnation. The very critics who had deplored the vehemence of *Judgment Day* now took me to task for the mildness of *Between Two Worlds.* With the aid of theatre parties booked in advance, we kept it going for a few weeks; but it was, in every sense, a failure.

7

There followed an incident so embarrassing that I find it hard to report, even after all these years. Tired and disturbed, I reluctantly fulfilled a promise to address a class conducted by Professor John H. H. Lyon at Columbia. I talked for about an hour on a familiar subject, the predominant commercialism of the Broadway theatre. I said that art was subordinated to business; that the emphasis was on trivial, tasteless plays that catered to idle people who could afford high ticket prices; that the dramatist who introduced new techniques or vital themes met with indifference or hostility. In the last few minutes of my talk, I charged the critics with fostering the theatre of sterile entertainment and with discouraging innovators and rebels. I said that, with a few honorable exceptions, they were stupid and illiterate; and I went on to characterize several of them, without mentioning names, of course, in most uncomplimentary terms. Quite spontaneously, I ended by saying that I intended to give up writing plays for the commercial theatre.

My strictures, though caustic enough, were far milder than the opinions I had often heard privately expressed by playwrights, actors and producers. Nevertheless, however justified my charges may have been, there can be no doubt that my public statement of them was injudicious and ill-mannered. In slight self-extenuation, I may say that I did not know that my audience included several young men from the School of Journalism, who rushed to the telephone to relay my remarks to the metropolitan dailies.

The consequences were most unpleasant. The newspapers gave full play to my attack upon the critics and my avowed intention to give up playwriting, completely ignoring the major part of my address, the condemnation of the commercial theatre. As I look back after nearly three decades, the speech strikes me as one of the most foolish of my many follies. It should have occurred to me that my remarks might be publicized, and that the critics would inevitably have the last word. Moreover, I should have foreseen that although the views I expressed had been held by me even before I became a playwright, my voicing of them now would certainly be attributed to my inability to accept adverse criticism of my own plays, and would make me seem a sorehead.

Having, so to speak, burned my bridges behind me, there was nothing for it but to stand my ground. So I attended the opening of a play, whose very name I have forgotten. My appearance created more interest than the performance. People crowded around me and asked me if I had meant what I said. Several critics told me they regretted my decision. As a matter of fact, I was on good terms with many of them. There were a few whom I held in contempt, others for whom I had little respect, but none with whom I had ever had a personal quarrel. At one time or another I had had cordial relations with Brooks Atkinson, Heywood Broun, Alexander Woollcott, Joseph Wood Krutch, Richard Lockridge, Gilbert Gabriel, John Anderson, Louis Sherwin, Ward Morehouse, Burns Mantle, Samuel Hoffenstein and Richard Watts, Jr.

The distasteful controversy went on and on. Every critic found occasion to comment. I was given ample opportunity to reply, but, as I have pointed out, the last word was always on the other side. My attack had, of course, aroused resentment; many of the comments were sarcastic or angry. It has always seemed odd to me that the artist, whose reputation and livelihood can be seriously jeopardized by adverse criticism, often undeserved, is expected to acquiesce graciously, and is branded a poor loser or an egomaniac if he strikes back. In time, of course, the controversy subsided; but, to my distress, I am still looked upon as a chronic critic-baiter, though I have never been anything of the sort.

Following my impulsive announcement at Columbia I dropped

Not for Children, the third play on my schedule. I am convinced now that I had long been unconsciously intending to call a halt to my writing and producing activities. In little more than five years I had written eight plays; all but *Not for Children* had been produced. Two plays written earlier had also had productions. Of the nine, I had directed eight, as well as three additional companies of *Street Scene* and one of *Counsellor-at-Law.* Six of the plays I had also produced, two of them in a theatre which I owned and operated. In the same period, I had written *A Voyage to Purilia* and two motion picture scripts, had made a lecture tour, five trips to Europe (two of them extensive), two to Hollywood, two to the Caribbean and one to Mexico. It was a pace that could hardly be maintained. It was not so much that I was feeling the strain— though I suppose I was—as that my obsessive desire for freedom made me rebel against being driven, even by myself. So I turned from playwriting to other things.

CHAPTER

XVII

Life as an Ex-Playwright

1

Though I intended to write no more plays, I did not entirely sever my connection with the theatre. For one thing, I still had the Belasco on my hands. The savings bank that held the mortgage was again threatening foreclosure, but I persuaded the president, a hard-fisted Scot, to give me time to find a tenant. I found one in the Group Theatre. The rental barely covered the carrying charges, but I wanted to encourage the organization which was trying to establish the sort of theatre in which I believed: a permanent company, with a definite philosophy and a long-range program.

One day Cheryl Crawford, one of the Group's directors, asked me to read half a dozen scripts which were being considered for production. I went through them with little interest, until I came to the last, whose vivid characterization, pungent dialogue and effective dramaturgy revealed a brilliant new talent. When I commended the play to Cheryl she said, "Well, you see, he's one of the boys in our acting company, so we didn't know just what to think." The play was *Awake and Sing*, by Clifford Odets. Its production by the Group was quickly followed by *Waiting for Lefty, Golden Boy* and *Rocket to the Moon*.

Another organization with whose aims I sympathized was the Theatre Union, a militant left-wing group headed by the young playwrights George Sklar, Albert Maltz and Paul Peters. It aimed to produce plays of protest—or, in the current phrase, "social significance"—for a "proletarian" audience. It had taken over the old theatre on Fourteenth Street vacated by Eva Le Gallienne after years of gallant struggle to keep her Civic Repertory Theatre alive. The sad truth is that, with the exception of *Stevedore,* written by Peters and Sklar, the plays presented by the Theatre Union were neither very good nor very well done. Nor were the proletarians weaned away from the movies. The sparse patronage was supplied mainly by middle-class liberals who, like myself, gave support to any theatre that tried to break away from the sterile Broadway routine.

At one point the Theatre Union, unable to put up the Equity bond to guarantee the actors' salaries, asked for my help, since I was one of the few producers whose signature Equity accepted in lieu of a bond. It was a considerable risk, for it made me personally liable for the salaries. Luckily, the Theatre Union managed to meet its obligations.

Shortly after my tilt with the critics, an old acquaintance, Kyle Crichton, invited me to discuss some theatre problems with a small group at dinner. Crichton, one of the editors of *Collier's* magazine, doubled as Robert Forsythe, under which name he wrote a column called "Redder than the Rose" for *New Masses*—the only bright feature of that now dreary doctrinaire publication. Present at the dinner which was at the home of William Browder, brother of the Communist Party leader Earl Browder, were Mike Gold and Joshua Kunitz, both of *New Masses,* and two or three others. My hosts, having taken my rebellion against Broadway as evidence of my ripeness for conversion to Communism, proposed that I organize a theatre designed to acquaint the masses with the philosophy of the class struggle. When I said that, since this was to be a theatre of and for the workers, I assumed the wage scales of the theatrical unions would be met, Kunitz replied impatiently, "These are technological problems with which we need not concern ourselves." I declined the invitation, of course, explaining that I was a playwright, not a political propagandist—adding, however, that if any constructive revolutionary movement ever developed in America I would be quick to join it. Whereupon Kunitz, in his best platform manner, said, "There are those who wait, and those who are already upon the barricades." I managed to depart without laughing aloud. Barricades, forsooth! A few days later Crichton, who had a sense of humor, wrote me an apology for the owlish behavior of the comrades.

2

In 1934 there appeared a remarkable book by a Midwestern housewife, Elizabeth Dilling. Entitled *The Red Network* and sub-titled "A Who's Who and Handbook of Radicalism for Patriots," this volume, appropriately bound in red, is a 352-page exposé of the revolutionary movement in America. After a general discussion in Part I, Mrs. Dilling gets down to specifics in Part II, which contains "descriptive data concerning more than 460 Communist, Anarchist, I.W.W., or Radical-Pacifist controlled or infiltrated organizations." Subversive agencies whose machinations are revealed include the American Friends Service Committee, the Federal Council of Churches of Christ, the National Association for the Advancement of Colored People, the National Catholic Welfare Conference, the American Federation of Labor, the Union Theological Seminary and the Young Men's and Young Women's Christian Associations.

Part III, the "Who's Who," lists "one or more affiliations of about 1,300 persons, who are or have been members of Communist, Anarchist, Socialist, I.W.W., or Pacifist-controlled organizations." In introducing the names, Mrs. Dilling remarks: "Mention in this Who's Who will be regarded by those who are proud of their affiliations as a badge of honor, by those ashamed of them as a blacklist."

In spite of the scornful implication, I found myself in the first category, for I could not help feeling honored by the association of my name with the names of Jane Addams, Clarence Darrow, John Dewey, Albert Einstein, Felix Frankfurter, Sigmund Freud, Mahatma Gandhi, Robert M. Hutchins, Fiorello La Guardia, Sinclair Lewis, Romain Rolland, Eleanor Roosevelt, Bernard Shaw, Leopold Stokowski, Rabindranath Tagore, Norman Thomas, Hendrik Willem Van Loon, H. G. Wells, William Allen White and Thornton Wilder. One would have thought that this nonsensical farrago would have been self-defeating. Unfortunately, it was not. Not only, as Mrs. Dilling states, was the listing based largely upon the "documentary evidence" of reports issued by the House of Representa-

tives committee headed by Hamilton Fish, and the even more infamous Lusk Committee of the New York State Legislature, but
the book supplied new ammunition for the reactionary press and
the "patriots" to whom it was addressed, in their campaign to wipe
out liberalism and all movements for social reform. It was another
manifestation of the dangerous obscurantism in American life that
finds recurrent expression in the rise of a Father Coughlin or a
Senator McCarthy, and in the actions of the Daughters of the
American Revolution, the American Legion, the John Birch Society,
the Ku Klux Klan and the House Un-American Activities Committee.

The list of my political delinquencies, brief in comparison with
those of such out-and-out revolutionaries as Jane Addams, John
Dewey, Albert Einstein and Eleanor Roosevelt, included my sponsorship of the travel agency that had arranged my trip to the Soviet
Union, and my authorship of We, the People, "an argument for
revolution." The chief count was my membership on the board of
directors of the American Civil Liberties Union. In fact, Mrs.
Dilling cites every member of the A.C.L.U.'s board, national committee and executive staff, besides devoting twelve pages to a discussion of the organization's activities.

For many years, it was standard practice at American Legion con-
ventions to adopt resolutions condemning the A.C.L.U. as pro-
Communist. The charge has never been substantiated, for the very
good reason that it is groundless. On the A.C.L.U.'s fortieth birthday Governor Rockefeller of New York, in a congratulatory message,
said: "It is of the utmost importance that our civil liberties be
preserved intact and untarnished. This we need not only for individual self-realization, but also as an example to the rest of the
world." On the same occasion the New York Times said editorially:
"The American Civil Liberties Union . . . has been indispensable
in investigating violations of civil liberties, in publicizing them and
in working through the channels of public opinion and of the law
to see that our constitutional principles as expressed in the Bill of
Rights remain a living force." Ten years earlier President Truman
had said: "The integrity of the American Civil Liberties Union and
of its workers in the field has never been, and I feel never will be,
questioned. Officers, directors and members of the Union have performed outstanding services to the cause of true freedom."

I quote these encomiums with pride, because nothing in my
civic life has meant more to me than my thirty-year membership

on the board of the A.C.L.U. Even before my election to the board, I was on its anticensorship committee, the National Council of Freedom from Censorship. For many years I have been a sort of spokesman for the A.C.L.U. in all matters pertaining to the suppression, by post-office, customs, police and censorship-board officials, of books, plays, films and broadcasts, and to such related fields as blacklisting, regulatory "codes" and the repressive activities of pressure groups. For four decades I have participated in many censorship cases and controversies, engaging in lectures, debates, committee meetings and appearances before legislative groups, writing articles and pamphlets, conducting an active correspondence with both advocates and opponents of censorship.

Attendance at A.C.L.U. board meetings has contributed substantially to my education. Week after week, year after year, there is a panoramic revelation of America's political, economic and social life, of its mores, prejudices and psychology. The complex field of censorship is only one of the many areas that come under constant surveillance. "Due process of law" covers such diverse matters as unlawful seizure and search, wiretapping, the third degree, denial of the right to counsel or of a fair trial. Academic freedom involves the right of teachers to express their opinions without restriction, the right of students to organize, the use of educational facilities for free discussion. In labor relations there are complicated questions of picketing and boycotts, democracy within trade-unions, the right of employers to oppose union activities. The separation of church and state guaranteed by the Bill of Rights gives rise to problems involving allocation of public moneys to religious schools; religious instruction and observances in public educational institutions; the regulation of Sunday activities.

Other matters that demand attention are lynching and mob violence; the improper deportation of aliens; the denial of passports to citizens desiring to leave the country or of visas to foreigners desiring to enter it; loyalty oaths; the questionable procedures of legislative investigatory committees. Perhaps the most important class of cases has to do with the rights of minorities: discrimination against Negroes, Jews, Catholics, Orientals, Mexicans, Puerto Ricans, Spanish Americans and American Indians in education, housing, employment and the use of public facilities. It is a long and varied catalogue of abuses in a country dedicated to freedom and equality before the law!

Association with my fellow board members has been a constant source of pleasure, stimulation and knowledge. Illness, death, assumption of public office, pressure of other duties necessitate frequent changes in the composition of the board, so there are always new and interesting personalities. In fact, only three of the present members antedate me in length of service: ex-Judge Dorothy Kenyon, a witty and determined champion of women's rights; B. W. Huebsch, for many years one of the heads of Viking Press; and Walter Frank, a lawyer whose long life has been devoted to civic causes. As I look back over the long roster of those with whom I have served, I am profoundly impressed by its high level of character, intellect, talent and attainment. A few names will suffice to indicate the caliber of the board's membership: Arthur Garfield Hays, Whitney North Seymour, Morris L. Ernst, Thurgood Marshall, Carl Carmer, Norman Cousins, Quincy Howe, Lewis Galantière, Walter Millis, John Hersey, August Heckscher, John Haynes Holmes, Norman Thomas.

3

The Group Theatre's tenancy gave me time to work on a plan for the eventual use of the Belasco as the home of a co-operative, nonprofit repertory company devoted to the production of fine plays at low prices. Organized under the name of Theatre Alliance, a group of actors and technicians that included Aline Bernstein, Sam Jaffe, Philip Loeb and Aline MacMahon joined with me in attacking the many problems that had to be solved: administrative structure, system of compensation, choice of plays, supplementary activities such as lectures, concerts and plays for children. The immediate concern was finance. I was willing to put in the theatre at the cost of the carrying charges, but production costs had to be provided for. We estimated that we needed a hundred thousand dollars to carry us through a first season—not a large sum for organization expenses and the production of five plays. We reasoned that there must be a thousand New Yorkers who would be willing to contribute an average of a hundred dollars toward the creation of an art theatre such as could be found in almost any fair-sized European city.

We wrote letters, issued publicity statements, gave small parties for the well-to-do, made personal calls on prospective contributors.

None of us had had any experience in raising money, or any interest in it. I found it quite distasteful, for I had never asked anyone for anything. We were cordially received everywhere. Everyone thought it a splendid project; everyone had an excellent reason for not contributing. Sam Jaffe asked me to accompany him to dinner at the Fifth Avenue apartment of a department store owner. Over coffee and Havanas, our host, anticipating us, discoursed eloquently on the economic situation: the decline in securities, the shrinkage of trade, the high taxes, the confiscatory policies of the Roosevelt Administration. Jaffe listened sympathetically, then said gravely, "Yes, I know a man who had seven million dollars and is down to four. He's been obliged to cancel his subscription to *Harper's Bazaar*." Of course we came away empty-handed.

So it went, all along the line. The combined efforts of all of us brought in less than ten thousand dollars. As a last hope, I wrote to the Federal Emergency Relief Administration, which was helping to finance projects that put people back to work. Jacob Baker, assistant to Harry Hopkins, head of the F.E.R.A., asked me to come to Washington. After making it clear that no funds were available for privately organized projects, Baker introduced me to Hopkins, who told me that both the President and Mrs. Roosevelt—particularly the latter—were anxious to find some way of helping workers in the arts who had been hit by the depression. Hopkins had heard numerous proposals from theatrical personalities, but all of them, he said, were either motivated by self-interest, impracticable, or beyond the scope of governmental participation. He asked if I had any suggestion. I said I had not given the matter thought, but I was sure that any theatre project must be organized nationally, on a regional basis, not centered in New York. Hopkins seized my arm. "That's what I've been waiting for somebody to say!" he exclaimed. "Go home and write it up."

Failure to obtain government funds made inevitable the disbanding of Theatre Alliance. To reimburse the contributors in full, which I felt honor bound to do, I had to bear the entire expense of the money-raising campaign. I let the Belasco go, too, glad to have it off my hands, for I had never wanted to be a theatre owner. So another attempt to establish an art theatre failed. However, one item in its program was realized. During my Paris years I had often attended concerts given in the interval between the day's work and the dinner hour. Theatre Alliance had hoped to arrange such concerts for Sunday afternoons, when the theatre was normally dark. The idea appealed to Ira Hirschmann, a civic-minded businessman with a deep interest in music. He organized the Society of the Friends of Music, which for many years gave excellent Sunday-afternoon chamber music concerts at Town Hall.

4

In a letter to Hopkins, I outlined a plan for the establishment, on a national scale, of a Federally sponsored theatre, a utopian dream of mine that I shall go on dreaming, knowing full well that there is little likelihood of its realization. The letter, far too long to re-produce here, suggested four basic principles: high standards of quality; low admission prices; permanence of employment for theatre workers; decentralization, and adaptation of regional proj-ects to local needs. It proposed the conversion of outmoded and unused theatres in every large population area into community centers housing permanent repertory companies which would pre-sent fine drama at prices within everyone's reach. Actors glutting the New York market would be encouraged to return to their home towns; stars would be invited to participate as guest performers. The repertory program would be supplemented by plays for chil-dren, high-quality motion pictures, concerts, lectures, forums, dance recitals, art exhibitions, instruction in the arts. Each theatre, though a unit in an over-all Federal structure, would be locally administered by some existing theatrical or educational group, so that the center would be a community enterprise and its maintenance a matter of civic pride. It was my opinion that, properly managed, many of these centers could eventually become self-supporting; in any case, Federal expenditure, in terms of the national budget, would be modest indeed. The benefits would be incalculable.

Hopkins, now head of a new agency, the Works Progress Ad-ministration, was devising means of providing work for the mil-lions who, in spite of the admirable measures of the New Deal, were still unemployed. Among his numerous projects were four that were designed to assist workers in the fields of art, music, writing and the theatre. I was asked to address a meeting of the National Theatre Conference, an organization of community the-atres, at the University of Iowa, on the occasion of the laying of the cornerstone of a campus theatre. Hopkins, the principal speaker, outlined enthusiastically the program for a Federal Theatre Project. He concluded his address with these significant words: "I am asked whether a theatre subsidized by the government can be kept free from censorship, and I say yes, it is going to be kept free from censorship. What we want is a free, adult, uncensored theatre."

Hallie Flanagan Davis, able director of the Experimental Theatre at Vassar College, was made head of the Theatre Project. The fact that she and Hopkins had been college classmates may have had something to do with her appointment, but her intelligence, idealism, experience and energy made her an excellent choice. Though most of my proposed program had not been adopted, for administrative, fiscal or other reasons, the basic principle of regionalism had been preserved. Hallie asked me to undertake the directorship of the New York region, an area that contained more unemployed theatre workers than all the rest of the country put together. I was reluctant about accepting what promised to be a very difficult assignment. Besides, I had rather been looking forward to getting to work on a novel.

The four arts projects were formally launched at a meeting in Washington attended by leaders in all the arts. Among the theatre representatives were Jasper Deeter of the Hedgerow Theatre in Pennsylvania, Frederic McConnell of the Cleveland Playhouse, Edward Mabie of the University of Iowa, Gilmor Brown of the Pasadena Community Theatre, Glenn Hughes of the University of Washington, Frederick Koch of the North Carolina Playmakers, and, from the professional theatre, Eddie Dowling, Paul Green and Charles Coburn. There were inspiring addresses by Hopkins and Mrs. Roosevelt; idealism and optimism were pervasive. For the first time in American history, the government was fostering the arts, even though the projects were intended primarily to reduce unemployment. Fired by the general enthusiasm, and urged by Hallie, I agreed to direct the New York region. First, however, I obtained Hopkins' assurance that there would be no censorship, and that I should have a free hand, with no superior but Hallie.

5

It is impossible within the compass of a few pages to tell the complex story of the Federal Theatre Project. In my book *The Living Theatre* I have given a chapter to it, but even that barely touches the subject. To those interested in a fascinating account of an undertaking unique in American life, I recommend Hallie Flanagan's 500-page book *Arena*. What follows concerns mainly my own relationship to the project, which is, of course, one of its minor aspects.

The New York regional project superseded a municipal activity, whose incompetent staff and feeble enterprises I took over, more of a hindrance than a help. Our headquarters were an abandoned bank building on Eighth Avenue, neither suitably arranged nor adequately furnished. On my first day I asked one of my assistants, a dreary little civil servant, to put in a supply of pencils, writing tablets, paper clips. He said everything would have to be requisitioned. When I told him to go ahead and requisition, he replied, "First we'll have to requisition some requisition blanks."

It was typical of what was to follow. I had wanted to occupy myself with the organization of acting companies and the supervision of play production, but office administration, labor management and public relations consumed most of my time. Employment was the major problem. Though the top pay for nonsupervisory jobs was twenty-four dollars per week, there were many hundreds of unemployed theatre people who wanted to get on the payroll. My own salary, the highest on the project, was two hundred and sixty dollars per month, based upon thirteen days' work at twenty dollars. Actually, I worked from early morning until late at night every day of the month, including Sundays. It amused me to receive scurrilous letters charging me with getting rich in a governmental sinecure.

Theoretically, employment was limited to persons on the home-relief rolls. This excluded many theatre workers who had been too proud to apply for relief. After much persuasion by Hallie and myself, the rules were modified; whereupon I issued this statement: "The Federal Theatre Project has been created for the purpose of providing worthwhile employment for professional theatre workers. Please bear in mind that you are not being offered relief or charity but WORK. The interviewers have been instructed to receive you with the same courtesy and consideration that would be extended by any professional employment agency, our object being to set up so high a standard of professional excellence in these projects that they will be able to continue on their own momentum after the Federal program is completed."

It took a long time to process the flood of applications, for each person's qualifications had to be determined. I laid down the policy that anyone who had had a reasonable amount of theatrical experience was eligible. The theatrical unions criticized me for not running a union shop, which Washington would never have sanctioned; the Communist hecklers, for not taking on everyone who, regardless of qualifications, professed interest in a theatrical career. We did take on a good many unemployables and incompetents, both union and nonunion, for thorough investigation was impossible. On the whole, however, the project employees were bona fide theatre workers who had proved their competence or were to prove it. I still meet people who tell me how much the project meant to them, not only economically but professionally and psychologically.

Even under optimum conditions the establishment of this large-scale project would not have been easy. As it was, the handicaps were almost insurmountable. To begin with, there was the active opposition of many powerful groups. All the anti-Roosevelt forces, which included F.D.R.'s foes both in and out of Congress and a large section of the metropolitan press, used the Theatre Project as a horrible example of the Administration's wastefulness and socialistic tendencies. For instance, at one of my weekly press conferences a reporter for the New York *Evening Sun*, which was running a daily "boondoggle" story to discredit the New Deal, asked me for some illustrations of the inefficiency of the Theatre Project. In astonishment, I said, "You mean you want me, who am knocking myself out to put this thing on its feet, to give you ammunition to snipe at it with?" He replied, "Well, if you won't give me a story, I'll make one up." And he did.

The Works Progress Administration, the very agency under which the project operated, was another source of obstruction. The local W.P.A. administrators were businessmen drafted into government service. They had no interest in the theatre, no understanding of its problems, no inclination to take on additional duties. The same formulas were applied to every activity, regardless of special requirements. Every item in our complicated operations, from the rental of rehearsal space to the purchase of a roll of canvas, had to be separately requisitioned—and in septuplicate! To prevent a delay of months, I had to sign every requisition personally. On my desk in the morning was a pile of requisitions as high as my chin. I signed all day, through telephone conversations, interviews and dictation. As soon as the bottom of a pile was reached, another was placed before me. Frequent calls to Washington did little to reduce the administrative difficulties. The record of those evasive, buck-passing conversations makes entertaining reading now, but at the time those of us who were trying to get things done were not amused.

Most distressing was the hostility of many professional theatre people. Because admission to the project's productions was never more than a dollar, and sometimes free, Broadway managers charged us with undercutting them. I tried to convince them that by introducing hundreds of thousands of young people to the theatre we were building up a vast future audience. Only a few were able or willing to take the long-range view.

Fiscal restrictions were severe. Since the projects had been organized primarily to provide employment, most of the appropriations had to go into wages for workers who had been on relief. The amount available for supervisory employees and for materials and equipment was painfully small. This worked no great hardship on the other projects. The artists went to work on murals in post offices and other public buildings (with resultant shrieks from Congressmen and irate citizens). The writers prepared a series of guidebooks for every state in the Union, a much-needed job that was well executed. The musicians were organized in bands and orchestras that gave concerts in parks, schools and factories. These activities required little supervision or equipment.

With the Theatre Project it was a different story. To find enough competent supervisors for the many production units that were organized, it was necessary to go outside the rosters of the unemployed. Equally urgent was the need for theatres and rehearsal space; materials for making scenery, property and costumes; lighting equipment, tickets, programs and so on. The utmost ingenuity had to be used to make shift with what was obtainable. It is to the credit of the project's designers and directors that so much of what was done was of high quality.

At the outset, I faced what seemed an impassable barrier. I was stunned to learn from the project's young legal assistant that no provision had been made for the renting of theatres. We had plans for numerous productions, but without theatres in which to ex-

hibit them it would have been futile to undertake them. I knew
there was no hope of getting action from Washington, so I took
things into my own hands. Using the authority vested in me, I
signed leases, in the name of the government, for seven dark Broadway theatres. It was unlikely that Washington would repudiate the
leases, so even if I were discharged—a contingency that did not
greatly alarm me—the Theatre Project would still have some showcases. Some weeks after I signed the leases, Lee Pressman, one of
the attorneys for the Treasury Department, came to see me. "Do
you realize," he said, "that it took ten thousand dollars' worth of
Treasury officials' time to find a legal formula for the ratification of
those contracts?" I replied that I thought it was money well spent.

In the midst of all this welter of administrative detail, we managed to proceed with the work of the project, which was, after all,
the production of plays. Ably assisted by recruits from the professional and nonprofessional theatre who took on supervisory jobs
at great personal sacrifice, we organized production units covering
a wide range of theatrical activity. They included the Negro Youth
Theatre, the One-Act-Play Unit, the German Unit, the Poetic Drama
Unit, the Yiddish Vaudeville Unit, the Classical Repertory Unit.
There were companies for the performance of Shaw, O'Neill and
Gilbert-and-Sullivan cycles; circus, marionette and dance units; a
Children's Theatre, which produced the charming and highly pop-
ular *Pinocchio;* an Experimental Theatre for unconventional plays
and new techniques of staging.

Another innovation was the Living Newspaper, devised to help
jobless newspapermen; it presented dramatizations of current news.
This became one of the most flourishing and successful of the project's activities. Still another exciting group was the Negro Theatre,
headed by John Houseman and Orson Welles, who took over the
Lafayette Theatre in Harlem and made some vivid productions
there—notably a brilliant *Macbeth,* set in nineteenth-century Mar-
tinique, with the witches performing voodoo rituals, and a lively
ball replacing the banquet.

For the Popular Price Theatre, a unit to which I gave all the
time I could spare, I selected T. S. Eliot's *Murder in the Cathedral,*
overruling members of my staff who objected on the ground that
a poetic play with a religious theme was not good box office! Even
in a government-sponsored art project, the concept of commercial

success died hard. I invited Halstead Welles, whose productions at Yale had impressed me, to direct. For the part of Becket we cast Harry Irvine, an experienced but little-known Shakespearean actor who was on the project's payroll. The lack of funds brought ingenuity and inventiveness into play. The production was tasteful, imaginative and theatrically effective; acting, staging, settings, music, costumes all were excellent.

The play was not only an artistic triumph but also a great popular success. We had put it into the Broadway Theatre, one of New York's largest, where, with seats priced at twenty-five and fifty cents, we played to capacity audiences, and could have done so for an entire season had not Ashley Dukes, the British playwright-manager who controlled the rights, limited us to six weeks. The production, ranking high in the annals of the New York stage, demonstrated what can be done in the theatre by dedicated craftsmen even under the most adverse conditions.

Throughout my tenure of office, I was harassed by complaints and accusations. I incurred the wrath of the Civilian Conservation Corps by withdrawing touring units which had been visiting the work camps. Reports had convinced me that living conditions in the camps, while perhaps adequate for robust young men, were wholly unsuitable for actors, some of whom were elderly or in ill-health. What hurt more was criticism from Negro sources. I had worked very hard to set up worth-while Negro units, but a shortage of qualified Negroes had compelled me to employ some white supervisors. For this I was charged with discrimination.

An annoying but ludicrous incident arose out of a project worker's charge that one of his fellows had made anti-Semitic remarks. Since the charge was denied, it was one man's word against another, so I did not see what I could do about it. Next day there was a stir in the street. Pickets representing the Project Workers' Union were parading with placards denouncing the Theatre Project as anti-Semitic. I immediately sent for the bright young leader of the union and told him that I was familiar with the Communist technique of seizing every opportunity to agitate, but that in view of my activity in the civil-liberties field I thought this demonstration made his organization look rather ridiculous. Luckily, he had a sense of humor; the pickets were quickly withdrawn.

6

A censorship situation led to my withdrawal from the project. The Living Newspaper, organized to present dramatizations of current topics of general interest, had chosen as its first subject Mussolini's invasion of Ethiopia. The staff writers prepared a script that included scenes in Rome, Addis Ababa, London and Washington, with excerpts from speeches by Mussolini, Sir Samuel Hoare and Roosevelt. A troupe of native African dancers on the project was worked into a scene at the court of Haile Selassie. It promised to be a vivid production. But without my knowledge some officious underling on the project wrote to the State Department, requesting clearance for Roosevelt's speech—one which had been broadcast and widely published. The State Department, which apparently had never heard of the Theatre Project, was thrown into a panic. A script of *Ethiopia* was urgently demanded. A few days later Jacob Baker ordered me to cancel the production. It was not the use of Roosevelt's speech that the State Department objected to, but the use of Mussolini's. It was feared Il Duce might take offense!

All of us who were connected with the production were bowled over. I called Baker to explain that all the official speeches used in the play were taken verbatim from dependable newspaper sources, without editing or comment; that all the factual material was presented objectively, without caricature or innuendo. When Baker refused to reconsider, I tried to reach Harry Hopkins; failing, I sent him telegrams reminding him of his assurances in his Iowa City speech and to me personally that there would be no censorship. He did not respond. When Baker came to New York, I told him that in view of my active opposition to censorship the cancellation of the show compelled me to resign. Baker pulled open a desk drawer, took out a typed letter, signed it and handed it to me. It was an acceptance of my resignation! Agitated though I was, the deliberativeness of this performance struck me as very funny.

A dress rehearsal of *Ethiopia* was scheduled for next day, so I struck a final blow against censorship by inviting all the drama critics to attend. They all came and, because of the circumstances, gave the production much more attention than it would otherwise have received. It was a fine show and the notices were very favorable, so the effort that had gone into it was not wholly wasted.

Though much work was yet to be done, I knew that my able associate, Philip Barber, was well qualified to carry on. My own activities had not been without results. Forty-five hundred workers had been given paid employment on the Theatre Project in place of a humiliating existence on the dole. About sixty per cent were actors, fifteen per cent technicians, the remainder writers, box-office employees, ushers, cleaners and so on. Most of those on the payroll were eager to work and acquitted themselves honorably and efficiently. On the artistic side, the units launched in those early months went on to provide entertainment and edification for many thousands previously unacquainted with the theatre or unable to pay Broadway prices.

Nationally, the Theatre Project's record was extraordinary. At one time forty-two separate units were in operation in twenty states, with a total of nearly thirteen thousand employees. A report made by Hallie Flanagan in the fall of 1938 gave some amazing figures. In its first three years the Theatre Project had produced more than nine hundred different plays, for a total of nearly 55,000 performances, many of them free, none charging more than a dollar. The attendance figures exceeded 26,000,000. Perhaps the most spectacular achievement was the simultaneous opening in twenty-one theatres of a dramatization of Sinclair Lewis' novel *It Can't Happen Here.*

But the project could not withstand its powerful enemies. It was constantly attacked in Congress as wasteful, immoral and Communistic. When Houseman and Welles announced a production of Marlowe's *Dr. Faustus,* one vigilant Congressman asked if the play's author was a member of the Communist Party. In the project's fourth year, Congress killed it by failing to make an appropriation. Its demise was perhaps the most tragic occurrence in the cultural history of the United States. Had funds been provided for continuance, upon an artistic basis divorced from unemployment relief, of those units that had clearly demonstrated their worth, the foundation would have been laid for a nationwide theatrical structure that would have brought enlightenment and enjoyment to millions, and stimulation to artistic creation. The cost, compared to the billions expended annually upon weapons of destruction, would have been infinitesimal.

7

I had expended so much energy on the Theatre Project that I did not feel like plunging at once into the writing of my long New York novel; so I decided to take my family on a trip around the world. Not wanting to make a standard travel-agency tour, I spent weeks working out an itinerary that would take us to the places we were most interested in.

Besides a desire to see the world, there was a more inward reason for taking a long trip, though I was not as aware of it then as I am now. For more than a year, I had had a love relationship with a young woman whom I shall call Laura. I am intentionally vague about her identity and the circumstances of our meeting, for, though she is dead, I want to protect her surviving family from possible embarrassment. It is enough to say that we were instantly attracted to each other and swiftly became lovers, in spite of the fact that she was much younger than I, had attended fashionable boarding schools and had been reared in an atmosphere of luxury and social snobbery. These disparities counted for nothing, for emotionally, sexually, psychologically and intellectually we were in complete harmony.

This love affair was unlike any other I had had. We had the same tastes in literature, art and good living, the same reactions to people, places and things. Communication between us was almost telepathic: we often anticipated each other's utterances and even thoughts. Humor was another strong bond: we laughed together constantly. Physically we were perfectly attuned. She was not what would be called a great beauty: a dark-skinned girl, with thick brown hair, a strong chin and a snub nose. Her mouth was exquisitely sensitive and her large brown eyes were the loveliest I have ever seen. Her personality was magnetic; she captivated everyone. Her way of expressing herself was quaint and vivid.

In the first year of our intimacy, we saw each other almost daily; less often during my crowded Theatre Project months. When I was free again, we were more eager than ever to be together. Richly content in our daily association, we never discussed the nature of our relationship or its future. Superficially that suited me very well; I was quite willing to enjoy the present without worrying about what was to follow. But, of course, it was not as simple as all that. This was no ephemeral romance; it was something new in my life, something that had struck deep. Yet I knew it must come to an end sooner or later, if nothing was done to stabilize it.

The obvious solution, as I well knew, was divorce and remarriage. However, I was reluctant about dissolving a marriage that had lasted for twenty years. Even though my wife and I had drifted further and further apart, I had misgivings about breaking up the home and severing family ties. My wife was fully aware of my relationship to Laura. Oddly enough, the two women struck up a kind of friendship, lunching or going to a matinee together; Laura was often at our dinner parties. It was an anomalous situation, but it did not seem to make any of us uncomfortable.

In a sense, my inertia, if it can be called that, was rationalization for another kind of resistance. In the forty-odd years that I had lived, I had never wholly surrendered myself to anyone. In family relationships, love affairs, friendships, I had always left an escape hatch open, always held back something to go on with if disaster came. Whether this withholding was due to my obsession with freedom, to some instinct of self-preservation, to cowardice or to niggardliness of spirit, I cannot say; that it was a central fact of my emotional life, I had always been acutely aware. Now I recognized that if I linked myself indissolubly to Laura there could be no holding back; unless I was prepared to give whatever I had to give, the commitment would be senseless.

The world tour offered a convenient excuse for not making an immediate decision. I had sufficient faith in the strength of our mutual feeling to believe that it would survive a four-month separation. If it did, we would find our way on from there. The possibility that it might not survive I preferred not to contemplate. I did not think it all out quite so methodically and cold-bloodedly, but those were certainly the considerations that influenced me.

8

We sailed in one of the attractive little American Export Lines ships that circle the Mediterranean. From the ship's radio news we learned that a Spanish general named Franco was on his way from Morocco with the intention of overthrowing the republican government. I discussed the report with some American consular officers who were en route to the Middle East; they agreed that the quixotic expedition was bound to fail. Long afterward I found out that ours was the last American ship to put in at Palma de Mallorca before the Franco forces took over.

The stopover at Alexandria gave us a few days in Cairo and enabled us to see the treasures lately removed from the tomb of Tutankhamen and to visit Giza, both by day and by moonlight. I rode the short distance from the Pyramid of Cheops to the Sphinx on a camel—a truly terrifying experience. Haifa made an unfavorable impression upon us. The new constructions springing up everywhere had the sleazy "modern" look of a get-rich-quick building contractor's project. I was struck by a huddle of hovels, made of flattened gasoline tins, in the midst of all the shining newness. "That's where those filthy Arabs live," said our young taxi driver. "But under the dirt floors they all have gold buried."

From Beirut we motored to Damascus, stoping en route at Baalbek, one of the world's great archaeological remains. Of the vast Temple of Jupiter, built upon an earlier Phoenician site, little has survived intact except one magnificent colonnade, whose majesty is somehow enhanced by the desolateness of the setting. Again I felt the surge of a deep emotional experience, whose effect was to be lasting.

Istanbul lacked the aura of romance and mystery with which my childhood reading had invested it. Under the whip of Kemal Ataturk, Westernization was proceeding rapidly. Gone were the veil, the fez, the baggy trousers; the appearance of the populace was drab and nondescript. Near our hotel were several movie theatres given over to the exhibition of Hollywood B pictures, mostly Westerns. I had never heard of any of them, nor of their stars and directors. Yet this was the image of America that was offered to the world.

In the crew of the modest little Soviet steamer that took us to Odessa were several lusty young women—not stewardesses, but working sailors. In Kharkov we saw a great sports parade: marching phalanxes of husky boys and girls, interspersed with floats illustrative of almost every form of sport. Our flight to Moscow took us over Russia's granary, vast wheat fields dotted with new barns and silos.

My attempts to locate Ernest were fruitless. Ivy Litvinov invited us to her home in the country. Her sixteen-year-old daughter, Tania, was making a parachute jump next day; the stunt was then all the rage among Soviet teen-agers. Though everyone in the household pretended to take it all casually, the tension and excitement were evident.

In Moscow I met with a high Soviet official, a sort of minister of fine art, presumably to discuss general cultural problems. But I was so indignant at the official censure of Shostakovich for his failure to write "socialist" music that I spent the whole hour denouncing the political censorship of art. The minister, of course, took the orthodox position that all art is political and that in a socialist state it must have a proletarian connotation. Later when my friend the playwright Alexander Afinegenov picked me up I told him about the argument. He shook his head disapprovingly. "Why do you waste your time in such discussions?" he said. "When you meet an important man like that, you should talk to him about the necessity of producing your plays in the Soviet Union."

The current rage among the Moscow intelligentsia was Nikolai Okhlopkov's Realistic Theatre. We saw a play called *Aristocrats,* which, surprisingly, portrayed the labor camps of the Arctic Circle as centers of benevolent moral and social regeneration. The arena-style production was about as far removed from "realism" as it was possible to go, depending as it did upon a variety of stylized devices that had little but novelty to commend them. To me it all seemed silly and rather effete.

Another curiosity was a production of *Hamlet* by a company from Uzbekistan. The nomadic Central Asian Uzbeks were rapidly being inducted into the new industrial society; their language had been alphabetized, illiteracy was disappearing. Along with this went the creation of an Uzbek National Theatre. The performance was painful. When the company's director, a Russian, asked my opinion, I suggested that instead of making these neophytes struggle with something beyond their comprehension they should be performing simple dramatizations of their own environment and culture. He said, "You do not understand. Before these people are capable of dramatizing their own lives, they must become thoroughly familiar with the classics of world drama."

What struck us most forcefully were the changes for the better that had taken place in four years. Though there were still shortages of some commodities and a complete lack of others, the food supply seemed to be adequate. The people looked better, too; raggedness and drabness were no longer much in evidence. Consumers' goods were more plentiful, but by Western standards the stocks were meager. When I happened to mention to Afinegenov the high price of laundry, he said, "Why don't you let me give you a few thousand rubles? I don't know what to do with them." In the political area there seemed to be, in spite of the Shostakovich incident, a certain amelioration. But this was illusory. A few months later the paranoid Stalin set in motion the infamous purge trials of his revolutionary comrades.

It was a seven-day trip on the Trans-Siberian Railway from Moscow to the Manchurian frontier, a comfortable enough though rather monotonous journey. We had two roomy sleeping compartments, connected by a lavatory. We even had hot baths, in the train crew's quarters. There was a diner all the way, serving meals that were more than ample. In fact, as a change from thick soups and heavy stews we would make a meal of the delicious black bread and sour cream, augmented by radishes bought from peasant women at the stations.

Everywhere in Siberia there was evidence of large-scale industrial expansion: factories and housing projects springing up, villages becoming metropolitan centers. On the outskirts of these swelling cities, thousands of people were temporarily housed in obsolescent boxcars. Long freight trains brought supplies and raw materials, returned with factory products. Along the line were many derailed cars, sprawling open, their contents scattered.

9

The Japanese soldiery was very much in charge at Manchuli —indeed, everywhere in Manchukuo. The thorough Russian border inspection we had just experienced seemed perfunctory compared to what we were subjected to here. I was questioned in great detail about what I had seen in Russia. To simplify matters, I said theatres and museums. No factories? No, only theatres and museums. Next, what schools did my children go to, and what did they study? And so on and on. Almost every article in our numerous bags was removed and inspected. When one of the guards walked off with my Zeiss binoculars, I was rather perturbed. But a bystander reassured us: "He just wants to see what the Soviets are doing." Sure enough, there stood the guard at the end of the platform, staring across the quarter-mile no man's land into the vast emptiness of Siberia.

It took another thirty-six hours to get to Harbin. We were edified by a handsomely printed, richly illustrated brochure that informed us that "the South Manchuria Railway Company is more than a mere railway company; it has been and still is the carrier of the light of civilization into Manchuria." On our train the light of civilization was being carried by heavily armed Japanese soldiers, who paraded the corridor incessantly, eying us sullenly. Every now and then one of them pulled down our shades, presumably because we were passing through a military zone. The fluttering shades did little to obstruct the view, but we saw no indication of human habitation.

Floods had wiped out part of the main line between Harbin and Mukden, but we managed to get places on a flight to Hsinking, the new capital of Manchukuo. The rickety plane flew low, passing directly over the flooded area. The spectacle was weird: whole villages completely submerged, as though at the bottom of a lake.

Hsinking had the aspect of a boom town. According to the useful literature of the South Manchuria Railway Company, it was being developed to "promote and intensify the friendly relations between Japan and Manchukuo." This intensification of friendliness was manifest in the gangs of coolies working under the eyes of armed Japanese overseers. Our taxi driver, a Pole, told us that the pay of Japanese workers was twice that of Europeans, ten times that of Chinese. He pointed out to us the "palace"—a converted brewery— of the pathetic Henry Pu-yi, feeble end product of the great Manchu dynasty, who, "accepting the heavenly mandate, graciously acceded to the throne of Manchukuo as her first Emperor." The real ruler was, of course, the Japanese ambassador, whose popularity was attested to by the high wall topped with electrified barbed wire that surrounded his official residence.

In Mukden John Davies, the American vice-consul, told me that the consulate staff had been greatly reduced because of the shrinkage of trade between Manchuria and the United States. He was very dubious about the future of Japanese-American relations. I was impressed by his intelligence and liberalism, qualities that were probably responsible for his persecution, some years later, by one of those Congressional committees.

About Peiping it is difficult to write without sounding rhapsodic. No city that I have seen excels it in interest or equals it in beauty, not even Venice, not even Paris. The innumerable palaces, temples and pagodas, individually rich, form an unmatchable ensemble. Peiping consists of four "cities," three of them walled rectangles nested in almost geometric symmetry—the outermost of the three, the Tatar City, containing the Imperial City, which in turn surrounds the Forbidden City; on the periphery sprawls the Chinese City. The high, thick walls are pierced by great gates. Broad, tree-lined intersecting avenues lead from precinct to precinct. From the roof café of the six-storied Grand Hotel we had a panoramic view of the great complex of the Forbidden City, and of the Coal Hill behind it, its arc surmounted by five pagodas. In the distance the triple circular roof of the Temple of Heaven was visible.

Seen from above or traversed on foot, the Forbidden City delighted the eye and elevated the spirit. The lavishness of color was overwhelming: rose-red walls; imperial-yellow curved roof tiles; gleaming white marble and alabaster bridges and sculpture; midsummer green profusion of foliage; delicate pinkish-white giant lotus that filled the surrounding moat. Three long visits were insufficient for the exploration of the maze of pavilions, throne rooms, banquet halls, bridges, balustraded courtyards and living quarters, and for more than a cursory look at the porcelains and bronzes, the ornate furniture and ceramic screens, the pictorial scrolls and the walls painted in *trompe l'oeil*. Also rich in ornamentation and architecture were the Lama Temple, the Temple of Heaven, the Winter Palace and the Summer Palace, built by the formidable Empress Dowager Tz'u Hsi. An excursion to the Great Wall and the Ming Tombs had to be called off because of the danger of being attacked by bandits.

At the hotel a ricksha with attendant coolie had been reserved for each of us. I was reluctant about employing human beings as draft animals, but I was assured that the coolies had no other means of livelihood; without it they would die of starvation in six months, instead of tuberculosis in five years. The standard rate of daily pay was one dollar Chinese, about thirty cents American. We paid our coolies ten dollars per week, for which they were very grateful, but American residents complained that we were ruining the labor market. The coolies were on duty day and night, cooking their meals in the broad hotel plaza and presumably sleeping there, too.

As devotees of Chinese cookery, we were outraged to find that the hotel provided only the standard bastard-French-international cuisine. Luckily, we met an American newspaperman, F. M. Fisher, who not only was a bit of an epicure but also spoke Chinese. Every evening, after cocktails on the Grand Hotel roof, where we usually picked up two or three other dinner guests, a ricksha caravan set off under Fisher's guidance for some obscure side street in the Tatar or Chinese City. While the special meal ordered by Fisher was being prepared, we drank tea and munched pumpkin seeds. Fisher always ordered a large bowl of scalding water, in which he washed all our dishes and utensils. Since most Chinese immigrants came originally from Canton, Chinese restaurants in the West usually serve only Cantonese dishes. But there are as many styles of cookery in China as in Europe. The cuisines of Canton, Peiping, Shantung and Szechuan are as distinctive as those of France, Germany, Russia, Sweden and Greece.

One rather fashionable restaurant served only duck, prepared in twenty different ways. The specialty was Peking duck, crisp thin slices of skin-covered meat folded in little pancakes which are spread with an unsweetened marmalade—a culinary masterpiece. It was there we met the San Francisco–born Anna May Wong, who was visiting China for the first time and was laughed at for speaking Chinese with an American accent. She was also criticized for her unflattering screen portrayals of Chinese dance-hall girls and spies.

One evening at cocktails I talked to Mrs. Edgar Snow, whose husband, an American correspondent, had gone off to try to make contact with the Chinese Communist army, which no foreigner had yet succeeded in doing. Mrs. Snow was fearful that he might never return. A year later, in England, my publisher, Victor Gollancz, told me he had just accepted for publication *Red Star over China*, by an American named Edgar Snow. It contained an account of the "Long March" and descriptions of Mao Tse-tung and other Chinese leaders whose names have become only too familiar.

The Chinese professors and students we met were chiefly interested in literature—one was translating the complete works of Thomas Hardy!—but Robert did have an opportunity to discuss the complicated political situation with a group of young Communists.

We were invited to lunch by the American ambassador, Nelson Johnson, a breezy Oklahoman who spoke three or four Chinese dialects and was well informed about China's culture and philosophy. When I asked him about the likelihood of a Japanese-American war, he said firmly that although there was bound to be an intensification of economic warfare there was no possibility of armed conflict. His opinion was in line with the tendency of American experts to minimize the aggressiveness of a Hitler, a Mussolini, a Franco, a Castro.

It is not easy for a Westerner to attune himself to the rhythms of Oriental art. A European cathedral or palace, or, for that matter, the Eiffel Tower or the Empire State Building, gives an immediate totality of effect, the over-all scheme is apprehended in its entirety. In China, except for the towering pagodas, the emphasis of the design seemed to be horizontal rather than vertical. Whether it was the Forbidden City, a hillside temple or a large family compound, introduction to the salient features was gradual. An unpretentious courtyard gave access to increasingly spacious areas and ever more elaborate structures, so that there was a gentle unfolding rather than an instantaneous, dramatic revelation. As in Chinese painting, the spatial arrangement was as important as the objects represented. It induced a serene satisfaction quite alien to the dynamics of the West, and impossible for me to analyze.

The Chinese theatre was anything but serene or orderly; the little I saw of it impressed me unfavorably. The ceaseless clangor of gongs, the restless spectators conversing, eating, coming and going, the informal behavior of the actors who were presumably off stage, produced an effect of confusion and discordance. The performances, based upon legendary materials, seemed to consist mainly of a succession of long, monotonous arias. Perhaps I was not seeing the theatre at its best; in New York I had greatly enjoyed Mei Lan-fang.

On the long trip to Nanking, we saw a countryside whose main features seemed to be the huge burial mounds that dominated the small farmsteads. Nanking's chief feature of interest was the mausoleum of Sun Yat-sen, a sort of magnified Grant's Tomb, approached by a flight of several hundred steps. We met a Chinese engineer who had given up a good job in a New Jersey plant to take part in the industrialization of his native city. He spoke bitterly about the obstacles: the objection of wealthy residents to the construction of factories; his loss of face with his silk-clad subordinates when he put on overalls to examine a defective machine.

Shanghai was an agreeable surprise. Our Peiping acquaintances had scornfully described it as a brash, vulgar, un-Chinese stronghold of blatant commercialism and colonialism. Commercial and noisy it certainly was, but it was colorful and lively too—a great seaport, harboring ships of every nation.

10

Before leaving New York I had written to the editor of a Japanese edition of my plays, informing him of our intended visit. In Moscow and in Peiping I had received letters from Japanese professors and journalists in several cities, announcing that they were on our "reception committees" and specifying arrangements that had been made for us. On the dock at Nagasaki was a smiling delegation, under whose guidance we made a quick tour of the city that was to become the second target of American atomic bombs.

The passage through the Inland Sea was enchanting. At Kobe— which is part of a vast metropolitan area that includes the great industrial center Osaka and the ancient capital, Kyoto—I began what I suppose were the most crowded three weeks of my life. Sightseeing was only a small part of our activity. Every day there were meetings, receptions, dinners, interviews. The newspapers carried daily accounts of our doings, accompanied by pictures, for the Japanese have a passion for photography. We were asked to dine with the editorial staff of the Osaka *Mainichi*, one of Japan's principal newspapers. I was questioned closely about American domestic conditions and foreign policy; as one tends to do in such situations, I stressed the more laudable aspects of American life.

One day we were drawn to the windows of our Kobe waterfront hotel by the sound of feminine wailing. A crowd of sobbing women was watching the debarkment of flag-draped coffins. A policeman who saw us at the windows waved us away with angry gestures. We learned that the coffins contained the bodies of soldiers whose civilizing mission in Manchukuo had apparently not been appreciated by the Chinese guerrillas.

In Kyoto, less commercialized and Westernized than most Japanese cities, we were fortunate in meeting Itsu Takeuchi, Japan's leading art critic, son of the brilliant painter known as Saiyo. He had traveled widely, had superb taste, spoke English and French fluently: a gracious, erudite man. In the garden of his home—designed and decorated with characteristic Japanese simplicity and purity—were monumental stone figures, brought from the interior of China on coal barges. We dined Japanese fashion, squatting on cushions; our host's sister did not join us, but helped the servants wait on us. We also attended a ceremonial related to some astronomical phenomenon. Men and women, all members of the House of Peers, wearing traditional dress, sat around a long cloth representing the Milky Way and passed little impromptu poems to each other. I tried to visualize a group of United States senators and their wives engaged in a similar activity.

Tokyo's Imperial Hotel, constructed by Frank Lloyd Wright, was one of the few large structures that survived the earthquake of 1923. It is an ugly building, heavy and squat, with a gloomy interior. Nor is Tokyo a very attractive city: big, busy, mostly modern, quite Western in character. At the home of the playwright Yuzo Yamamoto we dined in Western style, which made it all the more embarrassing to be waited on by his wife and daughters. Our name was a source of endless merriment to our Japanese friends. Every time rice appeared at table—that is to say, at every meal—it provoked great laughter. It was a good joke, I suppose; but after a while it began to pall a little.

Shortly after our return home, I received from a foreign office dignitary who had entertained us in Tokyo, a letter which in the light of subsequent events merits quotation: "To promote friendly relations between our two great pacific nations is not only my duty as Foreign Official in charge of the International Cultural Works Section, but also my most earnest desire as a Japanese who believes in human welfare through international understanding and co-operation." Was this just eyewash, or did he really mean it? I am inclined to think he did; Pearl Harbor was still five years off. However, the possibility of war was envisaged by many Japanese to whom I had talked—not military men, but professors, artists and journalists. When I asked what they believed would be the probable outcome of hostilities, they were all amazed that I could have any doubt about Japan's invincibility.

We saw as much as we could of the Japanese theatre. (The New York *Times* had commissioned me to write articles about it, as well as about the Russian and Chinese theatres.) Though it was as commercialized as the American theatre, being largely in the hands of two or three syndicates that also control the motion picture and broadcasting industries, the quality of many of the presentations was high. The classical noh plays were not performed during the summer months, but we were able to see several productions of the Kabuki Theatre, which popularizes and modernizes the traditional drama. Ennosuke Ichikawa, one of the great Kabuki stars, invited us to see the backstage apparatus, technical equipment not even remotely matched by any American theatre. Besides the Kabuki, there were the Girls' Opera Company (whose stars, particularly those who play male parts, have a fanatical following that a Hollywood actor might envy), revues, variety shows and contemporary plays. There was even a "proletarian" theatre, courageously conducted by U. Akita, who had served several jail terms for his unorthodoxy. We saw part of a dress rehearsal of Gorki's *The Lower Depths*.

I was interested to learn that some of my plays had been presented. The producer of *Street Scene* assured me it had been a great success. When I said that I did not remember receiving any royalties, he replied with an amiable grin, "Oh, we never pay royalties." However, piracy is not peculiar to Japan.

Japanese familiarity with modern Western culture astonished me. When I met with a group of students at Wasada University to discuss the American theatre, they questioned me about the playwriting activities of Lynn Riggs and the production plans of Eva Le Gallienne.

We boarded the Japanese steamer at Yokohama in a state of exhaustion; the tedium of the voyage to Seattle was a relief. Then home by the Great Northern Railway, traversing a land blighted by drought and strewn with the bleaching skeletons of cattle. Franklin Roosevelt had been renominated by acclamation and was on his way to a triumphal victory over Governor Alf Landon of Kansas.

11

Immediately after my return, I began work on my novel *Imperial City*. Like *Street Scene*, it dealt with the kaleidoscopic life of New York, only instead of concentrating upon a single house it attempted to present a panorama of the metropolitan scene. It centered upon the members of a wealthy, powerful family, whose diverse interests carried the story into fifty milieus and involved a great variety of characters and situations.

My long separation from Laura had not weakened our relationship. Through the fall and winter, we were constantly together. In the spring I went to Paris, where she joined me. We stayed at a pleasant little hotel in the Rue du Bac, a neighborhood familiar to me. Mornings we visited galleries or strolled along the quais; afternoons I worked; our evenings we devoted to a systematic exploration of restaurants, never dining twice at the same place. We celebrated the completion of the novel with a gala dinner at Foyot's, just a few days before it closed its doors forever.

While I was in Paris, Ronald Adam, a British actor-producer, put on *Judgment Day* on a sort of tryout basis at the little Embassy Theatre in Hampstead. The play was received with so much enthusiasm that Adam transferred it immediately to the Strand Theatre in the West End. I flew over from Paris for the Strand opening—the most exciting event of my professional career. Skillfully staged by Murray Macdonald and excellently acted, the play evoked fervid applause throughout and cheers at the end. In view of the patronizing reception in New York, the charges of distortion and exaggeration, the general pooh-poohing, it was perhaps excusable for me to gloat a little over the unanimous commendation of the British press, from extreme right to extreme left.

The London success was reported in the American press. A typical dispatch to the New York *Times* said: "Critics agree *Judgment Day* is one of the best plays seen in London in a long time." Now community and university theatres, which had shown no previous interest, began producing the play—for example, the Pasadena Community Theatre, the Cleveland Playhouse, units of the Federal Theatre Project. William McDermott, veteran Cleveland critic, said: "The complaint made of *Judgment Day* four years ago was that it was too exaggerated, that it couldn't be believed. Time has served Mr. Rice well. In that four years' period, Mr. Rice's exaggerations have come to seem prophetic and his passionateness of feeling moderate and justifiable."

The London production of *Judgment Day* infuriated the Germans. Ronald Adam told me an amusing, typically British story: When he applied to the Lord Chamberlain for the required license, the request was at first refused, on the ground that the German Embassy would protest. "How can they?" asked Adam. "The scene of the play is the Balkans, not Germany." "That's true, isn't it?" said the official in charge. "If they complain, we can say, 'Is that how justice is practiced in Germany? We had no idea!'" So the license was granted; there was no official protest from the Germans.

One night in London I sat on the stage as one of the crowd in the courtroom scene. It was gratifying to feel the waves of excitement come rolling across the footlights; no other play of mine has involved me so emotionally. After the long London run the play had a successful tour, and there were subsequent performances by the leading repertory theatres. Hardly a year has gone by without a production somewhere in the British Commonwealth. Not long ago, a London television showing was again applauded.

During my London stay Emma Goldman, the anarchist whose name had once been anathema to all right-thinking Americans, came to see me. I had known her only slightly: an unattractive but earnest and intelligent woman, who made her living by lecturing on the drama. She wanted to enlist my aid in combating the Russian infiltration of the Spanish Loyalist forces, which was turning the struggle for freedom into an instrument of Soviet foreign policy. With deep emotion she described the ruthless, even murderous, tactics of the Russian Communists. I was as outraged by what she told me as I was by the current purge trials in the Soviet Union, but of course there was nothing anyone could do about it.

There were urgent inquiries about the rights to *Judgment Day* from Hungary, Switzerland, Palestine, Loyalist Spain, France, Holland, and the Scandinavian countries. However, formal arrangements were made only for Norway, Holland and France. Elsewhere production was prevented by governmental censorship or by fear of antagonizing the Nazis. I happened to be in Holland in late summer. Just as I was about to leave The Hague for Amsterdam, I learned—

from the hotel porter!—of front-page stories to the effect that the burgomaster of Amsterdam, yielding to German pressure, had banned the production of *Judgment Day*, scheduled to open in a few days. My arrival in Amsterdam could not have been more timely. The producer called a press conference, which received wide coverage throughout Holland. The Amsterdam *Telegraaf* reported that the German Embassy in London was fuming about the play's production there, but that the general sentiment in diplomatic circles was "If the cap fits them, let them wear it."

When The Hague and Rotterdam also banned the play, there was an interpellation in the Dutch parliament by a Socialist deputy, who demanded to know whether the German ambassador was now the ruler of Holland. But fear of offending Hitler prevailed. As elsewhere, however, appeasement was futile; when it suited Hitler's purpose, Rotterdam was ruthlessly reduced to rubble and Holland overrun.

In France the situation was somewhat similar. The French producer was summoned to the Foreign Ministry, where he was reminded that though there was no censorship in France the police had authority to close a theatre if a production provoked political disturbances. Of course he took the hint and dropped the play. Eventually the only Continental production was in Oslo. A letter from my Scandinavian agent described the reception: "Immediately after the beginning of the play, a party of nacists protested by whistling and prevented it to go on in a normal manner. The police did what they could to turn out the perturbators, but the fact was that fifty per cent of the audience continued making trouble, and this party was more numerous than the party on the stage."

Later I learned that the Nazis had included my published works in a book-burning, the highest honor that has ever been paid me.

XVIII

Fellowship

1

With considerable anxiety I awaited the publication of *Imperial City*. I did not want to go back to writing for the Broadway theatre, but if the novel failed I might be obliged to do so, for economic reasons and because writing was the only career in which I was interested. Luckily, the book did very well in both America and England. The financial return was not comparable to that of a hit play, but it was comforting to know that I might be able to survive as a writer independently of the theatre. However, a wholly unexpected turn of events brought me back to playwriting.

In mid-November 1937 I attended a meeting of the council of the Dramatists' Guild. It was a dull day and a dull meeting. When it was over, I entered the elevator with Robert Sherwood and Maxwell Anderson. We agreed that a drink was in order. We went to a gloomy bar and, over our drinks, voiced our dissatisfaction with the theatre. My own views had been too well publicized to require much exposition, but Sherwood and Anderson spoke vehemently of their disenchantment with Broadway producers, particularly the Theatre Guild, which had presented many of their plays. They were harassed by disagreements about casting, revisions, and the disposition of subsidiary rights. If only their plays could be done as they wanted them done, without interference! We began exploring the feasibility of a group of playwrights organizing for the production of their own plays.

It happened that shortly after the production of *Street Scene* I had suggested this very project to Anderson, Philip Barry and George Kelly, but none of them had shown any real interest. There had also been an unsuccessful attempt by Arthur Hopkins to establish such a group. Now when Anderson and Sherwood asked if I would join them I immediately assented, for the proposed setup eliminated most of the conditions of the Broadway theatre which I had found unsatisfactory. We asked Sidney Howard if he wanted to come along with us; as we had anticipated, he was enthusiastic.

A few days later the four of us, all quite excited by now, met for lunch in the Hotel Plaza's Oak Room to discuss ways and means. We decided to seek a fifth member, for we felt that five playwrights could be reasonably expected to turn in three plays a year. If only one was even a moderate success, we would be on safe ground; a big hit every three years or so would provide a wide margin of safety. We discussed several possible candidates. I was afraid that the majority would be for Philip Barry, about whose adaptability to a co-operative enterprise I had developed doubts. The others, however, shared my opinion; we ended by agreeing to approach S. N. Behrman. We had hardly made this decision when, somewhat to our consternation, Barry, who had been lunching at another table unobserved by us, came over and said, "Whatever it is you're cooking up, I'd like a piece of it." Behrman was reluctant to take an active part in play production, but we overcame his objections.

At Anderson's suggestion, we called ourselves the Playwrights' Company, in emulation of the medieval guilds of artisans. We decided that a capital fund of $100,000 would be sufficient to see us through at least the first year of operations. (Today that would be barely enough to cover the cost of one production.) It occurred to us that John Hay Whitney, who had wide cultural interests as well as a great fortune, might be willing to back us. None of us knew Whitney, but Howard knew his attorney, John F. Wharton. We met with Whitney, but declined his offer of support when we learned that he expected to have a voice in our policies and decisions. We liked him well enough, but we wanted to be free of all outside control. Later I came to know Whitney quite well through my association as drama adviser with the John Hay Whitney Foundation, which grants fellowships in the arts to nonwhites—Negroes, Orientals, American Indians.

We decided to do half the financing ourselves, each of us investing ten thousand dollars. The remainder was quickly raised, chiefly by Sherwood at Long Island weekend parties. Among our investors were Averell Harriman, Dorothy Schiff, George Backer, Harold Guinzburg, Howard Cullman, Alicia Patterson and Raymond Massey. We had been so favorably impressed by John Wharton that, at my suggestion, we invited him to act as our general business adviser—a lucky stroke, for his aid to the company throughout its existence was invaluable.

We agreed that the company would produce any play written by its members, provided the budget did not exceed $25,000, a figure that, in 1937, was more than adequate for the average production. Plays calling for a greater expenditure required majority approval. Each playwright was to be in complete charge of his own production, calling upon his colleagues whenever he chose for script criticism, casting suggestions, comments at rehearsals and tryouts. Every one of us benefited immeasurably from the contributions of the others. In practice, none of us insisted upon his right to have a play produced when it met with general disapproval. During the company's existence, we all wrote plays that were not produced by it.

Though we had no objection to profits, none of us expected to get rich as a producer. What appealed primarily to all of us was the professional association. We had all known each other for a long time, were all about the same age, were all quite prolific and had had a substantial amount of success (four of the five had won the Pulitzer Prize). We all aimed our sights high, though we often missed the target. Further, we all enjoyed jokes; even at our business meetings the conversation was entertaining.

The announcement of our plans evoked derisive smiles and predictions of disaster. Broadway was sure that before the end of our first season we would be bankrupt and no longer on speaking terms with each other. Obviously it was an act of folly for a group of impractical, temperamental artists to attempt to usurp the role of the businessman. These dire prophecies proved false. The company survived for more than twenty years, in spite of a few economic crises and the disruptive effect of World War II. Its end was due to human mortality and to changing conditions in the theatre. The personal relationships could hardly have been more harmonious. Continued association led to deeper friendships rather than to estrangement. There were many hotly debated differences of opinion on artistic matters, and on political questions too. But there were no quarrels or personal antagonisms. We were cemented by mutual respect and common ideals.

2

Shortly after we organized, Sherwood asked me to read a new play of his, *Abe Lincoln in Illinois*, which covered the period between Lincoln's young manhood and his assumption of the Presidency. I thought it, and still think it, one of the finest plays ever written by an American. When Sherwood asked me to direct it, I was astonished and flattered. However, I was a little disconcerted when he told me that he wanted Raymond Massey to play Lincoln. I knew that Massey was a good actor, but I associated him with English drawing-room comedies. It was hard for me to visualize him as a gaunt, semitragic frontiersman.

What impressed me most about the play was its eloquent espousal of democracy, a vital theme in a world in which liberty was everywhere threatened. Hitlerism grew ever more menacing; the fascists were winning in Spain; a psychopathic Stalin was crushing all opposition, real or fancied. Disturbed by the cynical ruthlessness of the Soviet purge trials, a self-constituted committee composed of Roger Baldwin, George Counts, Arthur Garfield Hays, Waldo Frank and myself met with Ambassador Troyanovsky, at the Soviet consulate in New York. We told him that as individuals who favored better relations between our countries we wanted him to know that all liberal Americans were shocked by this perversion of justice. Troyanovsky responded, like a Southern segregationist, that this was a situation no outsider could understand. We all felt, however, that he was troubled by the hostility the purge had aroused in America.

I had sent an affectionately inscribed copy of *Imperial City* to Ivy Litvinov, though I thought she would probably never get it; I had heard that she was in disfavor because of her friendliness to foreigners, and that she had been sent to the provinces, where she was busy with her pet project of teaching Basic English. However, months later I received a letter headed simply "The Urals," in which she said: "I got your book at a moment when I don't know for which my hunger was greater—for a new book or a word of sympathy. Either would have been a joy—together they were a beatitude."

A German offer for *Imperial City* had been rejected by me. I suspected that the Nazis wanted to use the book as anti-American propaganda, for it depicted some of the less admirable aspects of the New York scene. Of course, it could have been pirated; but I suppose that would have been contrary to the German concept of "correctness." Even Hitler's seizure of power had been achieved by the "legal" expedient of expelling the Communist Reichstag deputies, thereby giving the Nazis a majority. (Since the war, *Imperial City* has been successfully published in both West and East Germany.)

One day a British newspaper correspondent asked me to join a group of British writers in a protest against the Nazi outrages. An hour later Theodore Dreiser, who also lived in the Hotel Ansonia, called up to inquire if I had signed. I said that of course I had and that I assumed he would, too. "Well, I don't know," he said. "I'm against Hitler, but I'm all for what he's doing to the Catholic Church." I knew that Dreiser had rebelled against his Catholic upbringing, but I could not believe he would carry his antagonism that far. I said I thought he was under a moral obligation to speak out against Hitlerism. Reluctantly he answered, "I guess you're right; I'll have to sign."

3

The Sherwood play, with its numerous settings and large cast, could obviously not be produced within our established $25,000 budget, but we were all so enthusiastic about the play that we did not even consider the cost. When, however, Maxwell Anderson told us that he was working on a musical comedy, *Knickerbocker Holiday*, with Kurt Weill, a refugee from Germany, we were faced with a bit of a problem. We had not expected to produce musicals and were a little dubious about the expenditure, particularly since I hoped to have a play ready, too. Nevertheless, we decided to go ahead.

Samuel Goldwyn, who wanted to make another New York picture, had taken an option on *Imperial City*. When he asked me to come to Hollywood for discussions, I was more than willing to go, for Laura, whom I had not seen in some months, was wintering there. Though we were always pulling away from each other, I because of my reluctance to commit myself fully, she because she saw no future in our relationship, our reunions were always ecstatic. This one was no exception. I left Hollywood with her promise to join me again in Europe in the spring. Nothing came of the *Imperial City* project. Goldwyn dropped his option, largely because of my unwillingness or inability to turn in a satisfactory story treatment.

Laura and I met in Paris, but stayed there only long enough to rent a little car for a leisurely circular tour of France, setting off across the battlefields of World War I, then by way of Nancy and Strasbourg to Dijon, France's gastronomic capital, and down the Rhone Valley to Arles, where we settled for a month or more while I worked on my play. Mornings we strolled about the town, sunned ourselves in the Roman amphitheatre or made excursions to the monuments in which Provence abounds. In the evening we drove to Marseilles for bouillabaisse at one of the restaurants on the Vieux Port, or to the fishing village of Martigues, known as La Venise Provençale, its little canals bright with colored sails, its Restaurant Pascal an epicurean rendezvous.

The play finished, we motored back to Paris by devious ways. When Laura left for America, I went over to London to visit friends and to see Raymond Massey, who was costarring with Tamara Geva in Sherwood's *Idiot's Delight*. My doubts about Massey's suitability for the role of Lincoln were dispelled; his versatility was reassuring. I sailed for home with a sense of great relief.

My play, *American Landscape*, met with general approval and was put down as the third item on the Playwrights' Company production schedule. I would have liked an early opening, but my commitment to Sherwood made it necessary for me to put it off. However, I did succeed in signing the fine old actor Arthur Byron for the leading role. Anderson and Weill had engaged Walter Huston, one of the best performers on the American stage, to play Peter Stuyvesant in *Knickerbocker Holiday*. Whatever the Broadway oracles may have thought of the Playwrights' Company, the actors were eager to align themselves with us. When Sherwood asked Alfred Lunt and Lynn Fontanne, who had appeared in his

great successes *Reunion in Vienna* and *Idiot's Delight*, whether
their Theatre Guild affiliation would prevent their working for the
Playwrights' Company, Lunt replied, "We go where the good
plays are."

4

It was with considerable trepidation that I approached the rehearsals of *Abe Lincoln in Illinois*, for I had never directed another
author's play and was afraid I might not do justice to Sherwood's
fine script. But things went smoothly. Massey had made a study of
Lincoln's traits and of Midwestern speech; more important, he was
imbued with the spirit of the play: his portrayal had simplicity
and deep, quiet emotion. We interrupted the rehearsal one day
long enough to listen to a short-wave broadcast from London.
Neville Chamberlain, just back from Munich, said that the agreement reached there guaranteed "peace in our time": a reassuring
declaration, though the price—the abandonment of Czechoslovakia
to Nazi domination—was a staggering one.

Knickerbocker Holiday was also in rehearsal, under the direction
of Joshua Logan. We were becoming increasingly worried about
finances. *Abe Lincoln* was costing $35,000, *Knickerbocker Holiday*
about $60,000. If both plays failed, we would indeed be out of
business in our first few months. (Today comparable productions
of the two plays would cost $125,000 and $300,000.)

Knickerbocker Holiday, with its depiction of Peter Stuyvesant
as the "indispensable man," was a not too subtle attack upon Roosevelt and what Anderson regarded as his highhanded measures of
social reform. The rest of us were strongly pro-Roosevelt, and
though, of course, we had no control over Anderson's script, we did
succeed, mainly by cajolery, in getting him to delete some of the
more pointed references to the New Deal. We all went to Hartford
for the tryout—the first, and therefore the most exciting, of many
such excursions. The circumstances were hardly auspicious: the
Connecticut River was in flood; there were six inches of water in
the hotel lobby. But the performance went sufficiently well to
justify cautious optimism.

Next we went to Washington for the opening of *Abe Lincoln*.
The response was good, but long experience had taught us all that

out-of-town enthusiasm does not ensure New York success. We
made good use of our time in Washington by tuning up performances and making minor textual alterations. There was one scene
in the play that had been a source of disagreement between Sherwood and myself from the time I first read it. Lincoln, deeply moved
by the courage and resolution of a pioneer whose child is desperately ill, utters a simple, touching prayer for the child's recovery.
It was the genesis of the play, for Sherwood had made it the turning point in Lincoln's life, the pioneer's idealism inspiring him to
dedicate himself to the cause of freedom. Sherwood told me he had
written the prayer on the back of an envelope while in a restaurant
and then had built the play around it. I felt that the scene had the
effect of being an arbitrary interlude, with little integral relation
to the rest of the play. Sherwood insisted that that was the one
scene he would not change. However, I kept persuading him to
work on it. The first change was the introduction of the pioneer
earlier in the play, so that the prairie meeting was a reunion of
old friends rather than an accidental encounter of strangers. Next
I suggested bringing in the town bravo, Jack Armstrong, who also
made an earlier appearance. By skillful interweaving, Sherwood
now made the scene a logical step in the development of the plot
and of Lincoln's character.

The play had been based largely upon Carl Sandburg's voluminous writings about Lincoln. I believe Sherwood's original title
had been "The Prairie Years," a borrowing from Sandburg. We
had several meetings with Sandburg, who later wrote a brief
preface to the printed text. Leafing through Sandburg in search of
atmospheric details, I came upon a remark of Lincoln's to the effect that the Todds must be important people, for they spelled
their name with two *d*'s, whereas one was enough for God. I told
Sherwood he must somehow work that into the script. It was one
of the play's biggest laughs.

It seemed appalling to us that the exclusion policy of the National
Theatre in Washington made it impossible for any Negro to see a
play that was an affirmation of the principles of democracy and that
touched specifically upon the race issue. Since no amount of persuasion had any effect upon the theatre management, we thought
of giving an extra free performance, open to Negroes only, on a
first-come, first-served basis. But Negro leaders convinced us that

the performance would merely have the effect of sanctioning segregation. However, the matter did not end there. Some time later Sherwood obtained from leading dramatists a pledge that they would not allow their plays to be presented at the National Theatre as long as Negroes were excluded. Thereupon Equity demanded a similar provision in its employment contracts. When the demand was rejected by the board of governors of the League of New York Theatres, a number of dramatists who, in their capacity as producers, were members of the League, called a membership meeting, at which I made a motion, seconded by Oscar Hammerstein, to overrule the board and adopt the Equity proposal. After heated debate, the motion carried. The National Theatre still stubbornly refused to change its policy, so for several years no professional touring company visited Washington. Unable to make a go of exhibiting motion pictures, the National finally capitulated and opened its doors to Negroes. The financial loss to actors, playwrights and producers had been heavy, but it is to the credit of the theatrical profession that there were few who did not think this important victory in the nation's capital well worth the price.

At the opening of *Abe Lincoln* in New York, at the Plymouth Theatre, Sherwood and I sat alone in the same little gallery from which I had watched *Counsellor-at-Law* seven years before. While we were waiting nervously for the curtain to go up, Sherwood looked through the telegrams of good wishes. Without comment, he handed me one from Clare Boothe Luce, which read: "This will be a night in the theatre."

When the curtain did go up, I was relieved, as director, to see that the performance was dynamic and the mechanics smooth. But though there was close attention throughout, I was disturbed by the audience's lack of warmth and excitement. I could see that Sherwood was worried, too. However, the opening scene of the third act, a skillful distillation of the Lincoln-Douglas debates, evoked a great round of applause; from then on the intensity of response increased. During the final scene we were startled and alarmed by hearing a woman's voice, coming apparently from the first row of the orchestra; we did not know what to make of it. At the final curtain there was a heartening demonstration.

The Sherwoods gave a large after-theatre party at the Barberry Room, to which they had invited many stars of the stage and of "café society." Everyone was in a congratulatory mood, but Sherwood, distrustful of first-night ovations, was not jubilant. He confided to me another worry. He had learned that the loud-voiced woman in the front row was his mother. Almost stone deaf, she had apparently believed that she was whispering to her companion. "I hope she never finds out that she made the disturbance," said Sherwood. "It might have a terrible effect upon her." Next day his mother phoned to tell him, with great delight, of her outrageous behavior at the opening.

The play had opened on a Saturday night, which meant a wait of twenty-four hours for the early editions of the Monday-morning papers containing the first reviews. No one who has not been through a similar ordeal can know how long those twenty-four hours can be. On Sunday evening Massey and the Sherwoods came to my apartment. We sat drinking and talking as the hours dragged on. I happened to mention my annoyance at a story in the drama section of the New York *Times* which outlined the entire plot of my forthcoming play, *American Landscape*. That was all that Sherwood, his nerves on edge, needed. He leaped to the telephone, called the *Times*, and, in the absence of all members of the dramatic staff, denounced the bewildered office boy for a breach of journalistic ethics. A week or so later, Brooks Atkinson wrote Sherwood to this effect: "Dear Bob, I'm sorry we were all out when you called. I know that we are bastards, but I want to assure you that we are not lousy."

At eleven o'clock Madeline Sherwood and I went down to Times Square. The papers were not yet out, so we lounged about until they appeared. Under an arc light at Broadway and Forty-third Street we read the notices in the *Times* and the *Herald Tribune*. The suspense was over; the play was a sure hit.

A few days later *Knickerbocker Holiday* opened. It too was a substantial success, thanks largely to Walter Huston. The play contained a romantic duet, "It Never Was You," which we all thought would be a song hit. Instead, to everyone's surprise, it was a number called "September Song" that was the hit. Huston could not sing, but his vaudeville experience had taught him how to put a song over, and his engaging personality made his rendition irresistible. The song still provides a good annual income for the estates of Maxwell Anderson and Kurt Weill.

I was less fortunate with *American Landscape*. From the beginning I was in trouble because of the physical condition of Arthur Byron. Ten days before the tryout, he told me that he felt he could not go on. Rather than call off the entire production, I made a quick replacement by bringing on Charles Waldron from Hollywood. Though a good actor, he lacked Byron's warmth and audience appeal. But I do not hold him responsible for the play's cool reception. After two disappointing weeks in Boston, we opened in New York for an unsatisfactory five weeks' run.

With *Abe Lincoln* and *Knickerbocker Holiday* thriving, the loss did not seriously affect the Playwrights' Company's financial position. Later in the season, Behrman's *No Time for Comedy*, with a cast that included Katharine Cornell and Laurence Olivier, was another great success. Our first season, with three hits out of four tries, was triumphal. What was more, the quality of the plays and the productions was far above the ordinary Broadway level. Best of all, these results had been achieved without friction or turmoil, in an atmosphere that we all found creative.

5

My marriage was slowly disintegrating. My wife complained constantly about my mother, now eighty and in failing health. Since I could hardly turn my mother out, I engaged a companion for her, to relieve my wife of responsibility. That meant giving up my study. I rented a small midtown apartment, where I spent most of my time, working, reading or just relaxing. Home life no longer had much to offer: my mother kept to her room; Peggy was at the University of Chicago; Robert, now drama editor of Ralph Ingersoll's new daily *PM*, was seldom in.

Laura had spent the fall in New York, but in early winter she left for California. Her going filled me with misgiving; I feared it might be the beginning of the end. Pride and honor kept her from making any demand, but I knew that she found our ambiguous situation increasingly intolerable. Yet I could not bring myself to end my marriage. I have often asked myself what restrained me, but have found no satisfactory answer. Perhaps more than anything else I was afraid that Laura and I would never be able to sustain, on the day-to-day level of marital life, the high pitch of our sporadic meetings. In other words, I preferred the risk of termination to the risk of anticlimax.

So, still clinging to my marriage, I sailed with my wife to France, en route to Yugoslavia and Greece. During our voyage, Mussolini marched into Albania. A visit to the Balkans did not seem propitious, so we went to Juan-les-Pins on the Riviera. Even that was a bit hazardous, for, as the American consul at Nice informed us, in the event of war the single railroad line and the highway along the coast would be restricted to military use.

While we were at Juan-les-Pins, I had a most extraordinary experience. One evening I bought a two-day-old copy of the London *Times,* as I did about once a week, not so much for the news as for the crossword puzzle with its trick definitions. When I had done the puzzle, I skimmed the paper, even glancing at the financial page, in which I had no interest whatever. Suddenly there leaped out at me, from amid columns of stock quotations, a single-paragraph dispatch from Mexico reporting the wreck of an international train, with heavy loss of life. Laura had told me of her intention to go to Mexico at some unspecified time. The instant I read the news item, I said to myself, "Laura was on that train!" After a sleepless night, I sent a cablegram to the Mexican address she had given me. Two days later I received an answer. She had indeed been on the train, but had escaped uninjured. If this was merely a coincidence, it was certainly a fantastic one. If it was not, there must be some form of thought communication of which we are not aware.

The political situation simmered down, so we went to Greece after all, spending three weeks in an examination of some of its marvels. Just before leaving Athens for Delphi, we had cocktails with the American Minister, Lincoln MacVeagh, who told us of some new discoveries made by the French archaeologists. At the French expedition's headquarters a bearded man in a smock informed us brusquely that the finds were not ready for public exhibition, but when I mentioned MacVeagh his manner changed and he led us into a little laboratory; there we saw the objects only lately removed from one of the "treasuries" which the cities of Greece maintained at Delphi: gold figurines and fragments of vases; votive offerings of no great artistic value but thrilling to behold, encrusted as they still were with the earth in which they had lain for twenty-five centuries.

We had booked steamship passage from England, but I heard that Pan American was beginning its transatlantic passenger service. Ever since the Lindbergh flight I had been hoping that someday I could fly the Atlantic. A quiet little man at Cook's, pleased by the notion of helping someone in this new venture, succeeded in getting a single place for me. My wife went to London with Peggy, who had joined us in Paris; I flew to Marseilles, the point of embarkation.

The double-decked hydroplane had accommodations for sixty-five passengers, but, since this was only the second westbound flight, a limit of eight had been set in order that more fuel could be carried. Among the other passengers were a Dutchman named Preester, one of Pan Am's chief engineers; Helen Rogers Reid, wife of the publisher of the New York *Herald Tribune;* and Paul Patterson, publisher of the Baltimore *Sun.*

The plane was scheduled to stop at the Azores for refueling. As we circled over the green islands that dotted the blue sea, we regretted that our stay would be so brief. Our regrets were premature. In alighting at the Horta mooring, the plane was slapped smartly by a wave, springing one of the plates. Preester, the Pan Am engineer, would not allow us to resume flight in that plane. That meant waiting a week until the next eastbound plane picked us up on its return flight. We groaned at the prospect of being marooned for a week on an island that except for its natural beauty had no attraction whatever.

Hard put to know what to do with ourselves, we wandered down to the dock, where a whale was being cut up, but the stench drove us back. Then it occurred to us that perhaps when the eastbound plane stopped for fuel we could fly back to Lisbon in it. We put it up to Preester, who made the necessary arrangements. The news of our mishap had, of course reached New York. I received a telegram from Robert: "Get a horse."

In due course the plane from New York arrived, and we gaily flew the twelve hundred miles to Lisbon, where we spent several delightful days as guests of Pan Am. On the return flight we stopped at Horta to transfer to our original plane. We took aboard some champagne, a fine dinner was provided, and afterwards we sat in the lounge over brandy and cigars as we flew into the setting sun and watched the moon rise behind us: nowadays almost a routine experience, but then a strange and thrilling one.

6

But the fun ended abruptly when I reached New York; there were harrowing days ahead. Awaiting me was a long letter from Mexico, in which Laura told me that she was marrying a man who had been asking her for years. The news, though not wholly unexpected, was shattering. I had lost forever the person to whom I had been more closely attuned than to anyone I had ever known. My first impulse was to fly to Mexico, but, unwilling to make a sudden, unannounced appearance that might be painful to her, I called her to tell her of my intention. She made it clear that the journey would be futile. In her letter she had referred, not without bitterness, to my casual treatment of her. Too disturbed to be objective, I reproached her for ending a relationship that had meant so much to us both. Yet I knew well enough that it was my own indecision that was at fault. Ironically, I knew, too, that my marriage, to which I had clung so persistently, was now effectively at an end.

In my unhappy state, I found distraction wherever I could, looking up people in whom I had no interest, engaging in meaningless flirtations. It was midsummer, but Sidney Howard happened to be in town making preparations for the production of a play for the new season. Though I felt affection for all my colleagues, I think I was closest to Howard. We not only agreed on most social and political questions, but I admired him for his warm nature, openhandedness and diverse interests. He had been a flier in the Lafayette Escadrille in World War I, was a connoisseur of all the arts, a much sought-after screenwriter, an enthusiastic farmer, and a playwright with an appetite for experimentation. We always had much to talk about.

Howard's second wife was one of the daughters of Walter Damrosch, who was president of the National Institute of Arts and Letters, to which I had been recently elected. I sometimes went to parties at the Damrosch house, where there were always many musical celebrities. But the household was dominated by Mrs. Damrosch, who was a daughter of James G. Blaine. I always felt that Damrosch, Howard and the other sons-in-law were overpowered by this fierce matriarch and her Amazonian daughters. It seemed to me that the demands of the social milieu in which

Sidney was obliged to live were hampering his work as an artist. The maintenance of an elaborate town house and a gentleman's farm stocked with blooded cattle made it necessary for him to spend much time in Hollywood. He persuaded himself that he liked film work, but it was clear that his real interest was the theatre.

We dined one night at a small Italian restaurant, where we sat for hours while Sidney talked about his first wife, the well-known actress Claire Eames, who had left him for another man. Though she had been dead for nine years, he had never become reconciled either to her desertion of him or to her death. He described minutely his trip from Italy to London to attend her funeral, the funeral itself, and the painful task of breaking to his young daughter the news of her mother's death. I just listened, for it was obvious that he felt a need to unburden himself of his obsessive memories. As one who had so recently suffered a heavy loss, I could listen with more than normal sympathy.

After dinner we strolled to Times Square, where Sidney bought make-up to be used by his children in a celebration at Tyringham in the Berkshires, where his farm was located. We walked down the block to look in on *Abe Lincoln in Illinois*, still playing to crowded houses. We stood at the back, congratulating ourselves upon our association with this fine play—rightfully awarded the Pulitzer Prize —and upon the auspicious beginning of our joint enterprise. As Sidney left for Grand Central Station, he said I would see him the following week when he came back to begin casting his play. I never saw him again.

A few days later Victor Samrock, our business manager, phoned to tell me he had just learned of Howard's death. I hurried down to the office, where I found Behrman, quietly weeping. The details were horrible and ironic. Sidney had gone to the barn, with the intention of using his tractor. Standing in front of it, he started it with a hand crank. The tractor was in gear; it moved forward, crushing him to death against the wall of the barn. It was unpredictable, senseless, appalling. At the funeral I was a pallbearer, a distressing duty indeed. From the house on the hillside to which we returned, we could look down upon the new grave in the village churchyard. Sidney's death, in his forty-ninth year, was far more than a personal loss to those who had loved him. It was a heavy blow to the Playwrights' Company, to the theatre as a whole, and to the cause of freedom in which he was a dedicated and effective fighter. I have known few men for whom I have had greater respect and admiration.

It was, I believe, on the very day of Sidney's death that the world learned of the signing of the Hitler-Stalin pact. A week later Hitler marched into Poland: World War II had begun. For anyone who remembered World War I and what it had cost in lives, in property, in the destruction of human happiness and the obliteration of moral and spiritual values, it was hardly credible that it was to begin all over again, with deadlier weapons and more implacable hatreds.

7

Shaken as I already was by the loss of Laura and by Sidney's death, the outbreak of war reduced me to a state that bordered upon demoralization. I knew from experience that work was my only salvation. Since I had no emotion left to expend, I once more wrote a lighthearted comedy, *Two on an Island*, another play about New York. It followed the pattern of an earlier play, *The Sidewalks of New York:* the story of a boy and a girl who come to New York in search of a career, crossing each other's paths frequently, but meeting only at the end of the play. For the numerous scenes, which included a sighteeeing bus, a subway car, the Metropolitan Museum of Art, a lunch counter and the head of the Statue of Liberty, Jo Mielziner devised a skeletonized production that was imaginative and amusing.

Among those suggested for the leading role was Betty Field, a young actress who was beginning to make herself known. She had attended one or two Theatre Alliance meetings, but I hardly knew her and had never seen her on the stage. I went to see her in an inane play in which she had little to do. But when she read for me I was so impressed by her personality and evident talent that I engaged her immediately. It was a happy choice. Her rare sense of comedy made her a delight to work with.

The tryouts in New Haven and Boston went well. In New York, the play was neither a success nor a failure. As often happens, the attendance struck a level that neither forced a closing nor afforded a margin of profit. Twenty years earlier the same receipts would have meant a year's run; twenty years later, a quick closing. As it was, the play ran for three months. The motion picture rights brought a good price, but the picture was never made, because the screen writers had the boy and girl meet in the first scene, thereby, of course, destroying the essential element of suspense.

The Playwrights' Company, besides establishing, in memory of Sidney Howard, an annual award to the most promising new playwright, decided to go ahead with Howard's play, *Madam, Will You Walk?* It was a fantasy that decried conformity and made a plea for individual self-expression. We all liked the script, but, knowing that Sidney had intended to do more work on it, we obtained permission from his widow for Sherwood to make whatever alterations seemed necessary. The casting of the leading part, a benign Satan, was difficult. At my suggestion we approached George M. Cohan, now past sixty and no longer very active. The part was unlike anything the Yankee Doodle Boy had ever attempted, but he was flattered to be asked to appear in a highbrow play, and after considerable hesitation he yielded to our persuasion.

From the beginning things went badly. Polly Howard resisted every change that Sherwood proposed. Every word that her husband had written was sacred, and she miraculously remembered conversations in which the very passages Sherwood wanted to edit had been pronounced indispensable by Howard. We gave Sherwood all possible support, but could make no headway against that humorless smile and finishing-school politeness. Only Sherwood's loyalty to Howard kept him from throwing up the job in disgust. There was conflict, too, between Cohan and the play's director, Margaret Webster. Accustomed to staging Shakespeare at the Old Vic, she felt ill at ease with Broadway's onetime darling. As for Cohan, he could not accustom himself to being directed by a woman—and an Englishwoman to boot! The whole venture came to a miserable end when Cohan's friends, after attending the Washington opening, convinced him that this was not the part New York wanted to see him in. He withdrew and the play closed. It deserved a better fate, as a production at the Phoenix Theatre years later proved.

Besides Anderson's *Key Largo*, which ran about as long as *Two on an Island*, we produced Sherwood's *There Shall Be No Night*, which won him another Pulitzer Prize, his third, a record surpassed only by Eugene O'Neill. Though it starred the Lunts and was widely

acclaimed, its New York run was less than two hundred performances. The play dealt with the Russian invasion of Finland, but
when it was done in England I was disturbed to learn that the
locale had been changed to Greece, with the Nazis as the invaders.
By that time we were in the war, and Sherwood, now one of Roosevelt's advisers, did not want to appear to be attacking one of America's allies. I felt that the defense of Stalingrad did not justify the
attack upon Finland, and that it would have been better to have
shelved the play entirely. I never discussed it with Sherwood, for it
was none of my business.

8

When *Two on an Island* closed, Betty went to California to fulfill a
motion picture contract. But first she and I took a short trip to
Guatemala. Then, in order to be near Maxwell Anderson, who had
asked me to direct his new play, *Journey to Jerusalem,* I rented a
house for the summer in New City, New York. Like Santa Fe,
Provincetown and Carmel, New City was the center of a colony of
artists and writers, of whom Anderson was perhaps best known. His
play *High Tor* took its name from a mountain nearby. Kurt Weill
had a house in New City, too.

Anderson, an introvert of simple tastes, had, like so many other
successful writers, steadily enlarged his scale of living. On a big
tract of farmland, bought years before for almost nothing, he had
built a costly, ugly house. An indulgent husband and father, he
maintained a staff of servants and several cars. His large earnings
did not keep pace with his ever-increasing expenses. Perpetually
plagued by money worries, he took distasteful Hollywood assignments or wrote impossible potboilers. His latter years were spent in
a desperate struggle to pay off his income tax indebtedness. Luxurious living harrowed his existence and impaired his career.

That summer was an anxious one for those whose eyes were
turned toward Europe. The "phony" war had become a grimly real
one, with the outflanking of the impregnable Maginot Line, the
overrunning of the Low Countries and the catastrophic fall of
France. In midsummer the aerial attack upon Britain began. Day
by day we watched and waited, hoping that the British could
hold out.

At a meeting of the Playwrights' Company in New City, Sherwood read us the text of a full-page advertisement he was preparing for insertion in the New York *Times*. Under the heading "Stop Hitler Now," it was, in effect, a plea for American intervention. Though I had been actively denouncing Hitlerism for nearly ten years, my pacifism was too deeply engrained to permit me to sign a petition for American participation in another war. When the advertisement appeared, it created a stir and, I believe, first drew Sherwood to Roosevelt's attention.

I joined a committee of writers and actors who were supporting Roosevelt's campaign for an unprecedented third term. In spite of Roosevelt's egomania and histrionics, I believed that he had the welfare of the people at heart; I strongly approved his socialistic measures. Mrs. Roosevelt invited the committee to Sunday lunch at Hyde Park. We had what is now known as a cookout, with Mrs. Roosevelt, in a bungalow apron, toasting the frankfurters over a charcoal grill. When her son Elliott shouted, "Hey, Ma, we're all out of beer!" she replied sharply, "You know there's always enough beer! Just look around for it." It was a domestic scene that made one happy to be an American. At length she came red-faced to the table at which Hervey Allen, I and some others were seated. Pushing back her wispy hair, she said, "You know, I'm always the last one to get anything to eat." After coffee she rose, tapped a glass with her spoon, and said, "We are now going to have a business meeting. Everybody will please be very quiet or leave." Roosevelt went right on talking to Katharine Hepburn, who had arrived in her private hydroplane. Mrs. Roosevelt tapped again. "The President of the United States will either be quiet or else leave." Roosevelt threw back his head and roared with laughter. A few moments later he left, in a car specially equipped with hand controls.

Journey to Jerusalem opened cold, had a cold reception, and closed after seventeen performances, supposedly confirming the Broadway dictum that plays with religious or political themes are "poison at the box office." Nevertheless, I returned to the political field, with another anti-Nazi play, *Flight to the West*. Suggested by my transatlantic flight, the entire action took place aboard a Clipper in the course of its transoceanic passage. I had written the principal part with Betty in mind, a character somewhat more mature than those she had previously played. The truly international cast included Paul Hernried (later Henreid), an Austrian baron of Scandinavian descent, who had just left England to escape internment as an enemy alien; Elenora Mendelssohn, a descendant of the composer and a goddaughter of Duse; another German refugee, a Russian, a Czech and a Dane. Minor parts were played by two young men who later made names for themselves: Karl Malden and Kevin McCarthy. Jo Mielziner ingeniously reproduced the interior of a Clipper.

We opened in Princeton, where Albert Einstein came backstage to express his approval of the play. "If it does not succeed," he said, speaking very slowly, "it is not the fault of the play, but of the public." The New York press was again divided. The audiences were enthusiastic, but far below capacity. Once more I was confronted with the situation of a play that strongly appealed to many theatregoers, yet whose receipts were insufficient to meet the heavy operating expenses. In a repertory theatre, or under less rigorous economic conditions, it could have run on indefinitely. Luckily, the cultural division of the International Ladies Garment Workers' Union offered to take over the play, so it ran for four months.

Those of us who had helped in the Roosevelt campaign were invited to Washington for the inaugural luncheon. The company was distinguished, but the food was almost the worst I have ever eaten. Mrs. Roosevelt took some of us on a tour of the White House, pointing out Lincoln's bed and a painting which Dolly Madison had saved from the British in the War of 1812. Five or six of us decided to visit Sherwood, who had been confined to his hotel by a cold. Direct access was blocked by reviewing stands, so we had to make a wide detour. As we turned into Pennsylvania Avenue, we were startled by the sudden blaring of a brass band. The inaugural parade was coming down the avenue just behind us! At the same time the crowd in the stands recognized Raymond Massey, who was one of us. There were shouts of "There's Mr. Lincoln!" and "Hello, Abe!" Unable to turn back, we marched down the avenue at the head of the parade for about a quarter of a mile, with people popping out of the stands to snap Massey's picture or shake his hand.

9

Besides directing *Abe Lincoln in Illinois* and *Journey to Jerusalem*, I had taken over the staging of Behrman's *The Talley Method*, which had only a brief run, though it starred Ina Claire and Philip Merivale, two of the finest actors I have ever worked with. Ina's comedic talent and superb sense of timing were extraordinary, but her flightiness, inability to remember lines, and loquacity did not ease a director's burden. Once when she said that she had to leave rehearsal early because a man was coming to her hotel to talk to her, Behrman remarked, "Ina, that is an objective that will never be achieved." Merivale was a well-educated, highly intelligent man and a good socialist. I was very fond of him and of his wife, Gladys Cooper, one of London's favorites. As a woman at a Mayfair dinner party said to me, "I never miss a Gladys Cooper play. She always says such witty things."

In the course of directing the plays of my three colleagues, I had come to know them very well and had tried to apply that knowledge to an analysis of their work. I believe that most serious writers have one basic theme or concept, reflecting some obsession, some compulsion, some inner conflict. In the work of each of my associates, I found, at least to my own satisfaction, a recurrent pattern.

Behrman, in spite of his wit and social talents, shrank from unpleasant problems and avoided, as far as he was able, contact with the crude realities of life. His awareness, conscious or unconscious, of his inability or unwillingness to be tough-minded is reflected in his plays, which usually portray an encounter between a clever, hypersensitive woman and a blunt, dominating man of the world, over whom she eventually triumphs.

Anderson's case was very different. His father, I believe, had been an itinerant preacher of some sort; in any case, Max had been subjected to stringent religious indoctrination. Though intellectually emancipated, he had, like so many others, never overcome his early conditioning. He had what might be called a crucifixion complex, an obsession with the concept of martyrdom, as a listing of his protagonists clearly shows: Jesus, Socrates, Joan of Arc, Medea, Mary Stuart, Anne Boleyn, the Earl of Essex, Sacco and Vanzetti, and the fictional heroes of *Key Largo* and *The Eve of St. Mark*. I had profound respect for his craftsmanship as well as for his integrity, idealism and earnestness. But though I commended his determination to restore poetry to the theatre, I felt that his attempts were not notably successful. I lack completely the poetic gift, but I think I recognize it when I see it, and I do not see it in Anderson's plays. He had great command of language, great eloquence, and a scholarly understanding of prosody; but it seemed to me that his verse never took wings. In fact, I found it often turgid and rhetorical, and, when spoken on the stage, singularly undramatic.

Sherwood's conflict was for me the most interesting and appealing of the three. The martyrdom theme, redemption through sacrifice, is present in his work too, but it is personal rather than mystical or metaphysical. Unlike Anderson, he had a background of sophistication, affluence and social position. With his sensual nature and hearty appetites, which he had every opportunity to indulge, he could easily have become a literary playboy, a fashionable figure in the worlds of letters and of society. In fact, he often veered in that direction. But he was held in check by a kind of *noblesse oblige,* a sense of moral obligation to devote his talents to the service of humanity. The resolution of this conflict is evident in his public activities; it recurs again and again in his plays. In *Abe Lincoln, Idiot's Delight, The Petrified Forest, There Shall Be No Night, The Rugged Path,* even in the posthumously produced comedy *Small War on Murray Hill,* we see the dilemma of a man torn between his personal desires and his compulsion to pursue an unselfish course. Behrman is a more brilliant writer, Anderson a sounder craftsman, but Sherwood excels in human appeal.

10

Betty's motion picture contract required her to return again to Hollywood as soon as *Flight to the West* closed. I went out to spend the summer with her. Irving Berlin had talked to me about writing the screen play for his musical film *Holiday Inn,* in which Fred Astaire and Bing Crosby were to be starred. I was by no means sure of my qualifications for the job, but when I arrived in Hollywood Mark Sandrich, director of the picture, persuaded me to undertake it.

Betty had rented a small house high up in Laurel Canyon, in a little byroad called Hermit's Glen, a secluded, wooded corner, yet only ten minutes from Hollywood Boulevard. Over the garage were two guest rooms, which I occupied. We had a long, quiet, happy summer. Our work kept us busy all day. Evenings and Sundays we drove out to dinner, visited acquaintances or idled by the swimming pool, reading, talking or listening to the radio. Hitler had invaded Russia; the news was alarming.

I plodded away conscientiously at the screenplay, but was unable to develop any real attack. The synthetic nature of scenario writing seems always to inhibit me. Nevertheless, I was a little puzzled when I was told that my script was lacking in "situations"; I had thought it was packed with them. I was enlightened, however, when I saw the completed picture, whose scenario was the work of an abler hand. For example, as Astaire, a night club entertainer, is making up, Crosby enters the dressing room bearing a jar of preserved peaches, which explodes, depositing its contents on Astaire's starched shirt front. I had to acknowledge ruefully that it was a situation that would never have suggested itself to me.

It was very hard for me to leave Betty. Our summer had been an idyllic one; we were deeply in love. When she finished her Hollywood assignment, she came to New York, where we were constantly together. But, unable to find a suitable stage engagement, she accepted another Hollywood job. Before she left New York our relationship reached a crisis. Like Laura, indeed like any sensitive woman, she found her ambiguous situation no longer tolerable. Apart from her professional success she had had few satisfactions. Her parents had divorced when she was very young; her early life had been insecure and unstable. Her mother, a silly, selfish hypochondriac, was constantly on the move, sometimes sending her to camps or boarding schools. She hardly knew her father; when her mother remarried, her coarse-grained, ill-tempered stepfather treated her harshly. She escaped in her teens to become an actress, but her professional life too had been a vagrant one without form or any sort of permanence. She wanted what most women want: security, roots, a home of her own, an enduring love relationship, children. Because of our attachment she had refused several offers of marriage; but now she felt that the decisive moment had come.

I was far from unreceptive to the suggestion of marriage. I had let Laura go mainly because of my reluctance to make an unreserved emotional commitment, but through losing her I had dislodged the inhibiting block, and I was quite prepared now to surrender myself unconditionally. My wife and I were now occupying separate apartments (though in the same building). It had seemed the only way of solving the ever present problem of my mother, and of relieving

my wife of all responsibility for her care. So there was now almost
no vestige of marital life worth preserving.

What troubled me most was the age difference between Betty and
myself: more than twenty years. But she insisted that age was of
no consequence when people loved each other; and in the two years
of our intimacy our love had been truly tested; in formalizing our
relationship, we would create for ourselves a world of domestic
happiness. The prospect appealed strongly to me; I had long felt
the lack of a satisfactory home life. Even the possibility of becoming a father again was attractive. I love children, and now that
mine were grown I missed having young ones. I asked for a little
time to think it over, but it did not take me long to make up my
mind.

It was not altogether easy to make the severance, though the link
had become so tenuous that it almost parted of itself. One of my
children thought it should have been severed years before; the other
thought I was right in holding the family together as long as possible. There are those who saw, those who will see, in my action the
familiar pattern of the middle-aged man—I was forty-nine—who
forsakes for a younger woman the wife to whom he has been married for twenty-six years. It is easier to make such generalizations
than to look at situations in terms of individuals. In every sense but
a legalistic one, my marriage had long since come to an end. For
many years there had been no pretense of fidelity on either side. Its
future promised no compensation for forgoing the positive values
that I saw in remarriage. A disbeliever in self-sacrifice that serves
no purpose, I made a pragmatic decision. Let those whose characters are nobler judge me.

Accordingly, I became a "resident" of the sovereign state of Ne-
vada, as a prerequisite to the legal dissolution of my marriage, a
revolting bit of hypocrisy, chicanery and collusiveness prescribed
by our antiquated and unrealistic divorce laws. For one who is not
interested in gambling, riding, frequenting night clubs or sitting in
bars, six weeks in Reno are an eternity. I had just finished a play—
never produced, because of my colleagues' lack of enthusiasm—and
was in no mood for work. One can read only for a certain number of
hours. In desperation, I became a moviegoer. There were five or six
movie theatres in Reno, most of them offering double features and
changing their bills twice weekly. I selected the programs that con-

sumed the most time, avoiding those with artistic pretensions. Of the fifty or more movies I saw, I do not remember the title, performers or substance of even one.

One Sunday I was mechanically eating a tasteless dinner, amid the unavoidable din of radio jazz and the clatter of the slot machines known as one-armed bandits. Suddenly the music stopped; there was an announcement of the attack on Pearl Harbor. I hurried back to my hotel, rented a radio, and kept tuning in on whatever station had a news program. Rumors of a threatened attack on New York were quickly dispelled. But it was inevitable now that we enter the war; perhaps it had been inevitable from the very beginning. So, for the second time in twenty-five years, the American people were committed to a world conflict whose causes and implications most of them did not understand.

At New Year's I flew to San Francisco to join Betty, who came up from Hollywood to spend the holiday with me. But fog grounded our return flights. Betty was due at the studio early next morning, and no train could get her back on time. After much scurrying, we found a taxi driver who undertook to drive her. Uneasily I watched her depart on the all-night, five-hundred-mile drive. I took a sleeper to Reno, arriving at five in the morning. My overnight absence added another day to my interminable sojourn.

As soon as the shoddy, farcical court proceeding was over, I flew to Hollywood. Since California required a waiting period, we left at once for Arizona, where we could be married immediately. At Williams we obtained a license from the town clerk, then found the local justice of the peace holding court in a vacated store. He was sitting as committing magistrate in a murder case. We sat there among deputy sheriffs, cowboys and Indians, Betty rather conspicuous and more than a little self-conscious in her mink coat and Hollywood hairdo. The defendant was a nineteen-year-old boy, who sat grinning moronically, evidently pleased by the attention he was receiving. He was charged with murdering his father. His lawyer intimated that he had acted to save his thirteen-year-old sister from the father's advances; the prosecutor suggested that it was jealousy that had prompted the killing. It was hardly the perfect setting for a wedding!

The judge held the accused for the grand jury, then turned his attention to us. As the room cleared, he shouted to one of the departing detectives, "Hey, flatfoot, I need you to witness a wedding!" The court clerk was the second witness; the ceremony was quickly performed. As we signed the register, the judge said, "From now on is a long time."

We spent a few days at the Grand Canyon and in Santa Fe, then went on to New Orleans for a gastronomic spree. While we were there Betty was summoned back to Hollywood for retakes, so we had to fly all the way back to California. The retakes consisted of one close-up, which was done in twenty minutes. In less than twenty-four hours we were on our way East again, this time straight to New York, eager to proceed with the plans we had made for our life together.

CHAPTER

XIX

A New Life : II

1

We had decided to live in the country, preferably in the vicinity of Stamford, Connecticut. Friends had warned us that it would take six months, more likely a year, to find a suitable house. It took us exactly ten minutes, for we fell in love with the first place we were shown. Situated on a hilltop in the middle of fifteen acres of rolling woodland through which tumbled a large brook known as the Rippowam River, it was a rambling, U-shaped, single-storied, wood-shingled house with four fireplaces and five porches. On the market for several years, it appealed neither to those who sought the quaint and old-fashioned nor to those who went in for modernity. For us, however, it was ideal: secluded, solidly constructed, with large rooms conveniently arranged; in short, the perfect place for work, enjoyment of country life and the rearing of a family. We obtained immediate occupancy, for Betty wanted the pleasure of moving into her own home before beginning another Hollywood assignment.

There now began for me a period of deep, serene and uncomplicated happiness such as I had never known before. For the first time in my life, I had a home that gave me a sense of solidity and permanence. Now, too, my longing for country life was richly fulfilled. But transcendent was the joy of my marital relationship. I surrendered myself to it completely, and in doing so found emotional sustenance and spiritual enlargement. The atmosphere was one of harmony and mutual responsiveness. Before the end of our first year of marriage our happiness was increased by the birth of a fine boy, whom we named John.

There was a little cottage on our property that could have been made into a pleasant home for my mother and her companion. But she did not want to leave New York. She was confined to her room now, and her greatest source of pleasure was receiving visits from old friends and from their children and grandchildren. So she moved to an apartment hotel, where I saw her frequently. As always, we had little to say to each other, but our love was undiminished.

2

In my new-found happiness, I was less agitated about the war than I would otherwise have been. Perhaps it makes for human survival that in the midst of disaster individuals persist in self-nurture and the pursuit of their own ends. I was not indifferent to world events, nor had my loathing of war abated; but I was not as wrought up as I had been twenty-five years earlier.

Moreover, since we were in the war, I felt that it was important to do whatever was possible to focus attention upon the defense of democracy, the objective for which the conflict was presumably being waged. I prepared material for the Office of War Information and the semiofficial Writers' War Board. Also, for radio performance I wrote a playlet in which Pierre Laval was tried for treason, with Lafayette and Joan of Arc as his accusers.

I continued to be active on the board of the American Civil Liberties Union. The liberties that were being defended overseas were in danger of curtailment at home. The threat of censorship was perennial; so were the attempts of the superpatriots to suppress all expression of opinion that was unorthodox or critical of the status quo. One major task was correction of the grave injustice inflicted upon thousands of Japanese, many of American birth, who had been forcibly removed from their Pacific Coast homes and indiscriminately herded into concentration camps. Though undoubtedly there were enemy agents among them, the great majority were loyal to America. The protests of the A.C.L.U. resulted in the institution of a screening process by which many of the internees were released.

Sherwood, besides occupying an important post in the Office of War Information—headed by Elmer Davis—had become one of Roosevelt's chief consultants on questions of public relations. One day an F.B.I. agent called upon me to ask whether I knew of any Communist affiliations that Sherwood might have. I managed to keep a straight face, but as he was leaving I could not resist saying, "If you want more information I suggest you try the White House, because Sherwood is living there now, helping the President write his speeches." The Hooverite nodded gravely.

Though Sherwood continued to attend meetings of the Playwrights' Company whenever he was in New York, he did no writing for the theatre during the entire war period. The company's whole setup had been predicated upon the continuing productivity of five playwrights. Howard's death and Sherwood's inactivity reduced our number to three, an insufficient source of supply for an organization that maintained its offices and staff on a year-round basis. We often discussed drawing in other writers, but never succeeded in doing so. Two or three whom we approached declined; other proposed names were rejected for personal reasons; we did not want the comradely nature of our company to be impaired by the intrusion of someone who might not be congenial.

3

My new home and new family occupied much of my time. So did my activity in the Playwrights' Company, the American Civil Liberties Union, the American Arbitration Society and the Dramatists' Guild, of which I was now president. I also did a great deal of writing, with generally unsatisfactory results. I wrote for Betty a play called *A New Life,* which dealt again with the struggle for liberty. She was expecting a second child, which was appropriate enough, for the entire action of the play took place in a maternity hospital. One stylized, expressionistic scene, set in the delivery room, was condemned by some as too harrowing, praised by others for its dramatic effectiveness. We had been puzzled about what to do when Betty would no longer be able to play, but we never had to meet the problem, for we closed after nine weeks. Two months later Betty gave birth to a charming daughter, Judith—or Judy, as she prefers to be called—only fourteen months younger than her brother John.

Next, Jed Harris persuaded me to dramatize Ira Wolfert's novel *Tucker's People,* a colorful book, full of human interest. Dealing ostensibly with the numbers racket in Harlem, it had an underlying theme that appealed strongly to me: the thesis that the main difference between the racketeer and the businessman who ruthlessly cuts down his weaker competitors is that the latter can always find legalized methods to achieve his ends, whereas the racketeer, who is engaged in an illegal activity, is forced to resort to violence.

Betty's contract required her to be in Hollywood for six months, so we all moved out there. I toiled away at the play, but nothing ever came of it, mainly because Harris had quarreled with Paul Lukas, whom he had wanted for the lead, and could not find a satisfactory substitute. Harris had a reputation for driving people to distraction. Everyone had warned me against working with him. But in the year or more during which we were in fairly close contact I never experienced any unpleasantness; on the contrary, I found him stimulating and often amusing.

The war news began to be a little more encouraging. Betty and I sat up all one night to listen to the radio reports of the D-Day landings on the Normandy coast. I had a strong personal interest in the war's speedy end. My son Robert was in the Seabees. After being shunted about from camp to camp, he had been sent to Hawaii. I was greatly worried, for the offensives against the Japanese-held islands had entailed heavy casualties. However, someone discovered that Robert was a newspaperman, so he was assigned to a destroyer, where he prepared stories about the ship's personnel for home-town publication. It was a lucky stroke for us, for his Seabees unit became engaged, with appalling losses, in the assault upon Iwo Jima.

When *Tucker's People* was finally dropped, I wrote a play based upon the life of Thomas Paine, a man of vision, courage and integrity, who has never been accorded his rightful place in history, largely because of *The Age of Reason*—the poorest and least important of his books—which attacks the myths and superstitions of Judaeo-Christianity. Theodore Roosevelt once called Paine "a filthy little atheist," a rather extraordinary characterization, since this sentence appears on the first page of *The Age of Reason*: "I believe in one God and no more; and I hope for happiness beyond this life." I did a great deal of research on Paine. It might have been better if I had done less, for I crowded too much into the play, making it discursive and episodic. I put it aside, intending to go back to it someday, for the material is rich. But of course I never shall.

4

In Europe the defeat of the Axis powers was imminent. The Italian front had collapsed, Paris had been liberated, the Allied armies were closing in on Germany. On the eve of victory came the shocking news of Roosevelt's death. I was among the millions who mourned; I had admired him for his espousal of liberty and for the sweeping social reforms that won for him the hatred of the beneficiaries of special privilege.

Though Germany surrendered, the Japanese still held out. With my son on a destroyer subjected to frequent attacks by suicide planes, I awaited the end with great anxiety. Then came the dropping of the atomic bomb on Hiroshima, which I regard as one of the most inexcusable acts in all history, an outrage against humanity whose awful aftermath we are now reaping. Quite apart from its immediate horrors, it sanctioned the immoral doctrine that the end justifies the means, and demonstrated that in a power struggle between nations human life and human happiness count for nothing.

The responsibility for this monstrous crime rests not only upon the political and military leaders who set it in operation, but upon the great scientists who developed the bomb with full awareness of its potentiality. No man, however dedicated to the pursuit of abstract knowledge, can hold himself above the battle, nor disclaim involvement in the proximate consequences of his activities. If the thinker and the scientist are to be mere super-robots, without moral responsibility, then the advancement of knowledge holds no hope for the betterment of mankind.

Undoubtedly other nations would have invented nuclear weapons. But it was our first use of them that stimulated their worldwide production and that stopped us from condemning them. On the contrary, we have been forced into the position of condoning their use, and of threatening its repetition if, in someone's opinion— just whose we cannot be sure—it serves our national interest to do so. We have only ourselves to blame for the dilemma in which we find ourselves.

It would be erroneous to say that the war came to an end. It has never ended. There has been merely an armed truce, punctuated by hostilities in every quarter of the globe. Every month a new conflict arises. The immediate objectives of World War II were attained by the defeat of Hitler, Mussolini and the Japanese warlords, and by the liberation of the occupied countries. But the over-all objectives, the termination of imperialism, the abolition of dictatorships, the establishment of world order based upon the principles of human rights and individual liberty, were not even remotely attained. Everywhere liberties are suppressed, whole populations are subjected to regimentation, swarms of refugees or deportees starve or rot in exile. Hatred, fear and suspicion are rampart; accusations, threats and counterthreats fill the air. While half the world goes hungry, the great powers pour their wealth and creative energy into weapons of destruction that, even before completion, are rendered obsolete by the invention of still deadlier weapons. Higher and higher the lethal piles tower, ready to topple explosively at the touch of a finger.

Only the United Nations, which, by providing a forum for the discussion and mediation of international disputes, points the way to the establishment of world government, offers a ray of hope. But its powers are limited and its authority is challenged by nations that will submit to no restriction upon their sovereignty. One can only console oneself with the rather mystical belief that the human race has not yet run its course and that somehow man's desire to survive will triumph over his destructiveness.

5

After V-E Day, Sherwood wrote a new play, *The Rugged Path,* a title suggested by an early Keats poem referred to by Lincoln in the first scene of *Abe Lincoln in Illinois.* A war play, its theme was again the struggle between a man's selfish desires and his sense of duty. It had much to commend it, but it lacked Sherwood's sure touch; in spite of considerable rewriting, it never came up to his best work. For the lead, he lured away from Hollywood Spencer Tracy, a fine actor as well as a very popular one. Like most actors long absent from the theatre, Tracy was very nervous about appearing on the stage. There is a world of difference between acting before a camera and acting before an audience. The screen actor can repeat a scene over and over until it comes out right. On the stage there is no second chance; the actor is committed the moment he appears. No actor ever escapes that little moment of panic just before he goes on. If he has been coddled for years in a movie studio, he feels even more defenseless.

The play opened in Providence, in a vast theatre packed to the doors with an audience attracted by Tracy's reputation. During the intermission almost the entire audience filed down the aisle to have a closer look at Katharine Hepburn, who was sitting beside me. She went right on talking to me, as though oblivious to this marked attention. Again in Boston there were crowded houses, but little critical or popular enthusiasm for the play. Tracy was unhappy and did not want to open in New York. Sherwood and I sat up one night with him until daybreak, finally persuading him not to withdraw. But his instinct was sound, for the play's New York run was brief.

Sherwood took the failure very much to heart. It is always hard to see months of mental and emotional effort go for nothing, especially in the theatre, where one expires in a blaze of publicity. Sherwood's disappointment was aggravated by his money worries. His early plays, written before taxes became confiscatory, had netted him a fortune, which he had entrusted to an investment counselor, a gentleman of high social position, who embezzled every penny. The culprit went to prison, but that did not help Sherwood.

It was a blow from which he never recovered, for he had believed that he had complete financial security. He lived on a lavish scale in New York and maintained a country house in England which he was reluctant to give up, though eventually he had to. During the war years, he had devoted himself entirely to governmental service. In the ensuing years he was preoccupied with financial problems. His book *Roosevelt and Hopkins,* besides winning him another Pulitzer Prize, this time in biography, was deservedly successful. He was also in great demand as a screenwriter. *The Best Years of Our Lives*, in which he had a participating interest, was highly successful. One of the broadcasting networks engaged him to write a se-

ries of television plays at unheard-of terms. But after the first effort
met with indifference and the second was shelved, he asked to have
the contract annulled. His real interest was in the theatre. It was a
misfortune for him and for the American drama that he never
wrote another play that won popular favor or that measured up
to his high level of achievement.

He was plagued by ill-health too. He had been gassed in World
War I while serving with the Canadian Black Watch, and apparently he had never fully recovered. In later life he suffered excruciatingly from a facial neuralgia known as *tic douloureux*. At
times the agony was so acute that he had to be given morphine in-
jections. He contemplated surgery, but was deterred by warnings of
the danger of facial paralysis. Few who knew him as an eminent
public figure and a distinguished writer were aware of his trials and
ailments.

6

For years I had been wanting to write a rather tragic play about an
inhibited little man who finds compensation for his frustrations in
extravagant fantasies in which, of course, he is the central figure. I
returned to the subject again and again, but was never able to find
a resolution that was not either anticlimactic or barrenly defeatist.
Suddenly it occurred to me to turn the play into a comedy about a
young woman. In no time at all everything fell into place; when I
sat down to write, it flowed along easily.

The play, *Dream Girl*, covers a day in a girl's life, from her
awakening in her virginal bed to her retirement with the young
man with whom she has unexpectedly eloped. Intellectually and socially sophisticated, but emotionally immature, she lives vicariously
in a world of fancy. She is involved with three men: her brother-in-
law, with whom she believes herself in love; a successful businessman with amorous designs; and a tough-minded newspaperman
who forces her to face reality. Scenes of actuality alternate with enactments of her fantasies, in which she sees herself as a participant
in a confessional radio program, as the mother of twins fathered by
her brother-in-law, as a murderess triumphantly acquitted of the
murder of a man who mocks her, as a partner in an illicit Mexican
romance, as an actress enthralling a first-night audience, and as a

streetwalker who ends her wretched existence by taking poison. The play had psychoanalytic overtones, but the approach was wholly comedic. The dream scenes employed all the clichés and stock situations of melodrama and treacly romance. I suppose I never had more fun writing anything.

The tone of the play reflected my happiness. As someone astutely remarked, the whole thing was a love letter to Betty. She undertook the part with understandable reluctance. Physically it is one of the most demanding ever written. There are only two or three minutes when the girl is not on stage; the transitions from reality to fantasy are frequent and swift, and require instantaneous changes of characterization and of costume. There is hardly time to breathe between scenes, much less to relax.

Against the advice of everyone, I cast an actor named Wendell Corey for the difficult role of the newspaperman. I had seen him in a poor play in which he had little to do. Nevertheless, I had him read for me, again and again; it is an ordeal for actors, but I have found it an invaluable aid. The more Corey read, the more I was impressed by his personality and ability. Betty, dubious about him at first, gradually came around. By the time the play opened, she was quite happy about his performance; so was I.

The need for frequent, rapid scene changes made the use of realistic settings impracticable; besides, it would not have been in harmony with the mood of the play. So Jo Mielziner and I decided to use merely three small movable platforms with stylized backings against which a few props could be set to suggest the various locales. Going even further, we manipulated the platforms in full view of the audience, covering the transitions with music, sound effects and modulations of lighting. Thus the flow of scenes and characters was never interrupted; something to engage the audience's attention was happening every moment.

In the drafty New York theatre where we rehearsed, I contracted a heavy cold. Rehearsal conditions in the professional theatre are almost intolerable. The actors are required to sit for hours on uncomfortable chairs; illumination is provided by a single, glaring overhead electric lamp that is distracting and ruinous to the eyes; the theatre is either stiflingly hot or unpleasantly chilly. All these conditions are remediable, but the false economy of producers and the inflexible regulations of the craft unions prevent any improvement.

I was in no condition to supervise the New Haven dress rehearsal, but the production schedule was unalterable. Disregarding my doctor's advice, I made the trip, dizzy with fever. The dress rehearsal took thirteen hours—from two in the afternoon until three next morning, with brief interruptions for food. To synchronize lights, sound effects, platform movements and costume changes, every scene had to be done over and over. Bundled in overcoat and muffler, sneezing and coughing, my head swimming, I sat through it all and managed somehow to escape hospitalization. Keeping me company were Joe Mielziner and the noted couturier and theatre buff Mainbocher, who had designed Betty's costumes.

In New York the play was an instantaneous success. For Betty it was a complete triumph. Her charm, versatility and comedic skill were recognized and applauded by the critics and the public. My faith in Wendell Corey was vindicated, too. The play was a boon to him, for at the end of his engagement he went to Hollywood, where he has had a very successful career.

But in the theatre nothing is ever wholly secure or serene. *Dream Girl* opened on a Friday night. On Monday Betty had laryngitis and was inaudible. There was a hurried company conference to decide whether to call off the performance or to go ahead with Betty's understudy, Helen Marcy. With the public storming the box office, we thought it advisable to risk going ahead—a great risk indeed, for we had not yet had time for understudy rehearsals. I attended the performance with great anxiety. Groans greeted the announcement of Betty's indisposition, but only a few people asked for refunds. Helen Marcy acquitted herself remarkably well and received an ovation. Her exploit was widely publicized: there were feature articles, interviews and photographs. It was one of those Cinderella stories; stock material in fiction, but of rare actual occurrence. It seemed that her career was made, yet she never had the luck to follow up her sensational debut.

7

Some months before the production of *Dream Girl*, my Uncle Will had died, in his late eighties. Though I had continued to contribute to his support, I had seen him infrequently in his late years. Stone deaf and crippled by arthritis, he had little to live for. Yet his going saddened me; I had always had an affection for him, and I could not forget his kindness to me in my childhood and youth.

Then, shortly afterward, the last link to my early life was severed by the death of my mother. I was not unprepared for it. She was in her eighty-eighth year and had long been declining. I mourned her bitterly and, after more than fifteen years, still constantly think of her. But I am thankful that, while she lived long enough to rejoice in my happy remarriage and to become acquainted with John and Judy, she was spared the knowledge of what was to follow.

Though Sherwood had resumed active participation in the activities of the Playwrights' Company, Behrman had withdrawn entirely. He no longer wanted to be involved with managerial responsibilities. There was no ill-will or dissension; we tried hard to persuade him to remain. His withdrawal again reduced our playwright membership to three, an insufficient base for sound operations, particularly in view of sharply rising costs. It was the beginning of an economic crisis that has now become so acute that the very continuance of the theatre as a commercial enterprise is threatened.

The organization of a touring company of *Dream Girl* presented serious casting problems. After long deliberation, I engaged Judy Parrish, an unknown but talented young actress. For the man's role I chose an actor who told me that he had become so discouraged by his failure to get ahead in the theatre that he was thinking of taking up some other career. I advised him to hang on a little longer. It was good advice; his name is Richard Widmark.

The play's New York success was duplicated in Chicago. Bad news brought me home immediately after the opening. Betty, who had gone back into the play after a summer layoff, was on the verge of collapse. She tried to keep going, but after a few weeks a complete breakdown compelled her to withdraw entirely. The accumulation of fatigue, anxiety and other factors had proved too much for her. It was more than a year before she was able to resume work. We carried on as best we could with substitutes, but Betty had become identified with the role. At the conclusion of a year's run we were obliged to close. Had Betty been able to continue, we could have gone on for another year.

Misfortune befell the touring company too. In the third month of the Chicago run Judy Parrish was stricken with rheumatic fever.

With no adequate replacement available, we canceled the projected road tour—a great disappointment, for we had expected it to be long and profitable. I have seen other productions of the play, but the only actress whose performance really delighted me was Lucille Ball. She lacked Betty's tender wistfulness, but her vivid personality and expert timing kept the play bright and alive.

8

From the time *Street Scene* was first produced, various composers, including Deems Taylor and William Schuman, had talked to me about the possibility of making an opera of it. Now Kurt Weill, who had expressed interest, too, said he would like to go ahead. I was delighted. I had great admiration for Kurt as a musician and deep affection for him personally. The prospect of seeing *Street Scene* in a new form and of working in a new medium was exciting. It was agreed that I should write the libretto. As lyricist I suggested Langston Hughes. I hardly knew him, but I liked the human and humorous quality of his verses and stories of Negro life.

Since the Playwrights' Company was not equipped, financially or technically, to undertake the production unassisted, Weill and I sought a coproducer. Rodgers and Hammerstein were enthusiastic about the project, but they wanted to do it on their own, without participation by the Playwrights' Company. To this Kurt and I would not agree. At length a coproduction arrangement was worked out with Dwight Deere Wiman, who, as the former partner of William A. Brady, Jr., had been one of the many managers who rejected *Street Scene*.

I did not feel qualified to direct a musical play, so we engaged Charles Friedman, who had successfully staged Oscar Hammerstein's modern version of *Carmen*. It was agreed that we should adhere closely to the original play, merely reducing the number of characters and condensing the dialogue. To give Hughes an opportunity for a blues number, I substituted a Negro janitor for the Swede of the original. But the essential elements of the play were unchanged.

We all worked together smoothly, but my situation was difficult. Betty, in her troubled state, had a horror of being alone. Time and again, when I was about to set out for a meeting with my co-workers, she begged me not to leave her. My colleagues did not complain, but I felt that in justice to them I should perhaps withdraw. However, they agreed to come and stay in my guest cottage, where I installed a piano for Weill. Then on the eve of rehearsals an organic ailment forced me to be hospitalized for a few weeks. Luckily, I had almost finished my part of the work.

In the cast were the fine operatic voices of Polyna Stoska, Norman Cordon and Brian Sullivan. Anne Jeffreys, from Hollywood, made an attractive heroine and sang well, too. Hughes's lyrics were simple, warm and singable. Weill's score was rich, melodic and dramatic, now tender, now moving, now satiric, now gay; it more than fulfilled my expectations. Friedman did an able job of direction. The murder scene gave him a little trouble, but I had staged it so often that I was able to help. Mielziner again created an effective setting.

The three-week tryout in Philadelphia was cataclysmic. The reviews were tepid, the attendance pitiable. Night after night we played to an audience of a few hundred scattered in the vastness of the Shubert Theatre. We had one packed house—on New Year's Eve, when of course every play sells out. Wiman, to lighten the gloom, invited us all to a champagne supper, where we tried to be merry. At one point Wiman's sister said, "I loved the show so much, I'd like to see it again at the matinee. Do you think I could get a ticket?" There was a moment of silence; then Forrest Haring, Wiman's business manager, leaned across the table and with perfect timing said, "Could you use a couple of hundred seats?" Our laughter was not gay.

Without doubt, those were the three longest weeks I have ever lived through. However, we kept working away just as though everything were going smoothly. I had been disturbed by the introduction of choreographic routines that seemed to me out of harmony with the over-all realistic tone. Therefore I was delighted when Moss Hart, after seeing a performance and expressing his enthusiasm, added, "But for God's sake take out all that musical-comedy stuff." The burden of revisions fell upon Weill. Alone among composers for the theatre, he did all his own orchestrating, so every time a change was made, he had to alter the score substantially. I was afraid he would crack up, but in spite of the apparent hopelessness of the whole venture he kept doggedly at it.

My gloom was deepened by the inability of Hughes, here in the cradle of liberty, to find hotel accommodations near the theatre. The rest of us were housed in a luxurious downtown hotel, while he was miles away. One small incident gave me comfort. Late one morning five or six of us, including Hughes, were conferring in the lobby of the Warwick Hotel. Someone suggested lunch. As we approached the dining room, the headwaiter, in his tail-coated majesty, showed signs of attempting to bar our passage. Ignoring him, we swept by en masse and seated ourselves at a large table. We were served without comment.

The Philadelphia operating losses were so heavy that we hardly expected Wiman to bring the production into New York. But he was a proud and a courageous man—and he had faith in the play. On the opening night in New York, a party of us had dinner at a restaurant just across from the theatre. We tried to be casual, but our hearts were heavy. I entered the theatre feeling as though I were on my way to the scaffold. Betty and I sat far back in the balcony, expecting the worst. However, the overture was warmly received, and when the curtain rose the attention of the audience was engaged. Ten minutes later Polyna Stoska's beautiful rendition of her long tragic aria evoked an ovation that literally stopped the show. From that moment on, success was unquestionable. We played for 150 performances, an extraordinary run for an opera; but when the usual seasonal decline set in, Wiman could hardly be blamed for not incurring further losses. So, in spite of continuing public interest, we were obliged to close, as do so many worthy plays before they have exhausted their potential audience.

9

Eight years had elapsed since my last visit to Europe. Remarriage and the birth of my children had kept me from attempting to go abroad during the war years, but now I was eager to return. I thought, too, that a trip would be helpful to Betty, and I looked forward to showing her Paris. A request from the New York center of the P.E.N. Club to represent it at the international congress in Zurich provided a convenient springboard. The P.E.N. Club—P for playwrights and poets, E for editors and essayists, N for novelists— is a world-wide organization that was founded in 1923, under the presidency of John Galsworthy. Its international meetings, held each year in a different country, had, of course, been suspended during the war. The Zurich congress was the first of many I have attended, for I subsequently became a vice-president of the New York center and then an international vice-president. I was in Vienna in 1955, London in 1956, Tokyo in 1957, Paris in 1958, Frankfurt in 1959, Rio de Janeiro in 1960, Rome in 1961, and again in London in 1962.

In the London of 1947 the ravages of the blitz were all too evident. There were flower gardens in Piccadilly; bomb sites had been converted into parking lots. You turned into a street lined with buildings and were startled to find only emptiness behind the façades. Some of Wren's lovely little churches had been destroyed or badly scarred. It was now possible to get a full view of St. Paul's, which had miraculously escaped the fire that had leveled its surroundings.

Everything was shabby, run-down or in short supply. When I thoughtlessly mentioned to a waiter that we had no napkins, he offered us one ragged bit of cloth. Meals were limited to three courses, one of which was bread. I had had numerous food parcels mailed to our London address. When we went visiting we took along dried fruits, chocolate, bacon, marmalade, sardines and other foods the like of which our friends had not seen in years. The extravagant gratitude was both amusing and touching. For those who could afford it, there were such unrationed items as gull's eggs; and we were invited to two or three luxurious dinners obviously supplied by the black market.

It was good to renew contact with my English friends, most of whom had come undaunted through the years of danger and deprivation. There was little talk about the war, and what there was was devoid of heroics. My admiration for England and her people was greater than ever. We visited Victor Gollancz at his country home in Berkshire, where he had conducted his publishing business during the war, housing his staff in cottages nearby. In the garden was the concrete bomb shelter where they had all taken refuge when the Luftwaffe came over, which was often.

Zurich, a pleasant, lively little city, had, of course, been untouched by the war. One member of the American delegation to the P.E.N. congress was Thomas Mann, who had taken up residence in California. He delivered the principal address, a discourse on Goethe, which, I was told, even those who knew German had difficulty in understanding.

A railway strike prevented our taking the train to Paris. No regular plane space was available, but we managed to get two places on an auxiliary plane which turned out to be an old German military transport, with bucket seats ranged along the sides. We were near the rear end, facing the door, which was warped and insecurely fastened by a rope. The safety belts, designed to hook onto soldiers' uniforms, were too short to encircle us. There was no insulation, and it grew decidedly chilly as we soared twenty thousand feet to clear the Alps. Suddenly I saw the radio operator sit up abruptly and scribble something on a scrap of paper, which he handed to the passenger nearest him. I looked down at the jagged peaks of the Mont Blanc massif, speculating on the prospects of an emergency landing. The slip of paper progressed back and forth across the aisle, reaching me at last. I read: "International football, first period: France 2, Italy 1."

Paris had suffered little material damage, though it is hard to understand how it had escaped the psychopathic ferocity of the Nazis. Yet, unlike London, a heavy pall seemed to overlie it, a general apathy that was strange to one who had known the city in happier days. Of course, Paris had been a captive city for four years, London had not. Yet it was a joy to revisit the Louvre, Notre Dame, the Sainte Chapelle, the Opéra, the cafés of Montparnasse, Montmartre and St.-Germain-des-Prés, a joy greatly enhanced by the companionship of Betty.

We went to Chartres and to Mont St.-Michel, visiting en route the invasion beaches incongruously named Omaha and Utah, where we saw the concrete pillboxes pitted by shellfire, and the rotting debris of the landing equipment. In the towns of Caen, Lisieux and Bayeux, where I had last been in 1939, there were rubble heaps everywhere; the once populous market places were meadows in which field flowers bloomed.

In Paris we dined two or three times with Harold J. Laski, who, as adviser to Ernest Bevin, was attending a conference of foreign ministers. At my favorite Alsatian restaurant, La Cigogne, I asked him how his omelet was. He put down his knife and fork and said with great deliberation, "It's not an omelet, it's a poem." I introduced him to a little subterranean cabaret, formerly a prison, called the Caveau des Oubliettes Rouges, where performers in period costumes sang the traditional folk ballads. Laski joined in the singing, in a sort of Cockney French. He was good company— one of the most erudite men I have ever met, and, with the possible exception of Ford Madox Ford, the greatest teller of tall tales. Like Ford, he would relate the most implausible personal experiences with an air of complete veracity. I think both men were so carried away by their narrative powers that they really believed the stories they told. Ford went on talking as long as you kept his glass filled; but Laski required no priming.

10

I was planning another novel, but it was still in its formative stage, so I accepted an offer from Samuel Goldwyn to make a screenplay of *Earth and High Heaven*, a story by a Canadian journalist, Gwethalyn Graham, dealing with a young woman who persists in her attachment to a Jew in spite of the opposition of her family. As a thoroughgoing assimilationist, I believe intermarriage to be one of the best means of breaking down sectarian barriers and lessening racial and religious prejudice. (When I was asked by the National Conference of Christians and Jews to write an article that would promote better relations, I proposed describing the numerous successful intermarriages of which I had personal knowledge. My suggestion was rejected; intermarriage, it seemed, was a subject that it was impolitic to discuss!)

Before undertaking the assignment for Goldwyn, I told him that I thought it unlikely that another picture about anti-Semitism could equal the success of Laura Hobson's *Gentleman's Agreement*, even though the stories were wholly dissimilar. But Goldwyn was determined to go ahead. However, he never made the picture—mainly, I suspect, because of his failure to get the support of leaders of the Jewish community. Stephen S. Wise, for example, refused his endorsement, on the ground that he did not approve of intermarriage.

Strangely enough, almost immediately after finishing this screenplay attacking anti-Semitism I became involved in a long-drawnout, acrimonious controversy with several Jewish organizations on a question of censorship. I had long been a militant opponent of censorship, whether by official action or by the unofficial pressure exerted by special-interest groups. Direct censorship was easier to combat, for official acts were usually subject to review by the courts, which evinced an ever-increasing tendency to support the free-speech guarantees of the Bill of Rights. Private organizations were harder to deal with, even when their "persuasion" implied economic or political reprisal, a type of pressure to which businessmen and officeholders are highly responsive.

There is hardly a racial, religious, ethnic or professional group that does not seek to suppress anything that it regards as contrary to its own beliefs or interests. Doctors, lawyers, veterans, clergymen, social workers, labor unions, associations of varied national origin, all seek to stifle derogation or adverse criticism. This type of control has become a growing menace to freedom of expression, especially in the motion picture and broadcasting fields. Among the worst offenders, mainly because they are the best-organized and numerically the strongest are the Catholic Legion of Decency, which seeks to impose its own standards of morality upon the whole community, and the American Legion, which often succeeds in penalizing those who do not subscribe to its peculiar brand of patriotism.

It has pained me to oppose the attempts of a worthy organization like the National Association for the Advancement of Colored People to ban such diverse material as *The Birth of a Nation, Uncle Tom's Cabin, Amos 'n' Andy*, minstrel shows and *The Green Pastures*, all of which allegedly malign or misrepresent the Negro. I have tried, with some success, I hope, to point out that any claim of special racial privilege is inconsistent with a struggle for equality. Langston Hughes stated the case very well when he said that as a Negro he felt he had as much right as a white man to be depicted as a criminal or a moron.

When Albert Deutsch, a New York newspaper columnist, saw the film version of *Oliver Twist* in London, he wrote a piece whose tone may be fairly described as hysterical, characterizing the picture as flagrantly anti-Semitic and demanding that it never be shown in America. Several Jewish organizations immediately took up the cry, though—familiar story!—no one on this side of the Atlantic had even seen the film. As a result of the hubbub, the American showing was deferred; it seemed probable that the picture would never be exhibited here.

For the next two years I was active in the campaign to bring about the release of the picture. I tried to persuade the Jewish organizations that it was one thing to criticize and condemn the picture, to urge people not to see it, even to picket the theatres in which it might be shown, but quite another to prevent it from being shown at all, for that constituted a restriction upon freedom of expression and a denial of the right of Americans to judge for themselves. In a democratic society there should be no sacred cows; no one should claim immunity from criticism or even from ridicule. It is the essence of the democratic process that all ideas and opinions, good and bad, true and false, be allowed unrestricted expression, in the expectation that eventually the good and the true will prevail. Restriction inevitably produces conformity and stultification and in the end leads to tyranny and enslavement. On the practical side, I suggested that suppression of the picture would fortify the belief that the movie industry is Jewish-controlled, and that the resultant increase in anti-Semitic sentiment would far outweigh any harm that the showing of the picture could conceivably do.

Deutsch's replies to my letters, though spirited, were courteous and well within the bounds of honest controversy. The same could not be said for the communications I received from the heads of several organizations, one of whom, a former justice of the New York Supreme Court, accused me of being a disciple of a profascist named Upton Close, of whom I had not previously heard.

Failing to make progress with the Jewish organizations, I brought the controversy into the open—often an effective technique, for the advocates of suppression then find themselves forced to take the defensive. I had plenty of support from such well-known civil-libertarians as John Haynes Holmes and Arthur Garfield Hays and from many newspaper columnists, including John Mason Brown, Bosley Crowther and John Crosby. In the end, the fight was won and the picture was released. Its exhibition created as little stir as it had in England and in Canada.

But the story has an even more significant ending. Some two years later another picture became an object of controversy. An Italian film, *The Miracle*, which had won prizes in Europe, was, upon its exhibition in New York, denounced as sacrilegious by the Catholic hierarchy. As a result, the license to exhibit was revoked: an action without precedent. Fortunately, this was a case that could be taken into court; more fortunately still, the exhibitor, Joseph Burstyn, was willing to make the fight. When the case reached the United States Supreme Court, I was one of the authors of the amicus brief filed by the American Civil Liberties Union— my only activity as a member of the bar! The Supreme Court not only reversed the ban on *The Miracle* but declared unconstitutional, on the ground of vagueness, the New York statute which forbade the exhibition of "sacrilegious" films.

To my surprise and gratification, I received a letter from Albert Deutsch which might well be studied by all censors and by all those whose special interests prompt them to advocate suppression. It says in part:

> My own reaction to the effort to impose a ban on *The Miracle* revealed to me a contradiction in my own thinking about censorship. I could not honestly condemn a move to ban *The Miracle* and at the same time endorse a move to ban *Oliver Twist*.
>
> Free speech in any form involves inherent dangers, but the way to meet these dangers effectively is to strengthen our democracy, including the right of free speech—not to weaken it at any point.
>
> I still condemn the producers of *Oliver Twist* for doing what they did, but I would not now deny them the right to display the product of their prejudicial slant.

I have said that the fight was won. Perhaps it would have been more correct to say that the skirmish was won, for the fight goes on. Not long ago, the same Jewish organizations that attacked *Oliver Twist* attempted to prevent a telecast by the Columbia Broadcasting System of a performance of Joseph Papp's fine Shakespeare-in-the-Park production of *The Merchant of Venice*. A letter of mine in the New York *Times* evoked the same accusations of fascism and Hitlerism. However, the network went through with the telecast, which won high critical praise and wide popular approval. The most effective answer to pressure is counterpressure.

11

In the course of my civil-liberties activities, I obtained a copy of *Communist Front Organizations*, a report issued by the California Senate's Tenney Committee, so called in honor of its chairman, State Senator Jack B. Tenney. Like its Congressional big brother, the House Un-American Activities Committee, it had spent years of its members' time and thousands of dollars of public money in "investigating," badgering and persecuting any organization or individual, particularly in the fine arts and in the professions, whose views deviated from the most hidebound political orthodoxy. Like Mrs. Elizabeth Dilling's privately printed *The Red Network* some fifteen years earlier, the report was appropriately bound in red. Its four hundred closely printed pages contained descriptions of some two hundred organizations alleged to be Communist fronts, and the names of thousands of individuals who by their membership were undermining the foundations of the American way of life: a truly alarming picture of the nation's peril.

It was not surprising to find five pages devoted to the American Civil Liberties Union, "definitely classed as a Communist front or 'transmission belt' organization." But I was a little startled to see the National Institute of Arts and Letters described as a "Communist front for writers, artists and musicians." I had long looked upon my membership in this august body as one of my few claims to respectability. It seemed, however, that a number of its members had signed a letter protesting the highhanded methods employed by the House Un-American Activities Committee under the chairmanship of J. Parnell Thomas, who later served a term in a Federal prison. Among the more than one hundred signatories to this treasonable letter were James Truslow Adams, Maxwell Anderson, Charles A. Beard, Bernard Berenson, Henry Seidel Canby, Bernard De Voto, Helen Keller, Joseph Wood Krutch, Sinclair Lewis, Archibald Mac-Leish, Marianne Moore, Eugene O'Neill, Robert E. Sherwood, Deems Taylor, Mark Van Doren and Thornton Wilder, as raffish a crew of conspirators as one is likely to find anywhere.

The list of individuals cited is even more extensive than Mrs. Dilling's, though there are certain omissions. Freud and Gandhi, for example, are not included. Einstein rates only six citations, and when I saw that I had received thirteen I felt rather puffed up, for it is not every day that one outdoes Einstein by more than one hundred per cent. Besides belonging to the A.C.L.U. and the National Institute of Arts and Letters, I had, it appeared, sponsored the Artef Theatre, along with Brooks Atkinson, Jed Harris and Orson Welles. I had also supported the Writers' and Artists' Committee for Medical Aid to Spain and had sponsored a Russian War

Relief meeting in Madison Square Garden, at which, as I recall it, General George Marshall was the principal speaker.

One would think that such a nonsensical hodgepodge would be self-defeating; and, indeed, those who were sufficiently independent could afford to laugh the whole thing off. But there were many whose job security or professional future was jeopardized by these irresponsible charges, or who were subjected to all sorts of harassments and annoyances. To give a minor example, Betty had contracted to do a motion picture, but when it came to signing she was told that she would have to explain her association with American Relief for Greek Democracy. Since she had never heard of this organization, she was puzzled and alarmed. Upon investigation I found that the Betty Field cited in the Tenney report was the wife of a New Jersey attorney. The studio apologized, of course, but the fact that its employment policy was governed by the citations was shocking evidence of the effect that the indecent activities of these legislative committees have upon decent people's lives.

12

My preoccupation with censorship and other civil-liberties issues did not interfere with the writing of my novel, a long book called *The Show Must Go On*. It was, in effect, the life history of a play, from the completion of the first draft to the end of the New York run. In my plays the characters have rarely been modeled upon people I actually knew, but in the novel I drew heavily upon my own theatrical experience. The leading characters were a rather naïve young playwright and a hard-boiled New York director-producer. While neither could be called a self-portrait, each presented certain aspects of myself. The central figure was a close approximation of Laura. The theatre which was the scene of much of the action was readily identifiable as the Belasco.

The Playwrights' Company had taken in Kurt Weill, for whom we all had great affection; besides, his keen interest in production made him most helpful to us. Sherwood, in an effort to retrieve his fortunes, collaborated with Irving Berlin on a musical comedy, *Miss Liberty*, which dealt with the inauguration of the Statue of Liberty and the journalistic war between Joseph Pulitzer and James Gordon Bennett. Moss Hart was the director. It seemed an invincible combination. But the show turned out to be a labored, listless work and did not last out the season. Sherwood was greatly disappointed by the poor financial return and by what he considered a loss of prestige. This setback, following the failure of *The Rugged Path*, led him to believe that he was losing his effectiveness as a writer.

Anderson and Weill had also written a musical play, *Lost in the Stars*, based upon *Cry, the Beloved Country*, Alan Paton's masterly novel about the South African race problem. The musical was a beautiful and noble work; yet we had difficulty financing it. Rocketing costs had long since forced us to seek outside backing for our productions, a disturbing departure from the company's original policy. In the end, the production of *Lost in the Stars* was made possible only by all of us going into our own pockets to provide the amount still needed. We never recouped our investment, but I was proud to be even remotely associated with a work that I regard as an important contribution to the American drama.

In the spring of 1949 Betty gave birth to our third child, a lively, impish boy whom we named Paul. *The Show Must Go On* appeared in due course and was well received both here and in England; later there were several foreign publications. I had enjoyed writing it, and it was comforting to know that I was not entirely dependent upon the theatre for a livelihood. Though I still enjoyed my association with the Playwrights' Company, I was uneasy about the changed economic conditions, which made it increasingly difficult to finance plays that did not have an obvious mass appeal, or to keep them running if they did manage to get produced.

After Paul's birth, Betty returned to the stage in *The Rat Race*, a play by Garson Kanin. One matinee day during the Philadelphia tryout, as I stood in the lobby, someone touched my arm. I turned and there was Laura. It was more than ten years since I had had any communication with her. But she had been often in my thoughts, constantly during the writing of *The Show Must Go On*, when I had relived all the days of our ecstasy. She seemed not to have changed at all: the same lithe carriage, the same vivid personality, the same alert, luminous eyes. After the matinee we had a drink with Betty; they were old acquaintances. Then, while Betty rested before the evening performance, Laura and I had dinner. We fell easily into our old give-and-take, catching up with each other's lives. She was living in rural Pennsylvania, was the mother of three daughters and was active in community affairs and local politics. She had had a cancer of the breast, but it had been successfully excised. When we parted after dinner, I was glowing with quiet happiness; I think she was, too.

After that we exchanged letters at long intervals, but I saw her only once again. A year or so after our chance encounter, we lunched together in New York. The old rapport was unimpaired, but there was no question of a resumption of the old relationship. Even if she had been completely unattached, it would have been unthinkable for me. I had committed myself wholly and irrevocably to Betty; since our marriage, no other woman had existed for me. Monogamy was not a matter of morals, but of emotion. Shortly after my marriage I had destroyed all of Laura's letters, scores and scores of them, brimming over with exuberant chitchat and expressions of love. It was hard to do, but I wanted to sever every emotional bond with the past. I kept only a pair of gold cufflinks that she had given me in Paris. I often wish now that I had kept the letters too.

At lunch she told me, not without self-consciousness, that she had long wanted to let me know that the effect of our relationship had been enduring. She was deeply grateful, she said, for the help I had given her in shaping her life. Afterward she wrote me: "As I once told you, you are very responsible for much of my philosophy and my outlook on life, and I have had a lot of time recently to look them over critically and find that they are just as I would like them to be; so again and again, thank you." It is a deeply cherished souvenir.

13

The Rat Race petered out quickly. Feeling that a long sea voyage would be beneficial to Betty, I booked passage once again on one of the little American Export Lines ships that made a circuit of the Mediterranean. A tragic event marked the eve of our departure. Kurt Weill had been hospitalized for some weeks, following a heart attack. We had been greatly relieved to learn that he would soon be discharged. Then had a second attack that killed him. He was only fifty and at the peak of his creative life: a fine human being, generous, intelligent, idealistic, warmhearted. I am not given to weeping, but as I stood beside his grave I could not keep back the tears. His death was a particularly severe blow to Maxwell Anderson, for they had been neighbors, friends and collaborators for many years. A musical play based upon *Huckleberry Finn* and *Tom Sawyer* was never completed. In the years since Kurt's death, his renown has grown. His works have had more and more recognition, thanks largely to the efforts of his widow, Lotte Lenya, who had created in Germany the leading roles in several of his operas. *The Three-Penny Opera,* written in collaboration with Bertolt Brecht, has recently completed an incredibly long run in an off-Broadway theatre.

Our tour took us to places that were familiar to me but new to Betty: Marseilles, with an excursion to Arles, Avignon and the Pont du Gard; Cairo, for two busy days. From Beirut we motored to Damascus, stopping over at Baalbek. Ever since my earlier visit I had wanted to use it as the locale of a play. I finally wrote the play, calling it *Love among the Ruins,* a borrowing from Browning. It was scheduled for production in the coming season. I welcomed the opportunity to obtain photographs to be used in designing the set, and to soak up the atmosphere of mingled grandeur and desolation. With the co-operation of Maynard Owen Williams of *The National Geographic Magazine,* whom I had met in Crete years before, I had been able to get some fine background material. But the Playwrights' Company was unable to finance the production. The play has never been produced, much to my regret, for I happen to like it.

Sherwood too had written a play that was not produced, a farce comedy about which everybody was dubious. Sherwood himself was far from satisfied with it. Failing to interest the Lunts, he kept working at the script, but nothing ever came of it. Anderson had nothing ready; he had not yet recovered from the shock of Kurt's death. All in all, it was a bad year for the company. There were more personal losses, too. Arthur Hopkins, my earliest theatrical acquaintance and the producer of my first play, died at the age of seventy-one. His luck had deserted him; once highly successful, he died almost destitute, and half forgotten. At the funeral services I sat beside another old friend, Walter Huston. When I lamented the passing of Hopkins, Huston said, "Well, we all have to go sometime." Less than three weeks later he was dead.

14

Following the *Oliver Twist* and *Miracle* controversies, I became
deeply involved in a civil-liberties issue of a rather different nature.
In June 1950 there appeared a paperbound book called *Red
Channels*, which, like its numerous predecessors, official and unofficial, contained a listing of alleged Communists or Communist
sympathizers, with appropriate "citations." Subtitled "The Report of
Communist Influence in Radio and Television," *Red Channels* confined itself, however, to naming individuals engaged in broadcasting.
Its publishers were three former Federal Bureau of Investigation
agents who had for some time been issuing a newsletter, *Counterattack*, which directly or by innuendo charged persons in the entertainment field with pro-Communist leanings.

A new wave of antiliberalism was sweeping the country. The in-
quisitions of the House Un-American Activities Committee and the
unscrupulous tactics of Senator Joseph McCarthy encouraged
veterans' organizations and other reactionary groups to intensify
their perennial campaigns against advocates of social change.
Anyone who favored a cause that also had Communist support was
regarded as a Communist sympathizer or tool. *Red Channels* pointed
out that the advocacy of "current issues in which the Party is critically interested: 'academic freedom,' 'civil rights,' 'peace,' the H-
bomb, etc.," could be "cleverly exploited . . . to point up current
Communist goals." It was all very simple. John Jones opposed
segregated schools. The Communist Party also opposed segregated
schools. Therefore, Jones, if not actually a Communist, was at least
a sympathizer or a stooge. If it could be shown that some action of
his had been praised in an obscure Communist publication, his
goose was really cooked.

Since charges of Communist membership invite libel suits, the
publishers of *Red Channels* were at pains to state that the "citations"
were mainly derived from the irresponsible but official reports of
the House Un-American Activities and Tenney committees. It was
further stated that some of the persons listed were "dupes or in-
nocents." However, there was no way of distinguishing the sheep
from the goats. The book's title and subtitle, together with the
cover design of a red hand grasping a microphone, certainly carried

unmistakable implications. As a friend of mine remarked, it was a little like publishing a list of females with a cover portraying a half-clad siren, and stating that not all those mentioned were necessarily women of ill-fame.

Among the names in *Red Channels* were Leonard Bernstein, Marc Connelly, Aaron Copland, Olin Downes, José Ferrer, Ruth Gordon, Judy Holliday, Burl Ives, Gypsy Rose Lee, Burgess Meredith, Arthur Miller, Dorothy Parker, William L. Shirer, Louis Untermeyer and Orson Welles. Even if it were possible to believe that these distinguished artists were either agents or unwitting tools of the Kremlin, it was hard to see how they could have used the broadcasting medium for the execution of their nefarious designs. Actors, of course, do not write the words they speak. Authors' scripts pass through many hands before they reach the air waves. Communist propaganda that escaped the scrutiny of advertising-agency and studio executives must have been so subtle that its penetration of the mass mind seemed highly improbable. Nevertheless, networks, sponsors and advertising agencies, single-minded in their pursuit of the dollar, adopted *Red Channels* as a guide to employment. In fact, it soon became known in broadcasting circles as the bible of Madison Avenue.

A spectacular incident brought this situation to public attention. The General Foods Corporation was sponsoring a television series based upon *The Aldrich Family*, long a popular radio serial. Shortly before the first telecast, Theodore Kirkpatrick, one of the publishers of *Red Channels*, called Mrs. Hester McCullough, a Greenwich, Connecticut, matron with a flair for nosing out subversives, to inform her that Jean Muir, who was to play the leading role, was among those cited. Miss Muir was charged with membership in organizations that favored equal rights for women, equal rights for Negroes and relief for Spanish refugees. She had also signed a message congratulating the Moscow Art Theatre on its fiftieth anniversary.

Mrs. McCullough got busy at once. She alerted Stephen Chess, Queens commander of the Catholic War Veterans, and Rabbi Benjamin Schultz, executive director of the American Jewish League against Communism. Telephone calls to the National Broadcasting Company demanded the dismissal of Miss Muir. Rabbi Schultz is reported to have told the network that he spoke for "more than two million members" of his organization. How he arrived at that figure or what the nature of his mandate was is not clear. At any rate, Miss Muir was promptly dropped, in spite of the fact that she not only denied any Communist affiliation, but also emphatically expressed opposition to Communism.

The episode received ample news coverage: front-page stories, editorials, comments from leading columnists. The dismissal of Miss Muir was generally condemned, though there were some expressions of approval. A talk with Miss Muir and her husband, Henry Jaffe, who was, in fact, attorney for the American Federation of Radio Actors, convinced me that nothing could be done about her particular case. She had been paid in full, and great care had been taken to avoid any charge that might have been the basis for a libel suit. General Foods issued a statement couched in characteristic public-relations doubletalk: "The use of controversial personalities in our advertising may provide unfavorable criticism and even antagonism among sizable groups of customers. . . . General Foods advertising therefore avoids the use of material and personalities which in its judgment are controversial." In other words: We would rather engage in blacklisting than run the risk of losing a dollar.

Patrick M. Malin, executive director of the American Civil Liberties Union, and I joined in a letter to General Foods, the essence of which was: "Just as we oppose censorship by public authority, we deplore suppression by private pressure." Further, at the request of the A.C.L.U. Merle Miller, one of its board members, made a study of the whole subject of blacklisting in the broadcasting industry, which was published under the title *The Judges and the Judged*.

Not long after Miss Muir's dismissal, another General Foods incident attracted attention. At the instigation of *The Tablet*, a Catholic publication, the company decided to drop Philip Loeb, a well-known actor, from the television series called *The Goldbergs*. Thereupon Gertrude Berg, producer and star of the show, threatened not only to withdraw but also to advise people not to buy General Foods' products. Consequently, Loeb was kept on. But shortly afterward the company withdrew its sponsorship for "economy reasons" and the show went off the air. When it was resumed, Loeb was not in it. He had been offered forty thousand dollars to cancel his long-term contract; his financial situation had impelled him to accept. But he felt that his reputation and his career had been irreparably damaged. Indeed, in what remained of his life he never got over it.

Despite the flurries of protest, blacklisting became an almost universal practice, in both the broadcasting and the motion picture fields. Ignoring the basic Anglo-American doctrine that an accused person is presumed innocent until proved guilty, studio and advertising executives preferred to accept uncritically the unsubstantiated charges of private individuals who were cashing in on their campaign of vilification. In fact, they told the accused that it was incumbent upon them to "purge" themselves! Later one of the *Counterattack* group withdrew from it and offered—for a fee, of course—to instruct its victims how this purge could be accomplished.

It is to the eternal credit of the theatre that it did not succumb to the general hysteria. Individual producers or directors may have been influenced by their political opinions in the employment of actors; but there was no blanket policy of exclusion and no knuckling under to pressure groups. When, at a meeting of the executive board of the League of New York Theatres, I introduced a resolution to the effect that, in casting, the fitness of the actor should be the controlling consideration, it was passed almost without opposition.

Unfortunately, it was impossible to adduce legal proof that the blacklisting amounted to a conspiracy, for there was no formal agreement among those who were practicing it. Even in specific instances, failure to engage an actor or a writer was not in itself evidence of blacklisting. One bricklayer or one longshoreman may be as well qualified as another, but with an actor or a writer there are questions of suitability, of personality, of compensation. Even more baffling was the fact that the actor or writer had no way of knowing that he had been rejected. He knew only that since the appearance of his name in *Red Channels* his engagements had been decreasing. One talent agent told me in confidence that he no longer thought it worth while to suggest clients who were listed, since they were certain to be turned down.

Among those blacklisted was my old friend Mady Christians, a fine actress and a woman of exceptional intelligence and sensibility. She had distinguished herself not only on the stage but also in

motion pictures and television. Now suddenly she found herself
deprived of her principal means of livelihood, denied opportunity
to practice her profession, stigmatized as a subversive. It was evident to everyone who knew her that her predicament was seriously
affecting her health as well as her state of mind. In October 1951
she died of a cerebral hemorrhage. She had had high blood pressure,
and there was little doubt that mental and emotional stress had
hastened her death.

From the funeral chapel I went to my office, where I wrote a
letter to the drama editor of the *Times*. To be sure to make the
Sunday edition, I called up Brooks Atkinson, whom I had seen at
the services. He told me to send the letter around at once, adding,
"I just had a call from London from an actor who said that Mady
was murdered." This is what I wrote:

Mady Christians is dead. A great actress, bred in a great tradition, a
fine, vital, liberal, warmhearted human being, her career was brought
to an untimely end by the relentless, sadistic persecution to which she
was subjected. No one who knew her or who saw her during the last
tortured months of her life can doubt that her death was hastened, if
not actually caused, by the small-souled witch hunters who make a fine
art of character assassination. She stood for what is best in American
art and in American life; and as a reward, she was slandered, falsely accused, hounded by the F.B.I., deprived of employment, faced with
destitution. There is no use appealing to the conscience of the Mc-
Carthyites: obviously they have none. But perhaps the martyrdom of
Mady Christians will set freedom-loving citizens thinking about what is
happening to art and to democracy in America.

The publication of the letter brought a flood of responses. A few
took the McCarthy–*Red Channels* line, but the majority sided with
me. My name had not been included in *Red Channels;* now the
publishers of *Counterattack* revealed the fact that I too was
"suspect." The old Dilling and Tenney "citations" were dusted off;
a few new ones were added. It seems I was among those who had
protested the exclusion from the United States of Hewlett Johnson,
the "Red Dean" of Canterbury. I shared the view of Winston
Churchill that toleration of the dean was not too high a price to
pay for preservation of the principle of free speech.

My letter to the *Times* had been reprinted in the *Daily Worker,*
which, according to *Counterattack,* made me a "hero" of the Com-

munist Party. It was pointed out that I was one of a group of "leading playwrights" who had long "front records." Others named as members of this group of Kremlin underlings were Clifford Odets, Lillian Hellman, Marc Blitzstein, Garson Kanin, Arthur Miller, Arthur Laurents and Oscar Hammerstein II. When Brooks Atkinson wrote a column deploring the effect that "ignorant heresy hunting and bigoted character assassination" were having upon the vitality of the American arts, *Counterattack* retorted that the article "read like a *Daily Worker* editorial."

While the furor about Mady Christians was still at its height, I became directly engaged in the blacklisting controversy. With nine other playwrights, I had a contract with the Celanese Corporation for the television presentation of two plays by each of us. It was provided that "the plan should so operate as to permit each playwright to have maximum casting and other production participation to the extent that he may desire it." It seemed like a good setup artistically as well as financially.

I was to be represented on the program by *Counsellor-at-Law* and *Street Scene*. When the former was put into production, I expressed my uncertainty about the actor who was being considered for the lead, a doubt which, it appeared, the agency shared. I suggested Paul Muni or Gregory Peck. Neither being available, I was asked for further suggestions. I named Lee J. Cobb, Edward G. Robinson, Sam Wanamaker, José Ferrer and John Garfield. The attorney for the Ellington Advertising Agency told me that none of them was acceptable—they were all in *Red Channels!* Of course it had not occurred to me to consult the bible of Madison Avenue before making my selections. In any case, Wanamaker, Cobb, Ferrer and Robinson were unavailable, Robinson for the excellent reason that he was appearing in the Playwrights' Company production of the anti-Communist play *Darkness at Noon*.

So it came down to Garfield, who, everybody agreed, was an excellent choice. But the agency's attorney would not accept him. I said I would not insist if someone equally good could be found. When no adequate substitute was suggested, I sent for Garfield, who, oddly enough, had had a small part in the original stage production of the play. I asked him point-blank if he was a Communist. He replied that he had testified under oath that he was not, a fact confirmed by his attorney, Louis Nizer. But the advertising agency took the position that he was a "controversial figure"; besides, his wife was suspected of dubious affiliations!

It seemed to me time to make a public issue of this outrageous situation by exercising my contractual right to withdraw from the program. To do so entailed a considerable financial loss; it also forced me to divert attention from my play *The Grand Tour*, which I was just putting into rehearsal. But I felt that it had to be done.

In a carefully worded letter addressed to the program's sponsor, I said: "As an anti-Communist . . . I have repeatedly denounced the men who sit in the Kremlin for judging artists by political standards. I do not intend to acquiesce when the same procedure is followed by political commissars who sit in the offices of advertising agencies or business corporations." And in conclusion: "It has been broadly hinted to me that if I took this step and made my reasons public, I could expect reprisals: in other words, the banning of my own plays on the air waves. That is a risk I am prepared to run. I could not live happily with myself if I allowed economic considerations to deter me from exposing an ugly blot upon American life and an ugly threat to American liberty."

I released the letter at a press conference held on the stage where I was rehearsing *The Grand Tour*. The story received the wide coverage I had hoped for. In the main, my action was supported in editorials and in the columns of such influential writers as John Gould, John Crosby and Max Lerner. I was deluged by letters, telegrams and telephone calls, most of them commendatory. In the midst of all this hubbub, *The Grand Tour* opened and closed in a week. It was far from a total loss, however, for it has had numerous foreign productions, and more radio and television performances both here and abroad than any other play of mine.

The publicity given to my withdrawal from the Celanese program prompted many persons already alarmed by the excesses of McCarthyism to make known to the network and to the program's sponsors their disapproval of blacklisting—exactly the sort of counterpressure I had hoped for. I soon received a visit from the agency's head, Jesse Ellington, who said he wanted me back on the program. I replied that I asked only for the assurance that casting would be determined by fitness and not by political considerations. He readily agreed and we issued a joint statement. Understandably enough, Ellington did not want to admit past blacklisting, but the announcement made it clear that there would be none in the future. Shortly afterward Aline MacMahon telephoned me to say that she had been offered a part in one of the Celanese productions, her first television engagement in several years. There followed a gradual abatement in blacklisting, both on Madison Avenue and in Hollywood. Recently, John Henry Faulk brought a damage suit against those responsible for his having been blacklisted. The jury awarded him the staggering sum of $3,500,000.

15

It had become evident that the three surviving members of the Playwrights' Company could not supply enough hit plays to keep the company solvent. My play *The Grand Tour* had just failed; so had Maxwell Anderson's *Barefoot in Athens,* a play about Socrates. Sherwood had not succeeded with the revisions of his farce comedy; and another play of his, *The Better Angels,* which dealt with the Mormons, was not ready for production. Neither play was ever produced, nor was another of Anderson's studies of the royal houses of England, *The Cavalier.* Our efforts to find new members, particularly younger ones, had failed. Play production was becoming more and more a wild gamble. It was increasingly difficult to get backing, especially for serious plays with limited appeal; the experimental play was ruled out almost entirely. Rising costs necessitated an increase in ticket prices, beyond the range of thousands of theatre lovers. In thirty years, despite the population growth, the number of Broadway theatres and of Broadway productions had shrunk by more than fifty per cent. There was a corresponding decline in road companies and in the cities that could be profitably visited.

The survival of the Playwrights' Company now depended upon the production of outside plays that promised box-office success, and upon the assurance of financing. Accordingly, we took in Roger L. Stevens, a large-scale real-estate operator with a passion for the theatre. He had already been associated with several Broadway productions and had connections that apparently made it easy for him to get backing for plays.

His first activity as a member of the company was to acquire the rights to *The Fourposter,* a sentimental comedy by the Dutch writer

Jan de Hartog. It had only two characters, ably portrayed by Hume Cronyn and his wife, Jessica Tandy. At the Wilmington tryout we all felt that the play was mildly entertaining but quite trivial; we thought its chances of success were dubious. It ran on Broadway for nearly two years. Because of the relatively low production and operating costs, it was the most profitable play the company ever produced. So the day was saved—financially, at least.

CHAPTER

XX

Catastrophe

1

When the Cronyns decided to take *The Fourposter* on tour, the Playwrights' Company engaged Burgess Meredith and Betty to replace them in New York. Betty's part was almost as long and as difficult as her role in *Dream Girl;* with only two characters in the play, she had to be on stage continually. She was reluctant to undertake it. Her health was not good, and she had psychological problems too. But to further the career that meant so much to her she had to go on working. I suspended my own activities in order to be able to help her in any way that I could.

There was a week's preliminary engagement at the Lydia Mendelssohn Theatre on the campus of the University of Michigan. With some medical assistance and such moral support as I could supply, Betty got through. Her fine performance as well as Meredith's delighted the audiences. Later in New York the reviews were enthusiastic, and the play continued to prosper. But for Betty every performance was an ordeal. There were nights when she found it almost impossible to go on. In desperation, she decided upon a measure she had long considered: a resort to psychoanalysis.

Her decision disturbed me greatly, not because of any foreboding about the future of our relationship, whose indestructibility I never doubted, but because of my skepticism about psychoanalytic therapy. I had become acquainted with Freud's theories in my early twenties. In fact, his writings had given me clues to human behavior that had had an important influence upon my work, particularly in *The Adding Machine, The Subway* and *Dream Girl.* They had also given me a clearer insight into the motives and determinants of my own conduct.

But it is one thing to use Freudian theory as an aid to better understanding of oneself and others, quite another to surrender unreservedly to a therapeutic technique that, as even its staunchest advocates admit, is far from an exact science. A firm believer in the theory of natural selection might well hesitate about becoming the subject of an experiment in eugenics, or might even be doubtful about the value of eugenical experiments. To put it another way, I would be reluctant to use a potent drug intended to relieve a particular ailment unless I was sure that its collateral effects had been carefully tested. I suppose that psychoanalysis, like medicine, must have its guinea pigs, but I did not want to be one, nor have someone dear to me be one.

Because of the close relationship between patient and analyst, I was extremely wary about the qualifications of the practitioners of this dubious technique. The character, personality or even the mentality of the skilled surgeon, heart specialist or oculist are of small importance to the patient, but these become dominant factors when one lowers all defenses and lays bare one's inner life. This exposure, it seems to me, should be made only to a person of exceptional integrity, sensitivity and self-discipline. I had had no occasion to consult analysts professionally, since fortunately I have had no phobia, anxiety, compulsion or inner conflict that I have not been able to cope with. But I had had social contacts with numerous analytic practitioners and only too often found them vain, dogmatic, insensitive, dissolute or downright stupid.

The most eminent of these was Alfred Adler, who on the occasion when I met him was loud and opinionated, constantly interrupting and contradicting—behaving so boorishly, in fact, that the other dinner guests were reduced to silence and the hosts painfully embarrassed. On an ocean voyage I sat at table with one of Freud's best-known disciples, author of several books on psychoanalytic theory. When, at the captain's dinner, some homosexuals appeared in female attire, he became almost apoplectic with rage, muttering that he would like to kill them. Some months later I heard that he had entered a mental hospital. At another dinner party I overheard the hostess warn one of the women guests not to get into a taxi with a well-known analyst who was the guest of honor. At still another party a highly regarded practitioner informed me, with a drunken leer, that she was analyzing a close friend of mine and knew all about my private life—a shocking breach of professional ethics, I thought. Another told me gleefully at cocktails that he had had a most satisfactory afternoon exchanging scatological stories with a group of eight-year-old boys. And an intimate friend, herself a psychiatrist, told me that her analyst, a man at the top of the profession, had taken advantage of her dependence upon him and forced her to submit to sexual relations. It is certainly not my intention to malign a whole profession upon the basis of a few incidents that may have been exceptional. Undoubtedly there are analysts who are conscientious as well as able; but we all tend to base our opinions—and our prejudices—upon personal experience; mine were not calculated to inspire confidence in the therapists.

What I worried most about was the effect the long, harrowing inquisition might have upon Betty. Acquaintances had told me of the agonies they had suffered. Some, finding them unendurable, had given up; others went on year after year, never seeming to find the curative self-understanding they were seeking. Others, who had "completed" their analysis, seemed worse off than when they began. They had become cynical and caustic; they had discovered no dynamic substitute for the harmful illusions that had been stripped away. Like the pilgrims at Lourdes, they had thrown away their crutches but had not learned to walk. Again I was basing my conclusions on my own limited observation. Undoubtedly there are individuals who have been materially helped by psychoanalysis.

In spite of my uneasiness, I made no great effort to dissuade Betty: the decision, I felt, must be hers. Had I foreseen the consequences, I would have fought desperately to make her change her mind. For her submission to analysis was to mean for me the abrupt ending of ten years of happiness and the eventual collapse of a marriage that had become the core and substance of my whole life.

Knowing that in the early stages of analysis the patient undergoes an upheaval that twists relationships and distorts values, I was pre-

pared for a certain amount of disturbance and tension. But I had
not expected a sudden disintegration of our gay, warm family life,
nor a replacement of harmony and rapport by a sense of strain and
estrangement that made communication no longer possible. Almost
overnight a wall sprang up, or rather a barbed-wire entanglement
that met all attempts at penetration with painful lacerations.

I tried to bring logic and reason into play, telling myself that if
I could only be patient enough, tactful enough, the situation would
cure itself in time. I had to rely upon that hope, because I had put
all my emotional and spiritual resources into this marriage, confident
that it would endure until the end of my days, and growing more
confident with each successive year of happiness. It may seem that
I had succumbed to self-delusion, that I had been living in a fool's
paradise. But it was not so; there was nothing delusory about my
happiness: it was solid and real. I did not regret my reckless self-ex-
penditure; its rewards had been lavish. Nothing could deprive me of
what I had had; that was pure gain. But it was not easy to contemplate the destruction of what had been fashioned with so much love,
so much joy, such high aspirations. I could only hang on and hope for
the best.

The hope was vain. Things went from bad to worse. The decade
of idyllic happiness was followed by years of acute misery. I tried
to keep myself occupied. I spent even more time than usual with
my children, finding solace in their companionship, and anxious, too,
that their emotional security, fostered by the atmosphere of love in
which they had been reared, should not be undermined. I worked
away at a new play, *The Winner;* but it was hard to concentrate. I
agreed with my colleagues that it required considerable revision, so
I put it aside.

There was one brief respite. The Theatre Guild engaged Betty for
a summer tryout of a play called *Second Fiddle*. I was asked to direct. Though the play had a certain charm, I was not particularly
interested in it. But I welcomed the opportunity to work with Betty
again. Besides, there was a part in it for our daughter Judy, who
even at the age of nine wanted to become an actress. I worked
zealously on strengthening the script and on the production, thankful for the renewal of comradeship and the revival of family spirit.
We played in Westport, Connecticut, and on Cape Cod. The play
went well enough, but the Theatre Guild decided not to bring it

into New York. So the contact was broken and the process of deterioration continued.

To my dismay, Betty, known for her charm and her comedic gift, accepted a most unattractive part in a very bad play by Dorothy Parker and Arnaud d'Usseau, *Ladies of the Corridor*. In the cast were Edna Best, Frances Starr and June Walker, onetime stars, all of whom had parts that were more rewarding than Betty's. At the Philadelphia tryout I was depressed by the hopelessness of the play and the utter waste of Betty's talent. Her unhappiness about her part, and the play's swift closing in New York, intensified her disturbed state.

2

I returned grimly to work, struggling now against an organic ailment that had been aggravated by my emotional and mental turmoil. I wrote a suspense melodrama in which I had so little interest that I did not even try to get a production. For a time I worked on a futile project to base a series of television plays on the paintings of Grandma Moses. I did not care much what I did, so long as I kept busy. Meanwhile, I had revised *The Winner*. I had written the play with Betty in mind. The part was well suited to her, but she was unwilling to do it. Reluctantly I allowed myself to be persuaded to engage an actress about whom I had grave doubts.

My ailment had become so acute that surgery was unavoidable. The only sensible course was to get it over with immediately. But I was determined to go ahead with the production of *The Winner*, partly because of a stubborn unwillingness to submit to physiological exigencies, but mainly because I thought the play might provide a source of revenue for my family in case I did not survive the operation. With three young children to look out for, and Betty's earning capacity impaired by the state of her health, I had the economic situation very much on my mind. So I persuaded my surgeon to take remedial measures that would tide me over until the play was produced.

Of all the foolish things I have ever done, this was certainly the most foolish. I still marvel that I was able to live through those three months. Not only was I in constant pain, but in my weakened condition I became afflicted with something new in my experience:

a plague of boils. The rehearsal period was bad enough, but the tryout in Buffalo, Cleveland and Pittsburgh was almost unendurable. Some of my colleagues came to Buffalo to offer words of encouragement, but from then on I was on my own.

Betty came out for one night, but that was worse than nothing, for her visit was obviously prompted by a sense of duty. I had never felt so alone or so miserable. The midwinter weather was bone-chilling. I did nothing but creep from my bed to the theatre and back again, except one day when I made a round-trip flight to New York for an emergency treatment. My condition was not helped by the deficiencies of my actress, nor by her resistance to corrective suggestions. All my torments availed little for, though the play did well enough on the tryout, it ran only four weeks in New York.

There was only one compensation—a sort of consolation prize, as it were. In one scene of *The Winner* a judge presides at the hearing of a will contest. In casting the play, it occurred to me to engage a Negro for the part, for here was an opportunity, for once, to show a Negro who was not involved in a racial problem, but was simply functioning normally as a professional man. I offered the part to Frederick O'Neal, whose performance more than justified my selection. One or two critics charged me with arbitrarily dragging the race issue into the play, whereas I had done exactly the opposite, for there was not one reference to the judge's race. However, to my great satisfaction, I received the Canada Lee Foundation award "for courage and leadership toward integration in the performing arts." To complete my gratification, the presentation was made by Alan Paton, author of *Cry, the Beloved Country,* for whom I had the highest admiration.

3

A few days before the opening of *The Winner,* I had sent a first-night invitation to Laura. She telegraphed: "Unfortunately I am hospitalized and see little chance of talking my way out by Wednesday. I hope your own hospital stay will be as brief and pleasant as possible. Perhaps some spring day we can compare surgical notes." That day was never to arrive. Just as I was preparing to enter the hospital, a friend of Laura's called to tell me that the recurring cancer had reached her lung and she had died on the operating table.

At any time the news would have been shattering. As it was, I was overwhelmed by a sense of cumulative disaster. But I reflected that it would have been even harder to bear had I married Laura.

In spite of my physical and mental state, I did not want to die. I was not afraid of death; I simply wanted to go on living. The will to live, coupled with a basically robust constitution, enabled me to survive the operation and to make a quick recovery. The friendly ministrations of a cheery, warmhearted nurse did much to help me. But the home to which I returned was not a happy one; it was hard for me to keep up my morale.

My one objective now was to hold the family together at any cost. Betty had been expressing increasing dissatisfaction with country life, so I proposed that we move to New York. A return to the city was wholly repugnant to me, but I hoped that under living conditions more agreeable to Betty we might be able to go back, if not altogether to the old happy order of things, at least to a viable family life. I could not bring myself to sell the Stamford house, so attached had I become to it in the twelve years we had lived there: the only home in which I had ever taken real pride or known complete happiness. Besides, I clung to the hope that one day we would all move back there. So I rented the main house, keeping the guest cottage for weekend visits and as a place of retirement when I felt a need for solitude.

To relieve the domestic tension and to keep myself busy, I accepted an invitation to spend two months at the University of Michigan, lecturing and staging a student production of *Dream Girl*. For one who had left school at fourteen, it was an interesting experience. Somewhat to the landlord's puzzlement, I rented an apartment intended for five students. I like spacious quarters— probably because of the congestion of my childhood home—and I preferred my own cookery to the town's fare. I soon had a wide circle of faculty and student acquaintances. The *Dream Girl* production went very well. I was able to find two very good graduate students for the leading roles. As a happy aftermath, they married. Later they moved to New York, where I have had the pleasure of seeing them and their growing family now and again.

I tried to readjust myself to life in New York, but without much success. Nevertheless, I went to work on a new play, *As the Sparks Fly Upward*, suggested by the Book of Job. The choice of subject was undoubtedly influenced by my own experiences of the past few years. Perhaps it was the plague of boils that set me off! Not that I was so fatuous as to identify myself with Job, or that the play's characters and episodes in any way related to my own life. But I was temporarily obsessed by the situation of a man who suddenly discovers that his house is founded upon a quicksand and not, as he believed, upon a rock. In deference to my colleagues' opinion that the play's defects outweighed its merits, I put it aside, then went back to it again, and kept working away at it. But at length I gave it up: another wasted effort.

4

When Betty went to Hollywood to appear in the motion picture version of William Inge's *Picnic*, taking our youngest child, Paul, with her, I set out with John and Judy, aged twelve and eleven, to attend the P.E.N. Club Congress in Vienna. On my previous visit, Vienna had lain grim and inert, the truncated head of a dismembered empire. Now it was patching up the wounds of another war, but the atmosphere was brisk and alert. Everyone was looking forward to the reopening of the reconstructed opera house. There was general jubilation over the ending of the Allied occupation, particularly the imminent departure of the Russians.

Though P.E.N. is a cultural organization, one hears echoes of the cold war at the sessions. The Soviet Union is not a member, but the representatives of centers in the satellite countries introduce inno-cent-sounding resolutions that are in effect political propaganda; whereas Western delegates protest censorship and the imprison-ment of writers for their political opinions. There is even a minority that favors expulsion of all centers in totalitarian countries, since P.E.N. members are pledged "to oppose any form of suppression of freedom of expression in the country and community to which they belong." My own feeling is that writers are not responsible for the policies of their governments, and that it is better to permit them to have contact with their fellow writers than to exclude them from the community of letters.

The children participated eagerly in everything, even attending a meeting of a labor union at which I made a speech. They were de-lightful traveling companions, gay and alert; we had a merry time.

It pleased me to receive compliments on their good behavior from many of the delegates; it is the prevailing European opinion that all American children are precocious, ill-mannered little brats.

En route to Dubrovnik, where I was representing the American National Theatre and Academy at a congress of the International Theatre Institute (an agency of UNESCO), we stopped in Belgrade to see a performance of *Dream Girl* at the Yugoslav National Theatre. We sat in the official box occupied by Tito when he attended the theatre. The effects of the war bombardments were, after ten years, still visible everywhere in Belgrade. On a high hill is a grim war monument, the work of the great sculptor Ivan Meštrović, who, though he lives in exile, an avowed enemy of the Tito regime, is regarded as a sort of national hero.

At the University of Belgrade I was impressed by the students' knowledge of American literature and their eagerness to learn more. The great difficulty was getting hold of American books. Because of the pinchpenny policies of Congress, the little circulating library of the United States Information Service did not begin to meet the demands of Belgrade's inhabitants. When I returned to America I did what I could to stimulate the sending of books, but of course my efforts were trivial. The cost of one bomber that is obsolete before completion would provide enough books to win thousands of friends for us throughout the world.

Dubrovnik, formerly Ragusa, on the Adriatic, is an ancient walled town that surpasses anything on the Italian or French Riviera and, on a small scale, almost rivals Venice in beauty. We attended the opening of Dubrovnik's annual theatre festival, one of the permanent features of which is the performance of *Hamlet* high up on the battlements of the old fortress, a setting far more dramatic than Elsinore.

Nehru was on an official visit to Yugoslavia, and Tito brought him down to Dubrovnik. I attended a gala outdoor performance of the excellent Yugoslav National Ballet in honor of the two leaders. As they entered with a small party, the audience rose and applauded; Tito and Nehru waved, took seats in the front row, and the performance began. There was no fuss or ceremony; no guards or evidence of security measures. I was surprised by the informality and casualness of it all.

After an extensive tour of Italy, whose high spot for me was mak-

ing the acquaintance of the Giotto frescoes in the austere Basilica of
San Francesco at Assisi, we flew to Paris. I wondered how the children would respond to its beauty and was delighted by their quick
perception of it. It was good to see them enjoying aesthetic experiences of which my own childhood had been devoid. There was
a big Picasso show in the Louvre, mostly paintings of his cubist
period. At first the children giggled; then they began discovering
the arms, legs and features of the *Seated Woman*, or whatever it
happened to be. Their apparent understanding of the paintings attracted the notice of bewildered visitors, and soon they were being followed about the gallery by a dozen adults, who listened at-
tentively to their interpretations.

By way of London, we went to Edinburgh for the festival. Edinburgh is an attractive city for a sojourn, if one does not mind rain
and pretends not to notice the food. The festival is splendid, offering a rich, varied program of drama and music. But at an all-Bach
concert I had a harrowing experience. During our four-month trip
I had tried to keep my marital problem in the background. We had
been continually on the move, meeting people and seeing things,
and I had had a happy time with the children, so I had been able to
avoid thinking too much about my troubles. I wrote frequently to
Betty, mainly detailed descriptions of the children's activities. She
wrote to us jointly, thereby avoiding intimacy. It had been my hope
that after the long separation we would somehow find our way back
to each other. But as we neared the end of the trip I had to face the
fact that the hope was illusory, that the future held no promise.
Seated in the concert hall, I was flooded by memories of happier
days. The noble purity of the music awakened an aching realization of what I had lost and a yearning to recapture it. I felt a con-
striction that was almost unendurable. It was all I could do to keep
from shouting in protest.

5

With our return to New York, the summer's happiness came to an
abrupt end. As I had feared, the barrier was more impenetrable
than ever. I did not know what to do or how to plan for the future.
My homecoming was further saddened by news of the death of my
dear friend Aline Bernstein. I had visited her shortly before I left

for Europe, and it had been pitiable to see her, once so gay and alert, confined to a wheel chair, hardly able to speak or lift her hand.

Soon there was another blow: the death of Robert Sherwood. He had long been in ill-health, his condition worsened by worries about finances and about his career. Though he had done well with the motion picture *The Best Years of Our Lives* and with his Pulitzer Prize–winning book *Roosevelt and Hopkins,* it had been fifteen years since he had had a success in the theatre, where his heart really lay. It became my melancholy task to write a memorial piece for the New York *Times,* in which I tried to show how his work reflected his character and his psychological conflicts.

It seemed to me that the time had come to dissolve the Playwrights' Company. We had long departed from the original purpose, the co-operative production of our own plays. Nor had we succeeded in drawing in a group of younger playwrights who would perpetuate the company's aims. The only newcomer was Robert Anderson, whose *Tea and Sympathy* we had produced with great success. But though he was an able writer, he was not prolific. My troubled state made my productivity very uncertain, too. Maxwell Anderson kept working away, but his anxiety to get something on led to hasty writing that impaired his work. What was more, the fun and the creativeness had gone out of the enterprise. The meetings, once so stimulating, were now routine and businesslike, becoming more and more infrequent as the activities centered upon the production of outside plays in which we took little interest. However, in view of the general reluctance to disband the company, I agreed to continue my membership.

Indeed, I was too disturbed by the crisis in my personal life to care much about anything else. Shortly after Sherwood's death, I returned from a Stamford weekend to find that Betty had left me, taking our two younger children with her. I was utterly stunned and bewildered. Then rebellion surged up in me. I could not deny her right to leave me if she chose, but I could find no justification for having my children torn from me. I began legal proceedings for their recovery, but when I contemplated the sordid bickering that would ensue, as well as the inevitable newspaper publicity, I could not bring myself to go ahead. I was unwilling to make a display of the collapse of a deeply cherished relationship, and to subject my children to it. So a private settlement was made. In consenting to a divorce, I knew that I was throwing away my one effective bargaining point, and that Betty's not overscrupulous advisers would be quick to take advantage of it. But I do not believe in involuntary bondage and was unwilling to prevent her from getting her freedom. Subsequently she obtained a Mexican divorce and then, as I had expected, remarried.

While the negotiations dragged on, month after month, I kept trying to find some way to adjust myself to the radically altered conditions of my life. I had to maintain my morale, not only for my own sake but also for the sake of John, who continued to live with me: the only benefit I had obtained from the settlement. I felt it necessary to maintain a household, if only to provide a place where my children could visit me in comfort. Besides, though long a rover, I was never a nomad. The intensive domesticity of my childhood and youth had been followed by forty years of marriage, so I had never been without some form of family life.

6

It was a barren time, a time of no progress and no hope. To keep myself occupied, I worked away at my Job play; I was in no state to attempt anything new. An invitation to head the American delegation to the P.E.N. congress in London was welcome indeed.

Two busy months in England provided, if not forgetfulness, a slackening of tension. As always, I enjoyed the contacts with writers from many lands. I met the leaders of the two major political parties: R. A. B. Butler at a session of the congress which he addressed, Hugh Gaitskell at tea in the imposing mansion of the Speaker of the House of Commons. We were also received by the Lord Mayor of London, ceremoniously attired. The American center gave a luncheon at the Guildhall, at which I acted as master of ceremonies, introducing the American ambassador, Winthrop Aldrich. With J. B. Priestley, André Maurois, Mark Aldanov and a few others, I went to Clarence House for tea with the Queen Mother and Princess Margaret, two gracious ladies who made one feel quite at ease. I found the tiny Princess far prettier than her photographs made her appear. Perhaps most pleasant of all was a visit to Cambridge, where a small party of us lunched with the master of Trinity and had tea with E. M. Forster, who, heedless of a downpour, took us on a tour of the gardens.

I spent about ten days in Liverpool assisting in the production of *Dream Girl* by the Repertory Company. It was pleasant to be working in the theatre again, even if only in an advisory capacity. But I was disturbed, as I had been in London, by evidences of growing racial tension. The influx of Negroes from the British West Indies had created uneasy situations in employment, housing and sex relations. The antagonism seemed to be localized and motivated largely by economic factors, but it was discouraging to see the color line being drawn in England too.

Going back to New York was even harder than it had been a year before; now there was not even a faint glimmer of hope. Further, John was off to boarding school in Vermont. I had heartily approved his wish to go. I felt that being away from New York would relieve the strain of constant awareness of the family division, as indeed it did. His absence left me entirely alone, with no pattern to my life and nothing to look forward to. I began half a dozen work projects, but made no progress with them. I kept as busy as I could: reading, going to plays and concerts, dining out and giving dinner parties, spending some weekends in Stamford with Judy and Paul, even making some new and stimulating friendships.

So, by this means and that, I struggled through another year. The next P.E.N. congress was in Tokyo, and again I was asked to lead the American delegation. I was eager to revisit Japan, and, finding that the flight to Tokyo and back was almost as long as circumnavigation of the earth, I decided to make a round-the-world trip of it.

Beirut had become a crossroads of international airlines, with a profusion of villas, luxury hotels and night clubs. But on a tour of the city I came suddenly upon a slum quarter as wretched as any I had ever seen: massed, tumble-down hovels swarming with ragged inhabitants. These were the Arab refugees from Israel, who subsisted without hope upon doles from the United Nations. There were conflicting stories about the reasons for their plight, but about their miserable state there could be no doubt.

In Karachi I was a guest of the Pakistani government, thanks to my friend Ahmed Bokhari, undersecretary of the United Nations, whom I had first met at a luncheon party given by Dag Hammerskjold in honor of Karl Ragnar Gierow, director of the Royal Theatre of Stockholm. I dined with Major General Iskander Mirza, President of Pakistan, soon to be deposed.

The refugee problem was very much in evidence in Karachi too. On a visit to the university, I saw, on the rooftops opposite, the same sort of shack I had seen in Beirut. Here lived the Moslem exiles from India, as badly off as their Lebanese counterparts. It was distressing, too, to hear of the difficulties encountered by the Pakistanis in crossing the Indian corridor that separates East from West Pakistan. I could not understand why Nehru, a disciple of Gandhi, did nothing to alleviate an antagonism that seemed based solely upon religious differences. Religious leaders preach love and brotherhood, but sectarian bigotry forever foments hatred, injustice and bloodshed.

During my stay in Bangkok I was able to fulfill a wish that had seemed impossible of realization. In 1931 I had seen at the great Colonial Exposition in Paris a replica of a section of the temple at Angkor in Cambodia. I was eager to see the original, but did not expect ever to be able to visit this remote region. Now I found that Siem Reap, the site of Angkor, two days distant from Bangkok by road, was only an hour and a half away by air. The Bangkok airport at dawn was truly international. Every few minutes a plane departed for Saigon, Manila, Hongkong, Athens, Cairo, Calcutta or Singapore; the waiting room was crowded with Sikhs, Japanese, Koreans, Hindus, Chinese and Arabs, all in their characteristic dress.

The remains at Siem Reap, consisting chiefly of the Angkor Wat, the temple, and Angkor Thom, the citadel, structures built from the tenth to the twelfth century by the Khmers and rescued from the overgrowing jungle only in the nineteenth, rank high among the creative marvels of the world. The abundance and magnificence of architectural and sculptural detail are overwhelming. The façades are covered with a rich tapestry of stone carving that depicts not only vivid scenes of marine and land warfare, but also —like Egyptian tomb paintings, the windows at Chartres and the façade of the cathedral at Amiens—vignettes of the manners and occupations of the people.

Hongkong, with its beautiful natural setting and brisk air of sophistication, reminded me strongly of San Francisco. Many of the Chinese residents were obviously wealthy; as everywhere, the well-to-do Chinese women had great chic. But again there was the pitiable spectacle of refugees, this time from the Communist mainland. Thousands were huddled in grass huts on the terraced hillsides of Victoria Island, where they scratched out some sort of living. It is to the great credit of the British that they are trying to relieve the situation. I saw several decent-looking housing complexes that were being made available to refugees. I drove with my half-Portuguese, half-Chinese guide to the border of Communist China, only a few miles from Hongkong, which is, in effect, an internment camp from which one can escape only by sea or air.

The American delegation to the Tokyo congress presented a fine cross section of contemporary American letters. It included John Steinbeck, Elizabeth Janeway, John Dos Passos, John Hersey, Lewis Galantière, Karl Shapiro, John Brooks, Elizabeth Vining, Ralph Ellison, Donald Keene and Robie Macauley. The Japanese, avid students of American literature, were greatly impressed. Again it was evident that these cultural contacts did much to generate good will and to further international understanding.

Except for the area around the imperial palace, which had been spared in the bombardment, I found Tokyo hardly recognizable. The process of Westernization had been apparent enough in 1936, but now the city seemed completely Americanized with its roaring traffic, hustle and bustle, *espresso* cafés, hamburger joints and night spots. As one sat in the bar of the Imperial Hotel over a Scotch-and-soda, watching a televised baseball game, walked through an up-to-the-minute department store, went to a theatre that showed the latest Hollywood releases, or simply roamed the streets, one might have thought oneself in Detroit. When I deplored the replacement of the charming Japanese costume by tacky Western dress, the retort was "Well, you can't hop a bus or operate a typewriter in a kimono."

At the Kabuki Theatre I marveled again at the perfection of the performance and at the contrast between its technical resources and the outmoded equipment of American theatres. I saw also a specially staged performance of a noh play, my first experience of the classical theatre of Japan, now regarded as rather esoteric and archaic. The legendary substance of the play was only of moderate interest, but the artistry was profound: the imaginativeness of the simple, stylized production; the haunting music; the exquisite harmony of gesture and dance. I was deeply moved, alien though the idiom was.

It was good to meet again some old Japanese friends: Ryoichi Nakagawa, translator of some of my plays, and Ennosuke Ichikawa, one of the great actors of the Kabuki Theatre. One night after a performance he took me to his home, on a hillside on the city's outskirts. The beautiful house and its appointments were all in the Japanese style, as was the dress of my host and hostess. There was only the electric fan to remind one of Commodore Perry and Detroit. To my delight, my good friend the art critic Itsu Takeuchi came up from Kyoto to see me. We had maintained a sort of contact over the years, interrupted by the war, of course. Once more I tasted the flavor of Japan as he took me to his little private hotel, far from the city's center, where we had a leisurely talk and a meal in the Japanese manner, served by the smiling, bowing proprietress herself.

In all the time I was in Japan, I heard no mention of the war. But on my homeward flight I had a grim reminder of it in a tour of Pearl Harbor.

XXI

A New Life: III

1

With no new play planned and no great desire to write, I saw nothing ahead but sterile idleness. I had agreed to give a graduate course on the theatre at New York University, but that made relatively little demand upon my time and energy.

As I faced the bleak prospect, I realized that I had come to a turning point, perhaps the most crucial in my life. I had to decide whether I wanted to live or die—not physically, for even in my darkest moments I never seriously contemplated suicide, but whether I would allow myself to surrender to a process of deterioration, a downward drift in a muddy, sluggish stream of inertia or despair. On the practical side, I had to make an immediate decision about my future mode of living, for my Stamford tenants were moving out. I had three choices: to sell my house and become a full-time New Yorker; to find new tenants and go on using my Stamford guest house for weekends and escapes from the city; to give up New York entirely and move back to the country.

I shuddered at the thought of spending the rest of my life in New York. In my three years' residence there I had known ease or forgetfulness only during my periods of absence. A native of New York, I had a deep affection for it, but I no longer found it tolerable as a place to live. Though I had a large, bright, well-arranged apartment, I felt alien and imprisoned. After twelve years of country living I could not reaccustom myself to the roar of the streets, the polluted air, the grime and litter. Even more disturbing than the physical conditions was my cognizance of all those thick, tangled, impinging lives. I was constantly aware of the tense, strained faces; the jangling voices; the jostling crowds dashing for buses and dodging through traffic, in order to get nowhere in a hurry. I wanted neither to accommodate myself to that tempo nor to expend my energies in resisting it.

Nor was the compromise solution—half city, half country— satisfactory, for my visits to Stamford only underscored my discontent with New York. All my inclinations were toward moving back to the country. But there was far more involved than just a physical transfer. The psychological problem was complex and critical. Would I be able to adjust myself to living all alone in that vast house that had for so many years been a center of busy, happy family life? Or would the daily reminders of happier times make existence there unendurable? I had no way of knowing. I knew only that continued life in New York held no promise. So I decided to risk the plunge.

It was a grave decision for me; it proved to be a lifesaving one. In the succeeding years I have never once regretted it. From the day I moved back, I felt relief and relaxation. Once again there began for me an entirely new life: a quietly adventurous life, unlike anything I had ever known; a life of almost complete freedom, complete self-sufficiency. In a sense, it had been thrust upon me. By choice, I would have wanted my family life to continue until the end of my days. Since that had become impossible, I preferred to make an affirmative project of going it alone, rather than permit myself to founder in a morass of frustration, nostalgia and self-pity. Though my resolve was forced upon me by circumstances beyond my control, it was, in fact, a logical product of my basic nature. In spite of much external activity and a social, even gregarious, life, I have always been essentially introverted and aloof. Solitude has never had terror for me; some of my best hours have been spent alone. Self-integration and freedom have always been my goals, as they have been the subject of almost everything I have written. I cannot claim to have attained them wholly—perhaps no one ever does—but I have found it possible to live affirmatively and enjoyably alone.

Apart from my continuing interest in the education and welfare of my children, my life was now free from duties and obligations. I could adopt whatever routine of living suited me. Every day became a clear page for meaningful imprinting, scrawling, doodling or just leaving blank. The choice was mine to make, and the making of it was determined solely by my own inclination.

In the five years that have elapsed since I moved back, I have not known a day of loneliness or been at a loss for something to do. On nonworking days there are always odd chores, or errands to run. When my housekeeper is off, I like to bumble about the kitchen. My correspondence is heavy, for I am my own agent and accountant, and secretary as well. I like to maintain contact, too, with friends scattered here and there. Keeping up with current events and with developments in the arts also takes considerable time. I have a working library that serves me well. The long-playing record makes listening to music easy; there is good music on the radio. Television offers baseball games and an occasional interesting discussion or documentary. My children, grandchildren and friends visit me weekends and during school holidays. New York, with its theatres, music and galleries, its board meetings, cocktail parties and dinners, is only an hour away: opportunity without obligation. Since my movements are unrestricted, I can travel at will: a lecture engagement, a quick trip to London or Paris, an extensive tour anywhere. It is a varied, flexible and relatively carefree mode of life. I enjoy it.

But what gives form and tone and zest to it all is just living in the country. In the city, one day is like another. Everything is rigid, angular, inflexible: the same walls of masonry, the same iron traffic crawling over the geometric patterns of streets. There is nothing to gladden the eye, nothing to stir the senses or exalt the spirit. In the country, everything is fluent and mobile. Contours are soft and pliant. No two days are alike. Colors and even shapes change with the time of year and the time of day. One is constantly aware of the processes of growth and decay, of the flow and ebb of life. The parade of the seasons is a vibrant diorama, not merely a notation in a calendar. Each morning one looks out upon a world that has undergone some degree of alteration. It is not necessary to do anything about it, even to take conscious note of it; the modulation is ambient and pervasive.

My house is on a hill, out of sight and sound of the highway,

surrounded by acres of woodland. The clusters of pine, rhododen-
dron, spruce and yew provide year-round greenery. The cycle of
the deciduous trees is eternally fascinating, from the first feathery
blurring of the bare branches, through the tenderness of spring
foliage, the lushness of summer, the quick flash and fading of
autumn color, and the return to bareness. The large brook that
cuts through my land has a varied life, too, dwindling down to
a trickle in a dry August, raging and boiling over its banks in a
spring thaw or autumn cloudburst. Once it flooded, tossing huge
boulders about and all but carrying away the bridge that is my
only means of access. As compensation for tearing out a large
section of driveway, the receding waters left behind a big, old-
fashioned icebox. At the appropriate season the brook is thronged
with wading anglers—three men to a fish, I am sure. In summer I
hear the distant shouts and splashes of neighborhood children. In a
prolonged cold spell it freezes over to make a highway for visiting
ducks. All in all, a lively, versatile stream.

I lack the green thumb and am physically indolent besides, so I
make no pretense at gardening. But there are skunk cabbages and
jacks in a bit of marshland; crocuses, lilies-of-the-valley and violets
spring up here and there; the forsythia and lilac bushes blossom,
then the pink dogwood in my patio and the rhododendrons; wild-
flowers are varied and profuse. Every day there is a little something
new. Animal life is abundant: squirrels, chipmunks, rabbits, wood-
chucks and marauding raccoons. Sometimes a squirrel tumbles
down a chimney; it takes strategy to get him out of the house
without damage to the bric-a-brac. My son Paul has reported foxes,
but I suspect him of wishful thinking. Several times I have spotted
deer in the winter woods.

Though I am neither an ornithologist nor a bird-watcher, it is
the birds that delight me most. They are plentiful, for the trees
and fields give them lots of elbow room and there is nothing to
molest them. Many stay all winter: jays, chickadees, juncos, nut-
hatches, cardinals, woodpeckers. One morning I opened my Vene-
tian blind, and there, just outside the window, on a snow-laden
pine, a bluejay and a cardinal sat vis-à-vis: a tricolor that made the
day for me. In spring the seasonal procession begins: robins, and
numerous but transient starlings. Wrens move into the house that
Paul built—the opening is too small to admit anything else; phoebes

nest under a rain gutter, thrushes in a bush outside my study. Others come and go: catbirds, scarlet tanagers, crows, goldfinches, bluebirds, towhees, grackles, and various sparrows and warblers whose differentiations often escape me.

The air is clean and sweet. The eye is soothed by the encompassing greenness or the unsullied whiteness of the snow cover. At night there is the lambent play of moonlight or the march of the constellations. The stillness is broken only by the sounds of nature: the conversation of birds, crickets and tree toads; the murmur of the Rippowam; the hiss of rain in the leaves. It is a boon to inhabit a tiny island of beauty and peace in a world in which there is so little of either.

2

My return to the country revived my interest in writing. As soon as I had finished the pleasant task of hanging pictures and arranging books, I took up a theme that I had put aside twenty years earlier. It derived from an essay by the English psychoanalyst Ernest Jones in which he suggests that Hamlet's inaction was due neither to infirmity of will nor to doubt about the guilt of Claudius, but to his self-identification with the murderer, who had actually realized Hamlet's Oedipean wish to kill his father and marry his mother. In other words, it was Hamlet's unconscious feeling of shared guilt that kept him from vengeance.

In a modern California setting, I developed a play upon this thesis. I did not, as some commentators suggested, attempt to "rewrite" *Hamlet;* I could hardly have been so fatuous as that. I merely took the central situation of *Hamlet* and tried to examine it in the light of modern psychology. The play had a "happy" ending, in the sense that the young protagonist comes to an understanding of his fixation and is thus enabled to shake off his bondage to his mother. The play's title, *Cue for Passion,* was taken from one of Hamlet's soliloquies. The finished play was put on the production schedule of the Playwrights' Company—of which I was still a member, though I took little part in its activities.

Meanwhile I was conducting a class of seventy graduate students at New York University. I was given the title of adjunct professor, to which, in view of my limited educational background, I could never quite accustom myself. My subject was the theatre as distinguished from the drama. At the outset my students were puzzled by my statement that I would hardly refer to plays, but would concentrate on the theatre as a means of communication and as a social institution; they could not understand how such an examination could occupy a whole year. As it turned out, the year ended with many phases of the subject still unconsidered. I attempted to relate the nature of the theatre in various countries— Germany, Russia, Japan, Mexico, China, England, the United States—to the state of national culture and to the social, economic and political environment. Then we looked at the various elements that constitute the complicated structure of the theatre itself: the physical characteristics of the playhouse; the contributions of director, actor and designer; the collateral problems of labor relations, censorship, dramatic criticism and finances; and how all these elements affect not only the interpretation but also the writing of the plays. I enjoyed giving the course—it had a certain creative quality; and besides, I like to talk. Eventually I made use of the material as the basis for a book called *The Living Theatre*.

For the leading roles in *Cue for Passion* I engaged two fine players: John Kerr, who had distinguished himself in *Tea and Sympathy*, and Diana Wynyard, one of London's leading actresses. The New Haven reception was encouraging and the Philadelphia response was good too. In Philadelphia there was a curious throwback to the *Red Channels* controversy. In the program's brief biographies the printer omitted the names of two members of the company, both of whom happened to be listed in *Red Channels*. When I demanded an explanation, I was assured that the deletions were due to lack of space. However, in later printings of the program, space was found.

The New York first-night audience was responsive and sympathetic. But whatever the play's chances of success may have been, they were quickly erased by a newspaper strike which made it impossible to advertise or even to inform the public that the play was running: another example of the hazards and ordeals that beset play production. By the time the strike was over, it was too late to save the play; it closed after a five-week run. Of course the failure disturbed me; but I did not take this defeat quite so heavily as I had taken others. Perhaps I had become inured to failure and had fortified myself against it. Or perhaps advancing age had made the vicissitudes of my professional career seem less important than formerly.

Early in 1959 Maxwell Anderson died, at the age of seventy. His last years had been darkened by ill-health, financial worries and professional stagnation. As with Sherwood, a fickle public was already beginning to forget him. At New York University I had been amazed to find how little interest my students, all of them play readers and playgoers, took in the work of these men who ranked so high among writers for the American theatre.

The only remaining playwright members of the company were now Robert Anderson and myself. It was obvious that the company's original objectives could no longer be achieved. In fact, it had become just another producing organization, with control vested almost entirely in Roger Stevens—still making worth-while presentations, but offering little or nothing to its playwright members. In any case, emotional considerations would have impelled me to withdraw, for it was the associations that had always meant most to me. Having attended the funerals of Sidney Howard, Kurt Weill, Robert Sherwood and Maxwell Anderson, I no longer wanted to go on, in spite of my affection for the surviving members and staff.

To my relief, my resignation was made unnecessary by the decision of the board of directors to dissolve the company. But it was not easy to see the disbanding of an organization that for more than twenty years had provided stimulation, professional opportunities, harmonious working conditions and, above all, inestimably precious comradeship. It had been a unique experiment that had made valuable contributions to the theatre and had demonstrated the feasibility of co-operation among workers in the arts. However, it is unlikely that a similar association could exist in the present economic state of the theatre.

3

I hesitated about attending the P.E.N. Club congress in Frankfurt, for I had vowed never to visit Germany again. But curiosity overcame bias; I wanted to see what changes the war had wrought, particularly in Berlin.

John and Judy, now sixteen and fifteen, accompanied me on a jaunt through northern Europe, from Bergen via the dramatic fjord country to Oslo and then on to Stockholm and Copenhagen. Everywhere we were fortunate in meeting hospitable theatre folk and P.E.N. members.

In Warsaw our P.E.N. friends cleared up what seemed a hopeless tangle about reservations at the Grand Hotel, a new structure equipped with all sorts of modern devices, many of them in working order. There was a fine tiled swimming pool, which needed only water to be usable.

In spite of its cruel scars and the shining modernity of its reconstructions, I found Warsaw a beautiful city. The old market place, lovingly restored, building by building and stone by stone, recaptured, for all its synthetic newness, something of the ancient quality. The city had been demolished by the Nazis with insensate savagery; even the monuments of national heroes had been systematically smashed.

Completely dominating the city was Stalin's gift to the people of Warsaw, a hideous skyscraper, the Palace of Culture. In front of this architectural monstrosity stood a colossal statue of the benefactor himself, an aesthetic eyesore and a thorn in the flesh of the Poles. There was a current joke to the effect that the best view of Warsaw was from the Palace of Culture, because it was the spot in the city from which you could not see the Palace of Culture.

It was hard to tell which the Poles despised more, their German destroyers or their Russian masters. I was surprised by the open and widespread expression of anti-Russian sentiment. Except for some obvious party hacks, the people we met made no attempt to conceal their hostility to the Russians. Though the means of life were obviously meager, the Poles had a distinctive verve and chic. The individual and national pride that had made it possible for them to survive so many ordeals was very much in evidence. In one of the city's parks, the sound of music drew us to an outdoor arena where, beneath a statue of Chopin, one of the nation's foremost pianists sat at a grand piano and played while hundreds of listeners stood in rapt silence. It was deeply moving.

Warsaw was preparing for a visit from Khrushchev—"our friend," as the Poles sarcastically called him. We missed seeing him by only a few hours. At the airport, military units and brass bands were already assembling. On the way to the airport, our German-speaking driver told us about his experiences as a prisoner of war. He had been put to work on a German farm, where his rations had been woefully insufficient. He had survived only by swapping the contents of his Red Cross packages for more substantial fare. "After all," he said with a shrug, "what does a prisoner of war need coffee for?"

The airport in Berlin did not correspond to my recollection of Tempelhof. Then I learned that we were in the eastern sector. On our ride from the airport and on a subsequent sightseeing tour, there was ample opportunity for an extensive view of East Berlin. It bore little resemblance to the city I had last visited in 1932. There were two grandiose new features. One was the Stalinallee, a broad boulevard lined with shops and apartment houses—an obvious bit of window dressing, but dull and unimpressive. The other was the vast Soviet military cemetery in the suburb of Treptow, with handsome architectural and sculptural embellishments and superb landscaping. For the rest, one saw only a succession of drab streets whose shabby, ill-kept buildings were interspersed with unredeemed bombed areas. The once proud, elegant Unter den Linden was now half wasteland, gloomily dominated by the sprawling Soviet Embassy.

In the western sector, everything was new and dynamic. The Tiergarten had been denuded of its trees, but the contiguous area had become the site of a great architectural complex comprising numerous apartment buildings and two very interesting churches, one Catholic, one Protestant. In form, design and color the whole scheme was the best example of modern planning that I had yet seen. The Kurfürstendamm, formerly an avenue of restaurants and night clubs, had become the center of West Berlin, with its shining new hotels, its shops displaying automobiles, furs and jewelry, its up-to-date movie theatres and its fashionable cafés. The only somber note was the half-bombed Kaiser Wilhelm Gedächtniskirche, which had been left unrestored as a reminder of the war.

During the Nazi regime Germany had been a closed market for me. However, when the war ended, my novel *Imperial City* was published in both West and East Germany, and *The Adding Machine* and *Dream Girl* were presented as part of the Army of Occupation's program to acquaint the Germans with contemporary

American works. Now, in prosperous West Germany, the theatre was undergoing a revival. I was able during my stay in Berlin to make arrangements with a large agency for the handling of stage and broadcasting rights in my plays.

4

The following year the P.E.N. congress in Rio de Janeiro provided an excellent excuse for putting off the writing of this book, as well as an opportunity for a tour of South America. The Rio meetings were followed by visits to São Paulo, a phantasmagoria of seething industry, soaring skyscrapers and tangled traffic, and to Brasília, Brazil's new synthetic capital, which lies five hundred miles from the seaboard, in a trackless wilderness. I found Brasília grandiose in concept, but crassly materialistic in execution. The general impression was one of monotonous angularity: symmetrical towers that, except for the greater use of glass, reminded one of a New York housing project. We were luncheon guests of President Juscelino Kubitschek. In the absence of Alberto Moravia, president of P.E.N., I was called upon to make the usual bread-and-butter speech to our hosts. I could not bring myself to express admiration of Brasília, so I merely said that I hoped the Brazilian people would match this ambitious work of construction with the creation of works of the imagination and the spirit. Kubitschek, well pleased, leaned across the table and grasped my hand.

I went on to Montevideo and Buenos Aires, where I attended a reception at the imposing headquarters of the Society of Dramatic Authors. When I asked one of my hosts how many members the society had, he replied, "About three thousand. But," he added, "they are not all good dramatists." A magnificent flight over the Andes took me to Santiago and on to Lima, for my chief objective was the Inca remains at Machu Picchu.

The massive ruins of the once impregnable fortress of Machu Picchu include remains of temples, throne rooms, plazas, courtyards. The stone-walled terraces of the precipitous slopes provided the means of sustenance; great staircases lead from level to level. There is no sculptural adornment to please the eye and quicken the heart, as at Angkor, though presumably there once was rich ornamentation of silver and gold. Yet one is overawed by the splendor of the setting, the magnitude of the constructions of grim, bare stone, the perfection of the setting.

Home again, I forced myself to recognize that if I really intended to embark upon this autobiographical venture I could no longer put it off. So I steeled myself and set to work on what promised to be a long and difficult task.

CHAPTER

XXII

Credo and Coda

1

Long and difficult it has been indeed: the most sustained and ambitious piece of work I have ever attempted. Though I have an exceptionally good memory, it has not always been easy to recall the sequence of events and the details of experiences. Even harder has been remembering how I felt about things at the time they happened. The psychological demand has been heaviest of all. To retrace one's whole life step by step, overcoming reticences and resistances, reopening old wounds, reliving hours of pain or despair, recalling grievous errors and ignoble behavior, mourning lost friends anew, is an emotional ordeal.

Why have I voluntarily subjected myself to two years of almost monastic discipline, to month upon month of physical labor and spiritual travail? Was I impelled by vanity and exhibitionism? And is it not presumptuous to assume that the story of one's life is sufficiently important or interesting to warrant the attention of others? The answer, I suppose, must be yes; but only, I hope, a qualified yes.

For though I am not averse to readers, I have written this book primarily for my own instruction and satisfaction. Inevitably, as one approaches the end of life, one engages more in contemplation and retrospection than in external activity. Certain questions propound themselves with increasing persistence. Has life in general a meaning or purpose? If so, is it discernible in my own life? Is there a "right" way of living? If so, how wrong have I been? Have my goals been worthy? Worthy or not, how far have I progressed toward them? What, if anything, have I learned? Weighing the benefits of life against their cost, where does the balance lie? I hoped that a review of my life might suggest at least partial answers to these questions. I think it has.

Further, I wanted to attempt a modest contribution to the study of certain aspects of American life in the twentieth century, particularly the state of the theatre and the relation of the writer to it, and the function and status of the political and social nonconformist. To what extent these aims have been achieved is not for me to determine. I can only say that I have tried to be objective and honest. Of course, one is bound to put one's best foot forward, to give oneself the benefit of the doubt, even to fail to recognize that a doubt exists. I can claim only that I have not been guilty of willful falsification.

The principles that serve as guides to the conduct of life seem to fall into three main categories: political and economic, or one's relation to society; ethical and moral, or one's relation to other individuals; metaphysical and religious, or one's relation to oneself and to the universe. What astonishes me is that, in nearly all respects, my beliefs are substantially what they were fifty years ago. This consistency may be due to stubbornness, lack of imagination or ineducability. I prefer, of course, to regard it as proof of the soundness of my adolescent concept of freedom, upon which my whole philosophy of life is based.

2

I became an advocate of socialism in my teens, and have been one ever since. By socialism I do not mean Marxism or Leninism, or any historical or economic dogma, but the development of a society in which the implements of production are employed primarily for the satisfaction of human needs, rather than for the enrichment and aggrandizement of a few individuals.

There is no greater fallacy than the identification of the imperialism and totalitarianism of the Soviet Union with true socialism.

There is no more relationship between the policies of the Kremlin and the aims of ideal socialism than there is between the practices of the Christian church and the teachings of Jesus. The essence of utopian socialism is liberty; its objective is the establishment of a society based upon the voluntary co-operation of free, enlightened individuals who are as much concerned with the well-being of their fellows and of the community as a whole as with their own. Only such a society or group of societies, presided over by some form of world government, can make decent provision for all humanity and ensure universal peace.

As erroneous as the equating of Sovietism with socialism is the assumption that capitalism and democracy are synonymous. As a matter of fact, they are almost wholly antithetical. The history of the rise of American industrialism in the nineteenth century reveals a cynical disregard for human rights and human welfare. It is indisputable that many of the largest fortunes and industrial enterprises were founded upon land grabbing, pre-emption of natural resources, illegal rebating, market rigging and stock jobbery, price fixing, bribery of legislators, judges and administrative officials, and, perhaps worst of all, ruthless exploitation of human beings. The blast furnaces of Pittsburgh claimed as many victims as the gas chambers of Buchenwald; the bricks and mortar of many a fine library, hospital and college dormitory were compounded of the bones and blood of contract labor and sweatshop workers. The attempts of workmen to organize were met with injunctions issued by corrupt or biased judges, or with the blackjacks and bullets of thugs hired as strikebreakers.

As the popular demand for curbs upon the greed, dishonesty and inhumanity of the industrial barons grew, the advance toward socialism began. Antitrust laws and legislation supporting labor's right to organize were enacted. Agencies were set up to restrain the excesses of capitalism: the Interstate Commerce Commission, the Federal Trade Commission, the Federal Communications Commission, the Securities and Exchange Commission, the Fair Employment Practices Commission. Sweeping socialistic measures assured a more equitable distribution of wealth and greater security for the individual: graduated income and inheritance taxes; the abolition of child labor; social security; the minimum wage; unemployment insurance. In the same category are public schools, public recreation facilities and free clinics, paid for mainly out of taxes on property. Nearly all these reforms and ameliorative measures were actively opposed by the capitalists, many of whom still clamor for a return to the old laissez-faire, cutthroat industrial feudalism. But any political candidate who advocated such a policy would have little chance of election.

I used to think that the overthrow of the "free-enterprise" system—that is to say, an economic order based upon unrestricted exploitation and lethal competition—could be achieved only by revolution. But the growing popular demand for social betterment, reflected in greater governmental concern with human needs, has long since convinced me that "creeping" socialism will gradually accelerate its pace.

However, for the utopian socialist the decline of capitalism is only a first step toward the goal of a humanitarian world society. That will indeed require a revolution; not outwardly, but in men's hearts and minds. Competition must give way to co-operation, the profit motive to a preoccupation with human welfare. Competition is inimical and destructive; moneygrubbing is debasing. It is false to say that the desire for gain is man's greatest incentive. The heights in art, science, statesmanship and learning have been attained by those who were not primarily interested in material advancement. On the contrary, the individual who devotes his life to buying cheap and selling dear, to outwitting or crushing his competitors, or to devising means for coaxing the gullible into acquiring things they do not need or want, is an earthbound creature, incapable of moral or spiritual growth.

This is a truth that artists understand. There is, of course, rivalry and antagonism among them. But though divas may engage in hairpulling and actors in scene-stealing, the true artist knows that the best results are obtained when each member of the ensemble complements and supports all the others. Writers and painters may envy or belittle each other, but one does not succeed at another's expense. The greater the number of good books, plays or paintings, the greater is the general interest in the arts; the appearance of an exciting new work benefits not only its author but all creators, and indeed all society.

Under true socialism there would be neither overproduction nor unemployment as long as anyone on the face of the earth lacked the necessities of life; for those who had plenty would share it with those who were lacking. The denizens of this noncompetitive world would devote their ample leisure to the development of their talents and tastes; to the cultivation of their minds, bodies and spirits; to a better understanding of their environment, their fellow men and themselves. As they learned to behave honestly and generously, the supervisory and police functions of the state would diminish, until the state itself disappeared and men truly governed themselves. There would be no need for armaments: war would have become unthinkable. I am aware that, in the present state of the world, such a prognostication seems foolishly fantastic. But what would an eighteenth-century man have said of the prediction that a piloted space ship, soaring two hundred miles, would encircle the earth in an hour? Is it too grotesque to suggest that men who are capable of mastering the physical world may also be capable of self-mastery?

3

My religious views too have undergone little change. I was fortunate enough to escape religious indoctrination in childhood, so I never had to overcome superstitious fears, dogmatism or self-righteous sectarianism. In adolescence I was drawn now and again toward one sect or another—Quakerism, Roman Catholicism, Christian Science—but I could never bring myself to an acceptance of ritual, dogma and denominationalism; nor was I ever willing to submit to the authority of self-appointed spiritual guides. I have attended many religious services, and if the church was beautiful and the music good I have derived considerable aesthetic satisfaction. But I have not been impelled to become a participant.

There is, however, another aspect of religion that has nothing to do with churchgoing or adherence to a creed or cult. It is one's personal metaphysics, or relationship to the unkown and the unknowable. For the orthodox this involves nothing more than an uncritical acceptance of sectarian tenets. For the speculative person it demands the adoption of an individual belief. It is not enough to ask him if he believes in God. He is bound to ask, "Which God?" or "What do you mean by God?" For there is indeed a wide range of choice between a personified Deity, capable of begetting ter-

restrial offspring, and an impersonal force or principle that somehow controls or influences the universe as a whole, or human life
in particular. Each person's predilection is determined by accidents of character and of conditioning of which he himself is often
unaware. I do not see, therefore, how any belief can be regarded,
in the abstract, as "right" or "wrong." Its rightness, it seems to me,
depends upon its usefulness to the believer, and the satisfaction or
comfort he derives from it.

For my own part, I have never been able to accept the concept
of a personal God, possessed of human characteristics, who takes a
partisan interest in the destinies of individual men and women.
This had always struck me as a decidedly literal projection by man
of his own image upon the cosmos. I am unwilling to acknowledge
the sovereignty of a jealous and vengeful God who exiles his creatures for yielding to the temptation he has set for them; who mani-
fests his displeasure with human behavior by drowning the entire
race except for one family; who tortures his devout servant in order
to win a bet from the Devil; and who sends she-bears to devour
mischievous children. Hardly less acceptable is the ever-loving
Father who countenances a Belsen or a Hiroshima and seems to do
nothing to avert the death of millions by plague or famine. I am
unwilling to entrust my present or future happiness to a guardian
who is so callous or so powerless.

At the same time, I find it impossible to believe that life is pur-
poseless and meaningless, that the bewilderingly complex structure of the universe, with its organization, balances and delicate
interrelationships, is the result of mere chance, or of the haphazard operation of blind forces. It may be mathematically demon-
strable that a platoon of chimpanzees banging away at typewriters
through the ages would eventually produce the works of Shakespeare. But that is not how the works of Shakespeare were produced. They were created by one man, in the course of a short
lifetime; they represent an advanced stage in the development of
the human brain and the human spirit. Physiologically, the differences between Shakespeare and the Neanderthal man, or for that
matter between Shakespeare and the chimpanzee, are slight; yet
the differences in perception, sensitivity and creativeness are almost immeasurable.

I see no reason to believe that the evolutionary process has ended with contemporary man. There may yet be developed a race of men with bodies like ours but with mental and spiritual powers far beyond anything we can imagine. While I have my doubts about that one far-off divine event to which the whole creation moves, I can readily believe in man's progression toward a wiser and more benign way of life.

Beyond this rather general belief in a co-ordinated and ever-evolving universe I have been unable to go. I have read widely in philosophy, but not deeply, for I seem to lack the mental capacity to follow to its conclusion a closely linked chain of abstract reasoning. Besides, I am skeptical about the ability of a finite mind to reduce the infinite to an all-inclusive, comprehensible system. I enjoy the dialogues of Plato, as I enjoy the transcript of a skillful cross-examination, or a lively debate; but it is a debate devoid of sporting interest, for the cards are stacked and you always know who is going to win. I have no faith in absolutes, or in ex-cathedra pronouncements. The only philosopher I think I understand is William James.

4

Even more essential to a man's conduct of life than his political and religious beliefs is his personal code of behavior. Here again I put the emphasis upon the personal because of my deep distrust of authoritarian moral prescriptions that are presumed to have universal applicability. Chief among these is the collection of precepts known as the Ten Commandments, generally ascribed to Moses, an obscure but articulate leader of antiquity; his attribution of their authorship to the Deity must surely be regarded as figurative. Though after twenty-five centuries they are still accepted by millions as a complete guide to correct living, it seems to me that even the most cursory examination of the Commandments reveals their inadequacy.

Only two of the ten offer affirmative recommendations: the injunctions to Sabbath observance and to filial piety. The remaining eight merely state what is nonpermissible. Three of them deal with polytheism, idolatry and blasphemy, the remaining five with murder, adultery, theft, perjury or malicious gossip, and covetousness. In the main, it is a penal rather than a moral code. A man might rigorously obey all the Commandments and yet be a tyrant and a bully, a stingy and cruel husband, a neglectful father, a hardfisted employer, an ill-tempered neighbor, a loudmouthed opinionated boor, a social snob, a provocative chauvinist, a religious bigot and a malignant racist: in short, a despicable human being.

Certainly I am not alone in believing that viability requires a more fecund soil than this stony bed of bleak negations. Or, to shift the metaphor, if the traffic is to move ahead there must be more green lights than red. I have never before tried to codify the principles of behavior that seem to me aids to constructive living. But since so many others have engaged in this innocent diversion, perhaps I too may be permitted to do so, preserving, of course, the classical decadal pattern. It should be noted that my code contains no absolutes, but merely suggests choices; and that since it is entirely personal, I am not proposing it for universal adoption. Here, then, is my decalogue:

> It is better to live than to die;
> to love than to hate;
> to create than to destroy;
> to do something than to do nothing;
> to be truthful than to lie;
> to question than to accept;
> to be strong than to be weak;
> to hope than to despair;
> to venture than to fear;
> to be free than to be bound.

However obvious and commonplace these tenets may seem, I can say unhesitatingly that if, throughout my life, I had used them as touchstones for my every thought, word and deed, I would be a better man than I am.

5

So much for my beliefs and principles. But what has the course of my life been? How is it to be summarized and evaluated? What have I learned? What have I accomplished? How do I stand in relationship to myself, to my intimates, to society, and to life as a whole? Surely these are questions that everyone with an inquiring mind must ask himself as he approaches his end—even though he does not go to the trouble of writing a long book in his attempt to find the answers.

What conclusions others will come to about me, I cannot know. As for myself, I regard my life, in spite of defeats, failures, sorrows, pain, shortcomings and errors, as a happy one, and, in my own terms, as a relatively successful one, due in large measure to certain fortunate accidents that made living easier for me than it might otherwise have been. Though I am not a great believer in luck, I do believe that some individuals are more favored by natural and environmental factors than are others. I happen, through no effort of my own, to be the beneficiary of such advantages.

In the first place, I was born with an exceptionally sound physical constitution. Apart from two organic ailments that were relieved by surgery, I have been remarkably free from illnesses, especially of the chronic or recurrent sort. I have never in my life had a headache, a backache, an allergy, a sinus infection, a nosebleed, an ulcer, high blood pressure, or any form of digestive disturbance. I am not affected by changes in altitude or temperature, or subject to air sickness, seasickness, insomnia, or nervous, mental or muscular disorders. My power of endurance is considerable, and I have no trouble relaxing between work periods. So my activities have rarely been interrupted by physical disabilities or nagging ailments.

Even more auspicious was my childhood conditioning. I was nurtured in an atmosphere of love, with no competitor for the affection of my elders. Love was showered upon me by my mother, to a lesser degree by my grandfather and uncle, and even, in a twisted fashion, by my father. Though I was often lonely, I never felt neglected. I was seldom punished and never, so far as I can recall, unjustly. Most important of all, I was never made to feel mean, unworthy or sinful.

Further, though my childhood and youth were beset with economic problems, I had the extraordinary good fortune of achieving financial security in early manhood. True, this was not entirely accidental, for I did write the play that became a success; but, the hazards of the theatre being what they are, I was certainly lucky in hitting upon a novel theme and in then getting the play into the right hands. The odds against me were almost incalculable. I might have written a far better play that failed completely. As it was, I was able—thanks to my conditioned thriftiness—to establish financial reserves that were sufficient to carry me through many lean years. Altogether, then, I began my adult life with an exceptional equipment of physical, emotional and economic security.

It is this endowment that has enabled me to move toward what has consistently been my life's goal: freedom. Freedom in my work, freedom of thought and action, freedom as a member of society, freedom in personal relationships. I have never lost sight of these objectives, and I think that, within the limitations of my character and abilities, I have gone a long way toward attaining them.

6

I have never regretted my choice of a career. A writer, if he is not plagued by economic worries, is about as independent as anyone can be. Since I have never wanted to amass wealth or to live sumptuously, and have found my wares sufficiently marketable to enable me to pay my way, I have written not only pretty much what I pleased, but also when and where I pleased, for I have had no taskmaster but myself, and I carry my workshop with me.

As a writer, I have not been idle. In half a century I have written some fifty full-length plays (about twenty of them unproduced); four novels, three of which have been published; a book about the theatre; an indeterminate number of short stories, one-act plays, articles, book reviews, motion picture, radio and television scripts; and the present volume. It is an output that falls short of that of Owen Davis, who wrote three hundred plays, to say nothing of Lope de Vega, who is said to have written eighteen hundred. Still, it is substantial.

What immediately suggests itself is the possibility that if the quantity had been less the quality might have been greater. It is a hypothesis that I have not failed to examine. I have often asked myself, too, whether preoccupation with the welfare of my family and participation in civic affairs have retarded my development as an artist. It would be comforting to lay that exculpatory unction to my soul. But the sad truth is that I have written as well as I could.

If it is true that a man's reach should exceed his grasp, I deserve commendation, for my aspirations have always exceeded my achievements. But since I became aware early of my artistic limitations, I have not essayed to scale unattainable heights or attempted Icarian flights. I have wished for the dramaturgic skill of an Ibsen, the intellectual brilliance of a Shaw, the tragic power of an O'Neill, the poetic gift of a Synge, the insight of a Chekhov. But Ibsen led a bleak, lonely life, Shaw was childless, O'Neill was racked by illness and self-torture, Synge died in his thirties and Chekhov in his forties; I would not have wanted to change places with any of them. It is so with personal traits too. I have had many acquaintances who have been my superiors in knowledge, wisdom, wit, graciousness, generosity or tolerance; yet I have never wanted to be anyone but myself—perhaps because I am logical enough to see that I never *could* be anyone but myself.

Whether or not I would choose the theatre if I were at the beginning of my career today, I cannot say. Always dominated by commercialism, the professional theatre in America has succumbed to it almost entirely. Rocketing costs have increased its dependence upon an audience that is likely to be better equipped with money than with taste. It is harder and harder for the experimental play or the play of ideas to get even a hearing. The theatre, of course, can never die; its appeal is universal and deeply rooted in human emotions. But the theatre as a business has, I think, seen its best days. The businessman will continue to fulfill the useful function of providing popular entertainment, but the theatre as an art must be returned to its artists.

That necessitates a willingness upon the part of the artist to forgo economic gains for artistic satisfactions, and a recognition by the community that the theatre is a vital part of the national cultural life which should be as free from the profit motive as are libraries, art museums and symphony orchestras. There are hopeful indications that the transition is in progress, but it will be a long, arduous process, in the course of which the existence of the serious playwright will be precarious.

7

In a society in which business comes first and cultural activities are generally regarded as marginal, or even as slightly immoral, subversive or unmanly, the position of the American artist is ambiguous. When he is noticed at all by the majority of the population, it is likely to be because of his financial success, his marital difficulties or his behavioral eccentricity. He is not in the mainstream of national life, and is seldom influential or vitally engaged in public affairs, as is his counterpart in many other countries. When President Kennedy invited Robert Frost to participate in his inaugural ceremonies, there was a tendency to regard this gesture as novel, daring and a bit freakish.

Nevertheless, the American artist is in many respects better off than his fellows elsewhere. I, for one, can hardly complain of lack of opportunity or recognition. Though I had neither money, social position, influential connections or a formal education, I was able to get an early footing in the theatre and to maintain a place in it. In recent years my activity has diminished, but many of my plays are still being performed, both here and abroad. Equally important to me is the fact that I have never been restricted by censorship, nor has anyone ever attempted to prescribe what I may or may not write.

Further, though I have repeatedly expressed radical and unorthodox opinions and have been "cited" by official and unofficial guardians of the status quo, I have never been persecuted or penalized for anything I have written or said. Now and again my plays may have been ruled out by television executives upon the ground that I am a "controversial" figure; but that merely involved a financial loss, not to be taken too seriously. On the whole, I have had more success and more freedom in my work than I would have been likely to have anywhere else. Just as I have never wanted to be anyone but myself, I have never wanted to be anything but an American.

8

Though I have always aspired to becoming a good writer, I have wanted even more to be a success as a human being. Much as I would like to be remembered briefly for my literary work—unlike Shaw, I cannot even hope for "a few years of immortality"—I would rather be remembered as a good father, a good friend, a good co-worker and a useful member of society.

As I scan the balance sheet of my life, I am disquieted by the heaviness of the debit side. I could wish to have been less egotistical, less opinionated, less caustic, less irritable, less impatient, less intolerant. I have worked hard to remedy my defects, but with only partial success.

But in self-defense I hasten to refer to the other side of the ledger. I may have caused hurt by coldness, neglect or selfishness, but I have never willfully or knowingly injured anyone. Nor have I ever betrayed a trust, taken unfair advantages, or lied to advance my own interests. I can truthfully say that I do not hate anyone. There are individuals whom I do not like, but dislike is not hatred; for hatred is, I believe, almost invariably the product of fear, and I have never been afraid of anyone. It is quite possible that I have enemies, but since I do not know who they are I can do nothing to dispel their enmity.

I have spoken of my good fortune in growing up in an atmosphere of love. Thankfully, my whole life has been rich in love: parental love, sexual love, the love of friends, the love of children. Nothing in my life has given me more joy than fatherhood; the happiest day of my year is the Christmas dinner, for which I manage to assemble my five children and five grandchildren.

In my offspring I am exceptionally fortunate; they all rank high in attractiveness, personality, intelligence, talent and character. What is more, they are all richly endowed with humor, that rare and precious quality that smooths the rough places, adjusts the perspective and stipples life with laughter. All my children have made careers for themselves or are in process of doing so. Robert, an able journalist, has long been on the staff of *The New Yorker*. Peggy, for some years editor of *Gourmet* magazine, is now a feature editor of *Woman's Day*. John, a Harvard junior and a member of the *Crimson* staff, is thinking of a journalistic or a diplomatic career. Judy, who is preparing herself for the stage, is a freshman at Sarah Lawrence. Paul, just finishing grade school, has a deep interest in the natural sciences: the only member of the family with scientific inclinations. My grandchildren are still in the formative years; Andy, my eldest granddaughter, is of marriageable age, though, so I may yet see a great-grandchild at the Christmas table.

9

If I live! That is a contingency a man of my age must recognize, even without taking into account the hazards of the highways and airways, and the stock-piling of nuclear weapons. But I am not obsessed by thoughts of death, or alarmed by its prospect. Since I have never believed in a future life, I have never been bemused by threats of hell or hopes of Paradise. I think that the purpose of life is life itself, and that we best fulfill that purpose by living as long as we can and as well as we can. If I knew that I was to die to-morrow, I think I would accept the fact with equanimity. But I would be deeply regretful too, as one would regret being suddenly called away from a lively and entertaining party.

For it has been a good party, and I should like it to go on as long as I am capable of experience and of enjoyment. My health is ex-cellent; my mobility and faculties are as yet unimpaired. There is much that I still want to do, to see and to learn. A visit to India is a project long deferred; there is the prospect of P.E.N. congresses in Iran, Australia, Finland, Israel. Paris, London and Rome are only a few hours away.

Though my literary career is undoubtedly in the descendant, I shall probably go on writing as long as I am able to pound a type-writer or hold a pen. I have a new play about ready for production; several others are at various stages of development. I should like to commemorate the fiftieth anniversay of the production of *On Trial* with another courtroom melodrama; I should like to write at least one more novel.

What saddens me is not my own aging and decline in creativity but the ever-increasing toll of those I have respected and loved. Every week makes new gaps in the ranks of all the brilliant and talented and lovely and good men and women I have been for-tunate enough to have known, gaps that for me can never be filled. But there are compensations: new and valued friends of a younger generation. And, best of all, a vivid interest in the progress of my numerous progeny.

So, as I reach my seventieth birthday, I come at last, with a sigh of relief, to the end of this long labor.

Stamford, Connecticut
November 1962

DATE DUE

FEB 27 '64			
MAY 1 1 '68			
OCT 2 1 1970			
GAYLORD			PRINTED IN U.S.A.